RICARDO
ON TAXATION

RICARDO
ON TAXATION

By CARL S. SHOUP

PROFESSOR OF ECONOMICS, COLUMBIA UNIVERSITY

COLUMBIA UNIVERSITY PRESS

MORNINGSIDE HEIGHTS, NEW YORK 1960

PREFACE

The present study, begun some fifteen years ago, was interrupted by other commitments. The delay was fortunate in at least one sense: it afforded an opportunity to utilize that notable collection, *The Works and Correspondence of David Ricardo,* edited by Professor Piero Sraffa, with the collaboration of Mr. M. H. Dobb (1952).

Professors Mark Blaug, Albert G. Hart, Peter B. Kenen, Ragnar Nurkse, George J. Stigler, and Jacob Viner made helpful suggestions on many points at various stages in the drafting of the manuscript. Professors Fritz Neumark and Aldo Scotto generously supplied references to the German and Italian literature.

Chapters I and IX were published, in earlier draft form, as articles in *Finanzarchiv* and *Public Finance (Finances Publiques),* respectively.

The research expenses of this project have been met from a grant made by the Rockefeller Foundation some years ago to Columbia University for a study of economic aspects of public finance, and from supplementary grants made recently by the Columbia Council for Research in the Social Sciences.

CARL S. SHOUP

June 1, 1959

PUBLISHED IN GREAT BRITAIN, INDIA, AND PAKISTAN BY THE OXFORD UNIVERSITY PRESS
LONDON, BOMBAY, AND KARACHI
LIBRARY OF CONGRESS CATALOG CARD NUMBER: 58-10338
PRINTED AND BOUND IN THE UNITED STATES OF AMERICA

CONTENTS

TABLES

CHAPTER I

RICARDO AND TAXATION

In the field of applied economics relevant to the England of the early nineteenth century, the name of David Ricardo (1772-1823) has come to be associated with money and banking and international trade far more than with taxation. Had this outcome been foretold, Ricardo would probably have been surprised, perhaps disturbed. He attached the greatest importance to an economically advantageous tax policy, and he laid what he thought were solid theoretical foundations for achieving it.

Writing in 1819, Ricardo said:

> If it were not for the necessity of taxation the business of Government regarding Agriculture, Commerce and Manufactures would be very easy indeed,—all that would be required of them would be to avoid all interference, neither to encourage one source of production nor to depress another, but the necessity of raising money by taxes renders some interference necessary. The aim of the legislature should nevertheless be to press on all equally, so as to interfere as little as possible with the natural equilibrium which would have prevailed if no disturbance whatever had been given.[1]

And again, later in the same year in a letter to his friend Hutches Trower:

> Political Economy, when the simple principles of it are once understood, is only useful, as it directs Governments to right measures in taxation. We very

[1] Letter of Oct. 13, 1819, to James Brown, Vol. VIII, p. 101, in *The Works and Correspondence of David Ricardo,* edited by Piero Sraffa with the collaboration of M. H. Dobb, Cambridge, University Press, for the Royal Economic Society, in ten volumes. Reference hereafter to this source, including the editors' Introduction (roman page numbers) and footnotes, will be in the form: S. VIII, 101. In some quotations, the mechanical style of punctuation has been altered for the sake of convenience. Brown was a business man who had sent Ricardo a paper on money. Ricardo's lengthy reply contains the passage here quoted.

soon arrive at the knowledge that Agriculture, Commerc[e], and Manufactures flourish best when left without interference on the part of Government, but the necessity which the state has for money to defray the expences of its functions, imposes on it the obligation to raise taxes, and thus interference becomes absolutely necessary. It is here then that the most perfect knowledge of the science is required...[2]

Ricardo had already done his share, and more, in supplying guide-posts to "right measures in taxation." In his *Principles*—the full title is *On the Principles of Political Economy, and Taxation*—the first seven chapters formulate the laws of distribution in a taxless state, and the next eleven chapters reveal how the operation of these laws is modified by the impact of taxation.[3] Thus Ricardo endeavors "to trace satisfactorily the influence of taxation on different classes of the community; ..." [4] And by the time the *Principles* was revised for the third edition, Ricardo's involvement in taxation had widened to the point of giving more attention to the question, What determines the taxable capacity of a country? In particular, he was concerned to demonstrate (in Chapter XXXII, "Mr. Malthus's Opinions on Rent") the "doctrine of the ability of a country to pay additional money taxes, although the aggregate money value of the mass of its commodities should fall," [5] in consequence of technological improvements in agriculture, or by a relaxation of import restrictions on corn. In terms of British economic policy: could the fixed money amount of taxation necessary to service the heavy post-war debt be raised more easily, or less, if the corn laws were repealed and the price level consequently fell?

Although it is not difficult to understand why taxation interested Ricardo—he lived in a period designated by Dowell as "Taxation in the Zenith, 1815-1842" [6]—the dates at which his interest began and intensified remain obscure, and the proximate stimuli something of a mystery. There is no mention of taxation in the Mill-Ricardo correspond-

[2] Letter of Nov. 12, 1819, S. VIII, 132-33. See also letter of Oct. 26, 1819, Trower to Ricardo, S. VIII, 110.

[3] Of the 416 pages in the Gonner edition (more suitable for this count than the Sraffa edition, as it contains fewer editorial footnotes), 120 pages—a short page being included as one page—make up the chapters on taxation, and another 27 pages comprise the two chapters on bounties, and restrictions on importation—altogether, more than one third of the book. In subsequent footnotes, the Gonner edition of the *Principles* will be cited as "G."

[4] S. I, 5-7; G, 1-3.

[5] See "Advertisement to the Third Edition," March 26, 1821, S, I, 8; G, 3.

[6] Dowell, *A History of Taxation and Taxes in England from the Earliest Times to the Year 1885*, II, 247.

ence prior to a letter of October 14, 1816, in which Ricardo informs Mill that he is about to start on the tax chapters of the *Principles.* Indeed, none of the Ricardian correspondence prior to that date, including letters to and from Malthus and Trower, even hints that Ricardo is to write what amounts to a treatise on taxation. Moreover, few references to taxation can be found in the other Ricardian papers dated before the first edition of the *Principles.* Yet the chapters on taxation were composed with extraordinary rapidity and were scarcely touched in the course of revisions that were made in the second and third editions of the *Principles.*[7] Thus there is every indication, though little concrete evidence, that Ricardo had thought deeply on tax problems well before he set himself to writing the *Principles.*[8]

An intimate friend of Ricardo's attracted him to the study of science, about 1797. Sraffa remarks: "The identity of this interesting character is unknown. It would be tempting to suppose that is was William Frend, [who was] a mathematician and the author of pamphlets on

[7] The dates of publication of the three editions are: April 19, 1817; February 27, 1819; May 18, 1821 (S, I, xix, l, liv). Revision of the entire *Principles* for the second edition seems to have taken no more than five days (compare Ricardo's letters to Murray, Nov. 18, 1818, and Nov. 23, 1818; see S. I, 1). The third edition, however, contained extensive revisions in the non-tax portion, including the addition of the famous chapter, "On Machinery." See S, I, xxxvii-lx.

[8] See Chapter XVI below. Taxation was the primary subject of interest to the Political Economy Club, in the first twelve months of its existence. Ricardo was a member from the beginning. Of the fourteen questions propounded at the meetings from the initial one on April 30, 1821 through that of May 6, 1822, seven dealt directly with taxation. They were: What would be an efficient countervailing duty on corn? (submitted by S. C. Holland); The quantity of money being constant, would a general tax upon all commodities in a country raise their prices? (Colonel Torrens); What is the effect of taxation on general prices in a country having no foreign trade? (T. Tooke); What would be the best mode of taxation? (G. W. Norman); Is it practicable to pay the whole or a considerable part of the national debt by a contribution on the capital of individuals; and, if practicable, would it be expedient to do so? (G. Brown); How far are rents and profits affected by tithes? (H. Warburton); Under a system of free trade, would an ad valorem duty upon all commodities render it necessary to impose a similar duty upon all imported commodities, with a view to the protection of the home producer? (J. Cazenove). Every one of these issues had been analyzed in some detail in the *Principles,* so we cannot say from this evidence whether Ricardo wrote on taxation because of the current interest in that subject or whether much of the current interest in it was stimulated by Ricardo's taxation chapters. In the six years following the May, 1822, meeting no more than five tax questions were posed. Interest in the subject revived markedly thereafter. Political Economy Club, Vol. VI, *Centenary Volume,* pp. 5 ff.

taxation and on the quantity theory of money."[9] Is it pure coincidence that so much of the *Principles* deals with those two subjects? Frend's writings included *The Principles of Taxation,* London, 1799; *The Principles of Taxation, or, Contribution According to Means,* London, 1804; and *The National Debt in Its True Colours,* 1817.[10]

No indication of an interest in taxation is apparent in the titles of the books, pamphlets, etc., that formed Ricardo's library, though the evidence on this point is incomplete. Ricardo's "commonplace books" contained two excerpts from speeches by Tierney and Lord Holland on assessed taxes.[11]

Ricardo is said to have owed much to the Physiocrats: the concept of society's net income, from which alone taxes can be paid, and the collateral concept of a taxable capacity, or taxable limit, of a nation; and the realization that tax shifting is the mechanism through which an economically permissible distribution of the tax burden can emerge from an initial assessment pattern that professes to tax some part of the gross income that is not also net.[12] Yet there appears to be no direct evidence that Ricardo's interest in tax analysis had been aroused by a study of Physiocratic doctrine.

1. THE TAXATION CHAPTERS IN THE *Principles*

From August, 1815, to the fall of the following year, Ricardo had struggled with the initial seven chapters of what was to be the first edition of the *Principles.* In turn cajoled, chided (for procrastination), and encouraged by James Mill, he finally got the manuscript off to his literary mentor by the middle of October, 1816, and informed him: "I shall now consider the subject of taxation that I may have a consistent theory in the first instance on paper." [13]

Mill, acknowledging receipt of the manuscript of the first seven

[9] S, X, 34.

[10] Seligman, *The Income Tax,* p. 88. According to Seligman, the 1804 edition of the *Principles of Taxation* is virtually the same as that of 1799 except for a long preface of 30 pages in the later volume. Frend's views on taxation are for the most part found also in Ricardo, but the two men differ on some aspects of debt policy. See Index below, Frend.

[11] S, X, 396, 399-402.

[12] Clewing, Die finanzwissenschaftlichen Ansichten von David Ricardo, p. 125.

[13] Letter of Oct. 14, 1816, S, VII, 84. As to Mill's influence on Ricardo generally, see Hutchison, "James Mill and the Political Education of Ricardo," *Cambridge J.,* VII (no. 2, Nov., 1953), 81-100.

chapters, made a brief show of interest in the forthcoming analysis: "I am happy to hear you are upon taxation; and shall be curious to see what comes forth, as soon as it is done. That is a point closely connected with some of the most abstruse principles of the science." [14] The last paragraph of his next letter to Ricardo closes on a stronger note: "Send me the rest of what you have done. I long to hear you on tithes." [15]

In a month the manuscript of the taxation chapters was on its way to Mill.[16] Neither the author nor his "schoolmaster" [17] expresses any gratification or surprise over the rapidity with which these chapters were composed.[18]

It took Mill about as long—in elapsed time—to read Ricardo's tax chapters as it had taken Ricardo to write them. The manuscript had been sent to Mill by Ricardo on November 17, 1816; Mill returned it on December 16, 1816.[19] In a letter of the same date he offered these comments:

> I have now gone over your inquiry into the subject of Taxation, with the same care as the former part of the work. I have also the pleasure to tell you that I am equally well satisfied. Now for the first time is the real operation of taxes explained; for this was a part of his subject on which Adam Smith was superficial, and added not a great deal to the knowledge of the world. Your doctrines are original, and profound, for it was by no means an easy matter to get down to them; and I have no hesitation whatsoever in saying that they are fully and completely made out. I embrace every one of them; and am ready to defend them against all the world. In this part however, there will be rather more to do in fitting it for the press, than in the other. I do not mean that you do not here shew the same command of good expression as in the former; for that is a thing in which there is now not any danger of your ever failing. But in this I see you have followed the order of your own thoughts, without much studying the order which would most facilitate introduction into the minds of your readers. In preparing it for the press, that is the principal thing which you will have to study. And in that I shall perhaps be able to give you some assistance. I have marginal contents of the whole, paragraph by paragraph, and shall study them at leisure with that view.[20]

Mill was sufficiently impressed by Ricardo's tax analysis to call attention to it in a footnote in his *History of British India,* published also in 1817: "See a Dissertation on the Principles of Taxation, the

[14] Letter of Oct. 25, 1816, S, VII, 86. [15] Letter of Nov. 18, 1816, S, VII, 99.
[16] Letter of Nov. 17, 1816, Ricardo to Mill, S, VII, 87-88. [17] S, I, xiv.
[18] Cf. letter of Dec. 16, 1816, Mill to Ricardo, S, VII, 106-111. [19] *Ibid.,* 111.
[20] *Ibid.,* 106-7. If Mill did give Ricardo such assistance, no record of it seems to have survived.

most profound, by far, which has yet been given to the world, by David Ricardo, Esq. in his work 'On the Principles of Political Economy and Taxation.'"[21]

Aside from Mill's reaction to the tax chapters in manuscript form, the only substantial comment on that section of the first edition of the *Principles* was the one offered by McCulloch in a letter of July, 1818. "There is no part of your work which I admire more," he wrote, "than that in which you treat of the theory of taxation. . . ." McCulloch's praise was tempered by uneasiness over what he thought was a weak stand by Ricardo on the subject of government extravagance: ". . . still it appears to me that you give as it were a reluctant assent to those arguments, and they are of the most decisive nature, which shew the impolicy and ruinous effects of a heavy taxation. . . . All governments are but too much inclined to tax and overburden their subjects. . . ."[22]

2. ADAM SMITH'S INFLUENCE

Along with the manuscript of the taxation chapters, Ricardo had sent Mill a letter, in the course of which he said:

> On the subject of taxation you will perceive that I have altered, I hope corrected, some of the views which I had heretofore taken. I hope I shall be able to convince you of the general correctness of my principles. I have dwelt very little on the effect of those taxes on which there can be no difference of opinion, and have not mentioned many which have been ably handled by Adam Smith. His language is so clear, and his explanations so satisfactory, that I feel a reluctance to weaken the effect of it by using my words instead of his, and always feel a propensity to quote him without a word of comment.[23]

Three questions are suggested by this passage.

First, what were the "views heretofore taken" by Ricardo on taxation which he had by now altered? This question seems destined to remain unanswered, given the scarcity of pre-1816 references to taxation in the Ricardian papers.[24]

[21] S, VII, 228, note 1.

[22] Letter of July 15, 1818, S, VII, 280-81. For Ricardo's reaction to this charge, see his letter of Aug. 22, 1818, to McCulloch, S, VII, 286-87, and Chapter III below.

[23] Letter of Nov. 17, 1816, S, VII, 88. It appears that Ricardo first read *The Wealth of Nations* in 1799. S, X, 35-36.

[24] For hints, but no definite information, see Ricardo's references to views which he held temporarily on the raw-produce tax (p. 60 below) and to a mistake respecting the profits tax (p. 117, note 40, below).

Second, what were the taxes "on which there can be no difference of opinion" as to their effects? One of them, perhaps, was the tax on land rent, for on this one Ricardo "dwelt very little," as we shall see.[25] Death duties, transfer taxes, and stamp duties are also treated but briefly in the *Principles*,[26] though it is difficult to understand how Ricardo could have considered their effects to be beyond the range of controversy.

Third, what were the "many" taxes that Ricardo did not even mention, because they had been so "ably handled by Adam Smith?"

In fact, Ricardo omits no major category of tax found in Smith's chapter, "Of the Sources of the General or Public Revenue of the Society," [27] unless capitation taxes based on rank or income are to be so classified.[28] The difference between Ricardo's and Smith's tax chapters lies rather in Ricardo's almost complete concentration on economic analysis, and in his lack of interest in illustrative material.

Smith devotes more space than Ricardo to the English land tax,[29] and also treats at some length taxes of other countries based on actual rent,[30] and the existing taxes on transfer of property,[31] but gives no analysis of a tax on the monetary metal, gold, to which Ricardo dedicates an entire chapter.[32] Otherwise, the major types of tax are discussed in considerable detail by both writers:[33] the tithe (a tenth part of produce, levied for the established church),[34] taxes on rent of houses,[35]

[25] S, I, 173-75; G, 154-56. See Chapter V below. [26] S, I, 153-55; G, 134-36.

[27] *Wealth of Nations*, Bk. V, Ch. II: C, II, 302-91; M, 769-858. "C," in this and succeeding citations, refers to the Cannan edition; "M," to the Modern Library edition.

[28] *Ibid.*, C, II, 351-53; M, 819-21.

[29] *Ibid.*, C, II, 312-14; M, 779-81. Ricardo, *Principles*, S, I, 185-88; G, 166-69 (commenting on Smith's and Say's analyses of this tax). Ricardo devotes the opening paragraphs of his Chapter XII to a uniform fixed tax per acre, but does not refer in that connection to the English land tax, which seems not to have approached the flat per acre tax in practice, and clearly differed from it in principle.

[30] Smith, *Wealth of Nations*, C, II, 314-21; M, 782-88.

[31] Smith, *ibid.*, C, II, 342-48; M, 809-15.

[32] Ricardo, *Principles*, Ch. XIII, S, I, 191-200; G, 171-80.

[33] But note the puzzling omission by Ricardo of the income tax.

[34] Smith, *Wealth of Nations*, C, II, 321-24; M, 788-91; and Ricardo, Ch. XI, S, I, 176-80; G, 157-60.

[35] Smith, *Wealth of Nations*, C, II, 324-31; M, 791-98; and Ricardo, Ch. XIV, S, I, 201-204; G, 181-85. Ricardo's treatment of this tax consists largely of direct quotation from Smith.

taxes on profits of particular trades, or on profits generally,[36] taxes on wages,[37] and taxes in the form of excises or customs duties on consumable commodities, luxuries, or necessaries.[38]

Even for the latter group of taxes, however, Ricardo's analysis involves very little duplication of Smith's. He disagrees with his predecessor's economic analysis at points, and gives his reasons; he covers some economic phenomena touched on lightly, if at all, in the *Wealth of Nations*, especially effects on the general level of money prices; he leaves almost entirely to Smith descriptions of and judgments on administrative problems. In Adam Smith's long chapter on taxation the reader is treated to a rich slice of real life, against a background of somewhat undependable economic reasoning; with Ricardo we move on a high level of economic abstraction, supported by generally dependable reasoning, based, however, on dubious postulates of a most sweeping nature. Ricardo's chapters are enriched by acute analyses of smaller economic problems. The two treatments of taxation are complementary in consumption, not rival.

Who was nearer the truth, Ricardo or Mill, in evaluating Adam Smith's contributions to tax analysis? "Superficial," said Mill; while Ricardo felt "a propensity to quote him without a word of comment." Mill was wrong; but Ricardo did not describe his own feelings very accurately, if we are to judge by the number of pages of the *Principles* given over to exposing fallacies in Smithian tax doctrine. The truth seems to be that Smith, far from being superficial, dug for himself logical traps so complex that Ricardo's intellect was stimulated and even tried to its limit. Ricardo did not follow Smith; he tracked him.[39]

[36] Smith, *Wealth of Nations*, C, II, 331-42; M, 798-809; and Ricardo, Ch. XV, "Taxes on Profits," S, I, 205-14; G, 186-97; and Ch. XVIII, "Poor Rates," S, I, 257-62; G, 242-47.

[37] Smith, *Wealth of Nations*, C, II, 348-51; M, 815-18; and Ricardo, Ch. XVI, S, I, 215-42; G, 198-226.

[38] Smith, *Wealth of Nations*, C, II, 354-91; M, 821-58; and Ricardo, Ch. IX, "Taxes on Raw Produce," S, I, 156-72; G, 137-53; Ch. XVII, "Taxes on Other Commodities than Raw Produce," S, I, 243-56; G, 227-41; Ch. XXII, "Bounties on Exportation, and Prohibitions of Importation," S, I, 301-20; G, 285-305; and Ch. XXIX, "Taxes Paid by the Producer," S, I, 379-81; G, 370-72 (see also Ch. XII below.)

[39] Sraffa calls attention to the fact that Ricardo's chapters on taxation closely follow Smith's in the order in which the several taxes are discussed. S, I, xxv. For a brief analysis of the effect exerted by Adam Smith on tax policy, see Kennedy, *English Taxation, 1640—1799,* pp. 141-50. Kennedy thinks it was not substantial, on this point differing with Dowell, *History of Taxation in England,* II, 167-70.

3. A TREATISE ON TAXATION?

The second edition of the *Principles* had been out only a few months when Ricardo found himself under pressure from his friend Hutches Trower to expand his tax analysis. Over the next two years, mention of such a project recurs in correspondence with Trower and Malthus. It is not clear precisely what kind of a tax treatise Trower and Ricardo had in mind; it was evidently to be something different from Chapters VIII-XVIII of the *Principles*, perhaps a detailed analysis of the current tax system of Great Britain.

The public mind [wrote Trower, in September, 1819] is now in a proper state to receive instruction on these matters [political economy]; and there is one branch respecting which they are lamentably ignorant. I mean the *principles of taxation*. The question of taxation is never agitated in Parliament without affording abundant proof of this deficiency. All taxes on necessaries are scouted as unwise and unjust, and efforts are constantly making to repeal them.—It is true, that you have already clearly and ably laid down those principles in your Book. But I cannot help thinking that much benefit would arise from having these principles more *fully* explained and insisted upon, and their *application to our particular situation pointed out*. Their importance is enhanced by the peculiar circumstances in which this Country is placed, by the enormous amount of the funded debt, which will render it *absolutely necessary*, in any future war, to depend *almost exclusively* upon supplies raised within the year. It is a question of great interest, and general application, and I know no person so qualified to engage in it, and do it justice as yourself. In short it would be a more enlarged and comprehensive view of a subject you have already treated; *applied to, and illustrated by*, the actual circumstances and situation of the Country. Except the Chapters in your Book I am not aware of any modern work upon the subject.[40]

At the moment, Ricardo was noncommittal, replying only: "On the subject of taxation a wide field is open for those, who will patiently think, to give instruction to the Public; but the first step must be to make the first principles of Political Economy known, and that remains yet to be done."[41]

Ricardo passed the suggestion on to Malthus, two months later. Expressing his pleasure at hearing that Malthus's *Principles of Political Economy* was to be soon in the press, he added,

...I regret that the most important part of the conclusions from the principles

[40] Letter of Sept. 19, 1819, to Ricardo, S, VIII, 70-71.
[41] Letter of Sept. 25, 1819, to Trower, S, VIII, 79.
[42] Letter of Nov. 9, 1819, to Malthus, S, VIII, 130-31.

which you endeavour to elucidate, will not be included in it, I mean taxation. In a letter which I have lately received from Trower, he is full of regret that the important subject of taxation receives so little attention from Political Economists: at this time he thinks it peculiarly important, and I cannot but agree with him. As soon as you have launched your present work, I hope you will immediately prepare to give us your thoughts on a subject in which are all [sic] practically interested.[42]

Meanwhile, Ricardo put Trower off with protestations of intellectual inadequacy and want of time:

The subject you mention is very important to be well analyzed, and explained —namely, the best means of raising the funds which may be necessary for future expenditure; it is highly interesting and merits the most patient investigation. The difficulty which encompasses it is almost sufficient to deter one from entering upon it. For my own satisfaction however, and not with any hope to throw much light on so very intricate a question, I would employ my time upon it, if I had any time at my command, which at present I have not: on some future day I will bend my whole mind to the consideration of this subject.[43]

Trower kept after Ricardo, almost with the persistence of a James Mill, but without the success. In September, 1821, Trower wrote:

I confess I feel, that, now, the subject, with respect to *Principles (of Political Economy)*, is set at rest; although, no doubt, there are many minor points still disputed by some writers. But, what I am anxious to see is *an ample application of these Principles to the practical operation of Taxation.* What we now want is a Text Book, to which Statesmen may refer, at once, to regulate their financial operations. Hitherto, Taxes have not been levied upon any settled principle, on the contrary, for the most part, they have been at war with all principle. Convenience has been the only guide. Whatever article seemed capable of bearing the burden of Taxation, and was likely to prove productive has been selected. But it is time to abandon this disgraceful, and ruinous mode of proceeding, and to avail ourselves of the benefits to be derived from the vast body of light, which has been lately thrown upon this important subject. The Time will come when our purse strings must be pulled again; and we ought to be prepared with a knowledge how best to wield our resources. For such a task I know nobody better qualified than *yourself;* indeed, you have already opened up the subject, in your excellent work; and I should rejoice to see you compleat what has been so ably begun.[44]

But by now Ricardo seemed even less disposed to undertake the project than he had been in November, 1819.

[43] Letter of Nov. 12, 1819, to Trower, S, VIII, 132. In this letter, too, he expresses regret that Malthus has not covered the subject.

[44] Letter of Sept. 13, 1821, S, IX, 68-69.

I, as well as you [he writes] would like to see an application of the Principles of Political Economy, as now understood, to the practical operation of taxation, and I hope it will not be long before such a work appears. Ministers will always look more to the facility with which they can raise money by a tax, and the produce they can obtain from it, than to its consequences on the prosperity and future resources of the country (witness the legacy duty);[45] this however is no argument against the general dissemination of good doctrines, for if a minister was not restrained by an honest legislature, he would receive no inconsiderable check from an enlightened public. You make a great mistake in supposing me capable of producing so important a work.[46]

In September, 1823, Ricardo died; the promise of four years earlier to "bend my whole mind" to the consideration of taxation had not been redeemed.

4. COMMENTARIES ON RICARDO'S TAX ANALYSIS

At this late date, after a century and a half of commentaries on Ricardian doctrine,[47] can there be occasion for intensive analysis of Chapters VIII to XVIII of the Principles, and related Ricardian material on taxation?[48] Strangely enough, the answer seems to be in the affirmative, as a brief review of Ricardian literature with respect to this point will indicate.

Among Ricardo's contemporaries, James Mill (1773-1836) and J. R. McCulloch (1789-1864) were stimulated to reproduce Ricardian tax doctrine: Mill in a series of chapters in his *Elements of Political Economy* (1821, third edition 1826), McCulloch in an article for the *Encyclopaedia Britannica,*[49] and, much later, in his *A Treatise on the Principles and Practical Influence of Taxation and the Funding System* (1845).[50]

[45] See Chapter III below.

[46] Letter of Oct. 4, 1821, Ricardo toTrower, S, IX, 87-88.

[47] Blaug, *Ricardian Economics. A Historical Study,* pp. 3-4.

[48] All passages dealing with taxation in Ricardo's speeches, pamphlets, and correspondence are covered by the present study, through references or analyses at appropriate points in the discussion of the taxation and bounty chapters of the *Principles* (the latter include Chapters XXII, XXIII, and XXIX, and parts of Chapters VII, XIX, XXV, XXVI, and XXXII).

[49] *Supplement to the Fourth, Fifth, and Sixth Editions of the Encyclopaedia Britannica* (1824), VI, 608-43. This article of McCulloch's is noted in Hollander, ed., *Letters of David Ricardo to John Ramsay McCulloch* (Publications of the American Economic Association, Vol. X, 1895), p. 812 (p. 178 of the *Letters).*

[50] "That portion of the 'Wealth of Nations' which refers to Taxes and Public Debts, the chapters on the same subjects in Mr. Ricardo's 'Political Economy,' and the treatise of Sir Henry Parnell on 'Financial Reform,' are the only works of any

Mill did not subject Ricardo's reasoning to critical analysis; after all, he was, in his view, one of Ricardo's "two and only two genuine disciples," the other being McCulloch.[51] It is thus no surprise that Mill's chapters on taxation follow so closely Ricardo's own analysis that, among the score of comments Ricardo sent Mill on the manuscript of the entire *Elements*, only two are directly concerned with taxation, and only one of these is significant.[52]

Ricardo had no opportunity to comment on McCulloch's article, which was unfortunate, for he might have dissuaded McCulloch from dogmatic statements that the price level must remain unchanged, under a general profits tax,[53] and must rise, under a general sales tax,[54] and that all import duties fall on domestic consumers while all export duties burden only the foreigner,[55] and he might at least have cautioned against the assertion that a tax on dwelling rental would be divided between the occupier and the landowner (the supply of building being assumed quite elastic) "in the proportion that the profits of the capital laid out on [the houses] bore to the rent of the land on which they stood." [56] But these points aside, the *Britannica* article follows closely Ricardo's reasoning and conclusions, sometimes almost copying whole sentences. McCulloch had been eager to get Ricardo's reactions to his manuscript; he proposed to send his friend "the proofs of the more difficult parts;"[57] and Ricardo had been quite willing: "I shall be anxious to see your article on Taxation." [58] Within a week McCulloch had given further notice of intent: "I shall write you shortly on some

eminence on fiscal policy of a comprehensive character that have appeared in this country.... Under these circumstances we cannot be said to have obtruded ourselves upon a field of discussion already fully occupied." Preface, pp. v-vi.

[51] Letter of Sept. 19, 1823, Mill to McCulloch, S, IX, 391. The only non-relatives provided for in Ricardo's will were "his friends George Basevi, James Mill and Thomas Robert Malthus." S, X, 105. "With very few exceptions,—perhaps with none,—Mr. Mill of all men possessed the greatest influence over him." Memoir of Ricardo, published in 1824, written by one of Ricardo's brothers, probably Moses Ricardo. S, X, 9; see also S, X, 14.

[52] S, IX, 126-33. The significant comment concerns land rent as an exclusive base for taxation; see p. 82 below.

[53] *Supplement to the Fourth, Fifth, and Sixth Editions of the Encyclopaedia Britannica*, VI, 618.

[54] *Ibid., p.* 629.

[55] *Ibid.*, p. 633.

[56] *Ibid.*, p. 618.

[57] Letter of Aug. 11, 1823, McCulloch to Ricardo, S, IX, 345. See also *ibid.*, p. 342.

[58] Letter of Aug. 21, 1823, Ricardo to McCulloch, S, IX, 362.

points connected with Taxation . . .";[59] but no more correspondence passed between them before Ricardo's death some three weeks later.

McCulloch's large book of 1845, *Taxation and the Funding System,* is a more wordy paraphrase of Ricardo on taxation, again with a few exceptions or qualifications, especially with respect to the taxation of wages. McCulloch gives somewhat the impression of struggling, quite hopelessly, to free himself from the fascinating, intricate web spun by a master system-builder. In the Preface to the *Taxation* volume he asserts that "Mr. Ricardo's investigations [of taxation] are too abstract to be of much practical utility . . ."; [60] a year later he seems to recant, in his introductory remarks to his edition of Ricardo's Works:

> That part of Mr Ricardo's work, in which he applies his principles to discover the incidence of taxes on rent, profit, wages, and raw produce, is more practical than the others; and must always be a subject of careful study to those who wish to make themselves well acquainted with this department of political science.[61]

It remained for a mathematician and philosopher, one who had only a peripheral interest in political economy, to provide a searching analysis of some parts of Ricardo's taxation chapters. In 1829 and 1831 William Whewell (1794-1866), a Fellow of Trinity College, Cambridge, read to the Cambridge Philosophical Society two papers on political economy, in which he translated some of Ricardo's prose into mathematics, with critical comments on, and extensions of, both postulates and reasoning. His analyses of Ricardian tax theorems are appraised in the chapters below, in connection with the particular taxes to which they refer. Whewell's commentary on Ricardo caused no stir at the time, and appears to have been quite neglected since.[62]

[59] Letter of Aug. 24, 1823, McCulloch to Ricardo, S, IX, 369.

[60] *Taxation and the Funding System,* Preface, p. vi. In 1860 McCulloch contributed another article on taxation to the *Britannica,* 8th edition. It was reprinted separately. See biographical sketch of McCulloch by G. Barnett Smith, in *Palgrave's Dictionary of Political Economy,* Henry Higgs, ed. (1926), II, 657-58.

[61] McCulloch, ed., *The Works of David Ricardo with a Notice of the Life and Writings of the Author,* p. xxvi.

[62] See biographical sketch of Whewell by Rev. T. J. Lawrence, in *Palgrave's Dictionary of Political Economy,* III, 665. Whewell was the tutor of Ricardo's younger brother, Mortimer (1807-1876) at Trinity College, Cambridge, about 1825: S, X, 63. Whewell's two papers appear in the *Transactions of the Cambridge Philosophical Society.* The first paper was No. IX in Vol. III (1830), pp. 191-230, "Mathematical Exposition of some Doctrines of Political Economy," read March 2 and March 14, 1829, and dated at Trinity College, March 30, 1829. The second was No. V in Vol. IV (1833), pp. 155-98, "Mathematical Exposition of some of the Leading Doctrines in Mr. Ricardo's 'Principles of Political Econ-

J. B. Say, in notes to a French edition of the *Principles*,[63] offers a number of objections to Ricardo's tax analysis, but they are vitiated, for the most part, by a failure to understand the Ricardian economic model. The few points of significance that Say succeeds in making are reproduced in the appropriate chapters below.

Finally, among Ricardo's contemporaries, even Mrs. Marcet's Caroline, who had taken such pleasure in the study of chemistry, was not deemed ready by Mrs. B. for exposure to tax analysis. Yet the twenty-two conversations on political economy in which she showed herself so splendid a pupil included several on money and banking, international trade, and the foreign exchanges.[64]

In 1848, with the appearance of John Stuart Mill's *Principles*, taxation theory and indeed the whole theory of public finance are reformulated and extended to a degree that makes it inappropriate to

omy and Taxation'," read April 18 and May 2, 1831, and dated at Trinity College, May 7, 1831. The first paper, devoted almost entirely to taxation (tax on wages, tax on profits, percentage tax on agricultural produce, fixed tax per acre, tax on rent), analyzes also the effects of the two Ricardian types of improvement in the technique of agriculture (S, I, 80; G, 57), and restates the "axioms" of Ricardo's macro-economic system. The second paper examines these "postulates" critically, and includes a mathematical treatment of the Ricardian problems of distribution of income, foreign trade, international gold flow, and the effect on relative prices of "the proportion and durability of fixed capital" (p. 173). Only a few pages are devoted to taxes (the same five treated in the first paper). Henry Sidgwick, in "Political Economy: Method," in *Palgrave's Dictionary,* III, 136, footnote, says: "The earliest systematic application by an Englishman of mathematical symbols to political economy would seem to be Whewell's mathematical exposition of some doctrines of political economy in the *Cambridge Philosophical Transactions,* vol. iii, pp. 191-230." For comment on Whewell, and for information on two earlier English economists and one American who applied mathematics to economic problems (T. Perronet Thompson, "E. R.," and Samuel Gale), see Robertson, "Mathematical Economics before Cournot," *J. Pol. Econ.*, LVII (no. 6, Dec., 1949), 535.

[63] Ricardo, *Des principes de l'économie politique, et de l'impôt,* trans. by F. S. Constancio, with annotations by Jean-Baptiste Say. 2 vols. 1819. The translation is of the first edition. This work is hereafter referred to as "Say, Notes on Ricardo."

[64] The Author of *Conversations on Chemistry* [Mrs. Jane Marcet], *Conversations on Political Economy,* 4th ed., 1821. Feeling quite venturesome, Mrs. B., Caroline's mentor, offers a bit of information on tithes, but betrays her nervousness by an uncharacteristic assignment of responsibility: "It is the opinion of a political economist of great eminence, Mr. Ricardo, that the farmer is eventually remunerated for the expense of tithes" (p. 245). In the last two editions of *Conversations* (6th, 1827; 7th, 1839), Mrs. B. seems to have formed opinions of

speak of Mill as either a supporter or a critic of Ricardian tax doctrine. Although he utilizes much of Ricardo's tax analysis, and discards other portions, he does not attempt a systematic critique of Ricardo's tax chapters.[65]

Marshall's *Principles,* breaking with the tradition established by Smith, Ricardo, and J. S. Mill, contains no book on public finance; he offers, however, a critical comment on Ricardo's analysis of a tax on agricultural produce.[66] Seligman's *The Shifting and Incidence of Taxation* contains a five-page summary of Ricardo's chief conclusions, and some incidental references to his analysis.[67] A somewhat more extended summary is provided by Musgrave in his *The Theory of Public Finance.*[68]

Even the commentators on Ricardo have neglected the chapters on taxation. Gonner, in his "Introductory Essay" to the 1891 reprint of the third edition of the *Principles,* summarizes Ricardo's conclusions, but does not reach the level of critical analysis that he achieves with respect to the rest of the volume. And in his article on Ricardo in Palgrave's *Dictionary,* Gonner allots only one brief paragraph to taxation.[69] Hollander's "Centenary Estimate" passes over the taxation chap-

her own on this subject. The price effect of the tithe "has been ably discussed by Mr. Ricardo" (pp. 247, 239, respectively), but not ably enough, if we are to judge by the distinctly non-Ricardian conclusions that she now reaches. Mrs. Marcet's successor in popularizing the new political economy, Harriet Martineau, was appreciably bolder, devoting five volumes to taxation *(Illustrations of Taxation,* 1834). But her *Illustrations of Political Economy,* 1832-34, ran to twenty-five volumes, and her *Poor Laws and Paupers Illustrated,* 1833-34, to ten. See Lindley M. Fraser, "Marcet, Jane," and "Martineau, Harriet," in *Encyclopaedia of the Social Sciences,* Vol. 10, pp. 108 and 168 respectively, and the same two titles in *Palgrave's Dictionary of Political Economy,* Vol. II, by Edwin Cannan, p. 690, and Hugh E. Egerton, p. 703, respectively.

[65] Mill, *Principles of Political Economy,* Ashley ed., Bk. V, Chs. II-VII. See Chapter XVI below.

[66] Among the later volumes that Marshall planned was one to be entitled *The Economic Functions of Government.* And the title of his course in Easter Term, 1885-86, was "Speculation, Taxation, etc. (Mill, IV and V)." J. M. Keynes, "Alfred Marshall, 1842-1924," in A. C. Pigou, ed., *Memorials of Alfred Marshall,* pp. 60, 52 respectively. See also the preface to Marshall's *Principles,* 5th ed., and C. W. Guillebaud, "The Evolution of Marshall's *Principles of Economics," Econ. J.,* LII (no. 208, Dec., 1942), 339, 349. For the analysis of the tax on produce, see Marshall's *Principles of Economics,* 8th ed., Appendix L.

[67] Fifth ed., pp. 147-51, 258-75, 292.

[68] See pp. 385-92.

[69] G, pp. xli-xlvii, and *Palgrave's Dictionary of Political Economy,* III, 308.

ters with three pages of general comment.[70] The stenographic record (unauthorized) of Mitchell's *Lecture Notes on Types of Economic Theory* includes some fifty pages on Ricardo, but the references to taxation are few and brief.[71] The balance has been partially redressed in the recent work by Oswald St. Clair, who devotes the equivalent of some forty pages of his *A Key to Ricardo* to analytical comments on certain parts of Ricardo's tax doctrine.

In the French, German, and Italian literature of economics and public finance, Ricardian tax analysis appears to have attracted no more attention than in the English.

Du Puynode, writing in 1868, has some thirty pages on the subject, but his comments are worth little, as he seems unable to follow Ricardo's chain of logic.[72] In the substantial section that Gide and Rist allow to Ricardo's thought in their *History of Economic Doctrines,* taxation is not mentioned, apart from a brief footnote on rent.[73] The title of Ricardo's chief work is cited simply as *The Principles of Political Economy.* Recently, Giraudeau has summarized some of the more important Ricardian tax theorems.[74]

In the German literature, von Falck's work (1882) on the development of shifting and incidence doctrine [75] and Schneider's monograph of 1923 [76] offer the most substantial critiques of Ricardian tax theorems. But neither of them subjects Ricardo's reasoning to intensive analysis; the objections offered are on a general level, and concern the validity of Ricardo's assumptions or the relevance of his conclusions. They thus make almost no analytical contribution. Diehl, in his two-volume commentary on Ricardo, allows but eight pages to taxation, in part because

[70] Hollander, ed., *Letters of David Ricardo to John Ramsay McCulloch, 1816-1823,* pp. 97-99, 124-25.

[71] See Vol. I, pp. 150, 157, 158, 164, 169, 182.

[72] *Études sur les principaux Economistes,* Ch. 3, "Ricardo," espec. pp. 214-38.

[73] On pp. 138-68; see note 1, p. 155.

[74] "La théorie de l'impôt chez Ricardo," *Rev. de Sci. Fin.,* XLIII (no. 2, April-June, 1951), 319-39.

[75] *Kritische Rückblicke auf die Entwicklung der Lehre von der Steuerüberwalzung seit Adam Smith,* pp. 48-70.

[76] Die Steuerlehre Ricardos. Typescript, dissertaton, University of Freiburg. A printed volume of the same title, published in 1927, author Wilhelm Greuling, can be disregarded, as it is simply a literal copy of Schneider's work. Finally, another, quite different, doctoral dissertation, at the University of Bonn, in 1951, by Clewing, Die finanzwissenschaftlichen Ansichten van David Riccardo, is on a still more general level, and of broader scope, not being limited to taxation.

he sees no point in repeating a criticism of what he considered a faulty theory of distribution on which much of the tax analysis is based.[77] A few paragraphs, or at the most a few pages, on Ricardian tax doctrine are to be found in Földes,[78] Held,[79] Kaizl,[80] and Mann.[81] Wicksell's monograph on shifting and incidence affords a useful critique of many aspects of the Ricardian economic system, with particular reference to taxation, but it is not a systematic study of Ricardo's tax doctrine.[82]

A number of Italian public finance scholars have referred more or less briefly to Ricardo's tax analysis.[83] Pantaleoni's treatise on shifting and incidence (1882) utilizes short quotations or paraphrases from

[77] *Sozialwissenschaftliche Erläuterungen zu David Ricardo's Grundgesetzen der Volkswirtschaft und Besteuerung.* There is a short section on the implications for nationalization of land that flow from Ricardo's theory of ground rent ("die Bodenverstaatlichungsbewegung"); and customs duties are discussed in a long chapter on "Ricardo's Doctrine of Foreign Trade." For an analysis of Ricardo's plan for a capital levy to retire the war debt, see the following, by Diehl: (1) "Die einmalige Vermögensabgabe," in *Schriften des Vereins für Sozialpolitik,* Bd. 156, Teil 1, 1918; (2) "David Ricardo und der finanzielle Wiederaufbau Englands nach den napoleonischen Kriegen," *Bankarchiv,* XIX (no. 9, 1920), 106-9, and XIX (no. 10, 1920), 122-27, espec. pp. 125-27. In his article, "Ricardo," in *Handwörterbuch der Staatswissenschaften,* 4th ed., 1926, Diehl gives only one paragraph, not very helpful, on Ricardian tax doctrine.

[78] "Ricardo. Mit besonderer Berücksichtigung der kriegswirtschaftlichen Probleme," *Jahrb. f. Nationalökonomie,* CXIV (3rd series, LIX, no. 6, June, 1920), 481-535.

[79] "Zur Lehre von der Überwälzung der Steuern," *Ztschr f. d. ges. Staatswiss.,* XXIV (nos. 3-4, 1868), 421-95.

[80] *Die Lehre von der Überwälzung der Steuern,* 1882.

[81] "Überwälzung der Steuer," *Handwörterbuch der Staatswissenschaften,* Vol. 8, 4th ed., 1928; "Die Wandlungen des Finanzliberalismus," *Schmollers Jahrb.,* LIX (no. 3, 1935), 271-97; and "Geschichte der angelsächsischen Finanzwissenschaft," in *Handbuch der Finanzwissenschaft,* Vol. 1, 2nd ed., 1950. For a socialist point of view, see Nachimson, "David Ricardos Steuertheorie," *Die Neue Zeit,* I (29th year, no. 8, Nov. 2, 1910), 244-54.

[82] *Zur Lehre von der Steuerincidenz.*

[83] Cabiati, "La finanza di A. De Viti De Marco," *Giorn. degli Econ.,* LXVIII (no. 11, Nov., 1928), 881-898; Fubini, "Contributo alla determinazione del concetto di imposta generale sul reddito," *Giorn. degli Econ.,* LXXII (no. 5, May, 1932), 297, "I dui tipi fondamentali di indagine nell'ambita dell'economia finanziaria," *Giorn. degli Econ.,* LXXIII (no. 12, Dec., 1933), 883-89, "Francesco Ferrara e David Ricardo," *Giorn. degli Econ.,* LXXV (no. 2, Feb., 1935), 85-101; Jarach, "Gli effetti di un'imposta generale ed uniforme sui profitti," *Atti Accad. scienze di Torino,* XLVI (1910-1911), 286-301; Steve, "Sul concetto di imposta generale," *Giorn. degli Econ.* (new series), VI (nos. 11-12, Nov.-Dec., 1947), 573-626.

Ricardo to serve as a base for Pantaleoni's own analysis, but contains no sustained critique of Ricardian tax doctrine.[84] Both Griziotti in 1917 and Sensini in 1920 examine Ricardo's analysis of war finance and his proposal for a postwar capital levy.[85]

[84] *Teoria della Traslazione dei Tributi.* See especially pp. 267-73, on taxes on wages and necessaries.

[85] Griziotti, "La diversa pressione tributaria del prestito e dell'imposta," *Giorn. degli Econ.*, LIV (nos. 3 and 5, March and May, 1917), 129-64 and 313-34. Reprinted in his *Studi di Scienza delle Finanze e Diritto Finanziario,* II, 193-261. Sensini, "La teoria di Ricardo sui diversi effetti del prestito e dell'imposta," *Giorn. degli Econ.*, LX (No. 2, February, 1920), 57-74. Two recent review articles on the Sraffa edition do not mention taxation: Einaudi, "Dalla leggenda al monumento," *Giorn. degli Econ.* (new series), X (Nos. 7-8, July-August, 1951), 329-34; and de Toma, "Ricardiana," *Giorn. degli Econ.* (new series), XI (Nos. 3-4, March-April, 1952), 211-28.

CHAPTER II

RICARDO'S MACRO-ECONOMIC SYSTEM

Ricardo had a public conscience and an abstracting mind. To start his intellectual engine turning over, two kinds of stimuli were needed: an economic issue of practical importance, and an erroneous or misleading diagnosis and prescription by someone who commanded attention—Adam Smith, Malthus, Say, a Parliamentary Committee, or, best of all, the Directors of the Bank of England. But once the machine was in motion, a powerful generalizing and system-building mechanism took over, and the raw materials of irredeemable paper money, fluctuating exchanges, gold movements, corn prices, 3 percents at 70, and Bank of England profits were converted into abstract analyses of measure of value, progressive and stationary states, distribution of national product among wages, profits, and rent, and comparative advantage in international trade. Thus the Ricardian macro-economic system possesses an air of abstraction from time and place, an aloofness from specific issues of policy, that explains much of its attraction for economists of later generations, but that may lead us to overlook the originating stimulus.

Moreover, this system, as presented in the first seven chapters of the *Principles,* gives an initial impression of coherence and completeness; it suggests a master builder who started construction only when the full set of blueprints was at hand. This impression is not confirmed, however, by the written record that develops as Ricardo reacts to the several problems of policy that emerged in the years 1809-1815; for example: When should the Bank of England notes again be made redeemable in gold, and should redemption be in coin or only in bullion? Should restrictions on the import of corn be continued? Should the export trade be favored, as tending to raise the general rate of profits? From his earlier pamphlets and correspondence it appears that Ricardo did not visualize his macro-economic structure as a whole until a large part of it was in place. But the work proceeded so rapidly, over a period of scarcely more than five years, and the results were assembled in so compact a form, that again we are apt to forget that the Ricardian economic system grew directly out of current problems.

The set of generalizations compressed into the first seven chapters of the *Principles* apparently touched off the production of a second set, the chapters on taxation. The impression that they are derivative from the first group, rather than arising directly out of issues of current policy, is supported by the lack of evidence that Ricardo had engaged in tax controversy before he sat down to compose Chapters VIII to XVIII (and Chapters XXII, XXIII, and XXIX) in the autumn of 1816. Ricardo's letters, speeches, and pamphlets extend and refine this abstract body of tax analysis; they do not supply it with starting points drawn from English fiscal problems of the day. The tax chapters give the impression that Ricardo, being certain that correct policy in these matters was vital to the country's welfare, was equally certain that such a policy could be derived from, and only from, a "systematic inquiry into the nature of economic relationships and their mode of development in different types of circumstances." [1] This inquiry had just been completed, in Chapters I-VII, and could be applied at once to the most pressing problem of government, the raising of revenue by taxation. There was no occasion to list and evaluate the tax measures then in force, or current tax proposals. Such a canvass would be a waste of time; the correct prescription was the thing.

Certain consequences ensue for the student of Ricardian tax doctrine. An understanding of Ricardo's tax theorems requires of the reader somewhat more grounding in Ricardo's macro-economic system than is needed for comprehension of much of his monetary analysis, for instance. Correlatively, the logical gaps that impair the system are just as damaging for the tax analysis; we shall encounter a notable example in Ricardo's theorem that virtually all taxes of general scope come out of profits eventually, no matter where initially levied.

Accordingly, for the background to analyze Ricardo's tax doctrine, we turn in the present chapter to a summary of his laws of economic growth, distribution, and value.[2]

[1] Robbins, *Theory of Economic Policy in English Classical Political Economy*, p. 171.

[2] The summary is based chiefly, of course, on Chapters I-VII of the *Principles*, but in part also on the remaining chapters and on Ricardo's other works and

1. RESTRICTIONS ON CORN IMPORTS AND THE THREAT OF THE STATIONARY STATE

Wartime impediments to the import of wheat, among them a substantial duty that varied inversely with the price, had induced English farmers to extend cultivation to markedly inferior lands, and to work the better lands more intensively. The marginal cost of wheat grown in England had increased correspondingly.

At the end of the war with France, England had to decide whether to maintain wheat production at something like the wartime level, or to rely largely on imports of the grain, purchased by export of manufactured goods. A severe fall in the price of wheat had stirred sentiment for even greater protection; but on the other side were those to whom maintenance of the war-extended agriculture was a misuse of national resources and a threat to the country's growth. Ricardo was a leader in this latter group. His *Essay on the Influence of a Low Price of Corn on the Profits of Stock,* published early in 1815, was not influential in shaping policy, for Parliament shortly thereafter enacted the Corn Law of 1815, which prohibited importation of wheat until the price reached 10 shillings a bushel. But the *Essay* was of great significance in the development of Ricardo's thought, for around it he developed in the next two

correspondence, assembled in the Sraffa edition. Specific page references are made sparingly; all that is offered here is a personal weighing and interpretation of well-known Ricardian propositions. Much aid has been derived from the following analyses of Ricardo's doctrine, published in recent years: Baumol, *Economic Dynamics,* pp. 17-19; Blaug, "The Empirical Content of Ricardian Economics," *J. Pol. Econ.*, LXIV (No. 1, Feb., 1956), 41-58, and *Ricardian Economics: A Historical Study;* Cassels, "A Re-interpretation of Ricardo on Value," *Q. J. Econ.,* XLIX (No. 3, May, 1935), 518-32; Hutchison, "Some Questions about Ricardo," *Economica* (new series), XIX (No. 76, Nov., 1952), 415-32, and "Ricardo's Correspondence," *Economica* (new series), XX (No. 79, Aug., 1953), 263-73; Kaldor, "Alternative Theories of Distribution," *R. Econ. Studies,* XXIII (No. 61, 1955-56), 85; Knight, "Ricardian Theory of Production and Distribution," *Can. J. Econ. and Pol. Sci.,* I (Feb. and May, 1935), 3-25 and 171-96; Paquet, *Le conflit historique entre la loi des débouchés et le principe de la demande effective,* pp. 22-24; Shove, "The Place of Marshall's *Principles* in the Development of Economic Theory," *Econ. J.*, LII (No. 208, Dec., 1942), 294-329; Stigler, "The Ricardian Theory of Value and Distribution," *J. Pol. Econ.,* LX (No. 3, June, 1952), 187-207; "Sraffa's Ricardo," *Am. Econ. R.,* XLIII (No. 4, Pt. 1, Sept., 1953), 586-99; and "Ricardo and the 93% Labor Theory of Value," *Am. Econ. R.*, XLVIII (No. 3, June, 1958), 357-67. Those reading Ricardo for the first time will find a useful companion in Oswald St. Clair's *A Key to Ricardo.*

years much of the system that appeared in the *Principles.* Indeed, the *Essay* contains those dynamic aspects that are of particular interest for his tax analysis: a continuing decline in the rate of profit, an increase in rent, and an eventual cessation of growth at the stationary state, that would inevitably result if wheat were not freely imported.

An economy like England's, with so many agricultural countries outside to draw from, had in Ricardo's view no forseeable limit to its growth if it continued to expand its manufacturing industries, and did not attempt to increase its farm production. Manufactured goods could be produced in ever larger quantities without the handicap of diminishing returns, and the cost of production would in fact be lowered continually by technological improvements.[3] A working force four times as large, for example, could produce four times the manufactures, and could import four times the foodstuffs without having to pay a higher price. A day's work in the factory would make possible the procurement from abroad of at least as many bushels of wheat as before. But if England insisted on growing more wheat as her population expanded, she would find it becoming steadily more costly, for farming, unlike manufacturing, operates under diminishing returns. A day's work by a farm laborer produces less and less wheat as cultivation is pushed out to inferior soils or as the good soils are worked more intensively. Thus a population four times as large would need much more than a quadrupling of the farm labor force if it insisted on feeding itself wholly or largely on domestic grain. Indeed, a time would come when the product of a marginal day's labor on the annual crop would add so little to the harvest that the increment would be barely enough to cover the minimum consumption of the farm worker and his family that would guarantee maintenance (not expansion) of the labor force. In looser terms, the marginal laborer would produce barely enough to cover his minimum living needs. Nothing would be left for the capitalist as interest or profit on the sums he had advanced to provide food, clothing, and shelter for the worker, and machinery, fertilizer, etc., that had to be used before the crop was harvested and ready for consumption. At this point, the country's growth must cease, and in fact it will cease somewhat earlier, since the product at the margin must allow a minimum portion,[4] never precisely stated by Ricardo,[5] as profit to the capitalist, to compensate him for trouble and

[3] S, I, 93-94; G, 71.

[4] See, for example, S, I, 115, 120-21, 290; G, 92, 99, 274.

[5] A numerical illustration in S, I, 36; G, 29 ("The greatest effects ... to that amount") implies a minimum rate of profit of 2.3 percent on the capital invested.

risk[6] and for the lapse of time.[7] The stationary state will have been reached. Manufactures will offer no avenue for continued growth; the rate of profit there will have sunk *pari passu* with that in agriculture, capital being mobile between the two uses.

2. THE PROGRESSIVE STATE: THE COURSE OF WAGES, PROFITS AND RENT

All this would be in the future, and even then only if Britain should be so short-sighted as to exclude foreign corn. Meanwhile she was a progressive state, not a stationary state.[8] In the progressive, growing state, agricultural labor at the margin is producing more than enough food to maintain the population unchanged. But who gets this excess of product at the margin?

To answer this question in Ricardian terms, we must rely on inference, for Ricardo never stops to specify the composition of family, the age distribution of the populace, and similar details that would support his conclusions on division of the product between labor and capital at the margin of cultivation in the progressive state.

As a first step, let us return for a moment to the stationary state, where the working force is neither growing nor declining. In the simplest case, each family consists of the father, mother, and two children who reach maturity (and, no doubt, some children who do not). We may define the working force as the man working in the fields plus the woman working in the home. Each year, for every man or woman dropping out of the working force through retirement or death, there is a replacement from the ranks of youth. The daily wage of the man, in market-basket terms, is just sufficient to guarantee that, out of the number of children born to the laborer and his wife, two survive to maturity, to become members of the labor force. This wage is the "natural price of labour,"[9] the natural rate of wages, just high enough to guarantee maintenance of the labor force unchanged in numbers. This natural rate, the market-basket minimum, is set by habit and custom well above bare physiological needs.[10] Nevertheless, in a given country and year, it is fairly rigid, not readily altered. Accordingly, no force can drive the wage

[6] S, I, 122; G, 101.

[7] On the time factor, see e. g., S, I, 37, G, 30-31; and on "interest," see S, I, 89, 110, 297-300, 363-64; G, 44, 66, 87, 282-84, 351-52.

[8] S, I, 109; G, 86. [9] S, I, 93; G, 70.

[10] S, I, 96-97, 332; G, 74, 318-19. For relevant passages from other sources, see St. Clair, *Key to Ricardo*, pp. 106-7.

actually paid (the "market rate" of wages) appreciably below this level, at least not for more than some years. At a lower market rate of wages, fewer children would reach maturity, and the death rate of those already in the working force would rise. With a smaller working force, cultivation would have to be restricted; it would be drawn in to more productive margins of cultivation. The worker at the margin would now be producing more than had the worker at the preceding, less productive margin. The excess product would be available for making good the loss in productivity caused by whatever it was that had temporarily impaired the market-basket wage—perhaps a diversion of some resources to government, or a permanent worsening of the climate.

Thus in the stationary state the natural rate of wages coincides with the market rate of wages, and whenever some external influence causes the market rate to diverge from the natural rate, forces are set in motion that tend to bring the two together again.

The only possibility of a permanent departure of the market rate from the natural rate hitherto prevailing arises from the fact that habit and custom may themselves be changed, under the pressure of the new market rate. Many years under a new low market rate of wages may degrade the laborer to the point where he will rear a replacement labor force at a lower standard of living than before. Similarly, sustained experience with a market rate of wages above the natural rate may decide the worker to raise his sights; a new, higher, natural rate of wages finally prevails,[11] and this consequence, with all that it means in benefits for the mass of mankind, is in Ricardo's view a compelling argument in favor of the progressive state, and hence in favor of a free trade in corn.

Turning again to the progressive state, the growing economy, we can see at once that the market-basket wage must exceed the natural rate of wages as defined above. The laborer's wage must be enough to support to maturity, not two children, but three or more. Or, to use a somewhat different approach: if capital is so plentiful, compared with the supply of labor, that the competing entrepreneurs offer more than the natural rate of wages, the population will increase; workers and their wives will spend at least part of the extra income in rearing more children to maturity.

There remains unanswered the question: Are the worker and the members of his family better off than when the market rate coincides with the natural rate? If the higher wage simply enables some of the children, who would otherwise have perished before reaching working

[11] S, I, 100-1; G, 77.

age, to attain that goal, the improvement in living conditions is real, yet the subsistence level is not exceeded. Thus the subsistence standard itself is seen to be ambiguous, except in terms of the question: Subsistence for how long? If the higher wage is accompanied by a larger number of births, and a somewhat larger number of deaths before maturity, but on balance a larger number of children reaching working age, and that is all, has there been an increase in the delights of domesticity? If, on the other hand, the death rate decreases, owing to better nutrition, and the birth rate increases so slowly that per capita consumption rises above the subsistence level, there is ready agreement that real benefits have accrued to the laboring poor. Ricardo does not distinguish sharply among these possible outcomes; we are not offered a contrast between two types of excess market rate of wages, one of which might be termed a subsistence excess market rate, the other a luxury excess market rate. In general, Ricardo's wage discussion implies only a subsistence excess market wage, but here and there passages more optimistic in tone may be found.[12]

Let us consider the implications of the subsistence excess market wage: no members of working class families are receiving more than enough to sustain life according to prevailing habits and customs, and some members are receiving even less than this and hence not surviving to maturity. Under these conditions, the labor force is expanding year by year. The product of labor at the margin of cultivation, a margin that is moving outward continually, is still so large, compared with the wage, that a substantial profit emerges and, accumulated as capital, is re-invested. Evidently, the rate of profit is still well above that minimum of reward at which accumulation ceases.

A simple numerical illustration may help fix the ideas. A purely agricultural, self-contained economy of 100 workers' families and 10 capitalists is observed at the start of a year when each capitalist has on hand 1,000 bushels of wheat. Wheat is the sole form of capital, and the sole wage-good. The minimum rate of profit that must be exceeded to induce accumulation and investment is assumed to be zero.

Each worker will produce 120 bushels of wheat; that is, only land of the best quality is in use so far, and the marginal product equals the average product, both being 120 bushels per man-year. For the time being, therefore, no rent emerges.

The number of children being reared in each family is in excess of

[12] Cf., e. g., S, I, 94, 163, 220, 292-93, footnote on 348, 406-407; G, 71, 144, 203, 276-77, footnote on 336, 400. On this issue St. Clair is instructive: *Key to Ricardo,* pp. 113-22.

pure replacement needs, and happens to be such that, at the minimum set by habit and custom, each worker's family must receive 100 bushels a year as wages.

Competition among the capitalists sets the wage at just 100 bushels a year, since there are 10,000 bushels bidding for 100 workers, and since the resulting wage, 100, is not higher than the worker's output, 120. The demand curve for labor, in this wages-fund economy, is a curve of unitary elasticity denoting the outlay of 10,000 bushels (the area under the demand curve at any given point), and the supply of labor for this year is completely inelastic at 100 workers. The demand curve stops its ascent at the point opposite 120 on the wage scale, and runs to the left horizontally to intersect the wage axis at 120, since the worker's productivity of 120 puts a ceiling on the wage that will be offered, no matter how few the workers.

By the end of the first year the capitalists have on hand 120 bushels of wheat times 100 workers, or 12,000 bushels of wheat, comprising 10,000 bushels return of capital, and 2,000 bushels profit. This is a rate of profit of 20 percent on the capital invested. Another way of computing a rate of profit, and one that Ricardo often employs, is to say that profit is 2,000/12,000 of the total product going to wages and profits, or $16^2/_3$ per cent. In these terms, we may also compute a rate of wages: 10,000/12,000, or $83^1/_3$ percent. At this stage, none of the product goes to rent; there are no landlords, the best grade of land being so plentiful that it is still a free good.

As the second year opens, we suppose that the labor force has grown to 125 workers.

The wage for the second year, on the same principles as those given for the first, is 12,000/125, or 96 bushels per worker, and we again suppose that this happens to be just enough to support at the minimum level the workers, their wives, and their children. This figure, lower than the 100 of the year before, implies some decrease in the number of children being reared in each family, though the number is still above a mere replacement level.

In this second year we introduce diminishing returns. While each of the 100 workers of the first year continues to produce 120 bushels, the added 25 workers must be employed on poorer land, all the best land having been taken up, and each of them produces only 110 bushels. This statement is of course an oversimplification, as no one worker can be identified as belonging to either group, and some of the larger labor force will be applied to cultivating more intensively the lands already in use. Thus it is more precise to say that of the 125 man-years employed, each of the first 100 man-years yields 120 bushels, while each of the last 25 man-years yields 110 bushels. Since all workers are paid the same wage, the result might seem to be higher profits for those entrepreneurs who make use of the first 100 man-years, but competition among entrepreneurs makes impossible such a difference in profits. The higher productivity of the first 100 man-years of labor applied to the better lands is taken by the landlords in rent.

Total product for the second year is therefore 100 workers times 120 bushels, plus 25 workers times 110 bushels, or 14,750 bushels. Each capitalist lays out 96 bushels per worker, and gets back 110 bushels per worker, a profit of 14 bushels, or almost 15 percent on the investment. Wherever a worker produces 120 bushels, the landlord gets the extra 10 in rent. Total profit is thus 14 bushels times 125 workers, or 1,750 bushels. Replacement of capital absorbs 12,000, and the remaining 1,000 bushels of the total product (14,750 bushels) goes to landlords as rent (10 bushels times 100 workers). Of the 13,750 bushels going to wages and profit, slightly less than 13 percent goes to profit, and slightly more than 87 percent goes to wages: a "rise" in wages and a "fall" in profits from the first year, in Ricardian terminology.

Ricardo's demonstration, derived from Malthus and West, that rent emerges as the economy grows, added a strong emotional appeal to his case against the corn laws. The case was strong enough anyway, and indeed, as Sraffa points out, Ricardo had developed much of his theory of profits on the basis simply of diminishing returns, without explicitly referring to rent.[13] Import restrictions on corn were unwise because they forced the country into diminishing returns. But they seemed more than just unwise, they became ethically repugnant, when it was realized that they served to channel a large part of the country's output into the hands of those who performed no economic function. In so far as land owners invested money in farm improvements, they were capitalists, not landlords. As landlords, they did nothing but receive rent, and consume it unproductively.[14] Ricardo must have felt that he had an irrefutable argument when he discovered that it was directed against both stupidity and avarice.

[13] S, IV, 7-8.

[14] Ricardo is never quite specific on the use landlords make of their income. They must consume it in the stationary state, to the extent that capitalists do not consume theirs; and we may infer they consume most or all of it in the progressive state.

We carry the numerical illustration partly through one more year. As the third year opens, the capital on hand is 13,750 bushels. The other 1,000 bushels, given to the landlords, will be consumed unproductively, Ricardo seems to imply, hence will not be available to feed productive workers. We assume that the working force has grown to 150 men. Accordingly, this year's wage will be 88 bushels. Hence the number of extra children in workers' families must continue its decline, to just the level where 88 bushels per family will barely suffice, per capita, to meet the habit-and-custom standard. And so on, year after year, until the stationary state is reached.

In this illustration, we may say that the market rate of wages remains unchanged through the years, in terms of the amount available for per capita consumption by workers' families. Or we may say that it declines in terms of the size of the market basket that the worker's wages purchase (100 bushels, 96 bushels, 88 bushels). Ricardo, however, would tell us that the wage rate had risen, for he usually measures the market rate of wages by the amount of labor needed to produce the market basket, even though the market basket is shrinking. In this illustration, the amount of labor going into the production of the market basket is $^{100}/_{120}$ of a man-year the first year and $^{96}/_{110}$ of a man-year the second year, that is, $83^{1}/_{3}$ percent and $87^{3}/_{11}$ percent of a man-year respectively. And therefore in this simple case, which does not involve changes in the amount of fixed capital, the wage rate rises similarly in terms of the proportion of the profits-wages segment of the national income that goes to wages ($83^{1}/_{3}$ percent, $87^{3}/_{11}$ percent). This last computation illustrates the Ricardian dictum that, as the progressive state moves toward the stationary state, profits tend to fall and wages tend to rise, and his correlative statement that wages can never rise but by a fall in profits. As a man-year of labor at the margin of cultivation becomes less productive, owing to resort to less favorable margins, a larger portion of the product at the margin must go to wages, hence a smaller portion to profits.

The natural rate of wages meanwhile remains fixed: let us suppose, at 50 bushels per worker per year. But this 50 bushels too is rising in value, if, with Ricardo, we measure value by the amount of labor input (with allowance for reward to capital), at the margin of cultivation. The natural rate of annual wage is $^{50}/_{120}$ of a man-year of labor in the first year, $^{50}/_{110}$ in the second year. Again, the rate of wages (now, the natural rate) has increased; the "value of labor" has risen.[15]

[15] See S, I, 18-20, footnote on 41, 49-50, 275, 289; G, 12-14, footnote on 34, 41-42, 260, 272.

Profit is falling, whether computed as a return on the capital invested (20 percent, 15 percent), or as a proportion of the wages-profits segment of the national product ($16^2/_3$ percent, 13 percent).

Rent increases, as a share in the total product, and in absolute amount measured in bushels. Moreover, if the illustration is expanded to include a manufacturing sector where cost remains constant no matter how greatly output is increased, it can be seen, with the aid of Ricardo's theory of value, that each bushel of wheat comes to exchange for more and more manufactured goods. The landlord gets more bushels, as the economy grows, and with each bushel can obtain more of other goods. He benefits enormously from restriction of corn imports and the consequent extension of domestic agriculture to less favorable margins.

In the absence of the mysterious influence assumed up to this point, by which the number of children in a family living in a progressive state is always just large enough to absorb, on a minimum-of-subsistence basis, the market basket afforded by the year's demand and supply conditions in the labor market, Ricardo's system provides no means of defining the ratio in which profits and wages divide between them that part of the national product which does not go to rent, even in the agricultural economy.[16]

3. VALUE IN EXCHANGE

In the one-product, purely agricultural economy assumed in the illustration above, distribution of the product is independent of exchange value; indeed, there are no exchanges of commodity against commodity. Once a manufacturing sector is introduced, or even if the agricultural sector is assumed to yield more than one product, the laws determining ratios of exchange among commodities must be ascertained if distribution of the total output is to be fixed.[17] It was this logical necessity, rather than pressure of current issues of policy, that led Ricardo into the thicket of value theory.[18] Exchange of commodities in general against gold, while involving the same problems, has special difficulties of its own, since it turns attention at once to foreign exchange and international trade; and

[16] Cf. Knight, "The Ricardian Theory of Production and Distribution," *Can. J. Econ. and Pol. Sci.*, I (Feb. and May, 1935), 3-25 and 171-96.

[17] See S, I, Introduction, by Sraffa, pp. xxx-xxxiii; Stigler, "Ricardian Theory of Value and Distribution," *J. Pol. Econ.*, LX (No. 3, June 1952), 203-204; Kaldor, "Alternative Theories of Distribution," *R. Econ. Studies*, XXIII (No. 61, 1955-56), 86-87.

[18] On the development of Ricardo's interest in the problem of value, up to the first edition of the *Principles*, see Sraffa's Introduction, S, I, xiv-xviii; and subsequently, S, I, xxx-xlix.

on these subjects Ricardo was certainly stimulated by current debate, which gave rise, in fact, to his first published statements on economic problems—the letters to the *Morning Chronicle* in 1809.

As the progressive state proceeds toward the stationary state, the labor cost of producing a bushel of wheat at the margin increases, while that of producing, say, a shirt, remains unaltered, except as both are influenced by technological changes. Under the labor-cost theory of exchange value that Ricardo adopted, with significant qualifications, a bushel of wheat comes to exchange for more and more shirts as the economy expands. How then is the laborer's minimum market basket, his family's subsistence goods, to be computed? If at one point in the progressive state a bushel of wheat exchanges for two shirts, and at a later point for four shirts, and if the subsistence wage in the first period is, in terms of wheat, five bushels, spent by the worker as three bushels of wheat and four shirts, what is the subsistence wage in the second period? Three bushels and four shirts still, which implies a corn wage of only four bushels, and a consumption pattern that is unaffected by the change in the corn-to-shirts exchange ratio? Or is it, say, two and a half bushels and ten shirts? Ricardo's somewhat curious refusal to be drawn into the problems of price-elasticities of consumer demand shut him off from an approach that might have allowed his analytical engine to construct an internally consistent theory of distribution in the progressive state.[19] His theory of distribution is less vulnerable in the stationary state, for, being stationary, this state does not experience changes in prices, and it can be constructed definitively, with the aid of arbitrary assumptions about the worker's market-basket pattern.

Finally, certain qualifications that Ricardo found himself obliged to make in his labor theory of value complicated the task of fixing the conditions for distribution of the product at the margin between worker and capitalist in the mixed-output progressive state, even ignoring the problem of the worker's market-basket pattern.

As a first approximation, in Ricardo's theory, commodities exchange for one another in the ratios of their inputs, consisting of labor hours and of profit on capital fixed as a percentage per year of investment. The commodities must of course be useful enough to the purchaser to induce him to pay the costs of production, or they will not be forthcoming. The relevant cost of production for agricultural produce is the wages-profit cost at the margin of cultivation.

[19] Cf. the three cases of variation in the value of labor, in Chapter I of the *Principles*, S, I, 18-20; G, 12-14.

Labor is not all of the same quality; a day's labor of a "working jeweller" is "more valuable" than that of a "common labourer;"[20] and Ricardo does not solve the problem of how to add heterogeneous units of labor. He tries to by-pass it by asserting that the ratio that an hour of one kind of labor bears to another, once it is arrived at, is subject to little variation thereafter. Emphasizing more the reasons for a change in an exchange ratio over time than the reasons why the ratio was what it was at a given point in time,[21] Ricardo appears to believe that he has overcome the heterogeneity problem, but it remains by-passed, not solved. To be sure, the ratio "depends much on the comparative skill of the labourer, and intensity of the labour performed,"[22] and we might infer that the skill and intensity are themselves proportional to the work and time involved in obtaining them, but Ricardo does not go so far as to assert this.

A variation in the ratio at which one commodity exchanges for another is therefore traceable, Ricardo concludes, to a relative change in the labor inputs, with allowance, too, for the time factor. Historical research may reveal to us which of two commodities A and B has undergone the greater change in input, so that we may understand why A and B exchange now at a ratio different from that of an earlier period, but it would be far more convenient if we could happen upon some commodity X whose input requirements never changed, for then a simple comparison of past and present exchange values of A and X, and B and X, would tell us at once whether the cause of the change in the A-B exchange ratio lay in the history of A's input or B's.[23] In fact, Ricardo regretfully concludes, no such commodity X exists.

Because Ricardo does include in cost of production a profit factor that is a function of the length of time the capital is tied up, the exchange ratio of A and B may alter over time, in his analysis, even though the relative labor inputs have remained unchanged. If the production of A uses more capital per man-year of direct labor than the production of B, a larger portion of A's sales price must go to profit and a smaller portion to wages than for B. Consequently, a rise in the rate of wages and a corresponding fall in the rate of profits will make A cheaper in terms of B. In general, if the rate of wages rises, computed as a percentage of the wages-profits share, commodities produced largely by direct labor will rise in price relative to those produced largely by capital instruments. Ricardo is inclined to rank this influence on exchange ratios as distinctly

[20] S, I, 20; G, 15. [21] See S, I, 21, 47; G, 16, 40. [22] S, I, 20; G, 15.
[23] S, I, 17-18; G, 12-13.

minor compared with that of changes in relative labor inputs; and he neglects the possibility that the proportions of direct labor and capital instruments in the production of a particular commodity might shift notably over time. In any case, this complication does in principle rule out the possibility of finding any one commodity that can be used as "a perfect measure of value for all things" in the sense of signalling where the cause of a change in an A-B exchange ratio is to be found.[24] And if a commodity, say corn, using much direct labor and little fixed capital, becomes more difficult to produce, what determines the new rate of exchange between it and a commodity, unchanged in cost, that uses much fixed capital relative to labor?[25]

4. THE LEVEL OF PRICES

The monetary medium, gold, is itself a commodity. Changes in the ratio at which an ounce of gold exchanges with other commodities, that is, changes in the general level of money prices, arise from changes in labor input per unit of output at the gold mine, or in other industries, provided the economy is a closed one, producing its own gold. But in the real world, and especially in England, which produces no gold at all, the size of the money stock in the country and hence the level of gold prices is determined by the workings of the law of comparative advantage in international trade, coupled with the labor cost of production in the foreign mines. Taxes or bounties, domestic or foreign, and other restrictions on or stimuli to imports or exports likewise influence the amount of the money stock in the country.

International trade in commodities is not regulated by relative labor-capital inputs as is domestic trade;[26] men and capital cannot move readily from one country to another, to redress differences in inputs relative to prices obtained. A country will import from another even though the absolute cost of the article in terms of input is smaller domestically, provided it has a still greater relative advantage in the production of something else, which it can then export in part, in exchange for the other commodity.

The country with absolute advantages is the one that will have the larger stock of gold relative to physical product, that is, the higher price

[24] S, I, 44-46; G, 37-38.

[25] Stigler, "The Ricardian Theory of Value and Distribution," *J. Pol. Econ.*, LX (1952), 204.

[26] S, I, 133; G, 113.

level.[27] This must be so if such a country's consumers are to buy abroad despite the absolute advantage in production at home. Gold is distributed by the impersonal forces of international trade in a manner that allows each country to produce according to its comparative advantage and to engage in international trade just as it would on a barter basis, in the absence of money.

The income velocity of circulation of the monetary stock, in the Ricardian system, is impliedly constant. The price level varies inversely with the money stock, and the economy's demand for money is of unit elasticity. Since the value of paper money obeys the same rules, the level of domestic prices under a paper money regime depends on the amount outstanding.

[27] See S, I, 137-40, 343; G, 117-21; 330. See Section 2 in Chapter XII below.

CHAPTER III

TAXES PAID OUT OF CAPITAL; TAXES PAID OUT OF INCOME

Since Ricardo was keenly interested in the factors making for economic growth, and feared the consequences of economic decay, it is not surprising that he starts his analysis of taxation by drawing a distinction between taxes that are paid from the capital of a country and those paid from its income, or revenue. But the reader is drawn at once into conceptual difficulties.

1. DEFINITION OF CONCEPTS

What does it mean, to say that taxes are paid out of capital? If capital today is smaller than it would have been had the tax and its accompanying government outlay not been in effect, the tax has come out of capital, in a comparative-statics sense. This is the concept we should have expected from an economist like Ricardo. Yet the main portion of Chapter VIII of the *Principles,* dealing with the total economy rather than the individual, is occasionally inconsistent or obscure unless it is assumed here and there that Ricardo is using " out of capital," in a looser sense, a historical sense. If the level of taxation of an economy has increased during a certain period, but its capital has also increased, the tax increment has not "come out of capital," in the historical sense; however much the tax increment may have slowed accumulation, its effect has not been powerful enough to overcome the net resultant of other forces. If the capital of an economy is observed to have decreased during a period, while taxation has increased, the increment is said, in this sense, to have come out of capital. The usefulness of such a concept is quite limited, perhaps negligible, for economic analysis. Yet Ricardo appears to employ it now and then.

"If the consumption of the government, when increased by the levy of additional taxes, be met either by an increased production, or by a diminished consumption on the part of the people, the taxes will fall upon revenue, and the national capital will remain unimpaired. . . ."[1] Does "be met" connote simply "be accompanied by," or, rather, "give rise to"? Does "remain unimpaired" mean "be not less than it was at the start of the period," or, rather, "be not less, at the end of the period, than it would otherwise have been"?

The sentence continues: ". . . but if there be no increased production or diminished unproductive consumption on the part of the people, the taxes will necessarily fall on capital, that is to say, they will impair the fund allotted to productive consumption."[2] Again, either concept will fit the language; but the sentences immediately following clearly seem to be in the historical mood: "In proportion as the capital of a country is diminished, its productions will be necessarily diminished; and, therefore, if the same unproductive expenditure on the part of the people and of the government continue, with a constantly diminishing annual reproduction, the resources of the people and the state will fall away with increasing rapidity, and distress and ruin will follow."[3]

Later in the *Principles,* in correspondence, and in the passages to be quoted below from "Funding System," the attributes that Ricardo attaches to the concepts, "out of capital," or "out of revenue," are sometimes those of comparative statics, sometimes those of a historical approach. Thus, in Chapter XVI ("Taxes on Wages"), in the course of criticizing Say for double counting of the damage done by taxation: "If a tax, however burdensome it may be, falls on revenue, and not on capital, it does not diminish demand, it only alters the nature of it."[4] And in a letter to McCulloch, Ricardo points out that if a tax on wages, or necessaries, is accompanied by a transfer of a wealthy consumer's gardeners into government service, the "rate of accumulation goes on as before . . .";[5] the tax has then been met by reducing private unproductive consumption. On the other hand, two further passages from Chapter XVI

[1] S, I, 150; G, 131. Ricardo neglected to insert "unproductive" before "consumption" here, when he was revising for the third edition; cf. footnote 14 on p. 43 below.

[2] S, I, 150-51; G, 131-32. Cf. Cannan, *History of Theories of Production and Distribution*, p. 72.

[3] S, I, 151; G, 132.

[4] S, I, 237; G, 221. For remarks on waste of sunk capital and loss of consumer satisfaction caused by a tax-induced shift of consumption, as under a heavy tax on salt, see Say, Notes on Ricardo, pp. 418-19.

[5] Letter of March 29, 1820, Ricardo to McCulloch, S, VIII, 170. See p. 70 below.

imply use of the historical approach; they are noted toward the end of Section 3 of the present chapter. And in Chapter XII, "Land Tax," the retrograde state is considered briefly, in terms that are of course not those of comparative statics:

> This portion [of the labor of the country placed at the disposal of the State] may become so large, that sufficient surplus produce may not be left to stimulate the exertions of those who usually augment by their savings the capital of the State. Taxation has happily never yet in any free country been carried so far as constantly from year to year to diminish its capital. Such a state of taxation could not be long endured; or if endured, it would be constantly absorbing so much of the annual produce of the country as to occasion the most extensive scene of misery, famine, and depopulation.[6]

2. HAD ENGLAND'S TAXES BEEN PAID OUT OF CAPITAL?

In the looser, or historical, sense, the heavy English taxation of the Napoleonic Wars had not been paid out of capital; but in terms of comparative statics, capital had surely been impaired.

The first conclusion is given unambiguously:

> Notwithstanding the immense expenditure of the English government during the last twenty years, there can be little doubt but that the increased production on the part of the people has more than compensated for it. The national capital has not merely been unimpaired, it has been greatly increased....[7]

Immediately, the analysis turns to comparative statics: "Still, however, it is certain that but for taxation this increase of capital would have been much greater."[8] To be sure, this is McCulloch speaking, Ricardo simply agreeing; the passage reflects a puzzling episode in Ricardo's intellectual exchanges with McCulloch. This sentence, and most of the paragraph, is a second-edition emendation, and consists of pure McCulloch, substituted by Ricardo, at the former's suggestion, for the Ricardian language of the first edition. Both passages are in comparative statics terms; but the first sentence of the McCulloch version continues the reference to Britain that marks the preceding paragraphs. Did Ricardo prefer McCulloch's language for that reason? Perhaps; but a simple desire to please his sympathetic critic is the more likely explanation.

The substitution came about in the following way.

McCulloch had expressed a fear that Ricardo might not see "the impropriety of contaminating a work destined to be immortal, with any thing that can be construed into an excuse or palliation of that system of

[6] S, I, 185; G, 165-66. [7] S, I, 151; G, 132. [8] S, I, 152; G, 133.

profligate extravagance according to which the economical affairs of the different European nations have long been managed." [9] Ricardo's reply invited specification of the passages which "you think hold out an apology to ministers for taxation," [10] for he had no clear idea of what was bothering McCulloch. He surmised, in a letter to Mill, that it might be the passage at the end of Chapter XVI ("Taxes on Wages"),[11] but he learned that the source of McCulloch's dissatisfaction was instead the eighth paragraph of Chapter VIII.

> I would beg leave to suggest [wrote McCulloch] the adoption of the following paragraph—"Still however it is certain that but for taxation this increase of capital would have been much greater. There are no taxes which have not a tendency to lessen the power to accumulate. All taxes must either fall on capital or revenue. If they encroach on capital, they must proportionably diminish that fund by whose extent the extent of the productive industry of the country must always be regulated; and if they fall on revenue they must either lessen accumulation, or force the contributors to save the amount of the tax by making a corresponding diminution of their former consumption of the necessaries and luxuries of life. Some taxes will produce these effects in a much greater degree than others; but the great evil of taxation is to be found etc." [12]

McCulloch's passage, inserted by Ricardo without the slightest change except for punctuation,[13] contains two logical lapses, one of which Ricardo noted in time for the third edition of the *Principles:* the consumption of necessaries that must be restricted if a tax is to fall on revenue is unproductive consumption, the food and clothing of valets or gardeners, not the necessaries of the farm hand, whose labor produces wheat that in turn will support future labor. The distinction between productive and unproductive consumption was much on Ricardo's mind by the time he came to revise for the third edition.[14] The McCulloch slip

[9] Letter of July 15, 1818, to Ricardo, S, VII, 281.

[10] Letter of Nov. 24, 1818, to McCulloch, S, VII, 337. See also letter of Aug. 22, 1818, Ricardo to McCulloch, S, VII, 286.

[11] Letter of Nov. 23, 1818, to Mill, S, VII, 334.

[12] Letter of Dec. 6, 1818, to Ricardo, S, VII, 353. See note by Sraffa, S, I, 152, note 2.

[13] Cf. "proportionably" and Ricardo's "proportionally" (S, I, 153; G, 134).

[14] S, I, 152, note 1 by Sraffa. The third edition saw a similar rectification of three other passages in Chapter VIII, "unproductive" being inserted before "consumption" or "expenditure"; see notes by Sraffa, S, I, 150, note 4, and S, I, 151, notes 1 and 3. Finally, Ricardo added in this edition a footnote on the concept of productive consumption, S, I, 151 (see p. 52 below), and a passage specifying that when taxes fall on capital they "impair the fund allotted to productive consumption." S, I, 151, note 2 by Sraffa.

that Ricardo failed to catch is the assertion that if taxes "fall on revenue, they must either lessen accumulation, or . . . ." It is precisely by falling on revenue, viz., by restricting unproductive consumption or by stimulating production, that a tax does not lessen accumulation.

The Ricardian passage that was displaced through the apprehensions of McCulloch had been free of McCulloch's logical lapses, and far more forceful:

There are no taxes which have not a tendency to impede accumulation, because there are none which may not be considered as checking production, and as causing the same effects as a bad soil or climate, a diminution of skill or industry, a worse distribution of labour, or the loss of some useful machinery, and although some taxes will produce these effects in a much greater degree than others, it must be confessed that the great evil of taxation is to be found . . . .[15]

3. FACTORS THAT DETERMINE WHETHER A TAX IS PAID FROM INCOME OR CAPITAL

Whatever may be the factors that determine whether a tax is to be paid from capital or from income, the fact that it is levied on one or the other of these bases is not "necessarily" significant. The tone of the following passage, which is clearly cast in terms of comparative statics, coupled with the analysis of death duties to be noted shortly, suggests however that Ricardo was considering at this point possibilities rather than probabilities, and that after all a tax based on capital is really less likely to come out of income than a tax based on income.

Taxes are not necessarily taxes on capital, because they are laid on capital; nor on income, because they are laid on income. If from my income of 1000 *l.* per annum, I am required to pay 100 *l.*, it will really be a tax on my income, should I be content with the expenditure of the remaining 900 *l.*; but it will be a tax on capital, if I continue to spend 1000 *l.*

The capital from which my income of 1000 *l.* is derived, may be of the value of 10,000 *l.*; a tax of one per cent. on such capital would be 100 *l.*; but my capital

[15] See note 2 by Sraffa, S, I, 152. In this first-edition version, the phrase "these effects" makes good sense; when it has to follow McCulloch's language, it becomes confusingly indefinite. Whether the tax is analogous to poor soil, or to a bad climate, or to a diminution of skill, etc., does not matter greatly, for analytical purposes, but it makes a great deal of difference whether the tax falls on capital, or falls on revenue, and, if the latter, whether it is said to lessen accumulation (McCulloch's error), or to reduce certain kinds of consumption. McCulloch was insensitive to the impairment of logic in the linkage of the new material with the old, and Ricardo was probably too eager to be done with McCulloch.

would be unaffected, if after paying this tax, I in like manner contented myself with the expenditure of 900 *l.*[16]

This illustration implies, by the way, that in the absence of the tax the individual would be spending all of his £1,000 income, of which at least £100 would be for unproductive consumption.

Taxes can be met out of income by increasing one's income. However, Ricardo nowhere suggests that this possibility is significant, at least in terms of comparative statics, and in a letter to Trower he is explicit to the contrary:

As a political economist I say that there is no tax which has not a tendency to diminish production, in the same way as a deterioration of soil or the loss of a good machine, but I mean nothing more than that it is an obstacle opposed to production. You say [where, is not known; none of Trower's letters contain such a statement] it is such obstacles as these which stimulate to exertion, and experience proves they are always overcome. I have no doubt that there is a degree of difficulty in production which acts in the way you mention; if too strong however it will oppose a physical difficulty which can not be overcome. I think the difficulties in our case are not precisely in the proper degree to ensure the greatest production. Still it is correct to record the obstacle and acknowledge it to be one. You compare the expences of the rich proprietors and the expenditure by Government of money received in taxes. With respect to future production it is indifferent whether this portion of the general revenue be expended by one or the other, excepting in this that in the expenditure of government a tax will be required for the future increased production as well as for that which is usually produced and this may prevent the production of the increased quantity altogether. A tithe on land which cannot afford a rent will prevent that land from being cultivated until the price of corn rises. If there were no tithe the same land might be cultivated for the proprietors benefit. If all I am to get is to be expended by the state I will not produce, if it is to be expended by me, I will. After it is produced it is not of much importance whether the state or I expend it, to the public at large, but it is of immense importance in determining me to be active or idle. Taxes for the benefit of trade itself such as for Docks, canals, Roads, &c. &c. are on a different footing from all other taxes, and produce very different effects, they may and generally do promote production instead of discouraging it.[17]

[16] S, I, 152-53; G, 133.

[17] S, VIII, 154-55, letter of Jan. 28, 1820, to Trower. Passages in J. L. Mallet's diaries for 1831 and 1835 indicate that the members of the Political Economy Club, McCulloch especially, had become quite un-Ricardian with respect to the income effect of a tax. *Minutes of Proceedings, 1899-1920 ... and Questions Discussed, 1821-1920,* VI, 226, 271. Cited by Erskine McKinley, "The Problem of 'Underdevelopment' in the English Classical School," *Q. J. Econ.,* XLIX (No. 2, May, 1955), p. 242.

But there is a force, Ricardo seems to say, that works effectively to make "most" taxes come from income. This conclusion does not accord well with the tone of the McCulloch passage noted above or the original Ricardian passage that it superseded. There is an oddly optimistic air at this point. Upon analysis the statement is seen to be essentially historical, the counterpart, for the individual, of the conclusion reproduced above that the national capital had increased over the preceding twenty years.

The paramount influence that causes most taxes to be paid out of income is "The desire which every man has to keep his station in life, and to maintain his wealth at the height which it has once attained . . ." ; this desire, we are told, "occasions most taxes, whether laid on capital or on income, to be paid from income . . .," a feat that is made possible either by a diminution in "the annual enjoyments of the people . . .," or because "they are enabled proportionally to increase their capitals and income." [18]

The phrase "once attained" emphasizes the historical approach. The taxpayer will cling to his capital status even in the face of increased taxation; he will do so by decreasing consumption below its previous level if he must, or by calling on part or all of an increase in income that would have occurred in any event. Capital therefore does not sink below the pre-tax level, and it probably increases, but not as fast, we may infer, as if the tax had not been imposed. This is all that Ricardo means when he says that "most taxes, whether levied on capital or on income, [are] paid from income." Moreover, he has in mind, at this point, only men of property.

Considering Ricardo's optimistic assessment of the preceding twenty years of English economic development, we might have expected him to place little emphasis on decreasing the level of "annual enjoyments" as the means of avoiding an absolute decrease in capital in the face of added taxation. But no, "It should be the policy of governments to encourage a disposition to do this in the people"; and from the context, especially the paragraph immediately following, "this" refers to diminishing the annual enjoyments, and has no reference to an increase in income. The government should "never . . . lay such taxes as will inevitably fall on capital; since by so doing, they impair the funds for the maintenance of labour, and thereby diminish the future production of the country." [19] One tax of that nature is said to be the legacy duty.

[18] S, I, 153; G, 133-34.
[19] S, I, 153; G, 134.

If a legacy of 1000 *l.* be subject to a tax of 100 *l.*, the legatee considers his legacy as only 900 *l.* and feels no particular motive to save the 100 *l.* duty from his expenditure, and thus the capital of the country is diminished; but if he had really received 1000 *l.*, and had been required to pay 100 *l.* as a tax on income, on wine, on horses, or on servants, he would probably have diminished, or rather not increased his expenditure by that sum, and the capital of the country would have been unimpaired.[20]

Ricardo's analysis seems open to several interpretations, depending on what a legatee is assumed to do in the absence of taxation. But the chief point in any case is that "The desire which every man has . . . to maintain his wealth," and his willingness to lower his standard of living to do so, if he must, are not influenced by the capital position held by the decedent. It is his own wealth that he will strive to preserve, not his ancestor's. To the legatee, the capital that has been accumulated by the decedent is not "attained" until it reaches him, and if the state extracts a part of it en route, only the remainder is capital which, once attained, must be kept intact, by a decrease in the level of consumption if necessary. Let the entire accumulation reach him, free of tax, and then it is this amount (plus his initial capital) that he will strive to maintain, even if the state imposes on him an income tax or luxury excises, or even, we may infer, a tax on his capital, to compensate it for the legacy tax it has abstained from; and he will lower the level of his annual enjoyments, if need be.

But we may also infer that the legatee-taxpayer will be under no pressure to lower the level of his annual enjoyments whenever his income is increasing, apart from the legacy, at a rate such that his annual capital accumulation is greater than the prospective tax. Under these conditions, the "maintenance" motive alone will not induce the legatee to strive for a higher capital position under an income or excise tax than under a legacy tax. The maintenance motive, with its ratchet effect of inducing the taxpayer to maintain the capital level he has achieved through inheritance, is not effective unless he is consuming so much of his income that he can pay the income tax or excise tax only by encroaching on his capital or by lowering the level of his consumption.

Accordingly, only in a restricted sense may we accept Ricardo's con-

[20] *Idem.* McCulloch, in the same vein: "The love of accumulation must on the average be always stronger than the passion of expence. The increased duty on luxuries would be met by a proportionable saving on those and other articles of expence. . . ." Letter of May 15, 1820, to Ricardo, S, VIII, 190. But cf. Ricardo, a few paragraphs earlier in the *Principles:* ". . . the great evil of taxation is to be found, not so much in any selection of its objects, as in the general amount of its effects taken collectively." S, I, 152; G, 133.

clusion that "most taxes, whether laid on capital or on income, [are] paid from income," and that legacy duties are an exception to this rule. The analysis applies only to taxes on men of property, since it is grounded on a presumed desire to maintain wealth. To give the argument force, we must assume that every propertied person in the economy is spending all, or virtually all, of his income. An increase of taxation will then usually be met by a decrease in unproductive consumption, with the exception of an increase in the legacy tax. This tax prevents the recipient's capital from increasing by as much as the decedent's capital decreases, and therefore lowers the sights for the economy as a whole with respect to maintenance of a capital position "once attained."

The analysis of such a situation may be of importance to an underdeveloped country characterized by great disparities in income and no appreciable growth in capital, provided that what capital there is is held by those in whom the "station-in-life" impulse is strong. But it seems of little or no significance for a country such as the England of Ricardo's day.

The legatee, we have seen, is not disposed to decrease his consumption to restore to its pre-tax level the estate of the decedent; and no more is the decedent-to-be willing to restrict his consumption in order to build up a pre-tax estate large enough to yield his heir what he would have planned to leave him had there been no prospect of a death tax. So much, at least, we may infer from Ricardo's acceptance of Adam Smith's conclusion that transfer taxes at death "fall finally, as well as immediately, upon the persons to whom the property is transferred."[21] The property owners of Ricardo's acquaintance, although eager to maintain their own stations in life, cared little for those of their heirs.

Ricardo returns to the luxury excises at the end of Chapter XVI ("Taxes on Wages"), and here again they are said, or implied, to be paid from income rather than capital. Again, too, the statement seems to be made in the restricted sense that the capital of the individual, or the country, as the case may be, will not be less at the end of the period than it was at the beginning, even under the tax.

The first passage:

> Taxes on luxuries have some advantage over taxes on necessaries. They are generally paid from income, and therefore do not diminish the productive capital of the country. If wine were much raised in price in consequence of taxation, it

[21] S, I, 153; G, 134.

is probable that a man would rather forego the enjoyments of wine, than make any important encroachments on his capital, to be enabled to purchase it.[22]

"Encroachment" here seems not to have the connotation, "absorption of what the taxpayer would otherwise have added to his capital during the year"; rather, it appears to mean, "encroachment on the amount of capital the taxpayer possessed at the start of the year." But this is admittedly conjecture.

The second passage appeared only in the first edition of the *Principles;* it is the one Ricardo altered in the mistaken belief that he was thereby meeting McCulloch's objection.[23] The passage reads:

After visiting with a tax the whole round of luxuries; after laying horses, carriages, wine, servants, and all the other enjoyments of the rich, under contribution; a minister is disposed to conclude that the country is arrived at the maximum of taxation, because by increasing the rate, he cannot increase the amount of any one of these taxes. But in this conclusion he will not be always correct, for it is very possible that such a country could bear a very great addition to its burdens without infringing on the integrity of its capital.[24]

This may mean that the minister is mistaken in thinking that he cannot increase the revenue from these luxury taxes by increasing the rates. More likely, it means that the minister may get more revenue from taxes on the income or property of well-to-do persons (not from taxes on necessaries), without "infringing on the integrity of its capital," if again we accept this conclusion in the restricted sense just noted above. We deduce this meaning from the manner in which Ricardo recast the passage for the second edition, even though in so doing he obliterated the main point:

After visiting with a tax the whole round of luxuries; after laying horses, carriages, wine, servants, and all the other enjoyments of the rich, under contribution; a minister is induced to have recourse to more direct taxes, such as income and property taxes, neglecting the golden maxim of M. Say, "that the very best of all plans of finance is to spend little, and the best of all taxes is that which is least in amount."[25]

Ricardo's willingness to scrap an important analytical point indicates how deeply he shared, with McCulloch, a conviction that England's government was wasting the country's resources, and should be held in

[22] S, I, 241; G, 224-25.
[23] See p. 43 above.
[24] S, I, 242, note 1 by Sraffa.
[25] S, I, 242; G, 226.

check by a presumption that any tax reduction was beneficial, any tax increase unfortunate.[26]

Thus far the discussion assumes that the government spends the tax revenue on unproductive labor. What if it uses the tax proceeds to redeem debt? Now, a tax may come out of capital without harming the country. Ricardo's reasoning on this point is found in his "Funding System" (1820), where he is demolishing the argument of Lord Henry Petty[27] that too rapid a redemption of the public debt would return too much capital to the stockholder, "without his having any means of deriving a revenue from it".[28] Debt redemption through taxation means simply that

> One portion of the people pay what another portion receive. If the payers employed the sums paid as capital, that is to say, in the production of raw produce, or manufactured commodities, and the receivers, when they received it, employed it in the same manner, there would be little variation in the annual produce.[29]

Ricardo continues:

> On the supposition, then, that the sinking fund is furnished by capital and not by revenue, no injury would result to the community, however large that fund might be,—there might or might not be a transfer of employments, but the annual produce, the real wealth of the country, would undergo no deterioration, and the actual amount of capital employed would neither be increased nor diminished.[30]

Comparative statics seems uppermost in Ricardo's mind, though the language is imprecise, as when he continues,

> But if the payers of taxes, for the interest and sinking fund of the national debt, paid them from revenue, then they would retain the same capital as before in active employment, and as this revenue, when received by the stockholder, would be by him employed as capital, there would be, in consequence of this operation, a great increase of capital,—every year an additional portion of revenue would

[26] See p. 75 below. "I have been a little puzzled what to do respecting MCullock I have not time to consult him respecting the passages he would have modified or omitted, and on looking over the book I see no opinion which I do not continue to hold. To shew him however my wish of attending to his suggestions I have altered the conclusion of page 329 [S, I, 242] and have said 'a minister is induced to have recourse to more direct taxes....' Will this do? or should I write to MCullock?" [as he did, the following day; see p. 43 above]. Letter of Nov. 23, 1818, Ricardo to Mill, S, VII, 334. For Mill's reply, see letter of Dec. 4, 1818, S, VII, 349.

[27] Marquis of Lansdowne (1780-1863).

[28] S, IV, 177, from "Funding System" (1820). [29] *Idem.* [30] S, IV, 178.

be turned into capital, which could be employed only in furnishing new commodities to the market.[31]

Ricardo goes on to scoff at fears of a general glut owing to so great an increase in capital.

When taxation is markedly lowered at the conclusion of a sinking fund program, all the debt having now been retired, what happens to the country's rate of capital accumulation?

Annual sums that used to be paid to government stockholders to redeem debt are now available for use by the erstwhile taxpayers. No harm can come of this, Ricardo seeks to assure us. We may readily agree, provided the former taxpayers save the amounts remitted in taxes, and assuming we have faith in Say's law. But Ricardo's argument that all is well even if these amounts are now spent on unproductive consumption is difficult to follow. Ricardo seems to have been overwhelmed by his enthusiasm for tax reduction at any cost. To be sure, capital now accumulates as rapidly as if, the debt being still in existence, no taxes were being levied for a sinking fund. But the sinking fund program was causing capital to accumulate still more rapidly (the taxpayers meeting their sinking-fund taxes out of their incomes). This benefit is lost by completion of the sinking-fund program. In general, tax remission will impair capital accumulation least when the tax is being paid out of capital.[32]

Debt redemption also lowers the flow of interest, and hence taxes to pay interest. If these remitted sums were saved, Ricardo would of course rejoice; Malthus would be apprehensive.[33]

[31] *Idem.*

[32] "Funding System," S, IV, 181-82, and cf. the passage, "Now, of this we are quite certain . . .," *ibid.* p. 183, to end of paragraph on page 184.

[33] Malthus, posing the extreme case of "a spunge . . . applied" to the national debt (repudiation), seems to be referring to interest on the debt which had been spent on consumption by the creditors: "With regard to the capitalists, though they would be relieved from a great portion of their taxes, yet there is every probability that their habits of saving, combined with the diminution in the number of effective demanders, would occasion such a fall in the prices of commodities as greatly to diminish that part of the national income which depends upon profits; and I feel very little doubt that, in five years from the date of such an event, not only would the exchangeable value of the whole produce, estimated in domestic and foreign labour, be decidedly diminished, but a smaller absolute quantity of corn would be grown, and fewer manufactured and foreign commodities would be brought to market than before." Ricardo comments: "I should think Mr. Malthus must be the only man in England who would expect such effects from such a cause." S, II, 435, *Notes on Malthus's Principles of Political Economy.* See also *ibid.*, S, II, 433, 443, 450; "Funding System," S, IV, 183-84;

4. UNPRODUCTIVE CONSUMPTION

If a tax can be kept from falling on capital by diminishing "unproductive consumption," the definition of that kind of consumption is crucial.

Unproductive consumption is consumption by unproductive laborers. Unproductive laborers are those who do not produce things like food or machinery that make possible or facilitate later economic activity. Whether this class of things may include intangible services is not clear, in Ricardo's doctrine; we may infer that he does not exclude them as firmly as Smith.[34]

In Ricardo's own words, inserted as a footnote in the third edition of the *Principles:*

> It must be understood that all the productions of a country are consumed; but it makes the greatest difference imaginable whether they are consumed by those who reproduce, or by those who do not reproduce another value. When we say that revenue is saved, and added to capital, what we mean is, that the portion of revenue, so said to be added to capital, is consumed by productive instead of unproductive labourers. There can be no greater error than in supposing that capital is increased by non-consumption. If the price of labour should rise so high, that notwithstanding the increase of capital, no more could be employed, I should say that such increase of capital would be still unproductively consumed.[35]

and the following letters: May 2, 1820, Ricardo to McCulloch, S, VIII, 181; May 4, 1820, Ricardo to Malthus, S, VIII, 185; March 2, 1821, Ricardo to Trower, S, VIII, 349.

[34] Smith at one point defined productive labor as labor that "fixes and realizes itself in some particular subject or vendible commodity, which lasts for some time at least after that labour is past." *Wealth of Nations,* Bk. II, Ch. III, C, I, 313; M, 314. See Knight, "The Ricardian Theory of Production and Distribution," *Can. J. Econ. and Pol. Sci.,* I (May, 1935), 186-89.

[35] S, I, 151; G, 132. Cannan, in *History of the Theories of Production & Distribution,* p. 73, is disturbed by the insertion of this footnote, and of the word "unproductive" (see footnote 14 on p. 43 above). "By these alterations and additions," writes Cannan, "the picture of the capital of a country as a store or stock of produce increased in any given period by the excess of production over consumption, is smeared over by the hand that painted it. In the first edition we were told that the addition to the capital consists of such productions as are over and above what replaces the annual consumption. In the third we are told that the whole produce is consumed, so that there cannot be any such thing as an excess of production over consumption." Cannan did not appreciate that Ricardo was matching the production of one year with the consumption of the next. The whole produce of Year 1 is consumed in Year 2, and, depending on who consumes it, production during Year 2 may or may not exceed the consumption of that same year. Cannan is referring specifically to that part of the note that reads "It must be understood . . . do not reproduce another value."

We infer that a rich man's valet, consuming food, and producing only personal services for his employer, is consuming unproductively, and so is his gardener who grows flowers for the table. The rich man's vegetable gardener offers a more difficult case. He might be viewed as consuming productively, even though the product is intended for his employer's table, since vegetables are capable of being diverted at the last minute to supporting laborers.

Presumably, a laborer may be in part productive, in part unproductive, by producing a mixed output, partly food that might be used by laborers, partly personal services for his employer.

Moreover, Ricardo indicates that a wholly productive laborer may be in part an unproductive consumer, in the sense that he is consuming more than he needs to, to supply this work; the market rate of wages is above the natural rate. For example, a full-time farm hand produces 100 bushels of wheat in a year, and receives 52 bushels, or its equivalent, as wages, while he could in fact sustain himself and rear his family on 40 bushels. In McCulloch's language,[36] one of the ways a tax may come out of income is by the taxpayers' "making a corresponding diminution of their former unproductive consumption of the necessaries and luxuries of life."[37] Now the phrase "unproductive consumption of the necessaries ... of life" might be taken to mean only the consumption of necessaries by individuals who were themselves unproductive (valets). But Ricardo did not so restrict it; witness the concluding sentence already given above, from the footnote added to the third edition of the *Principles*:[38] "If the price of labour ... unproductively consumed." If this unproductive consumption by productive laborers were curtailed in the event of a tax, the tax would come out of income.

Unproductive consumption also includes, presumably, consumption by those who do not work at all: typically, landlords and stockho'ders. But, as we have just seen, unproductive consumption is not restricted to them, and this is the striking feature of the classical concept, from the point of view of modern terminology, for it allows for two aspects of

[36] With "unproductive" added by Ricardo. See p. 43 above.

[37] S, I, 152; G, 133.

[38] S, I, 151; G, 132. Could this part of Ricardo's footnote reflect a pondering over the language he had adopted from McCulloch? See also the letter of July 9, 1821, Ricardo to Malthus, S, IX, 17: "If the labourer receives a large proportion of the produce as wages, all that he receives more than is sufficient to prompt him to the necessary exertions of his powers, is as much unproductive consumption as if it were consumed by his master, or by the state—there is no difference whatever."

unproductive consumption: the craftsman producing luxury furniture suitable only for the rich is consuming his food unproductively, and his patron will consume the furniture unproductively. The classical notion of unproductive consumption may be limited to one aspect only by restricting the concept of consumption to the using up of those kinds of commodities that can be, though they may not be, consumed by workers in the course of producing similar commodities.

In Ricardo's view, the government employee is unproductive; he consumes part of the economy's year-beginning stock of food, clothing, and shelter, and thus, part of the country's capital, without replacing it through his labor. Adam Smith had said that although government employees are unproductive, their services may be "useful," perhaps even "necessary," [39] and we may infer a grudging assent from Ricardo. Indeed, their services may be not only useful, but essential; without law and order, labor engaged by private capitalists could not be effective. Ricardo gives little place in his analysis to this facilitating function, but he must be presumed to have recognized it.[40] Ricardo's insistence on the unproductiveness of government employees arises less from the intangible nature of the product than from his deep distrust of state action and the clear wastefulness of wars. In any event, he has a point. If a certain psychological change causes the populace to becomes less law-abiding, some laborers must be diverted from farm and factory to the police force. Taxation increases, and so does "unproductive consumption." The stock of capital at the beginning of the next period will be smaller than it would have been had the additional police not been required, unless, of course, some countervailing change occurs. One such change could be a decrease in unproductive consumption elsewhere, releasing labor to make up the gap in production.[41]

Ricardo's assertion that increased taxation will not come out of capital if it is met either by an increased production or by a diminished un-

[39] *Wealth of Nations*, Bk. II, Ch. III, C, I, 314; M, 315. [40] See p. 43 above.

[41] "Dr. A. Smith compares the advantages attending the establishment of a bank to those which would be obtained by converting our highways into pastures and corn-fields, and procuring a road through the air. The highways, like the coin, are highly useful, but neither yield any revenue." Ricardo, *The High Price of Bullion*, S, III, 55. Alfred Marshall felt obligated to attempt definitions of productive labor and productive consumption, but was unhappy about them. "All the distinctions in which the word Productive is used are very thin and have a certain air of unreality. It would hardly be worth while to introduce them now: but they have a long history; and it is probably better that they should dwindle gradually out of use, rather than be suddenly discarded." *Principles of Economics*, p. 67.

productive consumption can, as we have seen, be taken in a comparative-statics sense. But the words "increased" and "diminished" must then be recognized not as being the opposite of one another, but as differing in their bases of comparison. Production, although labeled "increased," is in fact the same as it would have been in the absence of the tax. It is increased only in the sense of being above the level to which it would have fallen, under the drain imposed by government's use of resources, had not additional effort been put forth. It is input, not output, that is increased. The decrease in unproductive consumption, on the other hand—the alternate way to prevent the tax from coming out of capital—is a decrease from the level that would have obtained in the absence of the tax, for it is private unproductive consumption that is at issue.

5. TAXES ON TRANSFER OF PROPERTY, OTHER THAN DEATH DUTIES

At the end of Chapter VIII, Ricardo quotes with seeming approval some remarks by Adam Smith on taxes affecting transfer of land, loan contracts, and law proceedings. Two of the three, at least, are said by Smith to diminish the capital value of the taxed object. From this, we are to infer that such taxes are paid out of capital, for Smith generalizes: " 'All taxes upon the transference of property of every kind, so far as they diminish the capital value of that property, tend to diminish the funds destined for the maintenance of labour.[42] They are all more or less unthrifty taxes, that increase the revenue of the sovereign, which seldom maintains any but unproductive labourers, at the expense of the capital of the people, which maintains none but productive.' "[43]

Ricardo's approval of this passage is somewhat puzzling. Assuming for the moment that the tax on the transfer does "diminish the capital value" of the property, it does not necessarily follow that this represents a decrease in the country's real capital, or, if it does, that the decrease is not made good, by a reduction in unproductive consumption or an increase in production, by the seller. Perhaps the qualifying word "tend" was in Ricardo's mind when he did not stop to analyze Smith's conclusion.

[42] As Sraffa notes, Smith actually says "of productive labour." S. I. 154, note 2. *Wealth of Nations*, Bk. V, Ch. II, Appendix to Articles I and II, C, II, 347; M, 814.

[43] *Idem.*

More surprising is the absence of criticism by Ricardo of Smith's dogmatic statements on incidence.[44]

First, as to taxes on the sale of land. They fall, says Smith, " 'altogether upon the seller.' " And why? Because " 'The seller is almost always under the necessity of selling, and must, therefore, take such a price as he can get. The buyer is scarce ever under the necessity of buying, and will, therefore, only give such a price as he likes. He considers what the land will cost him in tax and price together. The more he is obliged to pay in the way of tax, the less he will be disposed to give in the way of price. Such taxes, therefore, fall almost always upon a necessitous person, and must, therefore, be very cruel[45] and oppressive.' "[46]

It is difficult to understand why Smith believed that sellers of land almost always had to sell, while buyers of land scarcely ever had to buy. Perhaps he was thinking of land of a kind bought and sold frequently, and therefore with an established market, that had to be compared closely with other forms of investment not subject to the transfer tax (government stock, for instance). Then, the differential tax on land would be taken into account by the purchaser: not only the tax to be paid on the immediate sale, but future taxes on possible future sales, to an uncertain extent. There being no cost schedule to influence the supply of land, its value would be decreased permanently by capitalization of the present and vaguely discerned future transfer taxes. But this is probably a strained and over-generous interpretation of Smith's implicit reasoning, and of Ricardo's acquiescence.

As to "Stamp duties, and duties upon the registration of bonds and contracts for borrowed money," no assertion is made by Smith that the value of anything is decreased thereby; he merely says that such taxes "fall altogether upon the borrower, and in fact are always paid by him."[47] No reasoning is offered to support this conclusion, which is not self-evident.

Finally, "Duties of the same kind [as stamp duties, etc.] upon law proceedings fall upon the suitors. They reduce to both the capital value of the subject in dispute. The more it costs to acquire any property, the

[44] See p. 12 above, for Ricardo's self-confessed "propensity to quote" Adam Smith on taxation.

[45] Sraffa says here (S, I, 154, note 1): "Adam Smith says 'very frequently cruel.'" In the Cannan edition the phrase is "frequently very cruel." *Wealth of Nations*, Bk. V, Ch. II, Pt. II, Appendix to Articles I and II, C, II, 346; see also M, 813.

[46] S, I, 154; G, 135; *Wealth of Nations, idem.*

[47] S, I, 154; G, 135; *Wealth of Nations, idem.*

less must be the neat value of it when acquired."[48] Smith does not specify which party bears the tax, but evidently it is the successful litigant. Again, there is no comment by Ricardo. In Parliament, however, he condemned the duties on law proceedings as

> the most abominable that existed in the country, by subjecting the poor man, and the man of middling fortune, who applied for justice, to the most ruinous expence [hear!]. Every gentleman had his favourite plan for repealing a particular tax, and this tax upon justice, was that which he should most desire to see reduced.[49]

After quoting from Smith at length without comment, Ricardo closes Chapter VIII with some remarks of his own that seem more to the point. Taxes on the transfer of property

> prevent the national capital from being distributed in the way most beneficial to the community. For the general prosperity, there cannot be too much facility given to the conveyance and exchange of all kinds of property, as it is by such means that capital of every species is likely to find its way into the hands of those, who will best employ it in increasing the productions of the country.[50]

And he quotes Say to the same effect.

We may therefore infer that to Ricardo transfer taxes are "paid out of capital" in the sense that they prevent the most effective use being made, either of particular capital instruments, or of money funds. He recurs to this point in "Funding System," but now in terms of ignorance rather than knowledge: "Under a complicated system of taxation, it is impossible for the wisest legislature to discover all the effects, direct and indirect, of its taxes; and if it cannot do this, the industry of the country will not be exerted to the greatest advantage."[51]

[48] S, I, 154; G, 135. *Wealth of Nations*, C, II, 346-47; M, 814.

[49] Speech of March 20, 1822, S, V, 147. William Frend lists "instances of inequitable taxation": "a poll-tax, land-tax, excise, customs, duties on law transactions, windows, houses, receipts...." *The Principles of Taxation*, p. 33. The duties on law transactions are "still worse" than the poll-tax, land-tax, excise, or customs: "for, if a man does not go to law, he does not pay his share to the state, and the fear of legal expences might expose him to injustice." *Ibid.*, p. 34. See also Bentham, *A Protest Against Law Taxes.*

[50] S, I, 154-55; G, 135. [51] S, IV, 189-90.

CHAPTER IV

SPECIFIC TAX PER UNIT OF AGRICULTURAL PRODUCE

Ricardo's conclusions on the economic consequences of a tax on farm produce, particularly foodstuffs, can be appreciated for their originality only if we keep in mind the law on this subject as it had been laid down by Adam Smith.

1. INCIDENCE ON CONSUMERS, NOT LANDLORDS

Smith had said that a special tax on the farmer would be shifted. The farmer would transfer his capital to some other use if he could not obtain a "reasonable profit," after tax, in agriculture.

Smith was referring to a tax "upon the profits of stock" employed in agriculture, but his reasoning applies as well to a tax based on output.

To whom could the farmer shift the tax? Not to consumers, said Smith. For that, each farmer would have to restrict production, to induce a rise in price. He would have to withdraw part of his labor, tools, and fertilizer from the land. But this action would not be in his interest.

> Each farmer occupies a certain quantity of land, for which he pays rent. For the proper cultivation of this land a certain quantity of stock is necessary; and by withdrawing any part of this necessary quantity, the farmer is not likely to be more able to pay either the rent or the tax. In order to pay the tax, it can never be his interest to diminish the quantity of his produce ....[1]

The "proper cultivation" evidently does not depend on price, in Smith's mind. One acre, it seems, properly absorbs just so much capital, and should produce just so much corn.

Accordingly, Smith concluded, the farmer will shift the tax to his landlord, by a reduction in rent.

[1] *Wealth of Nations*, Bk. V, Ch. 2, Part II, Art. II, C, II, 340, M, 807.

Ricardo approaches the problem of a special tax on agriculture by considering a specific tax per unit of corn, or "raw produce."[2] He does not criticize Smith's dubious reasoning directly, does not, indeed, even refer to Smith at this point, but he clearly disagrees. A tax on corn will be shifted, but not to the landlord. This conclusion is reached by application of the "doctrine of rent."[3] "Without correct notions of rent, no man can be made to understand that a land tax does not ultimately fall on the landlord, and it would be in vain to talk to him, till he did admit the new doctrine on the subject of rent."[4]

Ricardo implicitly assumes a completely inelastic demand for raw produce.[5] Whatever happens to price, an unchanged physical amount of corn must be produced. Consequently, all units of labor and capital[6] engaged in production of corn must continue so engaged even after the tax is introduced. But this is possible, for those units of labor and capital at the margin of cultivation, only if the price of corn rises to offset the tax. For those units, the tax cannot be recouped by a reduction in land rent, as no part of their product has been going to rent.

Both the extensive and intensive margins of cultivation are involved. At the extensive margin, the farmer is applying labor and capital to land so poor that its produce barely covers production costs, including a normal profit. Nothing is left to pay to the landowner. On more fertile land the farmer applies so much labor and capital that the product from the last "dose" barely covers its cost plus the customary profit.

In general, therefore, "Any tax which may be imposed on the cultivator, whether in the shape of land-tax, tithes, or a tax on the produce when obtained, will increase the cost of production, and will therefore

[2] Ad valorem taxes on agricultural produce are analyzed in Ricardo's Chapter XI, discussed in Chapter VI below.

[3] See letter of Feb. 6, 1815, Ricardo to Malthus, S, VI, 172-74.

[4] Letter of Sept. 25, 1819, Ricardo to Trower, S, VIII, 79. The term, "land tax," must be understood to exclude a tax directly on land rent.

[5] To some degree, this assumption was probably a simplifying device, to allow the main points of Ricardo's thesis to emerge more clearly. Ricardo recognized that an unusually abundant crop could all be sold; the price would have to fall, but not to zero. It would fall so much, however, that the farmer's gross receipts would decline; elasticity of demand would be less than unity. See Ricardo's comment in Parliament, March 5, 1822, S, V, 142. In a year of bad harvest, the restricted supply would be rationed by a rise of price. S, I, 162; G, 143-44. However, Ricardo apparently did think of the demand for corn as almost completely inelastic within a considerable range of price.

[6] "Capital" may be used alone in this context if it includes wages advanced to workers, not merely animals, tools, and other farm equipment.

raise the price of raw produce."[7] The phrase, "any tax which may be imposed on the cultivator," must be understood to include only a tax that extends to the cultivator working at the margin.

Earlier, Ricardo apparently had taken a different view of the incidence of an agricultural tax, but it is not clear what that view was. In a letter to Malthus, in January, 1817, Ricardo says,

> I fear I shall not have the satisfaction of receiving your acquiescence to my doctrines, particularly as I have reverted to my former views respecting taxes on raw produce. Whatever may be correct on that subject surely Adam Smith is wrong, as there are various passages in his book inconsistent with each other.[8]

The "former views," held as late as 1815, were evidently a belief that a tax on raw produce rested on consumers.[9] That was the view Ricardo was now (1817) expressing in his *Principles,* if we construe the statement that consumers bear the burden of the raw-produce tax as referring to the situation that obtains after the price of raw produce has increased, but before the consequent general increase in wages. Ricardo's chief concern, in these passages, is to demonstrate that a tax on farm produce does not burden the farmer particularly; it is passed on to all consumers. From there, its effects are diffused throughout the world of profits by a rise in wages.

But what had been the view to which he had moved during 1815 or 1816 and which he was now abandoning? There seems to be no assurance on this point. Could Ricardo be referring to that mistake concerning a tax on the profits of stock, to which he called Mill's attention in his letter of November 20, 1816? [10] A certain passage in the *Notes on Bentham* [11] might be involved, except for the fact that it was written in 1810 or 1811, too early to reflect the views referred to here; moreover, it does not directly contradict the theorem in question.

The conclusion that a tax on raw produce would be completely shifted to consumers had important policy implications, in view of the distress in which British agriculture found itself shortly after the end of the Napoleonic wars. Taxation of the farmer was widely held to be one of

[7] *Principles,* S, I, 156; G, 137. [8] Letter of Jan. 3, 1817, S, VII, 115.

[9] Ricardo presumably refers to his letter to Malthus of Feb. 6, 1815, S, VI, 173, and his statement of the same year in his *Essay on Profits,* S, IV, 33-34, note. See notes 20 and 21 below, this chapter. Sraffa, S, VII, 115, suggests that Ricardo may also be referring to a passage in his *Reply to Bosanquet,* S, III, 241-42 (quoted, in another context, on p. 104 below).

[10] See p. 117 below, footnote 40.

[11] See p. 79 below.

the chief causes of his difficulties.[12] This view must be mistaken, if farm taxes raise farm prices, without affecting the amount of produce taken. "The price of raw produce," Ricardo writes to McCulloch in 1816, "cannot for any length of time keep so low as to prevent farmers from getting the general profits of stock however high they may be taxed. All taxes I apprehend fall ultimately on the consumers." [13] In essays, speeches in Parliament, and letters,[14] Ricardo asserts repeatedly that the cause for agricultural distress must be sought elsewhere, chiefly in the succession of abundant harvests, coupled with a system of protective duties that had allowed the price of corn to rise to very high levels in earlier years.

Thus, in his essay, *On Protection to Agriculture,* published in 1822, Ricardo declares: "No point is more satisfactorily established in my opinion, than that every tax imposed on the production of raw produce falls ultimately on the consumer, in the same way as taxes on the production of manufactured commodities fall on the consumers of those articles." [15] If the "agricultural horse-tax, tithes, land-tax" [16] had never been imposed in the first place, the current price of corn would be still

[12] The problem was of course important quantitatively, even with respect to foodstuffs alone. About 1815, "in Great Britain one-half of the inhabitants were providers of food and brought to market one-half of their produce. . . ." Fay, "Corn Prices and the Corn Laws, 1815-1846," *Econ. J.,* XXXI (No. 121, March, 1921), 22.

[13] Letter of June 9, 1816, S, VII, 38. McCulloch replied (letter of Nov. 19, 1816, S, VII, 94): "I do not exactly understand what you mean by saying all taxes fall ultimately on the consumers. To me this seems just the same thing as to say, that all taxes fall ultimately on the public in general." But in this context, "ultimately" cannot mean "in the long run," since in the Ricardian system the tax comes to rest finally on profits, and on well-to-do consumers. "Ultimately" must mean after the lapse of a short period of time has allowed the price of raw produce to rise.

[14] In addition to the passages cited directly below in the text, see Ricardo's speeches in Parliament of Feb. 8, 1821, S, V, 74; of March 7, 1821, S, V, 84-85 (see p. 103 below); of April 5, 1821 (bills for repeal of malt tax and agricultural horses tax), S, V, 101-102; of Feb. 5, 1822, S, V, 123; of Feb. 11, 1822 (an important speech), S, V, 124-27; of Feb. 18, 1822, S, V, 131-32, 137. See also the letters of March 23, 1821, Ricardo to McCulloch (S, VIII, 357); of Feb. 8, 1822, Ricardo to McCulloch (S, IX, 157-58); and of Jan. 30, 1823, Ricardo to Trower: "I am rather singularly circumstanced—agreeing as I do with the reformers, on the subject of parliamentary reform, I can not agree with them that taxation and bad government has [*sic*] been the cause of our present difficulties: I believe that under the best possible government, and without taxes, we might have been involved in similar troubles" (S, IX, 267).

[15] S, IV, 240.

[16] S, IV, 255.

lower than it is, by the amount of these taxes.'[17] Some seven years earlier, in his *Essay on the Influence of a Low Price of Corn on the Profits of Stock,* Ricardo had said much the same thing:

I by no means agree with Adam Smith, or with Mr. Malthus, respecting the effects of taxation on the necessaries of life.... They both think that such taxes, incalculably more than any other, tend to diminish capital and production. I do not say that they are the best of taxes, but they do not, I think, subject us to any of the disadvantages of which Adam Smith speaks in foreign trade: nor do they produce effects very different from other taxes. Adam Smith thought that such taxes fell exclusively on the landholder; Mr. Malthus thinks they are divided between the landholder and consumer. It appears to me that they are paid wholly by the consumer.[18]

In a letter to Malthus at about the same time, Ricardo says:

I diff[er to]o, as you know, as to the effects of taxati[on] on the growth of produce. You appear to me not quite consistent in admitting as you unequivocally do that the last portion of land cultivated, yields nothing more than the profits of stock,—no rent, and yet to maintain that taxes on necessaries or on raw produce fall on the landlord and not on the consumer.[19]

It followed that reduction or repeal of differential taxes on agriculture could not bring the farmer relief. As the price of raw produce rose when the tithe or other special tax was introduced, so would it fall when the tax was repealed. This view is expressed forcefully in letters from Ricardo to Trower[20] and Cowell[21] in February and May, respectively, in 1822. Indeed, the farmer should look for relief to the repeal of other taxes, taxes on people or commodities generally.

To relieve him from such taxes would afford no inducement to produce more corn, because it would not make the production of corn relatively cheaper than the production of any other commodity. This is the essential difference between taking taxes off that affect the producer, and taking those off which affect consumers generally.[22]

And in *Protection to Agriculture* Ricardo suggests that if a special tax on agriculture were to be repealed,

[17] S, IV, 257. [18] S, IV, 33-34, note.

[19] Letter of Feb. 6, 1815, S, VI, 173. MS. torn at bracketed portions (Sraffa, note, *idem*).

[20] Letter of Feb. 20, 1822, S, IX, 165-66. Ricardo's statement here seems designed to assure Trower of doctrinal support, though he parts company "on the delicate topic of the repeal of taxes having been the cause of Agricultural distress," a proposition of Trower's that nearly broke up a meeting of the freeholders of Surrey. *Ibid.*, p. 165, text and note 2 by Sraffa.

[21] Letter of May 21, 1822, S, IX, 199-200. [22] *Ibid.*, p. 200.

a very reasonable doubt may be entertained, whether the competition of the sellers may not further diminish the price of the commodity in consequence of the repeal of the tax.[23]

In that same year of 1822, however, Ricardo makes an important concession to the proponents of tax relief. Writing to Trower, he admits that the price of agricultural produce might not fall immediately, upon removal of the tax. Still convinced of "the general prevalence of error" with respect to the origin of the distress in agriculture, "in attributing the want of a remunerating price to enormous taxation," he is

willing to allow that an immediate repeal of some of the taxes which affect agricultural produce, would materially relieve the farmer. There is an interval between the repeal of a tax which falls indirectly on a commodity, and the fall of the price of such commodity, that is favorable to the producer, and the benefit of this interval would be enjoyed by farmers. It might, if the distress is owing to temporary causes, be sufficiently long to enable them to surmount the difficulty which immediately presses upon them, it would however be quite unscientific therefore to say that it was the burthen of taxation which was the cause of the low price of corn.[24]

In what sense should the word "unscientific," in that passage, be taken? The explanation seems to be given in the essay, *On Protection to Agriculture:*

... it is perfectly consistent to maintain, that taxation is not the cause of some particular distress, and at the same time insist that a repeal of taxes would afford relief [to the distressed party]. When Lord John Russell's horse falls because he trips over a stone, and is enabled to get up again when relieved from the burthen of his harness, it would surely be incorrect to say that the horse fell because he was burthened with harness; though it would be right to assert, that the tripping over the stone threw him down, while the relief from the confinement of the harness enabled him to get up again.[25]

The analogy is incomplete; the removal of a tax, followed sooner or later by a corresponding fall in price, may perhaps be likened to replacement of the old harness by a different one, once the horse is on his feet.

Ricardo also admits that upon imposition of a tax there may be a period during which the price does not rise: "... taxes on production may be the cause of an excess of the supply above the demand ... when the

[23] S, IV, 256. There are some obscure passages at this point: the three sentences starting with "The first remedy is certain and efficacious..." but they do not seem to contradict the passages preceding and following.

[24] Letter of Jan. 25, 1822, S, IX, 152.

[25] S, IV, 257-58. For the allusion to Lord John Russell, see note 1 by Sraffa, S, IV, 258.

tax is a new one, and when the consumers are unwilling to re-pay, in the additional price, the additional charge imposed on the producer."[26]

But Ricardo seems to attach little importance to such delays in response, perhaps indeed has little faith that they will occur at all, for he adds, "... I think that no repeal of taxes could take place which would have any other effect than to relieve consumers generally of a part of the burthens which they now bear," and expresses a conviction that

> there are causes of distress, to the producers of a particular commodity, arising from abundant quantity, from which no practicable repeal of taxes could materially relieve, particularly if the commodity be agricultural produce, and if its ordinary price be kept above the level of the prices of other countries by restrictions on importation.[27]

2. EFFECT ON MONEY RENT AND ON CORN RENT

How does the rise in price of raw produce, resulting from the tax, affect land rent? Money rent is not changed; corn rent falls.

Ricardo's reasoning on this point may be paraphrased as follows. Since the demand for corn is assumed to be completely inelastic, there is no change in the physical amount produced, and price rises by the full amount of the tax. Thus the total amount of tax is exactly recouped by the increase in sales proceeds, and money payments to the factors of production are not lowered. Among these factors of production is land; hence the aggregate of money rent remains unchanged. Meanwhile, since the price of corn has risen, this unchanged total of money rent represents fewer bushels of corn.

It may be objected that the physical differentials in product remain unaltered; should not corn rent accordingly be the same as before? A dose of labor and capital at the margin still yields 160 quarters of corn, an intra-marginal dose 180 quarters. The rent, however, cannot remain at 20 quarters, for, the richer the yield, the greater the absolute amount of tax. With respect to the 180 quarters of corn from the intra-marginal dose, the tax is imposed on the differential 20 quarters as well as on the 160 quarters that go to capital and labor. Both of these physical shares are reduced by the tax. For example, if the tax is 8 shillings a quarter (8 bushels), and if corn sells for £4 a quarter before the tax and £4.8*s*. under the tax, the government seizes the equivalent of $^1/_{11}$ of the produce. The capital-labor share of the 180 quarters, formerly 160 quarters, is now only $145^5/_{11}$ quarters, but, at the new high price,

[26] S, IV, 256. [27] S, IV, 258-59.

yields the same money proceeds as before (£640). The landlord's share, formerly 20 quarters, is now only $18^{2}/_{11}$ quarters, worth £80, as was the 20 quarters before the rise in price.

Ricardo gives a numerical illustration, but it is incomplete, for it deals only in terms of an extensive margin. The following paragraphs expand the illustration to include an intensive margin.

First, let there be only two parcels of land, No. 2 and No. 3 of Ricardo's example. On parcel No. 2, the first dose of labor and capital, dose 2-a, produces 170 quarters of corn, the second dose, 2-b, 160 quarters. On parcel No. 3, only one dose is applied, dose 3-a, yielding 160 quarters. Corn sells for £4 per quarter before the tax is imposed; £640 is just enough to compensate one dose of labor and capital. The rent of parcel No. 2 is 10 quarters of corn, or £40.

A tax of 8 shillings a quarter is now imposed on corn, and the price rises by the full amount of the tax. Total revenue from the produce grown on parcel No. 3 increases to £704, just enough to pay the £64 tax. Similarly, the revenue from the produce of dose 2-b on parcel No. 2 increases to £704, just enough to pay the £64 tax. But the revenue from the produce of the intra-marginal dose, 2-a, must cover £68 tax, since it represents 170 quarters. Yet the labor-capital share of the produce is again only 160 quarters, hence cannot defray the extra £4 tax, which must therefore come from the sale of the landlord's share, 10 quarters. The landlord sells his 10 quarters for £44 (his rent) and from this takes $^{1}/_{11}$, or £4, for tax. Alternatively, he may be thought of as keeping his rental demand on the entrepreneur down to £40, thus allowing the latter to pay the entire tax himself.

If the example is now expanded to bring in parcel No. 1, three doses of labor and capital must be assumed applied to it, producing successively 180, 170, and 160 quarters. This parcel will yield £120 rent before the tax is imposed, and the same amount under the tax. The corn rent will decline. However, the proportion between the corn rents of parcel No. 1 and parcel No. 2 will be the same as before the tax.

3. REPERCUSSION ON WAGES FOR THE COMMON LABORER

Would the consumers of raw produce, to whom the tax is initially shifted, pass it on in any way? The laborers would do so, through an increase in wages—at least those laborers receiving "wages of the lowest kind." [28] Such wages

[28] S, I, 159; G, 140.

never continue much above that rate which nature and habit demand for the support of the labourers. This class is never able to bear any considerable proportion of taxation; and, consequently, if they had to pay 8*s*. per quarter in addition for wheat and in some smaller proportion for other necessaries [which contain, in varying degrees, raw produce], they would not be able to subsist on the same wages as before, and to keep up the race of labourers. Wages would inevitably and necessarily rise; and in proportion as they rose, profits would fall.[29]

All other consumers would bear the tax in proportion as they consumed the taxed produce; they would have no recourse. This group, consisting chiefly of capitalists and landlords, may include laborers receiving wages of more "than the lowest kind." Ricardo does not stop to consider them at this point, and the extent to which their wages may rise, if at all, is not explored. If the scale of "estimation in which different qualities of labour are held" [30] is to be maintained unaltered in terms of disposable wage, the remuneration of the skilled workers should rise by the absolute amount of the tax; if in terms of gross wage, by the percentage that the tax bears to the lowest workers' wages.[31] Later, Ricardo indicates that wages that are more than "moderate," or even merely moderate, may bear taxes.[32] Finally, what we may infer about the action of skilled workers' wages under a tax on necessaries or a wages tax depends on whether we are viewing the rise in the wages of the lowest kind as a short-run phenomenon in money terms, due to entry of government into the labor market, or whether we are trying to understand the relation between the market rate of real wages and the natural rate in the progressive economy, an issue that is here deferred for consideration in the analysis of Ricardo's chapter on wage taxation.[33]

Landlords, "instead of contributing their full share to such a tax, are the class peculiarly exempted," since they do not receive profits, the income share that is impaired by the tax. Hence the landlords "only con-

[29] *Idem*. In Chapter XXI of the *Principles*, S, I, 290, note, and G, 274, note, Ricardo atrributes the low level of "profits and interest" in Holland partly to "heavy taxes on the necessaries of the labourer..."

[30] S, I, 20; G, 15.

[31] St. Clair, *A Key to Ricardo*, p. 127, believing that the scale of estimation must be in terms of gross wage, not disposable wage, and inferring that Ricardo's conclusion (S, I, 159; G, 140) implies equal increases in wages, finds an inconsistency here. In any case, Ricardo certainly slurred over the point, in his tax chapters. For convenience in analysis, the terminology employed here ("disposable," "gross") views the raw-produce tax as being levied directly on the consumer.

[32] S, I, 348; G, 336; see p. 193 below. [33] See pp. 140-42 below.

tribute to the tax in proportion as they are consumers of raw produce."[34] Owners of government bonds ("stockholders") are exempt to the same degree, since their investment return, too, is not impaired.[35]

The farmer (the agricultural capitalist) would suffer partly as a consumer of raw produce, and partly as a capitalist through the general decline in the rate of profit that would accompany the increase in wages; but there would be no special decline of agricultural profits as such.[36]

The tax on raw produce can therefore be criticized as an unequal tax, "as it affects the income of the farmer, trader, and manufacturer, and leaves untaxed the income of the landlord, stockholder, and others enjoying fixed incomes...."[37] Evidently it is not to be considered unequal on the score of leaving laborers unaffected, for laborers, in the Ricardian system, are in general non-taxable economically.

The objection of inequality raised against the tax on raw produce can be removed by combining it with certain other taxes: "...by taxing directly the rent of land, and the dividends from stock. By so doing, all the objects of an income tax would be obtained...," without its inconveniences.[38] In the same vein, Ricardo writes to Trower in 1820:

> I never contemplate as a good and practical measure, a tax on profits, without also taxing all other sources of income. Profits can never be known without a minute scrutiny into the affairs of those concerned in trade, other sources of income are well known and may be easily come at. The landlord cannot well conceal the amount of his rent, nor the stockholder the amount of his dividend, and therefore it might become a question whether you should not tax the profits of trade indirectly, by taxing wages, or necessaries; and other incomes directly, as rent, dividends, annuities &c[a] &c[a] [39]

Again, the tax measures designed to insure equality do not include any tax on wage income.

The supreme confidence that Ricardo placed in his sweeping generalizations is nowhere better illustrated than at this point, where he is prepared to support a heterogeneous group of taxes on food (or wages), bond interest, and rent, as a perfect substitute for an income tax on all but laborers.

This policy proposal surely implies a belief by Ricardo that the rise in wages would not lag behind the rise in prices; Ricardo was not the man to suggest in place of the income tax a combination of levies that

[34] S, I, 184; G, 165. [35] S, I, 159-60; G, 140-41.

[36] For a similar conclusion respecting a special tax on agricultural profits, see *Notes on Malthus*, S, II, 130-31, 215.

[37] S, I, 160; G, 141-42. [38] S, I, 160-61; G, 142.

[39] Letter of Jan. 28, 1820, Ricardo to Trower, S, VIII, 154.

would force down the standard of living of the laborer for the months or years needed for a long-term process of adjustment through a change in rate of population growth. The passage quoted above—"they would not be able to subsist on the same wages as before, and to keep up the race of labourers"—does indeed suggest reliance on that kind of adjustment. But as the analysis proceeds, Ricardo rejects that view; upon the introduction of the tax on necessaries, prices rise and wages rise, at once. "In regard then to a tax on raw produce . . . it appears to me that no interval which could bear oppressively on the labourer, would elapse between the rise in the price of raw produce, and the rise in the wages of the labourer. . . ."[40]

What are the forces making for this immediate adjustment? Ricardo casts his argument in terms of the supply of and demand for labor, before and after the tax. The tax on raw produce will not "*necessarily* interfere with the quantity of raw produce; or with the number of people, who are both able to purchase, and willing to consume it."[41] The quantity of raw produce represents the demand for labor; the number of laborers, the supply. Both are unchanged from the pre-tax period.

> A tax on corn does not necessarily diminish the quantity of corn, it only raises its money price; it does not necessarily diminish the demand compared with the supply of labour; why then should it diminish the portion paid to the labourer? Suppose it true that it did diminish the quantity given to the labourer, in other words, that it did not raise his money wages in the same proportion as the tax raised the price of the corn which he consumed; would not the supply of corn exceed the demand?—would it not fall in price? and would not the labourer thus obtain his usual portion?[42]

The objection may be raised: the capitalists are in no position to increase their money demand for labor over what is was a moment before, when no tax was in existence, and the price of the taxed raw produce had not been raised. The sequence of events has been: (1) tax imposed on raw produce ("necessaries"); (2) rise in money price of raw produce, to maintain equiva'ence of profits in taxed and non-taxed industries; and now there is to be (3) a rise in money wages. While the capitalists can maintain their former total wage payment, they cannot do more. The key to the problem, however, lies in the fact that the capitalists will no longer employ the entire labor force. Government has entered the arena as employer, using for this purpose the revenue from the tax on necessaries. Private employers, en b'oc, engage a smaller number of laborers than before, at a higher wage rate than before, so that the total of wages they

[40] S, I, 166; G, 148. [41] S, I, 165; G, 146. [42] S, I, 166; G, 147-48.

pay is unchanged. Government, as employer, adds to the wage bill.

The same analysis may be made in real terms. Corn is taken by the government. With this corn the government bids for labor, in competition with capitalists. The total amount of corn offered for labor is no less than before, for the moment; long-term effects from diminution of rate of accumulation are not yet considered. Some laborers are drawn from private employment, presumably from trades producing non-essentials, to work for the government—these laborers have been released by capitalists who find the total amount of corn at their disposal reduced by the tax.

This explanation of the immediate rise in money wages is given explicitly, not in the chapter of the *Principles* here under study,[43] but in Chapter XVI, "Taxes on Wages."[44] However, an illuminating exchange of views with McCulloch indicates that Ricardo had the government's demand for labor in mind, even when he wrote the chapter on taxation of raw produce. In an article in the *Edinburgh Review* of January, 1820,[45] McCulloch had said that wages would not rise in proportion to the increased price of the taxed commodities, since competition among laborers would continue undiminished, and the demand for labor would not be increased. Ricardo disagrees:

> Suppose [the working classes] to be in that state of abundance [of the means for supporting their families] as to encourage the doubling of population in 25 years, and suppose a tax to be laid directly on wages, or on the necessaries on which wages are expended, of 20 pct., what effect will such a tax have on the real comforts of the labourers? None whatever, I answer, unless it diminishes the demand for labour [by "affecting the rate of accumulation," presumably], because

[43] Is it reading too much into Ricardo's analysis to assume that he was thinking at this point of the government's demand for labor? Even without the letter of March 29, 1820, to McCulloch to be noted shortly below, which seems decisive, it might be supposed that Ricardo's reference to a possibly unchanged total demand for labor and a possibly unchanged total supply of corn was not meant as a random shot. Yet several critics of Ricardo's have not given him the benefit of this interpretation. Cf. Cannan, *History of the Theories of Production and Distribution*, pp. 197-202; Gonner, G, 147, note (Gonner's capitalist should read the letter to McCulloch); Von Falck, *Kritische Rückblicke auf die Entwicklung der Lehre von der Steuerüberwälzung seit Ad. Smith*, pp. 61-64; Wicksell, *Zur Lehre von der Steuerincidenz*, pp. 68-69; Taussig, *Wages and Capital*, p. 177 [cited by St. Clair]; and St. Clair, *A Key to Ricardo*, pp. 129-31. St. Clair, though calling attention to the later passage in Ricardo's Chapter XVI, does not credit him with having it in mind when he wrote Chapter IX. See note 42 to Chapter X below.

[44] S, I, 220-21; G, 203-204. See pp. 127-29 below. [45] Art. IX, pp. 160-61.

it will be immediately transferred to the employers of labour, and will consequently diminish the profits of stock. Suppose wages not to be increased after the tax, every body could employ the same quantity of labour as before, and to that demand would be added the additional demand of government for labour, who cannot expend these taxes without employing soldiers, sailors and many other labourers. This of itself would soon raise the price of labour, and transfer the burden to the employer of labour. If I before employed 10 gardeners, after wages have thus risen, I may not be able with the same funds as before to employ more than 8, and thus the tax of 20 pct. falls on me—no more men are employed, but two men are dismissed from my service, and are taken into the service of Government. The rate of accumulation goes on as before,[46] and no other effect is produced than what would have been produced if a tax of an equal amount had been directly laid on me. Whatever may previously have been the rate of wages, the tax obviously never deteriorates the situation of the labourer unless it diminishes the demand for labour, by affecting the rate of accumulation. Taxes will generally affect the rate of accumulation, and therefore they are generally injurious to the labourer....[47]

McCulloch's rejoinder is not convincing:

But, admitting that the taxes are totally expended on the maintenance of home soldiers, it is plain, from the incomparably greater waste that must take place in providing for troops, and from the expenditure in the shape of *munitions de guerre,* that instead of the sums raised by Government setting the same quantity of labour in motion as they would have done had they not been thrown into the Exchequer, we shall be a great deal too liberal if we suppose them to have *half* that effect.[48]

Ricardo agrees that "war is attended with waste and extravagance,"[49] but correctly implies that this fact is not to the point in the short-run analysis of demand for labor.

What if the tax is raised to pay a subsidy to a foreign power, rather than to employ English soldiers and sailors? Will not wages fail to rise, in that case?

Suppose [says McCulloch] that in order to pay a subsidy to the Russians a duty of 6d. is laid on every quartern loaf, by what means will the labouring class be able proportionably to raise their wages? Yet such subsidies form a constant and important part of the expenditure of every war.... Hence when a country, in which the increase of capital and of population had been nearly equal has the misfortune to be involved in hostilities, I can have no doubt that if a sudden

[46] Because the tax has been met by reducing private unproductive consumption; the gardeners consume unproductively (see Chapter III above).

[47] Letter of March 29, 1820, Ricardo to McCulloch, S, VIII, 169-70.

[48] Letter of April 2, 1820, to Ricardo, S, VIII, 174-75.

[49] Letter of April 8, 1820, to McCulloch, S, VIII, 176.

check be not given to the principle of population, the condition of its inhabitants must be degraded. This, as it appears to me, is the great evil of excessive and especially of suddenly increasing taxation. Increased exertion might make some amends for the destruction of capital; but when the sentiments of the people are once depressed—when they submit to be sunk in the scale of existence—when, in short, the extortion of government has reduced them to the situation, for example, of the Irish, their capacity of improvement is at an end, and their condition becomes altogether hopeless and desperate.[50]

Ricardo had already answered this question in the *Principles,* Chapter XVI, "Taxes on Wages":

If when the tax [on wages] were levied, Government at once exported the produce of it as a subsidy to a foreign State, and if therefore these funds were devoted to the maintenance of foreign, and not of English labourers, such as soldiers, sailors, &c. &c.; then, indeed, there would be a diminished demand for labour, and wages might not increase, although they were taxed; but the same thing would happen if the tax had been laid on consumable commodities, on the profits of stock, or if in any other manner the same sum had been raised to supply this subsidy: less labour could be employed at home.[51]

But instead of reminding McCulloch of this passage, Ricardo's letter starts a discussion that drifts into confusion for both parties:

But I contend that the poor suffer from this dissipation of capital, not on account of the peculiar taxes which are imposed upon them, but on account of the disturbance which it gives to the usual demand for labour. It matters not, I say, whether the taxes be laid on wine, silks and velvets, the luxuries of the rich, or on the corn and clothing consumed by the laboring class, the specific evil is in both cases, not the tax, but the annihilation of capital to which the tax gives rise. ... If a loan was raised for a subsidy to Russia, or if the amount of the subsidy were supplied by a tax of 6d. on every quartern loaf, or a tax of 100£ on every pipe of wine; provided, in every case, the sum raised was equal in amount, it would be a matter of comparative indifference to the labouring class by which means it should be raised; the great evil is in the amount of the sum raised, and not in the mode of raising it.[52]

Ricardo is correct, within the framework of the assumptions of his economic system, if he is referring only to the short run. The corn, or other wage-good, is exported to Russia—in the most elementary case of this kind—and the English laborers and their families have less to eat and

[50] Letter of April 2, 1820, to Ricardo, S, VIII, 174-75.

[51] S, I, 221; G, 204. This passage was not altered in the second or third editions of the *Principles*. See John Stuart Mill's illustration in terms of the differing modes of war expenditure of France and Great Britain in the Napoleonic Wars. *Principles of Political Economy*. Ashley ed., p. 77, note.

[52] Letter of April 8, 1820, S, VIII, 177.

wear this year than if no such subsidy have been paid. If the subsidy is financed by a tax on necessaries, the prices of necessaries rise but wages do not rise. If it is financed by a tax directly on wages, wages do not rise. If it is financed by a tax on the consumption of the wealthy? Here the immediate consequences are not so obvious, but Ricardo seems to have in mind a discharge of domestic servants or other workers producing goods or services for the rich consumers, who are not thereupon added to the government payroll.

McCulloch replies:

I cannot help differing with you on the subject of taxation. Exclusive of the destruction of capital I think there is a very great difference in the effects produced by taxes on luxuries and taxes on necessaries. Suppose Ireland is obliged to remit a subsidy of 10 millions to Russia and that there are two methods of raising it—a duty on potatoes and a duty on claret and coaches. If the first method be adopted it is plain wages will not rise in proportion to the duty [Ricardo would agree]; for as the subsidy is to be remitted to a foreign country it cannot enable the Government to employ more labour. . . . But an increased duty on claret and coaches would be productive of these effects only in a very slight degree. The love of accumulation must on the average be always stronger than the passion of expence. The increased duty on luxuries would be met by a proportionable saving on those and other articles of expence; and few or no labourers would be thrown out of employment, inasmuch as this would in fact lessen the means of paying the duties.[53]

McCulloch appears in error, at least for the short run. If we continue the assumption that it is wage-goods that are exported to Russia via the subsidy, then either (a) wealthy consumers who were about to give wage-goods to workers in exchange for personal-consumption services or products such as wine will not do so, and workers in those industries will be unemployed, or (b) wage-goods that were to be given to productive workers will be diminished, and wages in these industries will be diminished—or, if labor is mobile between these types of industry, no unemployment will develop, but there will be a general fall of wages in terms of wage-goods, for the year in question. If claret and coaches are to be exported, laborers will not suffer. If forms of capital other than wage-goods are to be exported, labor will be less productive and will have its wages decreased, at least in the year following. These remarks are indeed but conjecture as to how Ricardo would have replied to McCulloch if either he or his correspondent had analyzed the problem in terms of types of export. In fact, Ricardo's reply does not help matters much. He

[53] Letter of May 15, 1820, to Ricardo, S, VIII, 189-90.

now declares that under an annual subsidy (Ricardo emphasizes the "annual" [and recurring?] aspect of the subsidy) from Ireland to Russia, financed by a tax on the necessaries of the poor, the wages of the laborer

> will undergo such a moderate increase as will compensate the labourer for the tax laid on his necessaries. It is the interest of all parties that they should so rise. I consider that the quantity of necessaries which the wages of a labourer will enable him to purchase, is really the efficient regulator of the population. The circumstances of the country require that the population should continue to increase at the same rate after the subsidy is granted to Russia as before, for there is no diminished demand for labour, and the question between us comes to this. Will the population be in the first instance very much depressed, and then afterwards violently stimulated, or will it continue in that course which the circumstances of the capital and the demand for labour originally required it to be? The value of things I believe to be influenced, not by immediate supply and demand only, but also by contingent supply and demand. You must not suppose that I am arguing in favor of taxes on necessaries, in preference to taxes on luxuries, for that is not the question—but I am endeavouring to ascertain in what these taxes really differ.[54]

Up to the last sentence in this passage Ricardo might be thought to have reverted to the initial problem: a comparison of the laborers' situation under no tax and no subsidy, with their position under a subsidy financed by a tax on labor's necessaries. Yet the point under discussion was: Given a tax-and-subsidy, does the laborer's situation differ, according to the nature of the tax? If we assume that Ricardo is continuing the analysis of this issue, the passage just quoted must, if it is to be consistent with his earlier letter, be considered a long-term analysis. We have been told, or so it seems, that in the short run the worker will suffer from the tax-subsidy measure, and he will suffer, regardless of the kind of tax utilized. We are now told that he will not suffer, again, it seems to be implied, regardless of the tax utilized. This latter conclusion can hold for the long term, but only, within Ricardo's own framework, if capital accumulation is not retarded. His passage does not make it evident how this result is to be achieved; it is not enough to assert that "It is the interest of all parties..." and that "The circumstances of the country require...." Indeed, his assertion that "there is no diminished demand for labour" is not understandable, in the context of the discussion up to this point.

McCulloch must have been as puzzled as we are now; in his next letter the subsidy issue is not mentioned,[55] nor does it reappear in any of the later correspondence between McCulloch and Ricardo.

[54] Letter of June 13, 1820, to McCulloch, S, VIII, 196.
[55] Letter of July 16, 1820, to Ricardo, S, VIII, 203-205.

In summary, and disregarding some parts of the letter of June 13, 1820, we may suppose that Ricardo's position on the two issues was as follows: The immediate impact of a tax-and-foreign-subsidy puts the laborer on a lower standard of living for the current year than he would have enjoyed if no such measure had been enacted; but it makes no difference, for this period, whether the tax be levied on the worker himself, or his necessaries, or on items of luxury. Over the long run, such a measure will continue to keep the laborer on a lower level than he would have occupied in its absence, if the tax used to finance the subsidy is one that impedes accumulation of capital. If the tax is instead met by a permanently lower level of luxury consumption, capital for domestic use can accumulate as fast as it would have done in the absence of the tax-subsidy measure, and the worker will not suffer. In the short run, the nature of the tax makes no difference; in the long run, it makes all the difference. We must recall that when the tax money is spent domestically, the government's demand for labor offsets the decrease in private demand for labor only in the immediate sense, in the short run; beyond that, all depends on how capital continues to accumulate.

This interpretation of Ricardo's long-run position on the foreign-subsidy problem is supported by passages in his earlier letter to McCulloch, just before McCulloch raised the subsidy issue. A full paragraph is worth quotation because of new vistas that Ricardo opens up in his long-run theory of wages:[56]

> The labouring classes in all countries have the very greatest interest in keeping the supply of labour rather under the demand, but they are then most happy when the funds for the support of labour, and consequently the demand for it increase with the greatest rapidity, and their means for supporting their families and contracting of marriages is at the highest level to which it can be raised. It is only because taxation interferes with the accumulation of capital, and diminishes the demand for labour, that it is injurious to the working classes. Sometimes it only retards the rate of accumulation, at other times it arrests it altogether, and on some occasions the taxes by being supplied at the expence of capital itself actually diminish the means of the country to employ the same quantity of labour as before.[57] Wages may be regulated, and may continue for a series of years, on a scale which shall allow the population regularly to increase from year to year in such a proportion as shall double it in 25 years. Under other circumstances this power of doubling may not be possible in less than 50, 100, or 200 years—or population may be so little stimulated by ample wages as to increase at the

[56] Letter of March 29, 1820, S, VIII, 168-69.

[57] For a similar warning, in the same context, with respect to the long-term consequences of taxation, see Chapter IX of the *Principles,* S, I, 165; G, 146-47.

slowest rate—or it may even go in a retrograde direction. Wages being regulated according to some one of these states may or may not be affected most injuriously to the working classes by taxation.[58]

Ricardo does not specify in which one of these states labor is affected most injuriously by taxation. It would seem that the greatest injury is done when population is stimulated little or not at all by "ample wages," for we may infer that under these circumstances population would not be checked at all by a decrease in the ample wages; population is not responsive to changes in wages. When population is not responsive, a decrease in wages is not counteracted by a decrease in population, or in its rate of growth. On the other hand, by "injuriously" Ricardo may have been referring to the degree in which the laborer's wages were close to the physiological subsistence level, so that any decrease in wage would carry with it the danger of real distress until population growth was altered accordingly. From this point of view, taxation that impedes capital accumulation is least dangerous to the working class when market wages are so "ample" (or, rather, would be so ample, in the absence of the tax), that the laborers have a substantial cushion between them and distress. Either interpretation could be supported by the context of the letter to McCulloch. Moreover, we are not told whether "ample" connotes a high per capita consumption level within the family, or simply a large family of which each member is at the subsistence level.[59]

In passing, the striking implications of one of the phrases above may be noted: "population ... may even go in a retrograde direction"; does this mean, even under "ample wages?" If so, Ricardo has in mind some powerful influence on population that has nothing to do with standard of living.

An issue similar in some respects to that of the foreign subsidy problem was discussed by Ricardo in Parliament, in 1819: use of tax proceeds to reduce the domestic public debt. In that year, the Chancellor of the Exchequer proposed to raise three millions to be applied to the sinking fund by new taxes on malt, tobacco, tea, etc. Ricardo, although opposed to the sinking fund as such, and "an enemy to taxation altogether,"[60] could not agree that the proposed taxes fell on the laborer

because imposed on the objects he consumed. If, indeed, they were imposed on the luxuries of the labourer, they might in some measure diminish his comforts; but the more the articles taxed approached the nature of necessaries, the more completely would they fall on those who employed labourers. It had been said,

[58] Letter of March 29, 1820, S, VIII, 168-69.

[59] See Chapter II above, pp. 30-31. [60] Speech of June 18, 1819, S, V, 26.

that these taxes would fall upon the poor-rates; but that amounted to the same thing; for the poor-rates formed, in reality, a fund destined to support labour, however inconvenient it might be to pay in that way.[61]

Of course,

all taxation had a tendency to injure the labouring classes, because it either diminished the fund employed in the maintenance of labour, or checked its accumulation. In the argument which he had used, he had supposed that it was necessary to raise a certain sum by taxes, and then the question was whether by taxing necessaries, the burthen would be particularly borne by the labouring classes. He thought not—he was of opinion that they would ultimately fall on the employers of labour, and would be only prejudicial to the labourers in the same way as most other taxes would be, inasmuch as they would diminish the fund employed in the support of labour.[62]

Here, at least as reported by Hansard, Ricardo does not specify whether he is thinking only of the long run, or whether, as in Chapter IX of the *Principles,* he is asserting that the laborer's wage will rise almost immediately following the introduction of the tax on necessaries and the use by the Government of the money. Speaking to a bill, on the floor of Parliament, he should not be assumed to be ignoring the short run; yet in this instance the Government is not to go into the market for labor, but rather is to redeem some of its debt. Apparently, if the analysis is short-run, we are to suppose that the private capital thus released will at once seek labor: another instance of Ricardo's refusal to consider seriously the importance of friction in the economic process.[63] The distinction between taxes on the laborer's necessaries and on his luxuries seems relevant only for the long run.

Ricardo's emphasis is on the family. But at one point he allows himself a remark on taxation of the single person: a passing reference, in the letter to McCulloch analyzing the effect of the Government's entry into the labor market.

The single man amongst the labouring class may bear and often does bear his portion of taxation, but the married labourers has [*sic*] the means of repaying himself by commanding increased wages, unless the amount of the tax is so heavy, however laid, that it disturbs the rate of accumulation.[64]

This passage is too lacking in logic to bear much analysis. If Ricardo has the immediate moment in mind, surely the single man no less than the married worker gets the advantage of the Government's entry into the labor market. If the married laborer cannot "repay himself" because

[61] *Idem.* [62] *Ibid.*, p. 27.
[63] Cf. the passage from "Funding System," S, IV, 177, quoted on p. 50 above.
[64] Letter of March 29, 1820, S, VIII, 172.

the tax disturbs the rate of accumulation, it must be because the market rate (actual rate) of wages is for the time being above the natural rate (the floor rate needed to maintain the population at its existing level). In that event married and single workers are again in the same position. Moreover, workers have to go through a "single" stage before they become married. Finally, even if we postulate a class of bachelor workers who remain single all their lives, Ricardo's conclusion seems invalid, for single workers are produced by married workers (at least in Ricardian terminology); the supply of single workers depends on the disposable income available to married workers. If married workers do not get enough, they will restrict the supply of married workers and single workers both, in the next generation. If anything, then, "the single man amongst the labouring class" might be supposed to get a bonus in the way of disposable income rather than "often .... bear his portion of taxation...."

4. EFFECT ON THE GENERAL LEVEL OF PRICES, AND FOREIGN TRADE

Another objection to a tax on raw produce that Ricardo disposes of involves two questions: can the general level of prices in terms of gold be raised by taxation; and if it can be, and is, so raised, will foreign markets be lost?

On the first point, Ricardo vacillates. In the text of the *Principles,* he answers in the negative; in a footnote added in the third edition, he reverses himself.

The average level of gold prices could not rise merely through taxation, "for the same quantity of money could not circulate the same quantity of commodities, at high as at low prices...."[65] Where could the additional gold for money come from? It would have to be imported; but high domestic prices discourage gold imports. Consequently, the

> probable effect of a tax on raw produce, would be to raise the price of raw produce, and of all commodities in which raw produce entered, but not in any degree proportioned to the tax; while other commodities in which no raw produce entered, such as articles made of the metals and the earths, would fall in price: so that the same quantity of money as before would be adequate to the whole circulation.[66]

[65] S, I, 168; G, 150.

[66] S, I, 169; G, 150-51. See also quotation from letter of March 27, 1815 Ricardo to Malthus, S, VI, 206, on p. 180 below.

The tax would change somewhat the pattern of foreign trade, but would not interfere materially with the total.

Nonetheless, most of the discussion of this "fourth objection" is taken up with an analysis of foreign trade under the alternative supposition that the tax would raise the general level of prices. And in the third edition appears the footnote that says, "It may be doubted whether commodities raised in price, merely by taxation, would require any more money for their circulation. I believe they would not." [67] The reasoning to support this view is given in another footnote, likewise introduced in the third edition, in the chapter on taxes on profits; comment on the reasoning is deferred to the discussion of that chapter which appears below.[68] Here, it is enough to summarize Ricardo's conclusions with respect to the consequences for foreign trade. "A tax which should have the effect of raising the price of all home productions, would not discourage exportation, except during a very limited time." [69] The high domestic price level would cause exports to fall; imports would remain undiminished; gold would have to be exported to pay for the surplus of imports, the domestic price level would fall. The fall in the price level would not discourage imports, which would have maintained their initial prices in English money while prices of domestically produced goods rose, and would continue to maintain them as prices of domestically produced goods fell. Again, the pattern of foreign trade would be altered somewhat, but not its total amount. The tax would remain something of a disadvantage, for it would "prevent the very best distribution of the capital of the whole world, which is never so well regulated, as when every commodity is freely allowed to settle at its natural price, unfettered by artificial restraints." [70]

The possibility of a general rise in prices that Ricardo is here debating arises directly from the increased cost of raw produce consequent upon the tax, and indirectly from the increased cost of other commodities of which raw produce is a component part. It does not arise from a spiral effect of wages on prices, for Ricardo implicitly denies that a general rise in wages could force a rise in the prices of manufactured products. A general rise in wages, we may clearly infer at this point, like a general commodity tax, cannot raise money prices if the economy imports its monetary metal; and if the monetary metal is obtained from domestic mines, prices will not rise unless the mines are exempt from the tax in question or from the general rise in wages. In one of Ricardo's earliest

[67] S, I, 169, note, and note 3 by Sraffa; G, 150. [68] See p. 118 below.
[69] S, I, 169; G, 151. [70] S, I, 172; G, 153.

notes on taxation, there is indeed an expression of the contrary doctrine;[71] but that view was evidently abandoned as the full structure of his macro-economic system took shape in his mind.

[71] "Commodities may rise from taxation tho' they are not subject to any direct taxation themselves. If a tax were laid on bread every commodity would rise, as there is no commodity to the production of which the labour of man is not necessary." Notes on Bentham's Sur les Prix (written between Dec. 25, 1810 and Jan. 11, 1811), S, III, 270. That is to say, a tax on necessaries will force a rise in prices of necessaries, which will cause a rise in wages, which in turn will force a rise in the prices of all commodities (including a second round, presumably, of rise in price of necessaries).

CHAPTER V

TAX ON AGRICULTURAL LAND RENT

Ricardo's analysis of a tax on agricultural rent, in Chapter X of the *Principles,*[1] follows directly from the doctrine of rent expounded in Chapter II; the tax cannot be shifted. It does not strike at the extensive or intensive margin of cultivation, there being no rent at the margin; hence the tax does not discourage production.[2] Ricardo's numerical illustration of this theorem specifies only an extensive margin, but it is to be understood that an intensive margin exists on lands No. 1 and No. 2.

Ricardo quotes Adam Smith: " 'Both ground rents [urban land rent, apparently], and the ordinary rent of land [agricultural land rent, apparently],' he says, 'are a species of revenue, which the owner in many cases enjoys, without any care or attention of his own. Though a part of this revenue should be taken from him, in order to defray the expenses of the State, no discouragement will thereby be given to any sort of industry. The annual produce of the land and labour of the society, the real wealth and revenue of the great body of the people, might be the same after such a tax as before. Ground rents, and the ordinary rent of land are, therefore, perhaps, the species of revenue, which can best bear to have a peculiar tax imposed upon them.'[3] It must be admitted," Ricardo comments, "that the effects of these taxes would be such as Adam Smith has described. . . ."[4]

[1] Planned initially as part of the chapter, "Taxes on Raw Produce," and made a separate chapter only after the book (first edition) had been printed off. See Sraffa, S, I, xxvi-xxx, and S, X, 403.

[2] Whewell of course agrees: "Mathematical Exposition of Some Doctrines of Political Economy," *Cambridge Philosophical Transactions,* III (1830), 221, and "Mathematical Exposition of Some of the Leading Doctrines in Mr. Ricardo's 'Principles of Political Economy and Taxation,' " *ibid.,* IV (1833), 178.

[3] S, I, 203-204; G, 183-84; Smith, *Wealth of Nations,* Bk. V, Ch. II, Pt. II, Art. I, C, II, 328; M, 795-96.

[4] S, I, 204; G, 184.

What does "no discouragement" mean, in this context? It may mean that recipients of land rent never save any of it, only consuming it unproductively; as a result, taxation of rent does not impair ability to save, there being no such ability to begin with, if we may assume that rent goes only to, and is the sole source of income for, a certain group of persons. A tax on pure land rent will then always "come out of revenue," never "out of capital," in the comparative-statics sense. This is the fact, in the Ricardian economic system; landlords, as such, do not save, nor do they possess the kind of capital that they can draw on for consumption, to maintain their standard of living in the event of a tax.

It seems more likely, however, that both Smith and Ricardo were thinking in terms of incentive at this point. In any case, we might conclude, here is a tax that should prove particularly attractive to Ricardo; it is paid out of revenue, and it has no tendency to discourage production. But no, an equity issue now takes command. Discriminatory taxation of land rent would run counter to another of Adam Smith's maxims, whereby the burdens of the State are to be borne by all in proportion to their means. "Rent often belongs to those who, after many years of toil, have realised their gains, and expended their fortunes in the purchase of land or houses;[5] and it certainly would be an infringement of that principle which should ever be held sacred, the security of property, to subject it to unequal taxation. It is to be lamented, that the duty by stamps, with which the transfer of landed property is loaded, materially impedes the conveyance of it into those hands, where it would probably be made most productive."[6]

Moreover, "exclusive taxation" of land would have unfortunate economic consequences, arising from the "risk" of that taxation. The land "would not only be reduced in price, to compensate for the risk of that taxation, but in proportion to the indefinite nature and uncertain value of the risk, would become a fit subject for speculations, partaking more of the nature of gambling, than of sober trade...." The land would therefore probably fall into the hands of "those, who possess more of the qualities of the gambler, than of the qualities of the sober-minded

[5] The first edition of the *Principles* does not contain "or houses"; see note 2 by Sraffa, I, 204.

[6] S, I, 204; G, 184. See also Ricardo's objection to "substituting for the tithes [which he considered a very bad tax indeed] a poundage on rents; this would be to tax exclusively a particular class of the community." Letter of Sept. 15, 1820, Ricardo to McCulloch, S, VIII, 238. For his objection, in turn, to imposing the tithe on lands hitherto exempt from it, see Chapter VI below. His dislike of "the duty by stamps" continues the theme begun at the end of his Chapter VIII.

proprietor, who is likely to employ his land to the greatest advantage."[7]

By "risk" Ricardo appears to mean the uncertain prospect of future taxes. This inference is confirmed by one of his comments on the first edition of James Mill's *Elements of Political Economy.* Mill is expounding the virtues of a tax on land rent, in a new country. Ricardo first points out that there would be a considerable period during which no rent would arise in such a country, and hence "no public revenue,"[8] and that the tax might in practice fall on profits from improvements made by the landlord. He then adds a third objection:

Under such a system of taxation great encouragement would be given to gambling. On the approach of war land would fall in proportion to the expectation of the duration of the war, and with every battle or treaty people would speculate according as their hopes or fears predominated. Land would be so uncertain a property that no safe provision could by means of the possession of it be made for children.[9]

And he concludes:

On the whole I should greatly prefer the present system of taxation. If land is to be peculiarly the subject of taxation it would be desirable to adopt the Asiatic mode, and consider the government at all times, both in war and peace, the sole possessor of the land, and entitled to all the rent.[10]

Gonner comments: "It is, however, doubtful whether the second objection [here, increase of speculation in land] would be valid in the case of nationalization [of land], provided that such be *introduced* without any general disturbance of security."[11] This argument is difficult to follow, unless by "nationalization" Gonner means only part ownership in the land by the Government, partial nationalization of any given parcel of land. Ricardo, incidentally, falls into the same kind of exaggerated terminology when he refers to Adam Smith's proposal as one "to tax exclusively" the revenue from land, to regard land "as a fit subject for exclusive taxation," though in between these two passages he employs the more moderate phrase, "unequal taxation."[12]

Ricardo's argument based on risk seems forced; his rejection of special taxation of land rent is based primarily on the importance he attaches to property rights.[13]

[7] S, I, 204; G, 184-85.

[8] Enclosure in letter of Dec. 18, 1821, Ricardo to Mill, S, IX, 132.

[9] *Idem.* Ricardo thus formulates a partial theory of tax capitalization, or tax amortization.

[10] S, IX, 132-33. [11] G, 184, note 2. [12] S, I, 204; G, 184.

[13] The administrative difficulty of isolating pure land rent for tax assessment does not appear to have been much on Ricardo's mind.

Much of Chapter X is in fact devoted to considering a tax imposed on rent in the broader sense of the term, which includes profits of the landlord in his capacity as agricultural entrepreneur supplying capital. Some part of such a tax must be shifted forward to the consumers of raw produce. At one point, Ricardo adds this proviso: "in a progressive country." [14] Is this to say that in a stationary or declining economy the tax would fall elsewhere? Ricardo does not develop this point, either here or in Chapter XV. We may infer that a discriminating tax on agricultural profits would in any case tend to raise the price of raw produce relative to the prices of other commodities. But let us assume that this tax is introduced into a stationary state where rates of wages and profits are at a minimum, and is not met by a decrease in unproductive consumption. An increase in production from the stationary state level is not a tenable alternative, hence the tax would cut into the capital stock of the country. The result would be a decrease in population, and a retreat to less expensive margins of agricultural production; consequently, the new price of raw produce would not be higher than the old price by the full amount of the tax. In a retrograde economy, already living off its capital, with the price of corn falling continuously, the tax would accentuate the shrinkage in population and output, and again the price of corn would not, at any given moment, be higher, by the full amount of the tax, than it would have been.

A passage in Chapter XVIII, "Poor Rates," deals specifically with taxation in the retrograde state, but the analytical issue is not the same; it concerns inability to earn a normal return on sunk capital, rather than a lower level of total cost at less intensive and less extensive margins. Ricardo is analyzing the effects of a particularly heavy tax on the profits from agriculture. He concludes that the excess of such a tax over the tax generally applicable to profits will be passed on to the consumer, provided the society is one "which is extending its agriculture. . . ." But

> in a stationary, or in a retrograde country, so far as capital could not be withdrawn from the land, if a further rate were levied for the support of the poor, that part of it which fell on agriculture would be paid, during the current leases, by the farmers; but, at the expiration of those leases, it would almost wholly fall on the landlords.[15]

In the former case the return on the investment would be kept up to the anticipated level, net after tax, by the necessity for still further invest-

[14] S, I, 175; G, 156. This phrase was added in the third edition; S, I, 175, note 1 by Sraffa.

[15] S, I, 260-61; G, 245-46.

ment, which would not be forthcoming unless the price of produce was rising adequately to cover the extra tax. In the second case, "so far as capital could not be withdrawn from the land," no such force would be operating. Thus income on sunk capital resembles rent.

As a part of this capital, when once expended in the improvement of a farm, is inseparably amalgamated with the land, and tends to increase its productive powers, the remuneration paid to the landlord for its use is strictly of the nature of rent, and is subject to all the laws of rent .... when once made, the return obtained will ever after be wholly of the nature of rent, and will be subject to all the variations of rent.[10]

[10] S, I, 262, note; G, 247, note.

CHAPTER VI

PROPORTIONAL TAX ON AGRICULTURAL OUTPUT

The tithes of Ricardo's day were usually a tenth part of the gross produce of agricultural land, payable in kind to the clergy. In many instances, however, the tithe had come to be held outside the church, and in many others had been extinguished by being exchanged for land or corn rents or fixed sums. Ricardo's chapter on tithes abstracts from this institutional background, with one exception, and is accordingly applicable to any tax expressed as a percentage of gross produce from agriculture. The exception arises when Ricardo is considering a compensating duty on imported corn; if collected by the church, such a duty would not lead to the reduction of other levies.[1]

Under stable agricultural prices, the effects of a tithe are the same as those of a specific tax per unit of product ("a money tax"): the price of raw produce is raised by the amount of the tax, money rents are unchanged, rents in terms of raw produce fall, and the proportions between the raw-produce rents remain as before.[2]

[1] S, I, 179; G, 160.

[2] Whewell agrees with Ricardo that, given what would now be called a completely inelastic demand, "the increase of price and the amount of the tax are equal, and the whole tax falls upon the consumers" ("Mathematical Exposition of Some Doctrines of Political Economy," p. 208). For further details, see Appendix A: 1, at the end of this volume. In his second paper, "Mathematical Exposition of Some of the Leading Doctrines in Mr. Ricardo's 'Principles'," pp. 176-77, Whewell's treatment of this case is more sophisticated, explicitly taking account of the fact that "prices rise so as to compensate the whole of the cultivator's loss and of the increased expenses of the labourer." The whole tax is now said to fall "upon the rich consumer." Assuming that the laborer spends half his wages for food, and that one third of the produce of an acre is paid in wages (pr = nlw, p. 171; pr = money value of produce of one acre; lw = number of laborers on one acre, times wage rate, p. 170; n = 3, p. 172), Whewell con-

1. THE GROWING BURDEN OF THE TAX, IN TERMS OF NET PRODUCT

Tithes become heavier or lighter than an initially equivalent specific tax if the price of the commodity rises or falls. The price fluctuations that Ricardo has in mind are those over the long term, caused, for example, by the need to push out to less favorable margins of cultivation in the progressive state, when importation of corn is restricted.

Today, we are inclined to say the same thing the other way round, and to charge the specific tax with the defect of becoming lighter or heavier, in real terms, as the price of the taxed commodity varies, while an ad valorem tax is viewed as the stable one, always taking the same proportion of the produce. But Ricardo had good reason to place the emphasis where he did, for he expected the price of corn to rise, relative to prices of manufactured goods, owing to increasing difficulty of production at the margin. A larger and larger proportion of the country's entire labor force would have to be devoted to the task of keeping the labor force alive; yet the tax would continue to demand one-tenth the output of that enlarging segment of the labor force.

Ricardo put it in slightly different terms, comparing the amount taken in tax with the "net produce of land" and with the "net income of [the] ... country."[3] He does not define "net" at this point, but from Chapter XXVI of the *Principles* ("On Gross and Net Revenue"), we know that it refers to profits plus rent.[4] It is "from the net income of a country that all taxes are ultimately paid, either in a progressive or in a

cludes that a tax rate of 10 percent will raise the price of corn by $^3/_{22}$ (see also p. 162). Whewell expands the analysis of the percentage tax on produce in his first paper, pp. 209-219, to take account of demand schedules that are not completely inelastic (unitary elasticity, elasticity of - $^1/_3$), of tax rates graduated with fertility of soil, and of marginal cost curves with varying slopes—though of course he does not use this terminology. He is chiefly concerned with determining the proportion of the tax that comes out of each of the three shares in income (wages, profit, and rent). Whewell's analysis of the proportional tax is impaired by failure to take into account consistently the intensive, as opposed to the extensive, margin of cultivation, and he does not discuss a specific tax per unit of product. But his extension of the Ricardian analysis is strikingly original. A detailed critique of Whewell's price-output analysis, although long overdue, is not attempted in the present volume, except for those parts that deal directly with Ricardo's reasoning in his tax theorems. See also Marshall, *Principles of Economics*, 8th ed., Appendix L, p. 834, for the case where demand for corn is not completely inelastic.

[3] S, I, 178; G, 159. [4] S, I, 347; G, 336.

stationary country," but in a progressive country "the net produce of land is always diminishing in proportion to its gross produce. . . ." [5] A tax that is a fixed proportion of gross produce must therefore increase faster than the net produce. Hence it "must necessarily be a very burdensome, and a very intolerable tax." [6] The church is "constantly obtaining an increased portion of the net produce of the land and labour of the country." [7] By the same reasoning, we may add, the tax is absorbing the output of an ever-increasing proportion of the total input.

That Ricardo took these prospects seriously is shown by his willingness to base investment advice on them. At that time, the landowner had an opportunity to commute the tithe by a single money payment. Trower asks Ricardo's advice: "How should you value *Tithes;* in reference to value of *money* or *land.* I say the *former.* I have been offered *mine* at 28 years purchase and I think I ought to purchase them at 26." [8] Ricardo replies:

> You ask me how I should value tithes—whether I should value them in reference to monied or landed capital. I differ with you, and think in reference to the latter. I think Tithes at 28 years purchase is a much cheaper purchase than Land at 28 years purchase particularly if you contemplate the increasing prosperity and population of the country. In an improving country Tithes always increase in a greater proportion than rent, because they are always the same proportion of the gross produce of the land; rent, even when it increases, is probably always a diminished proportion of the gross produce. Should the rent of your land in 50 or a hundred years rise 50 pc, I have no doubt whatever that the Tithes on the same land will rise very considerably more than 50 pc. If your Tithes are at a fair valuation, and not unusually high you would do well I think to purchase them at 28 years purchase.[9]

[5] S, I, 178; G, 159.

[6] *Idem.* ". . . this most oppressive and irritating tax," Ricardo calls it in a letter to McCulloch, Sept. 15, 1820, commenting on the latter's article on tithes in the *Edinburgh Review.* S, VIII, 237. See also S, VIII, 214, 222, 229.

[7] S, I, 178; G, 159. [8] Letter of July 22, 1821, S, IX, 31.

[9] Letter of Aug. 22, 1821, S, IX, 39-40. Twenty-eight years' purchase gives an interest return of 3.57 percent a year; twenty-six years' purchase, one of 3.85 percent. Discussion was continued, not very informatively, in letters of Sept. 13, 1821, Trower to Ricardo, S, IX, 70-71, and of Oct. 4, 1821, Ricardo to Trower, S, IX, 88-89. The central point, whether the total money value of annual gross produce from a given parcel of land will increase faster or slower than the annual rent of that land, depends on factors not brought out clearly in this Ricardo-Trower correspondence. In 1822, an anonymous English writer, "E. R.," in *An Essay on Political Economy,* who "is concerned with the general problem of the shifting and incidence of taxes," "treats mathematically and in great detail the effects on an economy of the commutation of tithes . . . . A comparison of his

Ricardo's concern for legitimate vested interests, most strongly evidenced in his opposition to special taxation of land rent, emerges in his correspondence with McCulloch on the latter's article on Tithes:

I do not quite agree with you in the justice of subjecting those to the tax whose lands have hitherto been exempted from it. Many tithe free farms are yearly brought to market, and an additional price is paid for them in consequence of the peculiar advantage they enjoy. It would surely be very unjust to subject such a proprietor to a tax after his paying a valuable consideration to be exempted from it.

And he extends the doctrine still further by the next sentence:

I think that it would be almost equally unjust to impose this tax on those who have retained the property in their own hands for the three hundred and fifty years of which you speak.[10]

analysis of the effects of commutation of tithes with Ricardo's wanderings on the subject seems to justify the mathematical method." Robertson, "Mathematical Economics before Cournot," *J. Pol. Econ., LVII* (No. 6, Dec., 1949), 534.

[10] Letter of Sept. 15, 1820, Ricardo to McCulloch, S, VIII, 237-38. For passing references to tithes, see *Protection to Agriculture,* S, IV, 218, and S, V, 45, speech of May 8, 1820.

CHAPTER VII

AGRICULTURAL TAX OF A FIXED AMOUNT PER ACRE

In the course of analyzing a fixed tax per acre, Ricardo makes a remarkable discovery: there is a type of tax that may benefit some of those who pay it, and this, regardless of the use made of the tax revenue. The theorem is stated in its most general form in a later chapter, "Poor Rates" (XVIII):

> if the tax paid by the cultivator of the worst land, be higher in proportion to the quantity of produce obtained, than that paid by the farmers of the more fertile lands, the rise in the price of corn, which will extend to all corn, will more than compensate the latter for the tax. This advantage will remain with them during the continuance of their leases, but it will afterwards be transferred to their landlords.[1]

Ricardo illustrates his thesis by a numerical example. The marginal parcel of land, paying no rent, yields 1,000 quarters (8,000 bushels) of corn. Ricardo does not specify the area; let it be a parcel of 1,000 acres. A tax is laid on all agricultural land, at the rate of £100 per 1,000 acres. The price of corn must rise by two shillings a quarter, if the poorest land is to remain in cultivation. And it must remain in cultivation, says Ricardo, for the same total of corn must be produced as before (inelastic demand). On a more fertile parcel of land of the same area, application of the same amount of capital yields 2,000 quarters, hence a rise of only one shilling in the price would recoup the tax of £100. The increase of two shillings, necessary to keep the poorest land in cultivation, will therefore add £200 to the value of the product of the better land, of which, £100 goes in tax, and £100 accrues to the landlord as increased rent.

Ricardo's general conclusion is incorrect; it is not true that a fixed

[1] S, I, 260; G, 245.

tax per acre necessarily benefits the landlords of the better lands. His error arises from failure to consider the intensive margin of cultivation.[2]

Gonner notes this omission, but goes too far in moving to the other extreme, declaring that "the consumer ... will not be taxed as Ricardo suggests, 'to raise the rent of the landlord.'"[3]

The correct answer is more complex; with respect to the land remaining in cultivation, the tax may benefit some landlords while injuring others, whether the reckoning be in terms of money or corn.

Any rise in the price of corn resulting from a fixed tax per acre will induce application of more doses of labor and capital to the better parcels of land. The tax does not strike the intensive margin. Its only marginal impact is at the extensive margin. The entire increment of produce obtained by putting more labor and capital on the better lands can be retained, by the cultivator or landlord, as the case may be; the state takes none of it.

Table 1 presents a pattern of gain and loss to owners of various parcels of land that illustrates the differential impact of a fixed tax per parcel. The Ricardian assumption of an unchanged total output is followed.

Ricardo did not approve of a tax of a fixed amount per acre. It violated Smith's fourth maxim: it "took out of the pockets of the people" more than it put into the Treasury. However, Ricardo felt bound to defend the tax against a charge of inequality made by Smith and Say. Smith thought

[2] Ricardo expected everyone else to remember it, however; see his remarks on Say's insistence that a tax on raw produce falls on rent, S, I, 413, note; G, 406, note. Say, to be sure, seems not to have grasped the concept of the intensive margin. See footnote 95 to Chapter XI below.

[3] G, 163, note. Whewell, in "Mathematical Exposition of Some Doctrines of Political Economy," pp. 219-21, presents a formula for determining "the parts of the tax [fixed tax per unit of area], which affect rent, profits and price," but under the assumption of a finite elasticity of demand for corn, in contrast to Ricardo's implicit assumption of complete inelasticity. By assuming a price elasticity of one-third (a 1 percent increase in price is accompanied by a decrease of $^1/_3$ of 1 percent in amount sold), pp. 201, 211, and making certain numerical assumptions concerning the proportions between the best, average, and marginal rates of production, he concludes that "the parts of the tax, which affect rent, profits and price, are .... as 15, 4, 8. In general, the part which falls on rent will be the greatest." By "the part affecting price," Whewell presumably means the added amount of gross receipts paid by consumers. His analysis does not, of course, confirm Ricardo's theorem, owing to the different elasticity assumption. In his second paper, "Mathematical Exposition of Some of the Leading Doctrines in Mr. Ricardo's '*Principles*'," p. 178, Whewell concludes that under Ricardo's assumption concerning demand, "the tax will wholly affect the price, and the results will be exactly the same as in a tax on raw produce."

the acreage tax discriminated against certain landlords; he believed the tax rested on rent. Say, likewise assuming that the tax came out of rent, concluded that it was an inadequate means of taxing agriculture, since it carried a marginal rate of zero: the tax absorbed no part of any increase in profit or rent that arose from additional doses of capital and labor on a given parcel of land. Say proposed instead a 20 percent income tax on the farmer or the landlord (he did not always distinguish these two parties clearly). Even admitting that there was an inequality to eliminate, this measure would not do it, in Ricardo's view; the special income tax would itself be shifted to consumers.

Ricardo thus concluded that no landlord and no farmer would suffer from the tax per acre, which therefore did not violate Smith's first maxim, equal taxation according to abilities. Ricardo not only failed to see that some landlords would be harmed—certainly those whose marginal acres would be ,forced out of cultivation by the tax—but he also implied a peculiar definition of equality in taxation. If some suffer not at all from the tax, while others reap a profit from it, hence bear a negative tax, has equality been observed?

In his comments on Say's numerical illustrations,[4] Ricardo assumes

Table 1. *ILLUSTRATIVE PATTERN OF GAIN AND LOSS TO LANDLORDS UNDER FIXED TAX PER PARCEL OF LAND*

PARCEL	UNITS OF OUTPUT FROM SUCCESSIVE INPUTS	RENT *Margin at 5*	RENT *Margin at 4*	TAX	RENT AFTER TAX *(Margin at 4)*
A	5-4	0	1	4	−3
B	6-5-4	1	3	4	−1
C	7-6-5-4	3	6	4	2
D	8-7-6-5-4	6	10	4	6
E	9-8-7-6-5-4	10	15	4	11
F	10-9-8-7-6-5-4	15	21	4	17

Under the tax, parcels A and B are withdrawn from cultivation; the price rises to a level that will compensate a unit of labor and capital producing only 4 units; the loss of production from A and B is made good by more intensive production on C to F. Compared with the pre-tax corn rent, the net corn rent after corn tax is smaller on C, just as large on D, and larger on E and F. If money wage and profit rate do not rise, price of output rises 25 percent. Compared with pre-tax money rent, the net money rent after money tax is smaller on C, larger on D, E, and F.

[4] In his notes on Ricardo's *Principles,* Say defends himself against the charge of assuming unequal rates of profit by explaining that the 4,000 francs and 10,000 francs (S, I, 189; G, 169) are rent, exclusive of profit. Notes on Ricardo, 316.

that the capital involved is in every case equal to the annual expense. The annual rate of turnover of capital is uniformly one. He does not face the problem posed by differing rates of capital turnover until Chapter XV of the *Principles* is reached, "Taxes on Profits".

Ricardo returns to his thesis that all taxes, now including the acreage tax, retard growth, since they allow the government to use resources that would have been productive in private hands, but he phrases the objection incautiously by declaring: "Every new tax becomes a new charge on production, and raises natural price." [5] We have already been told that a tax on pure land rent has no effect on price.

[5] S, I, 185; G, 165.

CHAPTER VIII

TAXES ON GOLD AND ON HOUSES

Ricardo's weighty Chapter XIII of the *Principles,* "Taxes on Gold," may be linked in analysis with his modest Chapter XIV, "Taxes on Houses," since both commodities exemplify goods the supply of which is slow to adjust to changes in cost of production.

1. FACTORS DETERMINING SPEED OF ADJUSTMENT

Inclusion in the *Principles* of a substantial chapter devoted to a tax on gold reflects Ricardo's interest in monetary theory rather than concern with current policy, since it was not a tax that England had employed, or was even contemplating. In any event, it illustrated well a point that Ricardo wanted to make on differential taxation in general. The rapidity with which market price adjusts to a tax depends on three factors: durability of the commodity, rapidity with which capital can be withdrawn from producing it, and nature of the demand. The analysis in Chapter XIII runs in terms of a tax on the production of gold, rather than on the existing stock, or on imports, except as noted in Section 3 below.

For a durable commodity, the stock in consumers' hands will be large relative to annual production. A check to production, from a tax, will then be reflected but slowly in price:

The agreement of the market and natural prices of all commodities, depends at all times on the facility with which the supply can be increased or diminished. In the case of gold, houses, and labour, as well as many other things, this effect cannot, under some circumstances, be speedily produced. But it is different with those commodities which are consumed and reproduced from year to year, such as hats, shoes, corn, and cloth; they may be reduced, if necessary, and the interval cannot be long before the supply is contracted in proportion to the increased charge of producing them.[1]

As the "least productive mines" were shut off by a tax,

The quantity of gold, and, therefore, the quantity of money would be slowly reduced: it would be a little diminished in one year, a little more in another, and finally its value would be raised in proportion to the tax; but in the interval, the proprietors or holders [of the gold mines, presumably], as they would pay the tax, would be the sufferers, and not those who used money.[2]

In this passage "quantity" must mean stock, not rate of flow from mines. We are not told how it is being "reduced," but we may infer a wastage of gold through wear and loss of coins, and an upward-shifting demand curve for gold as population and trade increase, the stock in a later year thus being below the level required to maintain the value of gold unchanged.

Capital "can be removed from trades which are less profitable to those which are more so, but with different degrees of rapidity."[3] The time period that must elapse before production is reduced will be great if there is much "difficulty in removing their capitals" from the taxed industry. Ricardo does not explain why the degree of difficulty varies from one industry to another, but we may infer that he has in mind the amount of fixed capital employed.

Finally, the nature of the demand for the taxed commodity has something to do with the speed of adjustment. Ricardo says:

Corn being a commodity indispensably necessary to every one, little effect will be produced on the demand for it in consequence of a tax, and therefore the supply would not probably be long excessive, even if the producers had great difficulty in removing their capitals from the land. For this reason, the price of corn will speedily be raised by taxation. . . .[4]

Ricardo distinguishes the demand for gold as money from the demand for gold in the arts:

The demand for money is regulated entirely by its value, and its value by its quantity. If gold were of double the value, half the quantity would perform the same functions in circulation, and if it were of half the value, double the quantity would be required... for money, the demand is exactly proportioned to its value... every man purchasing and selling only the same quantity of goods,

[1] S, I, 196; G, 176-77. See also, in Chapter XIV, "Taxes on Houses," S, I, 201; G, 181.
[2] S, I, 192; G, 172. [3] S, I, 191; G, 171. [4] S, I, 191-92; G, 171-72.

may be obliged to employ twice, thrice, or any number of times the same quantity of money....[5]

Thus Ricardo is implying the theorem that with a specified physical volume of business to transact within the economy, and under the extreme assumption of a fixed velocity of circulation, a halving of the stock of money will double the value of the monetary unit in terms of commodities, and similarly for changes of other magnitudes.

In a later chapter, Ricardo says:

It is undoubtedly true, that a taxed commodity will not rise in proportion to the tax, if the demand for it diminish, and if the quantity cannot be reduced. If metallic money were in general use, its value would not for a considerable time be increased by a tax, in proportion to the amount of the tax, because at a higher price, the demand would be diminished, and the quantity would not be diminished....[6]

The demand for gold in the arts, on the other hand, is completely inelastic; so, at least, we must infer from the following passage:

...although from its durable nature, and from the difficulty of reducing its quantity, [gold] does not readily bend to variations in its market value, yet that difficulty is much increased from the circumstance of its being used as money. If the quantity of gold in the market for the purpose of commerce only [that is, for use as money], were 10,000 ounces, and the consumption in our manufactures were 2000 ounces annually, it might be raised one fourth, or 25 per cent. in its value, in one year, by withholding the annual supply [2000 ounces]; but if in consequence of its being used as money, the quantity employed were 100,000 ounces [in place of 10,000 ounces], it would not be raised one fourth in value in less than ten years.[7]

In a year when production of gold was suspended, 2,000 ounces of gold, we may infer, would be withdrawn from the monetary stock for manufactures, despite the rise in the value of gold.

If the currency consists wholly or largely of paper, redeemable in gold, and if the gold itself is used almost wholly in manufactures, a decrease in production of gold will be followed quite soon by an increase in the value of the paper money:

[5] S, I, 193; G, 173. Gonner, criticizing Ricardo's statement that "the demand for money is not for a definite quantity" (*idem*), says: "The argument seems somewhat confused, since a diminution in the demand for money (gold) only takes place as its value rises; and therefore the value of the £900 left... [see illustration at S, I, 192; G, 172] would continually tend to increase." G, 173, note 1. But is not this what Ricardo has said, distinguishing, as he does, between the immediate and long-run effects?

[6] In Chapter XVI, "Taxes on Wages," S, I, 220; G, 203. [7] S, I, 193-94; G, 174.

As money made of paper may be readily reduced in quantity, its value, though its standard were gold, would be increased as rapidly as that of the metal itself would be increased, if the metal, by forming a very small part of the circulation, had a very slight connexion with money.[8]

2. "BURDEN" OF A TAX ON PRODUCTION OF GOLD

Ricardo is intrigued by his discovery that gold, under certain restrictive assumptions, can be taxed at little net cost to the community. If gold were produced only in one country, or its colonies, say Spain, and if it were used universally, and solely, for money,[9] the burden of unproductive expenditures by the government of Spain financed by a tax on the producers of gold would be partly offset by unsuspected benefits. The natural value of gold compared with all other commodities, in Spain and abroad, would rise, as the difficulty of producing it was increased by the necessity of paying a tax, and "as its market value in Europe is ultimately regulated by its natural value in Spanish America, more commodities would be given by Europe for a given quantity of gold."[10]

But that would not harm Europe, for, gold rising in market value, Europe would have to import correspondingly less of it to maintain monetary circulation. "No more goods then would be obtained in America, in exchange for all their gold exported, than before...."[11]

The benefit to Spain would arise from the fact that the tax would drive capital and labor from the gold mines to farms and factories. This would be a net gain, since Spain would be obtaining the same physical amount of commodity imports as before, for the smaller export of gold.

The possibility of gain from the restriction of gold mining exists, then, because for monetary purposes a smaller amount of gold can serve just as well as a larger, at a lower price level, of course. The apparent paradox in Ricardo's formula for a beneficial tax rests on the fact that under a system of private competition the production of one commodity—gold, for monetary purposes—is inevitably pushed beyond the limit that corresponds with the maximum of social welfare. This limit is, in fact, zero, in Ricardo's view, as given in his recommendations for a paper currency ("On Currency and Banks," Chapter XXVII of the *Principles*), although

[8] S, I, 194; G, 174. We should say, rather, "by being employed chiefly in nonmonetary uses." The phrasing of the first edition thus seems preferable. See note by Sraffa, S, I, 194. See also S, I, 168-69; G, 150: "It is not paper that regulates the value of gold as a commodity, but gold that regulates the value of paper."

[9] Ricardo does not make this assumption explicitly, but it is necessary for his argument.

[10] S, I, 195; G, 175. [11] S, I, 195; G, 176.

convertibility into bullion would be necessary, to guard against depreciation, and for payments in international trade.[12]

The degree to which Spain would benefit is at first stated in extreme terms of the quantity theory: "If in consequence of the tax, only one tenth of the present quantity of gold were obtained from the mines, that tenth would be of equal value with the ten tenths now produced." But this is under the assumption that "gold alone" is used for money. In reality, even if the king of Spain had a world monopoly of gold mines, "his advantage from their possession, and the power of taxation, would be very much reduced by the limitation of demand and consumption in Europe, in consequence of the universal substitution, in a greater or less degree, of paper money." [13] Ricardo does not elaborate on this qualification, or assess its importance; his interest is not in advising a hypothetical gold monopolist, but in demonstrating the waste to society in the use of gold as a hand-to-hand medium of circulation.

Ricardo's numerical example of a tax on Spanish gold mines involves not a tax per unit of gold produced, the type he has been discussing up to this point, but a fixed tax of 70 pounds of gold per mine. Perhaps Ricardo is unconsciously carrying over the fixed-tax concept from the immediately preceding chapter that dealt with a fixed tax on land area. Or perhaps he wants us to understand that the tax is proportionate to input; the three mines are assumed to utilize the same amount of labor and capital each (the intensive margin being again neglected). We shall assume here that the tax is fixed in amount, per mine. Mines No. 1, No. 2, and No. 3 are producing 100, 80, and 70 pounds of gold respectively.

Under the tax of 70 pounds of gold per mine, only the best of the three, producing 100 pounds, remains in operation. To cover wages and ordinary profit, the 30 pounds of gold left to the operator of this mine after the tax must exchange for as much of other commodities as did the 70 pounds he obtained before, after paying 30 pounds rent. Hence the price of gold must rise at least from 1 to 70/30, or by 133 percent. It "might" rise higher, "being a monopolised commodity," [14] and if it did so, the mine would yield some rent. The ratio of new output to old output, 100/250, suggests a rise of 150 percent in the value of gold. Ricardo's unwillingness to stipulate flatly a rise of this extent may reflect a realization that it would be some time before the money stock in the gold-using countries would be decreased, compared with what it otherwise would have been, by the same proportion as production. By "a

[12] S, I, 356-62; G, 344-50. [13] S, I, 196; G, 176. [14] S, I, 197; G, 178.

monopolised commodity" Ricardo does not mean one produced by a single firm, but a commodity like "wines of a peculiar quality, which can be made only from grapes grown on a particular soil, of which there is a very limited quantity,"[15] so that rent may exist at the margin of cultivation.

If the price of gold rises by 150 percent, the 100 pounds produced by the mine remaining in operation exchange for the same quantity of cloth, 10,000 yards, as did the 250 pounds of gold formerly produced by the three mines together. The mining capitalists and their labor formerly employed on Mines 2 and 3 now turn to cloth production, or the equivalent. Each of the two capitalist-labor groups is able to produce 2,800 yards of cloth, since they had each been producing gold for their wages and normal profit in an amount that would fetch 2,800 yards. Hence the increase in production of commodities by the Spanish economy is 5,600 yards of cloth, which largely offsets the tax, equivalent to 7,000 yards of cloth, that the king is now receiving. Thus the economy suffers a net loss of 1,400 yards of cloth through the tax and its accompanying unproductive expenditure of the king's. The 30 pounds of gold left to the owner and capitalist together of Mine 1 now exchange for 3,000 yards of cloth, of which 200 yards is rent and goes to the owner.

A large part of the tax—56/70 of it—is therefore a burden on no one. Accordingly, "the King of Spain, and the proprietors of the mines which continued to be worked, would together receive not only all that the liberated capital produced, but all that the other proprietors lost."[16] This is not as well stated as it might be, for it seems to imply that the producer of the still active mine has suffered no loss. The facts are as follows: the king gains 7,000 yards of cloth; the owner of Mine 2 loses 400 yards; the owner of Mine 1 formerly obtained 1,200 yards, and now receives only 200, and so loses 1,000 yards; the sum of these gains and losses, a net gain of 5,600 yards, equals the gain in production of cloth.

The net loss to the economy, equivalent to 1,400 yards of cloth, which arises from the unproductive expenditure of the king of Spain financed by the tax on gold mines, could be diminished by making the tax and expenditure smaller, provided Mines 2 and 3 could both be kept closed, so that the labor hitherto applied to them could be used to produce other things.[17]

[15] S, I, 12; G, 6. [16] S, I, 197; G, 177.

[17] The Spanish economy would be much better off under the lower tax, since as large a block of resources would be released, while unproductive expenditure by the king would be that much smaller.

In the second paragraph from the end of his chapter, Ricardo appears to continue with his numerical example in mind, except that he now reverts to a tax that varies with the amount of gold produced, in place of a fixed tax per mine. This paragraph is so compressed, both assumptions and reasoning being so largely implicit, that it scarcely bears analysis. If the reasoning here is supposed to apply to the numerical example given earlier, it is seriously in error; even a small tax of this kind, not just one that has been "pushed a little further," [18] would drive Mine 3 out of production, and hence would force some rise in the price of gold.

3. A TAX ON THE EXISTING STOCK OF MONEY

A tax levied on the existing stock of monetary gold does not, we should infer, reduce the money stock below what it would otherwise have been, unless the government is assumed to hoard the gold, or to export it. To this extent such a tax differs from one on production, which, by reducing future output, gradually affects the size of the money stock. Ricardo's analysis of a tax on the gold stock is brief and unsatisfactory: two sentences early in the chapter,[19] and a few lines at the end.[20] The first of these appears to give a valid analysis; Ricardo seems to say that a tax on stock alone will not raise the value of gold, perhaps asking us to infer that the government puts the gold back into circulation, as we should assume is the normal case with the proceeds of any tax. But at the end of the chapter Ricardo says that both a tax "on the actual quantity of gold in circulation" and a tax "on the quantity that is annually produced from the mines" have "a tendency to reduce the quantity, and to raise the value of gold. . . ." [21] He does not explain how the tax on stock produces this effect.

4. TAXES ON HOUSES

The kind of tax that Ricardo is analyzing in Chapter XIV of the *Principles* is levied on the annual rent of dwellings. It is collected from the occupier rather than the owner of the building. If the dwelling is owner-occupied, the tax is based on the imputed annual rental. With some exceptions, this is the type of local levy on real estate that has persisted in Great Britain to the present day, extending also to certain non-dwelling properties.

Ricardo likens houses to gold in this, that the stock existing at any

[18] S, I, 199; G, 179. [19] "If out of . . . by the tax." S, I, 192-93; G, 172.
[20] S, I, 199-200; G, 179-80. [21] S, I, 199; G, 179.

one time is diminished only slowly by subsequent use ("cannot be speedily reduced in quantity"), in contrast to "the produce of the land," which is "consumed and reproduced from year to year...." A tax on houses will "diminish the demand ... without diminishing their supply. Rent will therefore fall, and a part of the tax that[22] will be paid indirectly by the landlord."[23] But why only "part?" Under a fixed supply, and a not completely inelastic demand, all of the tax would fall on the building owner (the "landlord"). Moreover, this conclusion of Ricardo's may appear to be contradicted almost at once by the assertion: "A tax on the rent of houses may either fall on the occupier, on the ground landlord, or on the building landlord. In ordinary cases it may be presumed, that the whole tax would be paid both immediately and finally by the occupier."[24] But this conclusion is evidently meant to apply only to a small tax, for Ricardo at once adds—though the train of thought is broken by a paragraphing—:

> If the tax be moderate, and the circumstances of the country such, that it is either stationary or advancing, there would be little motive for the occupier of a house to content himself with one of a worse description. But if the tax be high, or any other circumstances should diminish the demand for houses, the landlord's income would fall, for the occupier would be partly compensated for the tax by a diminution of rent.[25]

As to the long run, Ricardo, quoting extensively from Smith, approves his conclusion that the builder must get his normal rate of profit, otherwise capital will be diverted from the building trade. Hence that part of the tax that does not fall on the occupier must in the long run rest on the ground landlord rather than on the building landlord.

Ricardo confesses that he, like Smith, can say little about the proportions in which the tax burden is divided between the several parties in the short period and in the long period. In the short period, during which the initial stock of houses remains undiminished, the proportion of the tax, if any, that will rest on the occupier seems to depend, as we have seen, on the size of the tax and the degree of prosperity of the country. Moreover, "It is ... difficult to say, in what proportions that part of the tax, which was saved by the occupier by a fall of rent, would fall on the building rent and the ground rent. It is probable that, in the first instance, both would be affected...."[26]

[22] "Ed. 3 inserts here 'that' (perhaps a misprint for 'then'); it is not contained in eds. 1-2." Note by Sraffa, S, I, 201.
[23] S, I, 201; G, 181. [24] S, I, 202; G, 182. [25] S, I, 202-203; G, 182-83.
[26] S, I, 203; G, 183.

With respect to the long period, the tax would "ultimately fall on the occupier and ground landlord, but 'in what proportion, this final payment would be divided between them,' says Adam Smith, 'it is not perhaps very easy to ascertain.' "[27]

Smith and Ricardo were held up at this point by their failure to extend the doctrine of rent to urban land. Smith had said—and Ricardo quotes this—that if the builder's trade afforded more than the ordinary profits, capital would be attracted to it and reduce the profit to its "proper level," but Smith had added immediately—and Ricardo quotes this too—: " 'Whatever part of the whole rent of a house is over and above what is sufficient for affording this reasonable profit, naturally goes to the ground rent. . . .' "[28] There is an indeterminateness here that Ricardo does nothing to remove.[29] If he had adapted the concept of the extensive and intensive margins of cultivation—here, "cultivation" of a building site by the application of building labor and capital to it—he might have arrived at conclusions at least as definite as those concerning a tax on agriculture. But he would also have had to consider the role played by housing in the subsistence market basket of the worker, and this problem, too, he left to one side.

Ricardo says nothing of the very short period which elapses from the time the tax is introduced to the time the occupier's lease expires. Since the tax is legally due from the occupier, he presumably bears the burden until time for renegotiation of the lease.

[27] *Idem.* [28] S, I, 202; G, 182.

[29] At least Ricardo did not fall into the trap that caught McCulloch, J. S. Mill, and Sidgwick. They distributed the incidence of the tax between landowner and occupier in the ratio that land rent bears to building rent. If, for purposes of exposition, we permit ourselves to distinguish one unit of product from another, then, as with bushels of corn grown to an intensive margin on a particular plot of land, so the units of dwelling accomodation that cumulatively constitute a house on a particular site must differ from one another in the proportion of their sale or rental prices that goes to land rent; and the marginal unit, like the marginal bushel, goes 100 percent to cover labor and capital costs. The flaw in the McCulloch-J. S. Mill-Sidgwick analysis can be seen readily by asking how the tax is divided if the occupiers' demand is completely inelastic within the range of the tax. See Edgeworth, "The Pure Theory of Taxation," in *Papers Relating to Political Economy,* II, 83-85, and Bickerdike, "Taxation of Site Values," *Econ. J.,* XII (No. 48, Dec., 1902), 472-84.

CHAPTER IX

TAXES ON PROFITS

In Chapter XV of the *Principles,* "Taxes on Profits," Ricardo is chiefly interested in ascertaining the effects on prices of a general tax on profits, under alternative assumptions of exempting or not exempting the profits of gold mining. Thus, at the top of page 206,[1] money is assumed to be taxed; in the first full paragraph on that page, it is assumed not to be taxed; in the last paragraph, it is taxed; in the following paragraph (page 207) it is not taxed—and so on. Often these alternatives are expressed in terms of value: "Whilst money continued unaltered in value..."[2] (*i. e.,* while profits of gold mining remained untaxed, so that all money prices rose), or "If money be taxed, or if by any other cause its value be altered...."[3] By money's remaining "unaltered in value" Ricardo means that the cost of producing money, in real terms, has remained unchanged.

Taxation of gold mining was an issue of no importance in Great Britain, a country without such mines, and toward the end of Chapter XV Ricardo turns to the problem of what will happen to prices if all profits are taxed in a country that obtains its monetary metal from abroad. He also makes a short excursion into farm taxation by analyzing an exemption granted to profits from agriculture.

1. DIFFERENTIAL TAXATION

A tax limited to a few products will force their prices up, until the normal rate of profit is again obtained, and this is so, whether the tax is based on output or on profit. Ricardo had already reached this conclusion in discussing a tax limited to corn or other raw produce. He now

[1] Page references are to the Sraffa edition, Vol. I.
[2] S, I, 208; G, 189. [3] S, I, 206; G, 187.

extends it to cover any commodity, including those "which are generally denominated luxuries," for example, wine, pleasure horses, and coaches.[4]

Nothing is said at this point concerning the effect of the rise in price on the amount purchased. The question is not an important one for manufactures, in view of Ricardo's assumption of constant cost; we know that in any case the price must rise by the full amount of the tax. As for agriculture, which encounters increasing cost, Ricardo has already specified that within a wide range of price the demand for raw produce is completely inelastic (see Chapter IV above).

In any event, price goes up by enough to remunerate the highest cost producer remaining in the taxed industry, and therefore in Ricardian terminology the tax cannot be considered a burden on producers. Thus Ricardo is reported as saying in Parliament, March 7, 1821:

He knew that taxation was an evil; but it could not be truly said that the taxation on agriculture prevented corn from remunerating the expense of its production. If the charges for growing or producing any thing were great, the price demanded for the article would correspond. If his hat or any thing else were taxed, he had, as the consumer, to pay an additional price for it; and where taxation went too far, it would diminish the consumption of the commodity so taxed. In other words, taxation tended to reduce the demand for the taxed commodity, but it did not prevent the remuneration of all the expenses of production for so much of the commodity as was in demand. It was wrong to say that corn could not be produced on account of the taxes on agriculture. The Member for Wareham had given a most convincing instance of the truth of this position, by explaining the duty on salt, which he stated to amount to 3,000 *l.* upon the value of every 190 *l.* Three thousand pounds duty were paid on salt, and yet salt yielded a sufficient profit to the producer. He did not mean to say that there was no hardship suffered by the consumer; but this proved that taxation alone did not prevent an adequate remuneration to the corn-grower.[5]

And in an important speech a year later:[6]

There were two descriptions of persons, producers and consumers, likely to complain to that House of the pressure of taxation. Against the producers he was prepared to say, he would shut the doors of that House. He would tell them they had the remedy in their own hands; that they must regulate their own price, by making the supply square with the demand. But to the consumers on whom the taxes really pressed, he would say, the doors of the House should be always thrown open. When they said that their income was unequal to their expenditure, and that taxes prevented them from procuring the comforts and enjoyments to which they were accustomed, he would say, that their prayers were entitled to the utmost

[4] S, I, 205; G, 186. [5] S, V, 84-85. [6] Speech of Feb. 18, 1822, S, V, 136-37.

attention, and that the taxes should as far as possible, be removed. Now, he would ask gentlemen, to whom they supposed the repeal of the malt tax would be a benefit—to the farmer who produced it, or to the general consumer? He should say to the consumer. And so on of the salt, the soap, and other taxes, which affected articles of general consumption. That would be his reason for calling for the repeal of these taxes....[7]

There remain two points to note before passing to Ricardo's discussion of a general tax on all profits.

First, Ricardo ignores the possibility that the tax would cover so large a segment of the economy that migration of capital to the tax-free sector would sink the rate of profits there.[8]

Secondly, Ricardo does not reproduce in the *Principles* an idea he had sketched six years earlier in his *Reply to Bosanquet:* the notion that a differential tax on any commodity the expenditure on which does not absorb a uniform proportion of all consumers' budgets will lead those consumers who are especially burdened by the tax to increase the price of whatever product they in turn sell.

If this tax again were laid on a commodity, the consumption of which, by each individual, was in exact proportion to his income, no other commodity would rise but the one taxed; but if it were not in such proportion, those who paid more than their just portion would demand an increased price for the commodity in which they dealt, and, by obtaining it, the society would be put in the same relative situation in which they were before placed.[9]

Perhaps the budgets of all the laboring class in Ricardo's day were so nearly alike, in their concentration on one or a few widely consumed necessaries, that the importance of this possible tax discrimination was not, to Ricardo's mind, substantial.

2. A GENERAL PROFITS TAX AND THE PRICE LEVEL

In the third, fourth, and fifth paragraphs of Chapter XV of the *Principles,* Ricardo analyzes the effect on the general level of prices produced by a tax on all profits, when the monetary metal, gold, is obtained from mines within the country.

If the gold mines are exempt from the profits tax, all prices rise. If the tax extends to gold-mining profits, no prices rise. Pre-tax relations

[7] The speech continues with some remarks on the alleged pyramiding of taxes by dealers or sellers.

[8] Whewell deals with the intermediate case, in his "Mathematical Exposition of Some Doctrines of Political Economy," pp. 203-205.

[9] S, III, 241-42.

among profits in the several lines of business, including gold mining, must be preserved, but now in terms of profits after tax. If mining were exempt, labor and capital would flow into it from the taxed industries until enough more of the metal was produced to support the higher price level needed to insure equality of profits. Or are we to infer that the mere threat of movement by labor and capital would be sufficient? Ricardo does consider the possibility that a higher price level could be supported without an addition to the stock of money.[10]

An illustration of the point is attempted in a numerical example that is elliptical, to say the least, and, in terms of Ricardo's own macroeconomic system, apparently in error. The example is as follows:

> If the tax be 100 *l.*, the hats, the cloth, and the corn, will each be increased in value 100 *l.* If the hatter gains by his hats 1100 *l.*, instead of 1000 *l.*, he will pay 100 *l.* to Government for the tax; and therefore will still have 1000 *l.* to lay out on goods for his own consumption. But as the cloth, corn, and all other commodities, will be raised in price from the same cause, he will not obtain more for his 1000 *l.* than he before obtained for 910 *l.*, and thus will he contribute by his diminished expenditure to the exigencies of the State; he will, by the payment of the tax, have placed a portion of the produce of the land and labour of the country at the disposal of Government, instead of using that portion himself.[11]

The "gain" of the hatter is evidently his profit, not his gross receipts. The tax is one of 10 percent on the original profit. How, then, can a mere 10 percent tax on profit, as distinguished from a 10 percent tax on sales, raise the price level 10 percent? Yet this is what Ricardo says it does, since £1,000 (precisely, £1,001), after the tax has been imposed, buys no more than £910 did before.

What seems to be implicit in this reasoning is a spiral rise of wages, prices, wages, prices, etc., resulting from the impact on the laborer of the initial rise in the price of necessaries. Wages rise, presumably because the share of the total product going to wages cannot be reduced, if the amount of labor supplied is to remain unchanged. Suppose, for example, that the laborers' share in the product is 70 percent and the profit share, 30 per-

[10] See Section 6 of this chapter, below; and cf. the language in a letter to Trower, Jan. 28, 1820, p. 113 below. St. Clair's emphasis on the existing stock seems more applicable to the case (not posed by Ricardo at this point) where the profits tax applies only to gold mining; *A Key to Ricardo*, pp. 322-23. It is also relevant to the case where the tax applies to all but gold mining; if a higher price level could be supported only by a larger gold stock, prices of commodities could not rise for some time. But if the tax is universal, Ricardo says prices will not rise; and a short-run emphasis on stock would lead to the same conclusion.

[11] S, I, 206; G, 187.

cent. We ignore rent, for simplicity, since it does not affect the analysis.[12] Concretely, suppose that the product other than gold—such product is called "commodities" here—is £10,000, of which £7,000 goes to wages and £3,000 to profit. A tax of £300 is imposed on profits other than those from gold mining. Prices of commodities are raised on the first round so that total sales equal £10,300. The cost of the wage earners' necessaries is therefore £7,210. This, by Ricardian doctrine, forces an increase of wages of £210; prices are raised, again, until sales proceeds equal £10,510. Wage earners' necessaries now cost £7,357. This fact provokes a further wage increase of £147—and so on, until finally the new wage total is £7,700 and the new profit total, before tax, £3,300. Total sales value of commodities is £11,000. After the tax of £300, profit is £3,000, as in the pre-tax period. But each £1,001 will now buy only what £910 bought before the tax was introduced. Moreover, profit after tax is only 27.27 percent of sales, compared with 30 percent before the tax was imposed.

Whether such a chain of reasoning was in fact in Ricardo's mind when he composed the numerical illustration reproduced immediately above is at least uncertain. In favor of such a thesis is the fact that in the earlier chapter on "Taxes On Raw Produce" (Chapter IX) Ricardo followed precisely this line of analysis, up to a point. A tax on raw produce raises the price of raw produce, whereupon wages rise, and profits decline. But the precedent of this analysis is incomplete; there is no rise in the general level of prices from the tax on raw produce, chiefly because Ricardo restricts the case to one where the taxing country imports its gold instead of obtaining it from a domestic mine. Moreover, the tax is a partial one, imposed on one class of commodities only, not a general tax.

In any event, Ricardo's illustration must be rejected, for the conclusion reached, namely, that prices would rise 10 percent, leaves the economy in a state of disequilibrium, owing to the fall in the profits of gold mining caused by the 10 percent increase in money wages.[13] Before the general profits tax was imposed, the gold mining capitalist paid £700 in wages and kept £300 as profit, out of every £1,000 of gold

[12] That is, it does not affect the attempt to make explicit what Ricardo left implicit. For completeness, he should have mentioned the role of landlords as consumers; see St. Clair, *A Key to Ricardo,* pp. 166-68. St. Clair's deduction from Ricardo's statement at S, I, 206 (G, 187) appears to be essentially the same as that presented here.

[13] My analysis published in *Pub. Finance,* V (No. 2, 1950), 101-18, was in error in failing to observe this gap.

produced. Now, he must pay £770 in wages, and thus gains only 23 percent profit on sales. Meanwhile the commodity capitalist is obtaining 27.27 percent on sales. No difference in rates of capital turnover are postulated that could account for the discrepancy. Capital would therefore flow from gold mining to commodity production, and prices would tend to fall. Accordingly, the rise in price would not be as great as Ricardo's example seems to imply, even initially. The price-wage spiral could proceed only a little way.[14]

3. SLOW-TURNOVER AND FAST-TURNOVER INDUSTRIES

In the paragraph beginning, "But although, if money be not taxed," up to the sentence in the same paragraph starting, "If under these circumstances, money rose in value,"[15] Ricardo reaches a conclusion relevant to modern income taxation. If a profits tax is to be wholly shifted to consumers under a completely inelastic demand, prices in some industries must rise by a greater percentage than in others. Even within an industry, firms differ with respect to the percentage increase in price requisite for complete shifting.[16] On this point a profits tax contrasts with a tax on sales.[17]

Ricardo's analysis is based on differences among firms and industries in the proportion of fixed to circulating capital—"durable and perishable capital." Some industries, for technological reasons, turn over their capital rapidly and others slowly. In current business analysis, this point is often made for inventory—grocery stores turn their inventory over rapidly, furniture stores slowly—but it is not so commonly recognized as being applicable to the entire property used in the business, including plant and equipment. The annual turnover ratio is obtained by dividing the total sales for the year by the total amount of property used in the

[14] See Appendix A: 2, at end of this volume.

[15] S, I, 207-208; G, 188-89.

[16] See Shoup, "Incidence of the Corporation Income Tax: Capital Structure and Turnover Rates," *Nat. Tax J.*, *I* (No. 1, March, 1948), and "Some Considerations on the Incidence of the Corporation Income Tax," *J. Finance,* VI (No. 2, June, 1951); and Beck, "Ability to Shift the Corporate Income Tax: Seven Industrial Groups," *Nat. Tax J.*, III (No. 3, Sept., 1950) and "Correction," *Nat. Tax J.*, III (No. 4, Dec., 1950).

[17] Thus the term "equal" (which Ricardo substituted for "in proportion") in the following sentence must be taken to imply unequal rates of tax on sales proceeds: "A tax imposed on goods, exactly equal to the tax on profits which each man would have to pay, will have precisely the same effects." Letter of Jan. 28, 1820, Ricardo to Trower, S, VIII, 154.

business (average for the year). It will be found that a steel manufacturing concern, for example, will have a much lower turnover ratio than a department store. Property used in the business should, for this purpose, include property operated under rent or lease.

We shewed [says Ricardo] that two manufacturers might employ precisely the same amount of capital, and might derive from it precisely the same amount of profits, but that they would sell their commodities for very different sums of money, according as the capitals they employed were rapidly, or slowly, consumed and reproduced.

The fast-turnover business will have the larger volume of sales if the two are earning the same percentage return on capital invested.

The one might sell his goods for 4000 *l.*, the other for 10,000 *l.*, and they might both employ 10,000 *l.* of capital, and obtain 20 per cent. profit or 2000 *l.* The capital of one might consist, for example, of 2000 *l.* circulating capital, to be reproduced, and 8000 *l.* fixed, in buildings and machinery....[18]

From the assumption made in the next sentence, with respect to volume of sales, it is clear that "2000 *l.* circulating capital" reflects annual current expenses of the same amount; the business firm must keep £2,000, on the average, tied up in inventory, cash, and accounts receivable. The £8,000 of fixed capital is to be taken as suffering no depreciation during the period in question. Under these assumptions, and assuming further a 20 percent annual profit on capital employed, this manufacturer would have to sell his output for £2,000 plus 20 percent of £10,000, or £4,000 altogether. Ricardo continues, "the capital of the other, on the contrary, might consist of 8000 *l.* of circulating, and of only 2000 *l.* fixed capital in machinery and buildings." [19]

The profit margins on sales of the two manufacturers must differ in order to give the same profit return as a percentage of capital. The slow-turnover manufacturer, with only £2,000 pounds of current outlay ("circulating capital"), must operate with a profit margin of 50 percent on sales, to obtain a 20 percent return on his £10,000 of capital. The fast-turnover manufacturer, with annual current expense of £8,000, and using only £2,000 of fixed, non-depreciating capital, needs a profit margin of only 20 percent on £10,000 of sales.

In Ricardo's example a tax of 10 percent is assumed to be levied on the £2,000 profit. If the tax is to be recouped in money terms (because the gold mine is untaxed), sales must increase £200 in each case. This conclusion evidently assumes no change in total cost accompanying the rise in money volume of sales, and hence no change in unit sales. The

[18] S, I, 207; G, 188. [19] S, I, 207-208; G, 188-89.

sales of the fast-turnover manufacturer must rise 2 percent, from £10,000 to £10,200. The sales of the slow-turnover manufacturer must rise 5 percent, from £4,000 to £4,200.

Ricardo is not interested in the problems posed by the competitive relations among industries and among firms. For him, the chief issue is the necessity of modifying his earlier statement that a tax on all profits except those of gold mining will leave commodities unaltered in relative value, since the money prices of all will rise. He now points out that, owing to the differing rates of turnover, "a tax upon income, whilst money continued unaltered in value [*i. e.,* not taxed], would alter the relative prices and value of commodities."[20]

4. UNEQUAL EFFECTS OF CHANGE IN MONEY STOCK

Toward the end of the paragraph that explains the differential effect on prices of a general profits tax, Ricardo starts an analysis, which continues through the next two paragraphs, of "a very important principle, which, I believe, has never been adverted to." This principle is that, "in a country where prices are artificially raised by taxation,"[21] an increase or decrease in the money stock, although causing the average level of prices to rise or fall, will affect prices of particular commodities in differing degrees, depending on the extent to which their prices have already been raised by taxes.

The analysis begins with the sentence, "If under these circumstances, money rose in value. . . ."[22] Two cases are studied: the first, where a general tax on profits has already produced unequal price increases; the second, where some commodities are taxed and others not. The second case is the simpler. Suppose that two commodities, A and B, are selling each for $1. A tax of $1 a unit is imposed on Commodity B, and its price rises to $2. Subsequently, there occurs a decrease in the stock of money. which forces down the general level of prices. The price of Commodity A falls from $1 to 50 cents. But Commodity B cannot similarly fall in price from $2 to $1; as long as the tax remains at $1, the price falls only to $1.50. Commodity A thus falls 50 percent in price; Commodity B, 25 percent. In principle, to be sure, the tax would not remain at $1 unless

[20] S, I, 208; G, 189. Whewell, "Mathematical Exposition of Some of the Leading Doctrines in Mr. Ricardo's 'Principles,' " pp. 178-81, casts this analysis in the form of algebra, but does not add to it or differ from it.

[21] S, I, 208-209; G, 190-91. [22] S, I, 208; G, 189.

the government sought to increase its percentage share in the community's resources.

In general, then,

in a country where prices are artificially raised by taxation, the abundance of money from an influx, or the exportation and consequent scarcity of it from foreign demand, will not operate in the same proportion on the prices of all commodities.... If ... money should fall in value, [and if] ... [the prices of commodities] should all rise in proportion to the fall in the value of money, profits would be rendered unequal; in the case of the commodities taxed, profits would be raised above the general level....[23]

Thus, if Commodity A rose to $2, Commodity B would rise, not to $4, but to $3.

In the other case, all industries are subject to a uniform profits tax, but the prices of some commodities have risen by a larger percentage than others, owing to differences in rate of turnover. Ricardo concludes that a rise in the value of money would in this instance, also, lower the prices of the several commodities by unequal percentages.

Continuing with the illustration he used in analyzing the unequal effects on prices of a general profits tax, he says,

The same cause which would lower the price of one from 10,200 *l.* to 10,000 *l.* or less than two per cent. [this is the fast-turnover industry] would lower the price of the other from 4200 *l.* to 4000 *l.* or $4^3/_4$ per cent. If they fell in any different proportion, profits would not be equal; for to make them equal, when the price of the first commodity was 10,000 *l.*, the price of the second should be 4000 *l.*; and when the price of the first was 10,200 *l.*, the price of the other should be 4200 *l.*[24]

Although Ricardo does not say so, we are evidently to infer that the income statements of the two concerns, after the fall in prices (the £200 profits tax still being in effect), read as shown in Table 2.

Gonner demonstrates, however, that Ricardo is in error at this point. If the price level falls, not only will gross receipts be reduced, but also current expenses ("circulating capital"), and the money value of the capital employed. Ricardo neglects to take account of these facts. Given a price decline of 2 percent, the total capital (fixed capital plus the stock of working capital at the beginning of the year), will be reduced in

[23] S, I, 209; G, 191-92. See also Speech of May 30, 1820, S, V, 54. Sir Edward West carries the analysis a step farther: "in consequence of the alteration of the relative cost of different articles, whilst the relative demand for them continued the same, there would be an alteration in the channels of capital..." *Price of Corn and Wages of Labour,* p. 120.

[24] S, I, 208; G, 189.

Table 2. *IMPLIED INCOME STATEMENTS OF FAST- AND SLOW-TURNOVER FIRMS AFTER FALL IN PRICES*

	Fast-turnover Firm	*Slow-turnover Firm*
Expenses (circulating capital to be recouped)	8,000	2,000
Tax	200	200
Profit after tax	1,800	1,800
Sales proceeds (total of three items above)	10,000	4,000
Capital invested	10,000	10,000
Profits as percent of capital	18	18

money value from £10,000 to £9,800. Gonner, using Ricardo's own figures, shows that a uniform percentage reduction in the gross receipts of the fast-turnover and the slow-turnover firms will leave them with a uniform percentage return on capital. The absolute rate of profit, however, falls for both companies.

So far as the two commodities in question are concerned, there is no alteration in respective profits [if both suffer the same percentage decrease in sales, hence presumably the same percentage decrease in prices]. In both cases the rate of profit is lowered, because ... the Government by supposition continues to exact the same fixed sum of £200.[25]

As Gonner points out, if the government's money amount of tax fell along with the fall in the general price level, from £200 to £196, both concerns would continue to earn 20 percent on the new low money value of capital, under a 2 percent fall in selling price.

But suppose that, the tax remaining fixed at £200, the rate of profit rises again to its initial level of 20 percent after tax. In this event, as Gonner notes, the sales proceeds of the two companies will indeed be in a different ratio to each other from what they were before the value of money rose (in both cases, the tax of £200 is assumed to be in force); see Table 3.

Gonner's illustration does not, perhaps, quite meet the specifications of Ricardo's example. Ricardo is analyzing a general tax on profits of all concerns except those in the gold-mining industry ("a country where prices are artificially raised by taxation"), whereas Gonner seems to be thinking of a narrower tax, like an excise, as indicated by these passages: "...capital would gradually be withdrawn from employment in the production of commodies thus taxed" and "...the manufacturer will obviously make an additional profit of £200. Capital then will flow into

[25] G, 190, note.

Table 3. CORRECTION AND EXTENSION OF RICARDO'S FAST- AND SLOW-TURNOVER ILLUSTRATION, BASED ON GONNER

	Fast-turnover Firm	Slow-turnover Firm
Period I: After the tax has been imposed, but before a general fall in prices		
Capital invested	10,000	10,000
Sales proceeds	10,200	4,200
Expenses (circulating capital to be recouped)	8,000	2,000
Tax	200	200
Profits: absolute amount	2,000	2,000
percent of capital invested	20	20
Ratio of sales of slow-turnover firm to those of fast-turnover firm	41.18%	
Period II: After a general fall of 2 percent in prices		
Capital invested:		
Fixed capital	1,960	7,840
Circulating capital	7,840	1,960
Total capital	9,800	9,800
Sales proceeds	9,996	4,116
Expenses	7,840	1,960
Tax	200	200
Profits: absolute amount	1,956	1,956
percent of capital invested	19.959	19.959
Ratio of sales of slow-turnover firm to those of fast-turnover firm	41.18%	
Period III: After the rate of profit has returned to 20 percent		
Capital invested	9,800	9,800
Sales proceeds	10,000	4,120
Expenses	7,840	1,960
Tax	200	200
Profits: absolute amount	1,960	1,960
percent of capital invested	20	20
Ratio of sales of slow-turnover firm to those of fast-turnover firm	41.20%	

such employment."[26] A more important omission is the neglect, by both Ricardo and Gonner, of the upward revaluation of capital that is implied by the initial rise in prices consequent upon the imposition of the tax. In the "Period I" section of the table above, the capital invested should be written up to some figure higher than £10,000 for each firm, in view

[26] *Idem.*

of the presence of the general tax. The degree of increase cannot be ascertained from the data of the example, for each block of capital goods is doubtless composed of a mixture of items, some of which had been produced by fast-turnover concerns, and others by slow-turnover concerns. Right away, before the rise in relative value of money, the profit rate drops below 20 percent, if sales proceeds amount to no more than those specified in the Period I figures. Similarly, the subsequent general price decline of 2 percent would not necessarily reduce the money value of these two firms' capitals by exactly 2 percent.

In a letter to Trower, January, 1820 (between publication of the second and third editions of the *Principles*), Ricardo repeats this numerical illustration, and carries it somewhat farther, but not in the direction indicated by the present comments. He assumes, instead, that the general price level declines still more, and he arrives at a conclusion that cannot be supported without some assumption about what happens to the price of the circulating capital. Here is the relevant passage:

> ...but if money should continue to rise in value and consequently the goods which sold for £10000 [after, first, the imposition of the tax, and second, a general fall in the price level due to monetary influences] should fall to £5000, then those which sold for £4000 would fall to £2000. Up to certain point then they fall in proportion to the capitals employed in their production, but subsequently in proportion to the value of the goods themselves. This is the opinion which I wished to express, whether it be a correct one is another question. On the hasty consideration which I can now give it I see no reason to doubt it.[27]

We do not have Trower's letter that evoked this defense and extension of the "opinion"; there seems to have been one, as Ricardo begins this part of his letter by saying,

> I have looked to the passages in my book to which you refer.[28] I quite agree with you that in most cases of taxes on income, or on profits, no effect would be produced on prices, and the burthen, which in every case would be equal, would fall on the producer, or the man enjoying the income. But I have supposed a case of our having the mines which supplied our standard, in this country, and that the profits of the miner were not taxed, then commodities would rise in price to the amount of the tax, or the miners business would be more profitable than any other, and consequently would draw capital to that concern.[29]

If sales proceeds are to fall, from £10,000 and £4,000, to £5,000 and £2,000, evidently the expense item (circulating capital to be recouped)

[27] Letter of Jan. 28, 1820, S, VIII, 154.

[28] Sraffa comments: "Presumably above, I [*Principles*], 205-210." S, VIII, 153, note 1.

[29] S, VIII, 153. Cf. St. Clair, *A Key to Ricardo*, pp. 328-29.

must fall in money value also. But nothing is said about this explicitly in Ricardo's note.

James Bonar and J. H. Hollander, commenting on this letter to Trower, appear confused:

The position seems to be as follows: The first effect of the tax will be uniform as regards profits, and therefore *not* uniform for prices, the high-priced articles and the low-priced (under competition) yielding a like rate of profits to the same amount of capital, but being various in number, and therefore not increased or diminished in price by the same figure per article; the eventual effect will be a uniform raising or lowering of the prices per article, through a change in the value of money generally. The first effect proceeds from the total to the items, the second from the items to the total.[30]

Having been led by a chain of logic to conclude that an increase in the stock of money in a country would not give rise to a uniform increase in commodity prices, if prices in that country, to begin with, had been "artificially raised by taxation," Ricardo takes a leap from the abstract to the real world by suggesting that the disparities in price increases observed in Great Britain during the period of "bank restriction," when the Bank of England notes were not redeemable, could be explained in this way. This would answer those who argued that the currency was not depreciated, because, if it were, all prices should rise by a uniform percentage, and this clearly had not been the case.[31] Ricardo believes he has shown his opponents a valid reason why lack of uniformity in price increases can coexist with a change in the value of the currency. He applies this reasoning, implicitly, in his evidence before the Secret Committee (of the House) on the Expediency of the Bank Resuming Cash Payments:

[50] Do you think a diminution of the circulation produces a diminution of prices in exact arithmetical proportion?

I think it has a tendency so to do, but it does not act exactly so nicely as that.

[51] Does it reduce the prices of all commodities equally?

I think not, in consequence of the inequality of taxation, otherwise I think it would.[32]

The testimony then turns to other aspects of a fall in prices.

[30] Bonar and Hollander, eds., *Letters of David Ricardo to Hutches Trower and Others, 1811-1823,* pp. 104-105, note.

[31] S, I, 209-210; G, 192. [32] S, V, 385.

5. LANDLORD'S STAKE IN HAVING FARM PROFITS TAXED

In the five paragraphs starting with "If the profits of all trades were taxed, excepting the profits of the farmer...,"[33] Ricardo studies the farmer and landlord under a profits tax that (a) exempts the farmer, (b) does not exempt him, (c) applies to him alone.[34]

The conclusions are "curious": The landlord is injured if the farmer is exempted; he is neither injured nor benefited if the tax extends to farm profits; and he gains if the tax is restricted to the farmer. How remote from the conclusions reached by Adam Smith, who believed that all taxes on farm profits would be shifted to the landlord! But they follow logically from Ricardo's analysis of rent.

As to the farmer, he too suffers if the profits tax applies to all business except farming; unlike the landlord, he still suffers if the tax is extended to include his farm profits; and if the tax is applied solely to farmers—Ricardo has answered this earlier, in his analysis of discriminatory taxes—the farmer will certainly not gain, in contrast to the landlord, and he will lose a little as a consumer of raw produce.

Ricardo does not call attention here to the general lowering of the rate of profit that is the effect of the rise in wages which, we are told elsewhere, must always follow a rise in price of necessaries.

The conclusions are valid, whether or not the tax extends to the profits of the domestic gold mines. Their tax status is implied rather than stated explicitly; we infer that the mines are taxed when we read, "by an alteration in the value of money,"[35] "if all commodities [except corn?] remained at the same price...,"[36] "if in consequence of a rise in the value of money...," "if, after the tax, the prices of corn and of every other commodity should remain the same as before..."; and exemption of the gold mines is implied by the phrases, "if ... money remained at the same value...," "but if the price of corn, and every other commodity should rise in consequence of the tax...."[37]

If farm profits and gold-mine profits are exempt from the tax, all prices rise except those of farm produce. The farmer and the landlord, too, receive no larger money income than before, yet they must pay

33 S, I, 210-13; G, 192-95.

34 This third case is covered in the footnote, S, I, 212; G, 195.

35 S, I, 210; G, 192.

36 S, I, 210; G, 193. Gonner says, in a note following the word "all," "[Insert 'other']."

37 S, I, 210-11; G, 192-94.

higher prices for everything they buy, except raw produce. To them, the tax on profits would be "a tax on expenditure."

Subjecting the domestic gold mines to taxation would not help the landlord and farmer, though their burden would take a different form. The "alteration in the value of money might sink all the taxed commodities to their former price," but corn would fall below its earlier price, "and, therefore, though the farmer [or the landlord] would purchase his commodities at the same price as before, he would have less money with which to purchase them." [38]

Thus, both landlord and farmer would suffer from a profits tax that exempted agricultural produce; but so too, we might add, would all manufacturing capitalists.

If the profits tax is extended to the farmer, the landlord is benefited; he regains the economic status he enjoyed before any profits tax was imposed.

This benefit arises in much the same way as the landlord's gain from a fixed tax per acre (see Chapter VII above). An intra-marginal dose of capital pays no more profits tax than a marginal dose, yet it produces more bushels of corn. A rise in the price of corn enough to recoup the tax on a marginal dose of capital, with its scanty yield, is more than enough to cover the same absolute amount of tax on the dose that yields many more bushels of corn. The excess recoupment is absorbed by the landlord through an increase in money rent, since there cannot be different rates of profit on the marginal and intra-marginal doses of capital. In Ricardo's numerical illustration, one dose of capital and labor at the extensive margin produces 160 quarters of corn; the tax is 10 quarters per dose; hence,

> Suppose the gross produce of the land of the quality No. 1 to be 180 qrs., that of No. 2, 170 qrs., and of No. 3, 160, and each to be taxed 10 quarters, the difference between the produce of No. 1, No. 2 and No. 3, after paying the tax, will be the same as before; for if No. 1 be reduced to 170, No. 2 to 160, and No. 3 to 150 qrs.; the difference between 3 and 1 will be as before, 20 qrs.; and of No. 3 and No. 2, 10 qrs.[39]

To be sure, Ricardo ignores the intensive margin and therefore does not state the amount of corn rent precisely. Land No. 1 might be assumed to produce 510 quarters by the application of three doses of labor and capital yielding 180, 170, and 160 quarters. Land No. 2 would produce 330 quarters with two doses of labor and capital. But his point is still valid: given an equal amount of tax on each dose of labor and capital,

[38] S, I, 210; G, 192. [39] S, I, 211; G, 193.

the differences in corn yield, available for rent, remain unchanged, and since the price of corn advances, money rent will rise.

Just the reverse occurs, as we have seen (Chapter IV above), under a tax on raw produce, or tithes. These taxes leave the money rent unchanged but diminish the corn rent.[40]

Ricardo says that the effect of a farm profits tax is "precisely the same"[41] as that of a fixed tax per acre, but in this he goes too far. He ignores the intensive margin in both cases, and it is here that a substantial difference emerges. The profits tax gives no incentive to extend the intensive margin by applying more doses of capital to the better acres. The rise in the price of corn is no more than enough to recoup the tax at the initial intensive margin. Under the tax of a fixed amount per acre, there is no tax effect at the intensive margin, hence no similar goal or limit for the rise in the corn price.

Although the landlord gets an increased money rent under the general profits tax, he is not a gainer in real terms; since "the prices of all goods, as well as corn, are raised [by the tax that does not extend to gold mines], the landlord loses as much by the increased money price of the goods and corn on which his rent is expended, as he gains by the rise of his rent."[42]

Alternatively, if the general profits tax included gold mines, and accordingly no commodities rose in price, "money rent as well as corn rent, would continue unaltered..." from pre-tax levels, and the landlord "would continue untaxed."[43]

The farmer, on the other hand, is not aided by extension of the tax to his profits; he is left, as before, injured by taxation. "By taxing the profits of the farmer you do not burthen him more than if you exempted his profits from the tax...."[44] But in another passage, Ricardo indicates that some damage to the farmer may arise by removal of the exemption: "he then would be in the same situation as other traders: his raw produce would rise, so that he would have the same money revenue, after paying the tax, but he would pay an additional price for all the commodities he consumed, raw produce included."[45] If we push the analysis a step farther, and assume that the rate of tax is lowered as its base is expanded, so that total tax revenue is unchanged, the farmer may be unharmed by removal of the exemption, and will be "in the same

[40] See Ricardo's letter to Mill, Nov. 20, 1816, S, VII, 90-92, reversing his earlier conclusion that a general tax on profits would injure the landlord.

[41] S, I, 212; G, 194. [42] *Idem.*

[43] S, I, 211-12; G, 194-95. [44] S, I, 213; G, 195. [45] S, I, 210; G, 193.

situation as other traders," provided they all have the same consumption pattern. As entrepreneur, he is not affected, in money terms, by extension of the tax to his profits; as consumer, he gains by a fall in prices of non-farm commodities and loses by a rise in the price of raw produce.

In revising the *Principles* for a third edition, Ricardo, no doubt reflecting on the "curious circumstance" of the landlord's benefiting by extension of the profits tax to farmers, was struck by the corollary: restrict the tax to farm profits, and the landlord will be better off than in the pre-tax period! Corn rent will remain as before the tax, the price of corn will rise, and the landlord will suffer as consumer only to the extent that he purchases corn. The tax "would, in fact, be a tax on the consumers of raw produce, partly for the benefit of the State, and partly for the benefit of landlords." [46]

This part of Chapter XV closes with a glance at the "stockholder," the holder of government bonds. He would want the profits tax extended to gold mines; he is injured, as a consumer, if prices rise, while, if they do not, he remains unaffected by the tax.[47]

6. A RISE IN THE PRICE LEVEL?

In the third paragraph from the end of Chapter XV,[48] and in an important footnote added in the third edition, Ricardo returns [49] to the problem of specifying the conditions that are necessary if a universal tax on profits is to raise the general level of prices. Two questions are involved. First, must there be an addition to the money stock, if prices are to rise under the influence of taxation? Second, will the tax bring into play forces that will cause such an increase in the money stock? Earlier in the chapter, where he assumed that the money stock was

[46] S, I, 212, note; G, 195 note. Wages would then have to rise, and profits generally would fall. For a denial of Malthus' assertion that landlords "pay ... many of the taxes which fall on the capital of the farmer and the wages of the labourer ...," see *Notes on Malthus*, S, II, 184. Longfield objected that consumption would diminish as the price of produce rose, and that Ricardo's erroneous assumption to the contrary, "combined with some confusion in reasoning," led him "to assert that a tax upon the profits of the farmer would be advantageous to the landlord." But Longfield does not explain in what respect Ricardo's reasoning was confused. Longfield, *Lectures on Political Economy*, p. 145.

[47] S, I, 213; G, 195. Of interest in this connection is Ricardo's cryptic comment on behalf of the stockholders, in a ltter to Trower, in 1822 (see p. 148 below).

[48] S, I, 213-14; G, 195-96. [49] See Sec. 4 in chapter IV above.

obtained from a gold mine within the country, the mine being exempt from the tax, Ricardo had answered both questions in the affirmative, the first implicitly, the second explicitly. Now he turns to the hypothesis relevant for Great Britain: "money, or the standard of money, is a commodity imported from abroad. . . ." The answer to the first question is here made explicit: "the prices of all goods could not rise . . . without an additional quantity of money. . . ."[50] But in the footnote, Ricardo says: "On further consideration, I doubt whether any more money would be required to circulate the same quantity of commodities, if their prices be raised by taxation, and not by difficulty of production."[51] In this respect, the text and footnote in the present chapter repeat the variant conclusions carried by text and footnote, respectively, in the earlier chapter, "Taxes on Raw Produce."[52] Here, however, the proposition in the footnote is supported by explicit reasoning. Additional details are supplied by notes that passed between Ricardo and Trower. It develops that the key to the problem, in Ricardo's mind, is the fact that the government makes use of the money abstracted from the private sector of the economy by the tax. It is worth quoting Ricardo at length:

> Suppose 100,000 quarters of corn to be sold in a certain district, and in a certain time, at 4 *l.* per quarter, and that in consequence of a direct tax of 8 *s.* per quarter, corn rises to 4 *l.* 8 *s.* . . . . If I before purchased 11 quarters at 4 *l.*, and in consequence of the tax am obliged to reduce my consumption to 10 quarters, I shall not require more money, for in all cases I shall pay 44 *l.* for my corn. The public would, in fact, consume one-eleventh less, and this quantity would be consumed by Government. The money necessary to purchase it, would be derived from the 8 *s.* per quarter, to be received from the farmers in the shape of a tax, but the amount levied would at the same time be paid to them for their corn; therefore the tax is in fact a tax in kind, and does not make it necessary that any more money should be used, or, if any, so little, that the quantity may be safely neglected.[53]

The difficulty in accepting this argument, in Ricardo's own terms, is that he ignores the necessity for an increase in the velocity of circulation, if

[50] S, I, 213; G, 195-96.

[51] S, I, 213, note; G, 196, note. At a meeting of the Political Economy Club on Feb. 4, 1822, Ricardo supported this thesis, and he writes to McCulloch: "The correctness of this view was doubted, and it was accordingly made the subject of conversation:—the majority of the company were I think convinced that the proposition was a true one." Letter of Feb. 8, 1822, S, IX, 159; and note 1 by Sraffa, *ibid.*, 158-59.

[52] The footnote in Chapter IX was likewise added in the third edition of the *Principles.*

[53] S, I, 213-14, note; G, 196, note.

the unchanged quantity of money is to carry an unchanged amount of product at a higher price level. This point is brought out clearly by Hutches Trower in a comment written on the back of a sheet of note paper on which Ricardo had jotted down a more detailed version of a similar numerical example. Neither Ricardo's note nor Trower's comment is dated, but "The argument of the Note . . . is so closely similar to that of the footnotes added to edition 3 in 1821 as to indicate that it belongs to this period."[54]

Here are Ricardo's note and Trower's comment, in that order, in full:[55]

A B and *C* each lay out £100 pr. Annm. in Corn, when its price is 40/ pr. quarter, they each buy 50 quarters. But Government imposes a tax of 10/- pr. quarter on corn, and consequently the price of corn rises from 40 to 50 shillings, and the whole 150 quarters consumed will cost £375, instead of £300. In consequence however of the additional price, *A, B,* and *C,* can each, only purchase 40 quarters, instead of 50;—and therefore they will together purchase 120 quarters instead of 150. There will remain 30 quarters to be disposed of [,] which will be purchased by Government at the market price of 50/- and therefore for £75. This sum of £75 is precisely the sum which Government has raised by the tax of 10/- on 150 quarters, I think therefore I have shewn that although it is true that 150 quarters of corn will be disposed of for £375 instead of for £300 no additional quantity of money will be required for the purpose of purchasing it.

Trower's comment:

No additional money is required to purchase it, because although more money is *paid* for the corn in consequence of the Tax, yet the cost of production of the corn, its natural price, is not increased. And the seller of the corn pays over to Government the extra price he receives in consequence of the Tax. This money, so paid to Government, is given to other persons, by whom that portion of the Corn is purchased, which used to be bought by the tax payers before the Tax was imposed.

So that the same £300 purchases the Corn whose price is raised by the Tax to £375. And it is enabled to do this in consequence of the *increased ratio* of its circulation, which the imposition of the tax occasions. Before the tax was imposed the 300 purchased 150 quarters of Corn for 300, now it first purchases 120 quarters @ 50/- amounting to 300; and then afterwards, that portion of it which was paid for the tax, vzt. 75, purchases the remaining 30 quarters @ 50/-

[54] Sraffa, S, IV, 320. Bonar and Hollander surmise that this note and comment were responsible for the two footnotes added to the third edition of the *Principles. Letters of David Ricardo to Hutches Trower*, p. 235.

[55] S, IV, 321-22.

amounting to 75. So that that portion circulates twice where before the Tax was imposed it only circulated once.

Thus the only effect of the Tax is to take from the payers of it the power of purchasing 30 quarters of Corn, and to transfer that power to other persons; and this is effected by causing the money to pass through the hands of the seller of the Corn to Government and from Government to these other persons. The increase in the ratio of circulation is equal to the amount of the Tax—vzt. 25 pCt.

But even Trower understates the amount of work that the money has to do in the new situation. In saying that "the increase in the ratio of circulation is equal to the amount of the tax," he ignores one of the two extra money flows. In place of one money flow from consumer to farmer for all the wheat, there are three flows—one from consumer to farmer, of the same size as before, though exchanging against a smaller quantity of wheat; another from farmer to government in payment of the tax; and a third from government back to farmer in purchase of the remaining wheat, or, alternatively, from government to its employees as wages and from them to the farmer to purchase the wheat. Before the tax is imposed, £300 moves from consumers to farmers for 150 quarters, at 40/ a quarter. Suppose the stock of money is £300; transactions velocity is 1. With the tax of 10/ a quarter in effect, £300 passes from consumers to farmers for 120 quarters of wheat at 50/ a quarter; £75 from farmers to Government as tax on production of 150 quarters; and £75 from Government to farmers in payment for 30 quarters of (taxed) wheat. The transactions velocity is $^{450}/_{300}$, or 1.5; the increase of 50 percent in velocity is greater than the tax rate (25 percent). If the Government spends its revenue in wages, and the government employees spend their wages on wheat, another £75 transactions must be added, and velocity rises to $^{525}/_{300} = 1.75$.

Indeed, the question arises whether even the initial price level can be maintained, without an increase in velocity. If wheat does not rise in price under the tax; if consumers are imagined to be somehow held to the purchase of 120 quarters at 40/ the quarter, perhaps by rationing; if farmers pay a tax of 10/ on the 120 quarters only (perhaps borrowing the money from consumers to do so); if the Government returns the £60 to farmers in purchase of their remaining 30 quarters of wheat—then the total of money flows is £240 + £60 + £60, or £360, and the transactions velocity has risen from 1 (pre-tax) to $^{360}/_{300}$, or 1.2. If the Government engages employees, who then buy wheat, velocity rises to $^{420}/_{300} = 1.4$.

Ricardo's footnotes in the *Principles* are a throwback to thoughts he had expressed more than a decade earlier: briefly, in his *Notes on Trotter's "Principles of Currency and Exchanges,"* in 1810, and in some detail in his *Reply to Bosanquet* in 1811.

Trotter had implied that the increase in "public revenue to remit into the Exchequer" had necessitated an increase in currency in circulation. Ricardo commented: "Taxation does not require any addition of money, or if any so little as not to be worth computing."[56]

The debate with Bosanquet involved the question of whether the Bank circulation was excessive. Bosanquet had cited Smith[57] as authority for the theorem that so long as the annual amount of taxes exceeds the amount of bank-notes in circulation, the paper cannot depreciate. Ricardo disputes Bosanquet's interpretation of Smith's passage—Smith did not say "annual" amount of taxes, and might better be taken to mean daily payment of taxes[58]—and then exhibits data for periods following 1793 to show that taxes can increase without an addition to the circulating medium, and, by implication, with no fall, at least, in the price level.

But the price level has risen; and a part of the rise may be "traced to the effects of taxation, to the increased scarcity of the commodity, or to any other cause which may appear satisfactory to those who take pleasure in such enquiries."[59] What does Ricardo (who certainly does take pleasure in such inquiries) think? He believed at this time (1811) that (a) "neither the income tax, the assessed taxes, nor many others,[60] do in the least affect the prices of commodities";[61] (b) a general tax on all commodities would raise the price level (though he does not explicitly say so); (c) no addition to the money stock is needed to maintain the new higher price level, since "That amount of money which is received by government in the shape of taxes, is taken from a fund which would otherwise have been expended on consumable commodities."[62] A numerical illustration is then presented:

[56] S, III, 384-85. [57] *Wealth of Nations*, Bk. II, Ch. II, C, I, 311; M, 312.

[58] *Reply to Bosanquet*, S, III, 237. Ricardo's equating of bank-note volume with daily amount paid in taxes is an unwarranted interpretation of Smith's passage, toward the other extreme; it allows no time for return of the currency by the Government to the private sector, to be again used for tax payments.

[59] S, III, 239.

[60] *I. e.*, "all other taxes which are not levied on commodities." S, III, 241.

[61] *Idem.* Ricardo adds that if the income tax were levied at a heavier rate on some than on others, part of it would be shifted.

[62] S, III, 243. "Although in the preceding statement I have conceded to Mr. Bosanquet, that in consequence of some of our taxes the prices of commodities will be increased, it does not appear necessarily to follow that more money will be requisite to circulate them."

In proportion as the taxes are great, must the expences of the people diminish. If my income amount to 1000 *l.*, and government requires 100 *l.* in taxes from me, I shall have but 900 *l.* to expend on such necessaries and comforts as are requisite for the use of my family. If government take 200 I shall have but 800 for such purposes. Now, as the amount of money actually expended by government and by me cannot exceed 1000 *l.*, no additional circulating medium would, I think, be required, although the taxes were 50 per cent. of each man's income. If the tax were laid upon bread, and, in consquence, the wages of labour were raised, the tax would eventually fall on all those who consumed the produce of the labour of man. It would make no real difference to these consumers if they had at once paid the amount of such tax into the exchequer, or if it had gone through the circuitous channel which it would then take.

Nor would any additional sum be required. Government would be in the daily receipt of a portion of the taxes, whether it was paid to the exciseman or to the tax-gatherer, and their expences in the one case would be precisely the same as in the other. Whatever the government expended would cause a diminished expenditure in the people to the same amount: the same amount of commodities would be circulated, and the same money would be adequate to their circulation.[63]

This statement certainly does not call attention very strongly to the supposed rise in prices. After the sentence "Although ... I have conceded to Mr. Bosanquet...," the rise in prices is not specifically mentioned. We must, presumably, suppose it to be implied throughout, but some additional doubt is cast by the tone and phrasing of an immediately succeeding paragraph:[64]

This is on the supposition that the people were sufficiently prudent or sufficiently rich to pay all the taxes from their annual income, and were not tempted or compelled to diminish their capital to satisfy the calls of government. If capital were however diminished, the aggregate amount of productions would also diminish; and if the money which was before necessary for their circulation were to continue of the same amount, it would bear a larger proportion to the goods, and it might therefore be expected that commodities would rise; but we must not forget that the amount of money in a country is regulated by its value, and as its value would in this case be diminished, it would become relatively excessive to the money of other countries, and the excess would therefore be exported.

By "This," at the start of this paragraph, does not Ricardo mean the assumed rise in prices, by the amount of the tax, without the need for an addition to the stock of money? If so, he then goes on to tell us that a still greater rise in prices may occur, temporarily, if taxpayers draw on their capital. Within a short period this rise would be cancelled by an outflow of gold. The final result, we may infer, would be: a higher price level than in the pre-tax period, with a smaller money stock than in the

63 S, III, 243. 64 S, III, 243-44.

pre-tax period. The implications for the price level that flow from the assumption that the tax is paid out of capital were not, unfortunately, explored when Ricardo came to write the *Principles.*

In summary, Ricardo in 1811 thought that if taxation was to raise the price level, an increase in the stock of money was not a necessary condition; in 1817 and 1819 (in the first and second editions of the *Principles*) he said it was a necessary condition; in 1821 he reverted to his earlier view. Perhaps he changed his mind twice on this subject, or perhaps when he drafted the *Principles* he simply forgot what he had written in the Bosanquet essay, and recalled it in time to add the footnotes to the third edition.

We turn now to the second issue: Will the general price level in fact rise, under a general tax on profits?

Granted, as Ricardo grants in the footnote, that a higher price level caused by taxation could be maintained without an increase in the money stock, there remains the question, would such an increase in the price level develop, and, if it did, would it be more than temporary? A negative answer is indicated in the passage just quoted from the *Reply to Bosanquet,* and is repeated in the *Principles:* even if such a rise "could" take place, "it could not be permanent," if the monetary metal were obtained from abroad. The rise in domestic prices would open a gap between exports and imports and gold would be exported, "till the relative prices of commodities were nearly the same as before." Thus, "It appears to me absolutely certain, that a well regulated tax on profits, would ultimately restore commodities both of home and foreign manufacture, to the same money price which they bore before the tax was imposed." [65] We are to infer, then, that if the analysis in the footnote is the correct one, Great Britain would end up with the pre-tax price level, but with a smaller money stock than before the tax.

This conclusion has a corollary that Ricardo did not see, or thought not worth mentioning. Abstracting from international trade, let us return to the case where the monetary metal is obtained from a mine within the country, and suppose that the mine is not taxed. If labor and

[65] S, I, 214; G, 196. See also, as reported by Hansard, Ricardo's speech of May 30, 1820: "...if all articles were taxed alike, [foreign] commerce in general would not be affected." S, V, 54. Perhaps similar considerations were in his mind when he said, in a letter to McCulloch, three years later, "I should deny that an increased Govt. expenditure could raise for any length of time the prices of those commodities even for which Governt. has a demand, but it is impossible to attribute to it the prices of all other things for which Govt. has no demand." Letter of March 25, 1823. S, IX, 276.

capital flow into mining, increasing the stock of gold, and if a tax-induced rise in the price level could be supported without any such increase in gold stock (following the reasoning in the footnote), then a still further increase in prices is to be expected; under these conditions, a general tax on profits would cause a rise in prices considerably in excess of the tax itself.[66]

[66] A tax on profits is given four pages in Whewell's "Mathematical Exposition of Some Doctrines of Political Economy," pp. 221-24, and slightly more than two pages in his second paper, "Mathematical Exposition of Some of the Leading Doctrines in Mr. Ricardo's 'Principles,'" pp. 178-81. Whewell does not take issue with Ricardo, but, in his first paper, attempts rather to extend the analysis by assuming a certain degree of elasticity of demand and certain rates of increase of cost, from the poorest to the best land. He therefore by-passes the problems raised and debated by Ricardo.

CHAPTER X

TAXES ON WAGES

Ricardo's analysis of a tax on wages moves along lines made familiar by preceding chapters of the *Principles.* But in the course of correcting errors found in Smith, Say, and Buchanan, Ricardo is drawn into illuminating discussions of some possible economic consequences of taxation: increase in government demand for labor; influence on luxury expenditures exercised by a tax on necessaries; impact of a given tax on the yield of other taxes; variations in relative values induced by taxes of general scope; shifting the burden of a domestic tax to foreign countries;[1] and payment of luxury taxes out of income rather than capital.[2] Ricardo also reconsiders the effect of a general tax on the level of prices and its consequences for foreign trade. The chapter is rich in insights into many aspects of economic effects of taxation.

1. GOVERNMENT'S DEMAND FOR LABOR

The first eight pages of Chapter XVI are devoted to a defense of Adam Smith against Buchanan.[3] Smith had concluded that a tax on wages would produce a rise in wages, and thus far, in Ricardo's view, he was correct. The price of necessaries determines the amount of money that must be paid to the laborer to enable him to acquire his "liberal, moderate, or scanty subsistence."[4] Buchanan objected, first, that wages do not rise and fall with the cost of necessaries. If the price of food rises because of a deficient supply, an increase in wages can do nothing but force a further rise in price. The short supply of provisions must be

[1] See Chapter XII below. [2] See Chapter III above.

[3] See letter of Dec. 16, 1816, James Mill to Ricardo, S, VII, 108.

[4] S, I, 215; G, 199. Ricardo is quoting Smith, *Wealth of Nations,* C, II, 348; M, 815

rationed by the price system. But Buchanan forgets, says Ricardo, that food prices may rise, instead, because of increased cost traceable to taxation, or because farmers must resort to a less productive margin of cultivation in order to feed a larger number of people. In these instances a rise in price is not accompanied by a reduction in the amount produced, and Buchanan's reasoning does not apply. "If, then, in consequence of taxation, ... the price of provisions be raised, and the quantity be not diminished, the money wages of labour will rise...."[5] But why is the quantity not diminished, and by what means is the labor force provided with the increase in aggregate money income necessary to clear the market at the higher level of prices? The answer emerges as Ricardo deals with Buchanan's second point. Buchanan had said, that if a tax were laid on wages, a worker already receiving "fair recompense" for his labor could in no way recoup the tax by obtaining still more from his employer. This dictum, unsupported by analysis, provides Ricardo with an occasion to consider the use made of the tax revenue, and thus to ascertain the net effect on the demand for labor. If the government expands its own payroll, its increased demand for labour is added to the undiminished private demand. Private demand in money terms is undiminished because "the owners of capital, who would have nothing to pay towards such a [wages] tax, would have the same funds for employing labour...,"[6] and, since the supply of labor is unchanged, money wages must rise. If, instead, the tax were levied directly on "people of capital,"[7] [through a tax on profits?] the total wage bill would not increase, as government demand would be substituted directly for private demand. In either case, therefore, disposable wages—wages after tax, if any—would remain unchanged. Buchanan, Ricardo complains, evidently neglects the government's demand for labor; so does Say.

If, instead, the tax is on "provisions" (Buchanan's first point), we may suppose the following chain of events to be implied: prices of provisions must rise if an unchanged amount is to be produced, other-

[5] S, I, 218; G, 201.

[6] S, I, 220; G, 203. In two long footnotes to Ricardo's sentences ending "... in proportion to the tax" (S, I, 220; G, 203), and "... employed at additional wages" (S, I, 221; G, 204), Say's denial of Ricardo's theorem that money wages will rise, under a wages tax, turns out to be a long-run analysis, hence no real contradiction of Ricardo. Say admits that the immediate effect is simply a displacement of demand for labor, not a diminution of it. But he confuses a tax taken out of a given laborer's consumption with a tax taken out of capital. Notes on Ricardo, I, 380-85.

[7] S, I, 221; G, 204.

wise capital would move into untaxed industries; the wages bill of government, financed by the provisions tax, when added to the unchanged wages bill of the private sector, forces money wages up, and enables laborers to demand an unchanged quantity of provisions at the new high price.

Ricardo explores alternative uses of the proceeds of a wages tax, demonstrating how important are the assumptions on this score. If the tax revenue is paid as a subsidy to a foreign state, there is no domestic government demand for labor, and the decrease in the worker's disposable income through the tax will not, or may not, be made good by a rise in wages. If the proceeds are "paid gratuitously to [domestic] employers,"[8] competition among them for labor, with the added funds at their disposal, forces a rise in wages.

Ricardo's introduction of the government's demand for labor into the analysis is, to be sure, followed some pages later by a passage that seems to make the rise in wages depend instead on labor's elasticity of supply:

> If the labourer's wages were before only adequate to supply the requisite population, they will, after the tax, be inadequate to that supply, for he will not have the same funds to expend on his family. Labour will, therefore, rise, because the demand continues, and it is only by raising the price, that the supply is not checked.[9]

A parallel is drawn with a tax on hats, or a tax on malt. In those cases, indeed, a supply that is elastic even in the short run is conceivable, but for the moment Ricardo seems not to notice the difference between short-run supply conditions of a single commodity, and of labor in general. Again:

> Suppose the circumstances of the country to be such, that the lowest labourers are not only called upon to continue their race, but to increase it; their wages would be regulated accordingly. Can they multiply in the degree required, if a tax takes from them a part of their wages, and reduces them to bare necessaries?[10]

It is not clear what fixes "the degree required" (this phrase was added in the third edition),[11] for when the market rate of wages is above the natural rate (the rate for a stable labor supply) there is no single "required" market rate above the natural rate. But it does seem evident that for the moment Ricardo is relying solely on supply conditions to explain the rise in wages. At once, however, he recollects that he has been making short-run pronouncements, while the supply is elastic only

[8] *Idem.* [9] S, I, 219; G, 202. [10] S, I, 220; G, 203. [11] S, I, 220, note 3 by Sraffa.

over the long run; he admits that "the number of labourers cannot be rapidly increased or diminished," and falls back on the fact that the demand for labor will increase as the government enters the labor market, spending the proceeds of the tax on wages. Ricardo's explanation of this demand factor starts somewhat awkwardly, in terms of "no necessary diminution of demand for labour," instead of emphasizing the increase in demand, in money terms. He seems to be reverting to the malt-and-hats type of tax, where the supply curve, being perhaps elastic even in the short run, is raised by the amount of the tax, along an inelastic demand curve. He even admits, unnecessarily, a qualification: "and if diminished, the demand does not abate in proportion to the tax."[12] The remainder of the paragraph makes it evident, however, that we are to interpret "no diminution in demand" as meaning that the demand curve, in money terms, shifts upward, along a labor supply curve that is completely inelastic in the short period. Hence demand absorbs the same amount of labor as before, at a new wage rate high enough to compensate the laborer for the tax on wages.

2. ERRORS IN SMITH'S REASONING

Although Adam Smith was correct in asserting that a tax on wages would put wages up, he was wrong, thought Ricardo, from that point on. Smith had concluded that the farmer, faced with a higher wage bill, would recoup from the landlord by paying a lower rent. This made no sense to Ricardo, whose farmers worked out to margins where there was no rent, hence, for portions of capital applied there, no possibility of recoupment from that source.

As to manufacturers, Smith said they would raise their prices, when forced to pay higher wages; but this too is a conclusion that cannot be accommodated within the Ricardian macro-economic system, unless the mine furnishing the monetary metal is within the country and is somehow exempt from the wage increase. And even if prices did rise, who would then finally bear the tax? The rise in the prices of necessaries would force a further increase in wages, prices would rise again, and a never-ending spiral would develop.

Smith was still more in error, thought Ricardo, when he drew alarming inferences for foreign trade from his conclusion that prices of manufactured goods would rise under the wages tax. The rise in prices, according to Smith, would lead to a reduction in exports. No, said

[12] S, I, 220; G, 203.

Ricardo, a general rise in prices of domestic manufactures does not "diminish the stimulus to a trade of barter, which all commerce, both foreign and domestic, really is."[13] Either the rise in prices would be temporary, because, we may infer, an outflow of gold would result, or the value of domestic money would sink on the foreign exchange market. Smith was consistent in his error, for he asserted that the embargo Spain had placed on the export of silver had been detrimental to her foreign commerce and hence to her manufactures. Ricardo devotes several pages to refuting Smith on this point, concluding that the only disadvantage the embargoing country suffers is that it maintains more "dead stock" (silver) than it needs, when it could have exported it in exchange for useful goods.

There is some inconclusive discussion of Smith's reference to an "observation of Sir Matthew Decker, that certain taxes, are in the price of certain goods, sometimes repeated and accumulated four or five times. . . ."[14] If Smith means by this that there exists what modern tax terminology calls "pyramiding," Ricardo seems to demur: the rich consumer will pay no more than the amount of the tax. Later in the *Principles,* Ricardo agrees that interest, if not profit, on the tax will be charged to the consumer by the taxpaying manufacturer.[15] If instead Smith thinks of this repetition and accumulation as a mechanism whereby equilibrium is finally attained after the entire tax has been shifted to the rich through their general consumption expenditures—an outcome that Ricardo does not in fact believe possible—there can be no objection, provided "there be no more paid than what is required by Government. ... If more be not paid by the people, than what is received by Government, the rich consumer will only pay his equitable share; if more is paid, Adam Smith should have stated by whom it is received..."[16]

[13] S, I, 228; G, 211. The same question is treated more directly and clearly by Ricardo in his essay, *On Protection to Agriculture,* S, IV, 213-16. The carelessness with which J.-B. Say read Ricardo is well illustrated here. Commenting on the paragraph ending with the passage just quoted in the text above, Say remarks that a commodity can be dear or cheap, even if money is not used, according to its cost of production. If it becomes more costly to produce, it must exchange for more of other things, even abroad. Thus Say fails to notice that Ricardo is speaking of commodities in general, within a single country, and that he has specifically called attention, in the same paragraph, to the difference between a rise in the cost of a few goods, and a general rise in costs. Notes on Ricardo, I, 400.

[14] S, I, 234; G, 218.

[15] See Chapter XIV below, analyzing Ricardo's Chapter XXIX, "Taxes Paid by the Producer."

[16] S, I, 236; G, 220.

Besides his direct attack on Smith's doctrine that a tax on wages would impair rent and raise the prices of manufactures, Ricardo offers a critique based on what he considers corollaries of that doctrine: corollaries manifestly absurd. One is that manufacturers would be benefited by the tax; another that landlords consume all the manufactured commodities; a third, that wages and the prices of manufactured goods would rise successively in a never-ending spiral.

Ricardo does not come off very well in this attack. He is in error in deducing the first and third corollaries, and his reasoning with respect to the second is impossible to follow closely.

In drawing his first inference, that Smithian doctrine implies a benefit to manufacturers from a tax on wages, Ricardo says:

> If the clothier, the hatter, the shoe-maker, &c., should be each able to raise the price of their goods 10 per cent.,—supposing 10 per cent. to recompense them completely for the additional wages they paid,—if, as Adam Smith says, 'they would be entitled and obliged to charge the additional wages *with a profit* upon the price of their goods,' they could each consume as much as before of each other's goods, and therefore they would pay nothing towards the tax. If the clothier paid more for his hats and shoes, he would receive more for his cloth, and if the hatter paid more for his cloth and shoes, he would receive more for his hats. All manufactured commodities then would be bought by them with as much advantage as before, and inasmuch as corn would not be raised in price which is Dr. Smith's supposition whilst they had an additional sum to lay out upon its purchase, they would be benefited, and not injured by such a tax.[17]

The clothier would have to pay more for his hats and shoes. He would receive more for his cloth, but only enough more to compensate him for the additional wages he had to pay, plus a profit on the working capital involved. After the clothier had devoted his increased gross receipts to paying the increased wages, it is not clear how he would be able to purchase as much as before of the hats and shoes at the new high prices. Perhaps Ricardo interprets the phrase "with a profit" to mean an additional profit large enough to compensate the entrepreneurs for the increased cost of their consumer goods, but it seems unlikely that Smith had so large an amount in mind. Perhaps instead Ricardo was thinking of the kind of wage-price spiral, this one leading to a new equilibrium, that he had used implicitly in his preceding chapter, "Taxes on Profits."

The second absurd corollary, that landlords are the sole consumers of manufactured goods (under Smithian wage-tax doctrine), is deduced by

[17] S, I, 223-24; G, 206-7.

Ricardo from the two assumptions that (a) the laborets bear no part of the tax, and (b) manufacturers benefit from it. Following a quotation from Smith, Ricardo comments:

In this passage it is asserted that the additional wages paid by farmers will ultimately fall on the landlords, who will receive a diminished rent; but that the additional wages paid by manufacturers will occasion a rise in the price of manufactured goods, and will therefore fall on the consumers of those commodities.

Ricardo then seems to pass over the word "consumers," going on to ask:

Now, suppose a society to consist of landlords, manufacturers, farmers and labourers, the labourers, it is agreed, would be recompensed for the tax;—but by whom?—who would pay that portion which did not fall on the landlords?—the manufacturers could pay no part of it ... If then neither the labourers nor the manufacturers would contribute towards such a tax; if the farmers would be also recompensed by a fall of rent, landlords alone must not only bear its whole weight, but they must also contribute to the increased gains of the manufacturers. To do this, however, they should consume all the manufactured commodities in the country, for the additional price charged on the whole mass is little more than the tax originally imposed on the labourers in manufactures.[18]

It is not possible to follow Ricardo's reasoning closely in the last sentence; to what does "this" refer? In any case, Ricardo forgets that manufacturers and farmers are also consumers who can bear a tax, and that even laborers may on occasion carry part of the burden as consumers, if they have an appreciable margin for luxuries.[19] Ricardo again, a few paragraphs later, neglects the well-to-do-consumer as a possible taxpayer. He is demonstrating the impossibility of a rise in farm prices as a result of a tax on wages, provided the tax applies equally to all industries, not merely to wages of farm labor. The same reason that would induce the farmer to raise his prices would be operating on the manufacturer; and "If they could all raise the price of their goods, so as to remunerate themselves, with a profit, for the tax; as they are all consumers of each other's commodities, it is obvious that the tax could never be paid; for who would be the contributors if all were compensated?"[20] But we may note that if prices did rise, the tax could be borne by the landlords and capitalists as consumers, although several rounds of price and wage in-

[18] S, I, 223-24; G, 206-7.

[19] See the note added to the *Principles* in the third edition, in Chapter XXVI, "On Gross and Net Revenue," S, I, 348; G, 336. St. Clair, *A Key to Ricardo*, pp. 168-71, notes this flaw in Ricardo's reasoning.

[20] S, I, 226; G, 209.

creases would be necessary (under a successive approximations approach) to reach the new equilibrium.

To be sure, Ricardo assigns a part of the wages tax to landlords, but only a small part, and not in their capacity as purchasers of commodities, but rather as direct employers of gardeners, menial servants, and similar laborers rendering direct consumer services. Landlords viewed as consumers would bear part of the tax through the wage increase that would have to be granted to such workers.[21]

Accordingly, although Smith's doctrine might well be erroneous, there is nothing inherently impossible about it. The picture to be drawn from Smith's analysis is that of a tax which raises wages, then the price of manufactured goods, then wages, then the price of manufactured goods, while on each round of wage and price increase a part of the tax is thrown off on consumers who cannot recoup through an increase in income. Ultimately, then, under Smith's doctrine, the tax would rest in part on landlords in their capacity as rent receivers, and in part on landlords, farmers, manufacturers, and perhaps some laborers, in their role of well-to-do consumers.

The third absurdity with which Ricardo charges the Smithian wage-tax doctrine is an implication that wages and the prices of manufactured goods chase each other upwards in a never-ending spiral.

> But if the labourers pay no part of the tax, and yet manufactured commodities rise in price, wages must rise, not only to compensate them for the tax, but for the increased price of manufactured necessaries, which, as far as it affects agricultural labour, will be a new cause for the fall of rent; and, as far as it affects manufacturing labour, for a further rise in the price of goods. This rise in the price of goods will again operate on wages, and the action and re-action first of wages on goods, and then of goods on wages, will be extended without any assignable limits. The arguments by which this theory is supported, lead to such absurd conclusions, that it may at once be seen that the principle is wholly indefensible.[22]

Again Ricardo overlooks that part of Smith's argument calling for some of the tax to be thrown off on rich consumers at each round of price and wage increase. Moreover, the absorption by rent of increases in farm wages will dampen the spiral. The role of these two influences in leading to a new equilibrium may be illustrated in a numerical example. All the figures are in money terms. Problems of money supply are ignored, to simplify and concentrate the analysis.

[21] S, I, 233; G, 216-17. [22] S, I, 224-25; G, 207-208.

Let initial sales of farm products total 600, of which 200 goes to rent, 200 to wages, and 200 to farmers' profits. Let initial sales of manufacturers be 400, of which 200 goes to wages and 200 to profits. Then wages total 400; profit, 400; rent, 200; and sales, 1,000.

A tax of 40 is imposed on wages. According to Adam Smith, wages rise from 400 to 440. Half of this increase, accruing as it does to farm laborers, is absorbed by a fall in land rent from 200 to 180. The other 20 is passed on by manufacturers through an increase in sales prices.

Let the initial sales of manufacturers (400) be taken off the market by landlords, 80; by manufacturers and farm entrepreneurs, 160; and by laborers, 160. Then, of the 20 increase in money sales of manufacturers, the laborers must meet $^2/_5$, or 8. Wages therefore rise 8 on the second round, of which 4 is absorbed by a further reduction in land rent, while 4 is passed on in a higher money volume of manufacturers' sales—and so on. A new equilibrium is reached, under the Smithian system, with the following figures:

Sales volume of farm products	600
Sales volume of manufacturers	425
Total	1,025
Wages	450
Profits	400
Rent	175
Total	1,025

Ricardo's refusal to believe that the repetition and accumulation of the wages tax can lead to a new equilibrium is the more strange in that he himself, in Chapter XV, "Taxes on Profits," had just implied a similar kind of self-limiting mechanism of cost and price increases, in saying that a 10 percent tax on profits would result in a 10 percent rise in prices.[23]

At first, under Ricardo's doctrine, the worker suffers not at all from a tax on wages; wages rise immediately. But "ultimately," his wages are lower than they otherwise would have been, for the workers employed by government do not produce commodities than can be consumed later.

[23] See p. 105, above. Whewell, "Mathematical Exposition of Some Doctrines of Political Economy," pp. 192-93, 229, points out the defect in Ricardo's reasoning on his never-ending spiral. See also Whewell's second paper, "Mathematical Exposition of some of the Leading Doctrines," pp. 181-85, especially pp. 181-82, for division of tax between capitalists and consumers. See Appendix A 3 below.

The demand for workers in real-wage terms therefore declines from the level it would otherwise have attained. However, the term "ultimately," or, as we should say, "in the long run," means "almost right away, to some degree." This can be illustrated by a numerical example, somewhat similar to that used in Chapter II above, in which we suppose that a hitherto inactive government suddenly imposes a tax designed to let it absorb, for defense purposes, half the labor force of a 100 percent farm economy. At the start of the year, there are 1,000 laborers in this economy, 100 competing entrepreneur-capitalists, and an inactive government. Each capitalist is assumed to have on hand 400 bushels of wheat. Each laborer can produce 80 bushels of wheat (we abstract from diminishing returns). No capitalist wants any of his capital unemployed for the year, and will accept a zero profit rate on it if necessary. No laborer can afford to be idle during the year. A demand curve for labor of unit elasticity, from the point, 80 bushels per worker and 500 workers, on to any larger number of workers, crosses a completely inelastic supply curve of labor at the point, 40 bushels per worker and 1,000 workers. Each capitalist would thus be prepared to employ 10 workers, at a wage of 40 bushels, and would expect to have 800 bushels of wheat on hand at the start of the following year. The year-end stock of wheat would be 80,000 bushels. However, the government, hitherto inactive, now announces a tax of 50 percent on wages, to defray the salaries of its prospective armed forces. The capitalists have to alter their plans. There will now be only 500 workers available for private employment, 5 to a capitalist. Each capitalist offers a wage of 80 bushels instead of 40 bushels.

The government taxes each private worker 50 percent of his wage, as he receives it, and transfers the proceeds at once to the government workers, who are assumed to be exempt from the wages tax. Thus the government is viewed as taking half the enhanced pay of the private worker and turning it over to the government employee. Alternatively, the government employee too may be assumed taxable; the government gives him a paper claim to an 80-bushel wage, but cancels half of it by taxation.

The year-end stock of wheat is only 40,000 bushels instead of 80,000 bushels. The aggregate of disposable wages for the year is as large as the aggregate of wages would have been in the absence of the tax. Thus the tax has been shifted forward completely, in a wage increase. The rate of profit for this year, on the other hand, has dropped from 100 percent to zero. For the second year, each capitalist can offer only 40 bushels in wages, in place of the 80 bushels he would have offered in the absence of wage taxation. And if the illustration were refined to take account of Ricardo's views on capital accumulation, capitalists might consume some of the wheat, or send it abroad, before accepting a zero rate. In any event, the worker's wages are lower in the second year than they would have been if no wage tax had been levied in the first year. This decrease in wage is the long-run consequence of the tax, reflecting the effect of all taxes upon accumulation.

In summary, then, it is of no consequence, in the Ricardian system, whether a general tax is levied on wages, or on profits, or on necessaries: in each case it is profits that bear the burden. Tax necessaries, and they rise in price; wages consequently rise, hence profits fall. Tax wages; wages rise and profits fall. Tax profits, and the taxpayer has no recourse. The "principle of the division of the produce of labour and capital between wages and profits, which I have attempted to establish, appears to me so certain, that excepting in the immediate effects, I should think it of little importance whether the profits of stock, or the wages of labour, were taxed."[24] The tax on necessaries does, to be sure, differ somewhat from the other two: such a tax

> will necessarily be accompanied by a rise in the price of necessaries, but the [tax on wages] ... will not; towards a tax on wages, consequently, neither the stockholder, the landlord, nor any other class but the employers of labour will contribute. A tax on wages is wholly a tax on profits, a tax on necessaries is partly a tax on profits, and partly a tax on rich consumers.

And Ricardo adds, at this point, "The ultimate effects which will result from such taxes then, are precisely the same as those which result from a direct tax on profits."[25]

The three taxes are also alike in their effect on relative prices, except as the tax on necessaries raises the prices of necessaries relative to luxuries. All three taxes depress the prices of those commodities the production cost of which consists in a larger degree of profits, and in a smaller degree of wages, than the average commodity (gold, if the monetary metal is produced within the country). Such commodities are those in which the use of durable capital equipment, for example, plays an unusually large part. Their prices fall, in the Ricardian system, whenever the rate of profit declines while the wage rate rises. The taxes in question, it will be recalled, raise wages and lower profits. Correspondingly, commodities produced with an unusual proportion of labor cost will rise in price, under the three taxes.[26]

Ricardo's demonstration of the similarity of effects of the three taxes

[24] S, I, 226; G, 209. [25] S, I, 215; G, 198. [26] S, I, 239; G, 223.

runs smoothly, in terms of his own system, except at one point. He is speaking of the long-run effects:

By taxing the profits of stock, you would probably alter the rate at which the funds for the maintenance of labour increase, and wages would be disproportioned to the state of that fund, by being too high. By taxing wages, the reward paid to the labourer would also be disproportioned to the state of that fund, by being too low. In the one case by a fall, and in the other by a rise in money wages, the natural equilibrium between profits and wages would be restored.[27]

Ricardo here confuses short-term and long-term effects. A tax on profits leads to a fall in wages, compared with what they otherwise would have been, in a later period, because the rate of capital accumulation is slowed, and the worker's market rate of wages is therefore not as far above the natural rate as it would have been. A tax on wages leads to a rise in wages, but this rise occurs immediately. The correspondingly lower rate of profit then impedes accumulation of capital, and in the long run disposable wages (wages after wage tax) will be at a lower level than if the tax had not been imposed.

3. ELASTICITIES OF DEMAND

Some clues to Ricardo's thoughts on elasticity of demand are to be found in the chapter on wage taxation.

As in the earlier chapters of the *Principles,* Ricardo attributes to "corn," or "bread," a demand that is virtually inelastic, at least within the usual range of price. "If the commodity taxed be corn, it is not necessary that my demand for corn should diminish, as I may prefer to pay 100 *l.* per annum more for my corn, and to the same amount abate in my demand for wine, furniture, or any other luxury."[28] Price inelasticity for corn thus brings into play income elasticity for luxuries. Since the amount of corn purchased remains unchanged at the new high price, disposable income available for the purchase of all other commodities is decreased.

And again: "I do not believe, that if bread were taxed, the consumption of bread would be diminished, more than if cloth, wine, or soap were taxed."[29] This statement implies complete price inelasticity in the

[27] S, I, 226; G, 209. [28] S, I, 237; G, 221.

[29] S, I, 237, note; G, 221, note. This is a footnote commenting on Say's assertion that "Every increase in the price of a commodity, necessarily reduces the number of those who are able to purchase it, or at least the quantity they will consume of it." Say's rejoinder reasserts his view that the demand even for wheat is somewhat elastic throughout. Notes on Ricardo, I, 421-22.

demand for bread, for if a luxury like wine were taxed, Ricardo's consumer would surely not decrease his consumption of bread.

As to price elasticities for luxury items, Ricardo's views seem only vaguely formed. One passage might be interpreted to mean that he thought the demand for wine, at least, was of unit elasticity: "If I cease to expend 100 *l.* on wine, because by paying a tax of that amount I have enabled Government to expend 100 *l.* instead of expending it myself...."[30] If the tax in question is one on wine, and if the consumer pays, say, £1,000 for a certain quantity of wine before the tax; after the price has been raised by the tax, we may infer that he continues to pay £1,000, but for a smaller quantity of wine. The percentage decline in consumption matches the percentage rise in price. This inference is not inconsistent with a succeeding passage.

> Taxes on luxuries ... are generally paid from income... If wine were much raised in price in consequence of taxation, it is probable that a man would rather forego the enjoyments of wine, than make any important encroachments on his capital, to be enabled to purchase it.[31]

On the other hand, we encounter passages that imply, for a given consumer, a completely inelastic demand for luxuries up to a point, then a completely elastic demand.

> Whatever habit has rendered delightful, will be relinquished with reluctance, and will continue to be consumed notwithstanding a very heavy tax; but this reluctance has its limits, and experience every day demonstrates that an increase in the nominal amount of taxation, often diminishes the produce. One man will continue to drink the same quantity of wine, though the price of every bottle should be raised three shillings, who would yet relinquish the use of wine rather than pay four.[32]

Finally, one of Ricardo's speeches in Parliament implies a belief that the elasticity of demand for a commodity not a necessity of life decreases steadily as the quantity increases, moving from a region of elasticity greater than unity to one of elasticity less than unity. A straight line

[30] S, I, 238-39; G, 222.

[31] S, I, 241; G, 225. The phrase, "paid from income," means, in this context, paid without encroaching on the taxpayer's capital, in the historical sense; see p. 40 above. Shove, in "The Place of Marshall's *Principles* in the Development of Economic Theory," *Econ. J.*, LII (No. 208, Dec., 1942), remarks in a footnote (p. 301) on "Ricardo's striking discussion of taxes on luxuries (*Works*, [McCulloch edition] pp. 144-5 [S, I, 241-42; G, 224-26]) which comes very near to Marshall's position in regard to the effect of elasticity of demand on the yield of a tax."

[32] S, I, 241; G, 225.

demand curve would illustrate the case. He supposes that "in a particular country a very rare commodity was introduced for the first time—superfine cloth for instance." At first, 10,000 yards are imported. If imports are doubled, "the aggregate value of the 20,000 yards would be much more considerable than the aggregate value of the 10,000 yards. . . ." But if imports continued to increase until the price fell so low that the cloth "came within the reach of the purchase of every class in the country, from that time any addition to its quantity would diminish the aggregate value." As to corn, Ricardo seems to say that any increase in the amount put on the market will decrease its aggregate value. Finally, as to money, unitary elasticity is the rule of demand, as he had already concluded in Chapter XIII of the *Principles:* "if the quantity were increased, the value of commodities would alter only in proportion to the increase. . . ." [33]

4. EFFECT OF ONE TAX ON BASE FOR OTHER TAXES

Ricardo touches briefly on a point of considerable interest to modern tax theory, especially that branch of it concerned with estimates of tax yield.

> Whether taxes be taken from revenue or capital, they diminish the taxable commodities of the State. If I cease to expend 100 *l.* on wine, because by paying a tax of that amount I have enabled Government to expend 100 *l.* instead of expending it myself, one hundred pounds worth of goods are necessarily withdrawn from the list of taxable commodities. If the revenue of the individuals of a country be 10 millions, they will have at least 10 millions worth of taxable commodities. If by taxing some, one million be transferred to the disposal of Government, their revenue will still be nominally 10 millions, but they will remain with only nine millions worth of taxable commodities.

[33] Speech of May 7, 1822, S, V, 171. Whewell, after considering the possibility of unitary elasticity (an unchanging amount is spent on a given commodity as its price changes), thought it more likely, following Tooke, that demand for corn would prove to be of less than unitary elasticity, in the event of a crop shortage. For small changes he assumed that the increase in price would be proportional to the decrease in supply (linear demand curve): for corn, "up to the magnitude of $^1/_{10}$," a "$^1/_{10}$ defect of supply gives $^3/_{10}$ increase of price." But instead of 3, he uses "the general number e in most cases." "Mathematical Exposition of Some Doctrines of Political Economy," p. 201. In any case, "the increase of price *ceteris paribus* must be a *function* of the defect of supply. . . ." *Idem.* Whewell saw clearly that price was determined by the solution of simultaneous equations of cost of production and demand. *Ibid.*, pp. 202-203.

Ricardo might have gone on to point out that the total yield of a tax system cannot be estimated by merely adding the estimates made separately for each tax, unless each of these tax estimates has taken into consideration the effect of the tax in question on the base. Instead, he drifts off into the usual comment: "There are no circumstances under which taxation does not abridge the enjoyments of those on whom the taxes ultimately fall. . . ." [34]

5. A RECAPITULATION

As we leave Ricardo's chapter on the taxation of wages, and recall the earlier chapter on the taxation of necessaries, the perplexing question recurs as to what meaning can be attached to the opening sentence of Chapter XVI: "Taxes on wages will raise wages, and therefore will diminish the rate of the profits of stock," [35] and to the similar dictum in Chapter IX, "Taxes on Raw Produce": "A tax, however, on raw produce, and on the necessaries of the labourer, would have another effect—it would raise wages." [36] A comparison of the course of argument in the two chapters reveals striking similarities.

In Chapter IX, as we have seen, the theorem at first is based on "the effect of the principle of population on the increase of mankind." [37] Ricardo then claims that no "considerable interval" [38] would necessarily elapse before wages would rise. He recognizes specifically that the supply of laborers cannot be adjusted as rapidly as the supply of hats. But he assures us that this fact is not relevant, since imposition of the tax does not necessarily result in any "excess in the supply of labour." [39] And why not? Because, we infer, the government replaces the private sector as a demander of labor.

In "Taxes on Wages," similarly, appeal is first made to the principle of population: an "able passage from Mr. Malthus's work" seems to Ricardo "completely to answer [Buchanan's] objection." [40] If "the lowest labourers" are "called upon" to increase their race, wages are "regulated accordingly," and they cannot "multiply in the degree required, if a tax . . . reduces them to bare necessaries." Of course, "the number of labourers cannot be rapidly increased or diminished," but "in the case supposed, there is no necessary diminution of demand for labour . . ." [41] since—and now Ricardo is explicit—government's demand for labor must be taken into account.

[34] S, I, 238-39; G, 222-23. [35] S, I, 215; G, 198. [36] S, I, 159; G, 140.
[37] *Idem.* [38] S, I, 161; G, 142. [39] S, I, 165; G, 147. [40] S, I, 218; G, 201.
[41] S, I, 220; G, 203.

It is difficult to escape one or the other of two conflicting interpretations: (1) that Ricardo has only the very short period in mind, practically no more than the first year of the tax, when he says that the tax will "raise wages"; (2) that he is likening the tax to the worsening of conditions of production at the margin that accompanies a resort to poorer soils and more intensive cultivation under the pressure of population growth. Perhaps the inferences suggested in Chapter II above may be utilized at this point: the excess of the market rate over the natural rate of wages in the progressive state implies merely a larger number of children, still at the subsistence level (though this supposition does not fit well with the assertion that laborers cannot increase their race if they are reduced to bare necessities). In these circumstances, a diminution of the worker's wage would force a fairly rapid reduction in the number of persons annually arriving at the working age. But misery would result, and misery is one thing from which the wages tax is absolved. Moreover, the diminution in the growth of the labor force would be a consequence of a slowing down in the rate of capital accumulation, owing to increased governmental use of resources, and there is nothing in this to guarantee an "increase" in wages, in any of the Ricardian senses of that term.

Nor does appeal to the stationary state support Ricardo's assertion that the tax will increase wages; a wages tax introduced in a stationary state would force a retreat by the economy to a less expensive margin of cultivation, through a contraction of population, where the rates of profit and wages after tax would be as before. Wages before tax would have risen, but not at the expense of profits.

Perhaps the most tenable conjecture respecting Ricardo's train of thought is as follows. First, he never did intend his analysis of the wages tax to apply to the stationary state; he showed little interest throughout the *Principles* in exploring such an economy. Second, he wanted to remind the reader on every possible occasion that because of the principle of population a laborer could not usually be expected to reduce the per capita consumption of the members of his family for any length of time, for any purpose whatsoever, even in the progressive state. Third, upon further reflection he concluded that the adjusting factors of malnutrition and early death had no role to play in the first year of a new tax, in view of the accompanying increase in demand for labor by the government.[42]

[42] Cf. the suggestion advanced by Wesley C. Mitchell, as reported in the unauthorized *Lecture Notes on Types of Economic Theory*, I, 157, 158, that the explanation of Ricardo's wages-tax analysis is to be found in "the logical shifts

which a man who tries to build up a theory of economic behavior by Ricardo's method is compelled to resort to." In his chapter on wages, "wages was the one subject that Ricardo was discussing, and when he was discussing wages by itself as a sole problem he could use his eyes, he could recognize the facts of this problem to the full." But in the chapters on "the effects of machinery, ... profits, ... [and] the incidence of taxation ... Ricardo is primarily interested in some other variable [than wages]. ... A person who is working with Ricardo's analytical methods cannot successfully handle a problem with two variables. ... Now, if you are going to suppose that a tax was laid on wages, you could tell nothing about the shifting of the incidence of the tax so long as you keep thinking about the variability of the natural rate of wages [or, we might add, the possibility of the market rate's exceeding the natural rate]. ... But if you suppose for the purpose of this argument that wages is a constant, accepting the 'iron law of wages,' then you can carry through your discussion of a fixed rate of wages with perfectly logical precision." While there is force in this interpretation, it does not call attention to the importance that the short-run influences assumed, in Ricardo's mind, when he came to write the chapter on wage taxation. And it understates the degree of integration that Ricardo achieved between the two chapters. Pantaleoni likewise pays no attention to the government demand factor; he sees Ricardo's incidence doctrine for wage taxation as being based simply on a minimum-of-subsistence assumption. *Teoria della Traslazione dei Tributi*, pp. 271-72. It is something of a mystery why so many authoritative interpreters of Ricardo have passed over in silence the explicit (Chapter XVI of the *Principles*) or the implicit (Chapter IX of the *Principles*) injection by Ricardo of the government-demand factor. See note 43 to Chapter IV above.

CHAPTER XI

WAR FINANCE

The title of Chapter XVII of the *Principles* gives no clue to its chief contribution, a discussion of war finance. The "taxes on other commodities than raw produce" that Ricardo analyzes are treated in the two opening paragraphs, which deal briefly with the taxation of manufactured commodities, and in the latter half of the chapter, which covers the taxation of commodities "at a monopoly price" (certain wines, works of art) and a tax on malt. There the discussion tends continually to revert to the taxation of raw produce.

The first two paragraphs of Chapter XVII merely repeat propositions advanced in earlier chapters, or make explicit what has already been implied, such as the fact that necessaries of the laborer include certain manufactured products. An implied reference to the constant-cost assumption for manufacturing is to be found in Ricardo's denial of Say's assertion that the burden of a manufacturer's tax will be shared between manufacturer and consumer. Say thought that the manufacturer could not make the consumer pay the whole tax levied on his commodity because "its increased price will diminish its consumption." Ricardo charges Say with forgetting his own doctrine, that "the cost of production determines the price." [1]

The next five paragraphs of Chapter XVII present what is still one of the most illuminating brief analyses of borrowing compared with taxation as a method of war and post-war finance. Together with Ricardo's

[1] S, I, 243, note; G, 227, note. Say replied that because of the difficulty of removing capital from one industry to another, the owner would retain some of it in the taxed trade, perhaps for as long as half a century, even though it were earning less than the normal return. Notes on Ricardo, II, 3-4. See also *ibid.*, pp. 32-35. Cf. the note by Ricardo on sunk capital, at the end of Chapter XVIII of the *Principles*, S, I, 261-62; G, 246-47.

article for the *Encyclopaedia Britannica,* "Funding System," (1819) it forms a notable contribution.

1. BACKGROUND OF RICARDO'S ANALYSIS: THE BRITISH WAR DEBT[2]

The public debt was an object of concern in postwar Britain.[3] The Great War with France, 1793-1815, had been financed at first almost entirely by borrowing; not until the end of 1797 did Pitt recommend to Parliament that it do more than provide new taxes only for the interest on the deficit.[4] The capital value of the debt rose from £240 million in 1792 to £839 million in 1817.[5]

The annual debt charge in the postwar period absorbed a portion of the total national expenditures that would be considered alarming today: 54 percent in 1817. To be sure, this ratio was not unprecedented; as Table 4 shows, Britain had been accustomed to devoting from one third to one half of national government expenditures to debt service. Moreover, the charge included a certain amount of outlay for debt redemption, as it covered all payments on terminable annuities (see note on sources to Table 4).[6] Nevertheless, the 1817 percentage was disquieting,[7] if only because the total of government expenditure was so much higher, at least in money terms, than before the war: £59 million

[2] For the geographical scope of the data given here in the text, see Table 4.

[3] See Gottlieb, "The Capital Levy and Deadweight Debt in England—1815-40," *J. Finance,* VIII (No. 1, March, 1953), 34-46.

[4] Kennedy, *English Taxation, 1640-1799,* p. 167.

[5] Much of the debt, however, was in perpetual annuities, and the capital value stated for them was merely the amount that the Government would have to pay if it decided to redeem. Thus a "3 percent" loan, a £3 annuity, floated for £75 (4 percent basis) would be counted in the public debt at £100, the price at which it could be called for redemption. Moreover, a large part of this debt was later purchased by the Government "at thirty and forty per cent. less than the original sum lent to it." Frend, *The National Debt in Its True Colours,* p. 4. Also, it is not always clear whether the figures include government stock held live in the sinking funds.

[6] In one of the new issues of this period, the main unit, £100 in 3 percent stock, was accompanied by the following "douceurs" (sweeteners): an annuity of 13*s.* for 77 years, £25 in 4 percent stock, and four tickets in a lottery for an extra £10 per £1,000 subscribed. This package offering was known as "the Omnium." Pressnell, *Country Banking in the Industrial Revolution,* p. 429. Tayler, *The History of the Taxation of England,* pp. 49-84, presents details of some of the public debt issues; see also Dowell, II, 450-81.

[7] See Shehab, *Progressive Taxation,* pp. 70-71.

in 1817, against some £18 million in 1792.[8] The annual debt charge had risen from £9 million in the latter year to £31 million in 1817. During the period 1815-1823 it was probably not much less than 10 percent of the national income of Great Britain in any of those years and may have exceeded that percentage in some of them.[9]

On the other hand, the Government succeeded in balancing its peacetime budgets, on the average. The accounts for the period are not entirely consistent, but in any event it is clear that the debt outstanding, funded and unfunded together, was either stabilized, or gradually reduced, during the years 1816-1823.[10] This result was achieved in the face of repeal of the income tax in 1816 and the war duty on malt the same

[8] The population of Great Britain increased from about 10.6 million in 1800 to 12.3 million in 1812 and 14.4 million in 1822. See Deane, "Contemporary Estimates of National Income in the First Half of the Nineteenth Century," *Econ. Hist. R.* (2nd series), VIII (No. 3, April, 1956), p. 353, and Dowell, *History of Taxes and Taxation in England,* II, 249: "In 1815 ... the population of the United Kingdom, if we allow rather more than eleven millions for England, two for Scotland, and six for Ireland, numbered between nineteen and twenty millions."

[9] Deane, "Contemporary Estimates of National Income," Table 8, p. 353, estimates the national income of Great Britain at £330 million in 1812 and £288 million in 1822. See also Shehab, *Progressive Taxation,* p. 70, note 4.

[10] Acworth, using data from Parliamentary Paper No. 366 of 1868-69, "which contains not only balanced accounts for all the years from 1688 to 1869 prepared on a uniform basis (except that the accounts previous to 1800 are net, those subsequent to 1800 gross) [apparently, net and gross of cost of collecting taxes], but also a mass of explanatory information on almost every branch of the public finances" (*Financial Reconstruction in England,* p. 139), shows a reduction in the funded debt, for the period 1816-1822 inclusive, of £19.8 million, and of the unfunded debt, of £6.1 million, the total debt falling from £861.1 million to £835.2 million. These figures are net results, after taking into account the amount of funded debt redeemed each year by the sinking fund and by other means, and the amount of stock created. *Ibid.,* p. 140. A table drawn from the same source, however, showing annual surplus and deficit after debt charges but before appropriations to the sinking fund (*ibid.,* p. 137), indicates a heavy deficit in 1816, and thereafter a surplus or deficit ranging only from − £2.1 million to + £3.4 million. The cumulative result for 1816-1823 is − £13.0 million, or, if the deficit of £20.4 million of 1816 is omitted, a surplus of £7.4 million. "The Statutory Sinking Fund amounted at this time [1816 and 1817] to £14 millions," and the Government had hoped to be able to meet it by a surplus of tax revenue over expenditures, instead of floating debt to feed the fund, but this aim they had to forego when the income tax and war duty on malt were repealed. However, "there were certain outside resources to draw upon;" perhaps these explain the reduction of the total debt, 1816-1822. See *ibid.,* pp. 32-33, and, for war indemnities, etc., *ibid.,* pp. 12-19.

Table 4. *NATIONAL GOVERNMENT EXPENDITURE, PERCENTAGE IN DEBT CHARGE, AND DEBT OUTSTANDING: ENGLAND, GREAT BRITAIN, OR UNITED KINGDOM, SELECTED YEARS, 1700-1842*

(money figures in millions of pounds sterling)

	Year	*Country (n.s. = not specified)*	*Total Annual Expenditure*	*Annual Debt Charge*	*Percent, Annual Debt Charge of Total Expenditure*	*National Debt*
I: Data from Dowell	1700	Eng.	3.2[a]	1.2	38	12.5
	1739	Gr. Br.	4.8[b]	2.0	42	46
	1755	Gr. Br.	5.6[c]	2.6	46	72.5
	1775	Gr. Br.	9.6[d]	4.6[e]	48	126
	1792	Gr. Br.	16.8[f]	9.3[e]	55	237[g]
	1815		[h]		[h]	860[i]
	1826	n.s.[j]	51.1[k]	29.2	57	[h]
	1842	n.s.[j]	51.7	29.5[l]	57	[h]
II: Data from Acworth	1792	U.K.	18.3	9.4	51	240
	1817	U.K.	58.7[m, n]	31.4	54	839
III: Data from Hargreaves	1793	Gr. Br.	[h]	9.5	[h]	245
	1815	Gr. Br.	[h]	31.4	[h]	834

Sources: I: Data from: Stephen Dowell, *A History of Taxation and Taxes in England,* II, pp. 68 (1700), 109 (1739), 128 (1755), 163 (1775), 206 (1792), 281 (1826), 323 (1842), and II, 453. II. Data from: A. W. Acworth, *Financial Reconstruction in England, 1815-1822,* pp. 24-25. "Debt charges" apparently includes only interest, not contributions to the sinking fund; but it does include all payments on Terminable Annuities (*ibid.,* 54). The Statutory Sinking Fund amounted to £14,000,000 a year, in 1816 and 1817 (*ibid.,* 32). In 1821, Ricardo said that "the whole of ... [the stockholders'] annual interest amounts only [sic] to £29,000,000," and that "the whole public revenue of the country from which [the stockholders and public officers together] ... are paid amounts only to £54,000,000...." Letter of Sept. 18, 1821, Ricardo to Wheatly, S, IX, 73. III. Data from: E. L. Hargreaves, *The National Debt,* p. 291. The national debt figures refer to "the *unredeemed* capitals of the debt, and no allowance is made for the capital value of the Terminable Annuities." *Idem.*

[a] Includes average for 1698-1700 of military and naval expenditures (£1.3 million).

[b] Includes average for 1736-38 of military and naval expenditures (£1.8 million).

[c] Includes average for 1753-55 of military and naval expenditures (£2.0 million).

[d] Includes average for 1773-75 of military and naval expenditures (£3.8 million).

[e] "Interest," instead of "debt charge."

[f] Includes average for 1790-92 of army and navy expenditures (£6.25 million). The data are presumably for Great Britain.

[g] Dowell, II, 209. For Great Britain.

[h] Not given.

[i] Dowell, II, 249. For the United Kingdom.

[j] Presumably United Kingdom.

[k] Includes average, for unstated years, of military and naval expenditures (£15.0 million).

[l] "Interest ... including management and terminable annuities," instead of "debt charge."

[m] The 1817 figure of £58.7 million includes £5.2 million for cost of collection of revenue, an item not included in the 1792 total of £18.3 million. If the £5.2 million is excluded, the 1817 percentage for debt service rises to 31.4/53.9 = 59 percent, in place of 54 percent. Thus the cost of civil government (national) rose only from £2.7 million in 1792 to £4.4 million in 1817, excluding in both years the cost of collecting the revenue.

[n] "From 1817 till 1854, the year of the Crimean War, public expenditure remained at a figure between £50 millions and £60 millions, excepting in the years 1833 and 1834—in these it fell just below the £50 million mark." Acworth, pp. 25-26.

year, and with the aid of higher excise rates on soap (1816), and on alcoholic drinks, tobacco, coffee, and tea (1819), and increases in some import duties (1819).[11]

Although the interest charge was not growing in money terms in the immediate postwar period, it increased in real terms, as the price level fell steeply, after a brief postwar rise. The Gayer-Rostow-Schwartz index, reproduced here in part,[12] shows a rise from 1815 to 1818, marked by a short decline in 1817, and then a continued fall, until by December, 1822, the wholesale price level index was only 86.3 against 139.3 four

[11] Dowell, *History of Taxation in England,* II, 264-67, and IV, 319.

[12] See Gayer, Rostow, and Schwartz, *The Growth and Fluctuation of the British Economy, 1790-1850,* I, 468, for monthly index of domestic and imported commodities, wholesale. The following items are of particular interest for present purposes (December of year given, except as noted): 1790, 89.2; 1792, 90.1; 1797, 109.1; 1800, 161.2; 1812, 164.4 (peak of all Decembers); 1815, 118.7; 1816, 132.3; 1817, 127.8; 1818, 139.3; 1819, 120.3; 1820, 103.5; 1821, 94.3; 1822, 86.3; 1823, September, 99.3; 1823, December, 99.8; 1824, 106.9. Deane, noting that "modern investigators seem to have found a far greater fluctuation in general price levels than seems to have been apparent to contemporaries," adds: "It may be that their indices are overweighted by those prices which were most sensitive to the effects of war and its aftermath." "Contemporary Estimates of National Income," p. 346.

years earlier. In the month of Ricardo's death it was 99.3.[13] As Pressnell says, "A short boom in 1817-18, and the slump which followed, formed a division between the first [postwar] period, and the next period, which was characterized by resolute progress towards a restoration of the prewar currency, and by deepening agricultural distress. The halting of the deflationary trend in 1822 led into the third period of reflation and boom, which culminated in 1825 with the crisis and subsequent overhaul of the banking system."[14]

Meanwhile, substantial conversion of the debt to reduce the interest charge was not accomplished until 1822.[15]

On balance, the result was an increase in the burden of the debt service in real terms during Ricardo's lifetime. The debt charge came to be regarded as an important cause of agricultural distress, sharing blame with the deflationary pressure thought to be exerted by the return to the gold standard (1819). The government bondholders ("stockholders") became a target for abuse and the subject of proposals designed to force them to part with some of their unjust enrichment.[16] "In this county," writes Ricardo to Trower, in 1822 (from Bromesberrow Place, Ledbury),[17] "they [the "landed gentlemen"] are very favorable to an income tax, because, they say, it would reach the Stockholder," adding, "as if the stockholder was now exempted from his just share of the taxes."[18]

[13] For certain other price indices for the period 1807-1823, see Acworth, *Financial Reconstruction in England, 1815-1822,* p. 141.

[14] Pressnell, *Country Banking in the Industrial Revolution,* p. 470.

[15] Acworth, pp. 128-29; Hargreaves, *The National Debt,* p. 155.

[16] See Ricardo's essay, *On Protection to Agriculture,* S, IV, 228 ff., especially p. 229: "the fund-holder, this devouring monster, as he has been called [by Cobbett] . . . ," and note 1, *idem,* by Sraffa. On opinions as to how the fund-holder had fared as a result of the war, see also Ricardo's *Essay on the Influence of a Low Price of Corn on the Profits of Stock,* S, IV, 39-41; his speeches in Parliament, Feb. 26, 1823, S, V, 251 ff. and June 11, 1823, S, V, 313-14, 320-21; and, in his correspondence, the following letters: Ricardo to McCulloch, June 9, 1816, S, VII, 37-38; Mill to Ricardo, Oct. 6, 1816, S, VII, 75; McCulloch to Ricardo, Nov. 19, 1816, S, VII, 93-94; Ricardo to McCulloch, Dec. 4, 1816, S, VII, 102-106; Ricardo to McCulloch, June 18, 1821, S, VIII, 390; McCulloch to Ricardo, June 21, 1821, S, VIII, 392; Ricardo to McCulloch, June 30, 1821, S, VIII, 396-98; Ricardo to Trower, Aug. 22, 1821, S, IX, 39; and Ricardo to Wheatley, Sept. 18, 1821, S, IX, 73. For some remarks on the opposite case, where prices rise and the fund-holder's power to consume is diminished while that of the capitalist is increased (because the tax burden in terms of commodities is lightened), see Ricardo's letter of May 20, 1817, to Barton, S, VII, 156-57.

[17] The country place of his son, Osman.

[18] Letter of Dec. 14, 1822, S, IX, 246. Could Ricardo have had in mind the

Ricardo's computations led him to believe that the increase in real burden of the debt arising from the monetary reform was not substantial. Writing in April, 1822 (*On Protection to Agriculture*), he asserted that the measures taken for restoration of specie payment by the Bank of England could not account for a greater fall than 10 percent in prices; the rest of the decline, at least for agriculture, was due to abundant harvests. "To that amount [10 percent], taxation has been increased by the measure for restoring specie payment...."[19] And later, in the same essay:

The whole amount of taxes paid to the public creditor and sinking fund, is 36 millions; suppose the other fixed charges to be four millions, then the whole taxation on which the altered value of money has operated, is 40 millions. I estimate the increase 10 per cent, or four millions, which fall on all classes,—landlords, merchants, manufacturers, labourers, and, though last not least,—stockholders.[20]

Quantitatively, then, no case could be made for the proposition that the fund holders were ruining the farmers by their deflationary gains.[21] Qualitatively, the objection was valid; and in the last chapter of the *Principles* Ricardo points out that if the money amount of taxes remains unchanged when money increases generally in value, the result is "undoubtedly to increase the burthens of society."[22]

2. IMMEDIATE EFFECTS OF WARTIME BORROWING

Payment of interest on the public debt, we are told in the opening paragraphs of Chapter XVII of the *Principles*, is not itself "the real expense"; we must look, rather, to the expenditure financed by the loan.[23]

objection raised by William Frend, that stockholders had been unfairly treated by the income tax, with respect to those issues of stock that had been sold under guarantee of tax exemption? Frend, *The National Debt*, pp. 22-28.

[19] S, IV, 228. See also Acworth, Chapter VII, especially pp. 103, 110-11.

[20] S, IV, 262, note. See also the following speeches in Parliament in S, V: 149-50 (April 3, 1822); 165-66 (May 7, 1822); 233-34, 237 (July 10, 1822); and letter of Feb. 20, 1822, Ricardo to Trower, S, IX, 166-67. Cf. the figures on interest and sinking fund contributions in "Sources" note to Table 4 above.

[21] For the hypothetical case where the price of corn would fall because of relaxation of import restrictions, and the consequent implications for the fundholder, see Chapter XIII below, and S, I, 417-21; G, 410-14.

[22] S, I, 423; G, 415. Ricardo makes the same point in his evidence before the House of Commons Committee on the Expediency of the Bank Resuming Cash Payments, S, V, 386.

[23] S, I, 244; G, 228.

When, for the expenses of a year's war, twenty millions are raised by means of a loan, it is the twenty millions which are withdrawn from the productive capital of the nation. The million per annum which is raised by taxes to pay the interest of this loan, is merely transferred from those who pay it to those who receive it, from the contributor to the tax, to the national creditor. The real expense is the twenty millions, and not the interest which must be paid for it.[24]

Ricardo is emphasizing the shift of resources from private use to government use. The shift must occur, whatever means are employed to finance it. In a letter to McCulloch, 1820, he says:

...I fully agree that [the] usual effects [of war] are to destroy or to prevent the accumulation of capital. But I contend that the poor suffer from this dissipation of capital, not on account of the peculiar taxes which are imposed upon them, but on account of the disturbance which it gives to the usual demand for labour .... Destroy that capital by a loan of 30 millions in the year, with only taxes to pay its interest; or raise the thirty millions within the year by taxes on luxuries, or on the necessaries of the poor, and the effect will be the same—the poor will suffer because 30 millions of capital is withdrawn from active employment.[25]

If the government does not borrow to meet the extraordinary expense of war, private persons may have to do so. The heavy war tax imposed by the government may drive individuals to borrow in order to meet their tax bills. "In one case it is a private transaction between A and B, in the other Government guarantees to B the payment of interest to be equally paid by A." [26]

"It is not, then, by the payment of the interest on the national debt, that a country is distressed, nor is it by the exoneration from payment that it can be relieved." [27] Ricardo quotes with approval Say's observations to the same effect, including Say's confirmation of Melon's doctrine of the right and left hands.

Whether war expenditures are met from taxes or from public loans seems, at this point in Ricardo's analysis, to be of no economic consequence, at least with respect to allocation of resources or level of output. To be sure, the particular individuals whose finances are impaired by the method adopted might have made better use of the money from the

[24] *Idem.* In a letter to McCulloch, March 23, 1821, Ricardo says, in passing, "I have a great deal to say on the different effects which follow from a taxation to support expenditure and a taxation to pay the interest of debt, but on which I cannot now write." S, VIII, 360.

[25] Letter of April 8, 1820, Ricardo to McCulloch, S, VIII, 177.

[26] S, I, 245; G, 229. [27] S, I, 246; G, 230.

viewpoint of the whole economy than do those who are spared; in this sense, one of the two methods of financing is probably better than the other. But there is no way of knowing which one it is.

McCulloch thought that the capital given to the state in war loans "would, if it had remained in the hands of the subscribers, have... been chiefly devoted to the increase of fixed capital, or machinery."[28] In McCulloch's view, the Government's use of the money would occasion more immediate demand for labor than would the increase of fixed capital, though being less beneficial in the long run. Ricardo objects to this unfavorable picture drawn, for the short run, of machinery compared with government. "The employment of machinery I think never diminishes the demand for labour—it is never a cause of a fall in the price of labour, but the effect of its rise." This was before he started work on the third edition of his *Principles,* where he inserted the famous chapter "On Machinery." And he continues:

> Loans, then, if made from capital, will be supplied from circulating and not fixed capital particularly if the expenditure of government, even with a slight diminution of capital, should as it generally does increase the demand for people. Fixed capital such as buildings, machinery &c[a]. cannot furnish the means of loans—they, after they are once erected must be employed as capital or thrown by as useless.[29]

The significance of the word "then" in this passage is not evident; Ricardo's statement that loans will be supplied only from circulating capital does not depend on the preceding assertion that the employment of machinery never diminishes the demand for labor. Moreover, McCulloch's point is not squarely met. McCulloch is referring to liquid capital that is about to be embodied in machinery; Ricardo, to capital already sunk in machinery. More important, neither McCulloch's assertion nor Ricardo's response attacks directly the problem of determining which one will make the best use of the money if it is left to him: the potential taxpayer who is spared temporarily if the money is borrowed, or the potential bondholder whose services are dispensed with if war expenditures are covered by taxation.

Ricardo's analysis in the *Principles,* as given up to this point, seems designed chiefly as ammunition against proposals that the national debt be repudiated in whole or in part, or that the interest contracted for be

[28] Quoted by Sraffa, from an article in the *Edinburgh Review,* Jan., 1820, S, VIII, 171.

[29] Letter of March 29, 1820, Ricardo to McCulloch, S, VIII, 171.

reduced, in order to relieve the public distress.[30] "Justice and good faith" alone are sufficient grounds for rejecting repudiation.[31] In addition, no economic gain from such action can be assured, since, as debt interest is not a "real expense," the economic issue is whether "the party exonerated from the payment of the interest of the national debt would employ it more productively than those to whom indisputably it is due," and the answer to this is by no means clear.[32]

But on page 247 of the *Principles,* Ricardo ceases his apparent attempt to minimize the differences between wartime borrowing and wartime taxation. Financing by debt is now contrasted sharply and unfavorably with financing by taxation. Some of the disadvantages of wartime borrowing arise the moment the debt is incurred; they supply arguments against going into debt in the first place. Others develop over the subsequent period of servicing the debt; they furnish reasons for retiring the debt by a capital levy if the country has been so unwise as to finance the war by borrowing. We turn first to the former group.

The first disadvantage of financing a war by borrowing rather than by taxation is that it makes the citizenry less thrifty by blinding them to their true situation.

If the expenses of a war be 40 millions per annum, and the share which a man would have to contribute towards that annual expense were 100 *l.*, he would endeavour, on being at once called upon for his portion, to save speedily the 100 *l.* from his income. By the system of loans, he is called upon to pay only the interest of this 100 *l.*, or 5 *l.* per annum, and considers that he does enough by

[30] McCulloch proposed "to reduce the interest on the national debt in proportion to the fall in the price of corn since the time when the debt was contracted." He later repudiated this proposal. See note 2 by Sraffa, S, VII, 93. The issue is discussed in the following letters: June 9, 1816, Ricardo to McCulloch, S, VII, 37-38; Nov. 19, 1816, McCulloch to Ricardo, S, VII, 93-94; Dec. 4, 1816, Ricardo to McCulloch, S, VII, 102-106; Dec. 6, 1818, McCulloch to Ricardo, S, VII, 351-52; Jan. 3, 1819, Ricardo to McCulloch, S, VIII, 4. See also Acworth, pp. 66-67. Gonner, though acknowledging the "evil ethical effects" and the "grave economic difficulties" that repudiation would bring, seems surprisingly sympathetic to the idea: "But from a purely fiscal point of view, so far as the *one* transaction was concerned, considerable advantages would be derived from shifting the loss from the shoulders of the community in general, progressive and unprogressive classes included, to those of the stockholders, who cannot be regarded as numbered among the more industrial and progressive." G, 231, note 1.

[31] S, I, 245; G, 230. Frend strongly opposed repudiation: "...extinction, as they call it, of the national debt by a spunge. Disgraceful ideas!" *The National Debt,* p. 13.

[32] S, I, 246; G, 230.

saving this 5 *l.* from his expenditure, and then deludes himself with the belief, that he is as rich as before.[33]

We may paraphrase this by saying that a man feels richer with a bond than with a tax receipt, even though the existence of bonds implies future tax payments by virtually everyone.

Ricardo expresses his idea even more forcefully in "Funding System"; it is so well put as to be worth quoting at length:

It would be difficult to convince a man possessed of 20,000 *l.*, or any other sum, that a perpetual payment of 50 *l.* per annum was equally burdensome with a single tax of 1000 *l.* He would have some vague notion that the 50 *l.* per annum would be paid by posterity, and would not be paid by him; but if he leaves his fortune to his son, and leaves it charged with this perpetual tax, where is the difference whether he leaves him 20,000 *l.*, with the tax, or 19,000 *l.* without it? This argument of charging posterity with the interest of our debt, or of relieving them from a portion of such interest, is often used by otherwise well informed people, but we confess we see no weight in it. It may, indeed, be said, that the wealth of the country may increase; and as a portion of the increased wealth will have to contribute to the taxes, the proportion falling on the present amount of wealth will be less, and thus posterity will contribute to our present expenditure. That this may be so is true; but it may also be otherwise—the wealth of the country may diminish—individuals may withdraw from a country heavily taxed; and therefore the property retained in the country may pay more than the just equivalent, which would at the present time be received from it. That an annual tax of 50 *l.* is not deemed the same in amount as 1000 *l.* ready money, must have been observed by every body. If an individual were called upon to pay 1000 *l.* to the income-tax, he would probably endeavour to save the whole of it from his income; he would do no more[34] if, in lieu of this war-tax, a loan had been raised, for the interest of which he would have been called upon to pay only 50 *l.* income-tax. The war-taxes, then, are more economical; for when they are paid, an effort is made to save to the amount of the whole expenditure of the war, leaving the national capital undiminished.[35] In the other case, an effort is only made to save to the amount of the interest of such expenditure, and therefore the national capital is diminished in amount. The usual objection made to the payment of the larger tax is, that it could not be conveniently paid by manufacturers and landholders, for they have not large sums of money at their command. We think that great efforts would be made to save the tax out of their income [this passage seems to imply that they have been consuming, unproductively, a substantial part of their incomes], in which case they could obtain the

[33] S, I, 247; G, 231.

[34] That is, he would save no more than the amount of tax imposed on him; hence he would save much less than if the war were financed at once by taxation.

[35] This seems to be comparative-statics analysis, but it also has historical overtones. See Chapter III above.

money from this source; but suppose they could not, what should hinder them from selling a part of their property for money, or of borrowing it at interest? That there are persons disposed to lend, is evident from the facility with which government raises its loans. Withdraw this great borrower from the market, and private borrowers would be readily accomodated.[36]

Ricardo's concession, evidently made in passing, to the charge-posterity argument is unfortunate ("It may indeed be said .... that this may be so is true ..."). The wealth of the country may increase absolutely, but surely not in relation to what it would have been if the war had been financed by taxes rather than loans. Posterity is harmed by wartime borrowing simply because the postwar stock of capital will be smaller than if heavy war taxation had checked wartime consumption.[37] Ricardo is viewing the stock of wealth at the outbreak of war as being carried forward to the postwar period and supplemented by continued accumulation. The part of the postwar interest and debt redemption charge that is carried by that initial block of wealth will of course be the smaller, the greater has been the accumulation meanwhile. But posterity bears no heavier burden than would have been its lot if less had been saved and accordingly "the proportion falling on the present amount of wealth" had been more—quite the contrary.

Returning now to the 40-millions illustration in the *Principles,* where it is said that the taxpayer believes he is as well off as ever if he manages to save from his expenditure only the £5 annual tax to finance his share —£100—of the newly created national debt:

The whole nation, by reasoning and acting in this manner, save only the interest of 40 millions, or two millions; and thus, not only lose all the interest or profit which 40 millions of capital, employed productively, would afford, but also 38 millions, the difference between their savings and expenditure.[38]

This puts the case too strongly, by slipping into double counting; 40 millions of capital are lost initially, and 38 millions of it that might have been recouped by a diminution of consumption stay lost.

[36] S, IV, 187-88. For a similar analysis, see letter of March 29, 1820, Ricardo to McCulloch, S, VIII, 170; and for some shrewd observations on the prestige value of owning property, even though it be at the price of an annually recurring tax, see letter of Sept. 15, 1820, Ricardo to McCulloch, S, VIII, 238.

[37] See Pigou, *The Political Economy of War,* p. 74. For an extensive discussion of the issue of the relative burdens on the present and future generations, with numerous references to the literature and some analysis of Ricardo's reasoning, see Griziotti, "La Diversa Pressione Tributaria del Prestito e dell'Imposta," in his *Studi di Scienza delle Finanze e Diritto Finanziario,* II, 193-261, reprinted from *Giornale degli Economisti,* March and May, 1917.

[38] S, I, 247; G, 231.

Ricardo is at once too optimistic with respect to the 2 millions of taxes levied for interest and too pessimistic with respect to the 40 millions borrowed. There is no guarantee that the recipient of the interest will not employ it in unproductive consumption;[39] and some part of the 40 million loan would probably be supplied by lenders' restricting such consumption.[40]

A second disadvantage of the policy of borrowing to finance a war is that it removes the threat of heavy taxation, and this threat would make a country "less disposed wantonly to engage in an expensive contest..." Moreover, "if engaged in it," under heavy taxation, "we shall be sooner disposed to get out of it, unless it be a contest for some great national interest." This remarkable assertion appears in Ricardo's article, "Funding System," but not in the *Principles*.[41]

Third, "By war-taxes, we should save many millions in the collection of [postwar] taxes," and "we might get rid of those great sources of the demoralization of the people, the customs and excise."[42] Moreover, there would be no management charges (paid to the Bank of England, presumably) for handling the public debt.[43] The first of these considerations serves also as a reason for a postwar levy to retire the debt. Neither argument appears in the *Principles*.

3. EFFECTS OF SERVICING THE DEBT IN THE POSTWAR PERIOD

Concerned though he was with the immediate effects of financing a war by borrowing, Ricardo was still more disturbed by the problems bequeathed to the postwar period. They appeared so acute that massive

[39] Gonner touches on this point, saying, "The two millions a year represents a tax chiefly paid by the producing class to those who do not produce." G, 232, note.

[40] Malthus thought that for a country to finance a war by taxation "might completely keep down its efforts," a point that Ricardo does not meet; and that "It might every year positively diminish its capital...," to which Ricardo replies, "Do not loans every year positively diminish the capital of the country?" *Notes on Malthus*, S, II, 444. Malthus thought the national debt helped to increase the "middle classes of society"; Ricardo cannot conceive how it could do so. S, II, 445.

[41] S, IV, 186; see also S, IV, 197-200. See also Ricardo's letter to Trower, March 25, 1822, S, IX, 180, quoted in footnote 77 to the present chapter, below. Perhaps Ricardo was merely following Adam Smith: *Wealth of Nations*, Bk. V, Ch. III, C, II, 411; M, 878; cf. "less wantonly undertaken."

[42] S, IV, 190. Frend had a similar view of the excises. *The Principles of Taxation*, p. 9, note.

[43] S, IV, 190.

debt redemption should be undertaken with little delay. Sounding the alarm on this issue in his article, "Funding System," [44] and in his parliamentary speeches and correspondence, Ricardo allows his tone to become uncharacteristically shrill. "This would be the happiest country in the world, and its progress in prosperity would be beyond the power of imagination to conceive, if we got rid of two great evils—the national debt and the corn laws." [45] By paying off the national debt "we should get rid of one of the most terrible scourges which was ever invented to afflict a nation. . . ." [46] In parliamentary debate, Ricardo "would tell his hon. friend, if no means were taken to pay [the debt] off, that he was sleeping on a volcano." [47] To Trower he expresses his fear of "the disadvantages we labour under from the pressure of our enormous debt," [48] and to McCulloch, of "the overwhelming incumbrance which palsies all our efforts." [49] Writing to Sir John Sinclair, Ricardo says, "I would pay [the national debt] off entirely, and never allow any new debt, on any pretence whatever, to be contracted." [50]

If the debt is not redeemed, outright repudiation is all too likely. In the *Principles,* Ricardo predicts that if war breaks out again before the debt is very considerably reduced, all expenses of the conflict will have to be met by taxation, "or we must, at the end of that war, if not before, submit to a national bankruptcy. . . ." [51] As if horrified by the implications of that phrase, Ricardo adds at once, "not that we shall be unable to bear any large additions to the debt; it would be difficult to set limits to the powers of a great nation; but assuredly there are limits to the price, which in the form of perpetual taxation, individuals will submit to pay for the privilege merely of living in their native country." [52] At times, Ricardo is even more pessimistic; he sees repudiation coming, in any event, if the debt is not paid off quickly.

From what I observe I am confident that this [debt redemption by capital levy] will not be the mode in which we shall get rid of the debt. Our burthens may, and will probably, continue to weigh us down for many years to come, but finally

[44] For an account of the circumstances that led to the writing of the article, "Funding System," for the *Encyclopaedia Britannica,* see note by Sraffa, S, IV, 145-46.

[45] Speech in Parliament, May 30, 1820, S, V, 55.

[46] "Funding System," S, IV, 197. [47] Speech of March 6, 1823, S, V, 268.

[48] Letter of Dec. 25, 1815, S, VI, 345. [49] Letter of Feb. 28, 1820, S, VIII, 157.

[50] Letter of May 11, 1820, S, VIII, 187.

[51] S, I, 249; G, 233. See also letter of Dec. 28, 1819, Ricardo to Trower, S, VIII, 147.

[52] S, I, 249; G, 233-34.

they will be forcibly thrown from our shoulders, and the stockholders instead of complaining, with injustice, as I think, that they were not to be paid at 100 for their 3 pcts., will have justly to complain of losing both their principal and interest.[53]

Ricardo was even willing to have the country go through the motions of maintaining a sinking fund in time of war, when total expenditure would almost surely exceed total tax revenue, because he thought the public might thereby be induced to tolerate a somewhat larger tax bill.

If a loan of twenty millions is to be raised annually, while there is in the hands of the commissioners [of the sinking fund] ten millions which they annually receive, the obvious and simple operation should be really to raise only ten millions by loan; but there is a convenience in calling it twenty millions, and allowing the commissioners to subscribe ten millions. ... By calling the loan twenty millions, the public will be induced more easily to bear the taxes which are necessary for the interest and sinking fund of twenty millions. Call the loan only ten millions, abolish, during the war, the very name of the sinking fund in all your public accounts, and it would be difficult to show to the people the expediency of providing 1,200,000 *l.* per annum by additional taxation, for the interest of a loan of ten millions. The sinking fund is, therefore, useful as an engine of taxation....[54]

The heavy taxation needed to service the debt does not, to be sure, put the country at any disadvantage in international trade, but it does lead the taxpayer to consider whether he would not do well to emigrate. Even though the tax revenue flows back into domestic hands as interest payments, still,

it becomes the interest of every contributor to withdraw his shoulder from the burthen, and to shift this payment from himself to another; and the temptation to remove himself and his capital to another country, where he will be exempted from such burthens, becomes at last irresistible, and overcomes the natural reluctance which every man feels to quit the place of his birth, and the scene of his early associations.[55]

But did Ricardo believe that such emigration of capitalists had in fact occurred, in the England of his day, to a degree that accounted in part for the current distress? The evidence on this phase of his thought is conflicting. The country was in a state of great distress, in 1819, chiefly

[53] Letter of Feb. 28, 1820, Ricardo to McCulloch, S, VIII, 158.

[54] "Funding System," S, IV, 172.

[55] S, I, 247-48; G, 232. See also Ricardo's speech in Parliament, Dec. 16, 1819, S, V, 32-33; and his letters of August 7, 1817, to Mill, S, VII, 171; of March 22, 1818, to Trower, S, VII, 259-60; and of March 23, 1821, to McCulloch, S, VIII, 358. Adam Smith had expressed the same fear: *Wealth of Nations,* Bk. V, Ch. III, C, II, 413; M, 880.

because of "the inadequacy of the capital of the nation . . .," and of this, in turn, Ricardo seemed to say, "the national debt, and the consequent amount of taxation, was the great cause," by having induced emigration of capital.[56] But in 1823, writing to Trower, Ricardo said, "I can not agree . . . that taxation and bad government has [*sic*] been the cause of our present difficulties: I believe that under the best possible government, and without taxes, we might have been involved in similar troubles." [57]

Continued heavy taxation of any kind is likely to cause resources to be distributed among the several branches of industry differently from the way in which they would be distributed in the absence of taxation and government expenditure. This will be so, regardless of how earnestly the legislator may strive for what we should call today a "neutral" tax system.[58] The consequence, in Ricardo's view, is an inefficient allocation of resources, resulting in a smaller total product.

Ricardo writes to Trower, in 1815,

> I am every day becoming a greater enemy to the funding system. Besides its other evils it disturbs so cruelly the prices of commodities as to give us a serious disadvantage in all foreign markets. If the supplies were always raised within the year, and if in consequence one class of the people were obliged to borrow from another in order to discharge their quota of the taxes,—a [private] debt as large as the present [public debt] might exist, but the effects would in my opinion be beyond all comparison less injurious.[59]

A very heavy tax during the relatively short period of the war, on the contrary, causes "little permanent derangement . . . to the industry of the country." [60] But this assertion, made in his article, "Funding System," contrasts somewhat with two immediately preceding paragraphs, in which Ricardo defends heavy war taxation against a charge of injustice. It had been objected that such taxation would favor the professional, salaried, and working men, since the huge sums required could be raised only by substantial taxes on propertied individuals. This inequity, Ricardo replies, would soon be eliminated by a movement into the favored activities, which would lower the rates of compensation there. Ricardo seems at this moment unconcerned with the degree of "derangement"—to be sure, it would not be "permanent"—implied in this tax-

[56] Speech of Dec. 24, 1819, S, V, 38. [57] Letter of Jan. 30, 1823, S, IX, 267.

[58] Ricardo was reported as saying in Parliament that the national debt "destroyed the equilibrium of prices . . ." and "hung like a mill-stone round the exertion and industry of the country." Speech of June 9, 1819, S, V, 21.

[59] Letter of Dec. 25, 1815, S, VI, 345. [60] "Funding System," S, IV, 189.

induced shifting of vocations. And the degree of mobility that he assumes in the labor market is extraordinary:

These large taxes, it may be said, must fall on property, which the smaller taxes [to cover the interest charge] now do not exclusively do. Those who are in professions, as well as those who live from salaries and wages, and who now contribute annually to the taxes, could not make a large ready money payment; and they would, therefore, be benefited at the expence of the capitalist and the landholder. We believe that they would be very little, if at all benefited by the system of war-taxes. Fees to professional men, salaries, and wages, are regulated by the prices of commodities, and by the relative situation of those who pay, and of those who receive them. A tax of the nature proposed, if it did not disturb prices, would, however, change the relation between these classes, and a new arrangement of fees, salaries, and wages, would take place, so that the usual level would be restored.

The reward that is paid to professors [professional men?], &c. is regulated, like every thing else, by demand and supply. What produces the supply of men, with certain qualifications, is not any particular sum of money, but a certain relative position in society. If you diminished, by additional taxes, the incomes of landlords and capitalists, leaving the pay of professions the same, the relative position of professions would be raised; an additional number of persons would, therefore, be enticed into those lines, and the competition would reduce the pay.[61]

Service on a war debt necessitated high rates of excise, and these in turn gave rise to smuggling; Ricardo appears to believe that redemption of the whole debt would allow such a lowering of rates as largely to solve the problem of smuggling. By getting rid of the debt, "Should we not get rid of the immorality of smuggling,[62] and of the excise laws? By getting rid of smuggling, should we not benefit trade? For all the profit of the smuggler was a tax on the whole community." [63]

[61] S, IV, 188-89.

[62] In Brussels: "Mrs. Ricardo keeps a keen look out after silk and lace the two commodities in which she appears prepared to lay out all her money. I am incessantly telling her that I will have no smuggling, and if any thing is seized I will be an evidence against her. I cannot satisfy myself that smuggling is not a dishonest and an immoral act, I am resolved to discourage it by every means in my power." Letter of July 17, 1822, in *Journal of a Tour on the Continent,* S, X, 189.

[63] Speech of March 6, 1823, S, V, 268. For another, minor, disadvantage attendant on taxation to service a war debt, see Ricardo's speech of May, 30, 1820, S, V, 54.

4. RICARDO'S PROPOSAL TO REDEEM THE DEBT BY A CAPITAL LEVY

Ricardo's prescription for removing Britain from the perils it faced with its postwar debt was presented in some detail before an unreceptive audience, his fellow members of Parliament. A capital levy of general scope should be imposed: "the whole capital of the country ought to be assessed for the discharge of the public debt."[64] Foreigners would be exempt from the tax.[65] By encouraging redemption of the land tax, the government might obtain additional sums that could properly be applied to reduction of the debt.[66] The debt should be bought in at the market price, then about 70 for the 3 percents, not redeemed at par.[67] Most of the war loans had been raised in a 3 percent stock issued at a heavy discount; the price had been at one time as low as 50.[68] The rate at which the capital levy would have to be imposed if the debt were to be redeemed at par would no doubt have been a significant factor in determining whether to adopt the other alternative, but Ricardo never troubled himself to attempt even a rough estimate of the tax rate necessary, under either mode of payment. This gap in his presentation doubtless reflected, not an attempt to slur over a fact that might have stiffened opposition to his proposal, for Ricardo never lacked forthrightness, but rather a

[64] Speech of Dec. 24, 1819, S, V, 38. Ricardo is reported as opposing the use of a "property tax" for this purpose, although this means would be better than nothing; he is evidently referring to the income tax, which in British tax law bore the title of "property tax" after 1803. In his article, "Funding System," Ricardo proposes a "tax on property," which in this context surely does not mean an income tax (S, IV, 197). See also Ricardo's speeches in Parliament, Feb. 11, 1822, S, V, 126-27; May 16, 1822, S, V, 187; and Feb. 21, 1823, S, V, 249; and his remarks at a meeting in honor of Joseph Hume, Dec. 7, 1821, S, V, 472.

[65] Letter of May 11, 1820, Ricardo to Sir John Sinclair, S, VIII, 187.

[66] Speech of Feb. 21, 1823, S, V, 250; see also speech of Feb. 28, 1823, S, V, 259.

[67] For retirement at market price, see letters of Dec. 19, 1819, Ricardo to Heathfield, S, VIII, 144; Dec. 28, 1819, Ricardo to Trower, S, VIII, 147-48, and Feb. 28, 1820, Ricardo to McCulloch, S, VIII, 157-58. For Heathfield's conversion to Ricardo's views, see Acworth, p. 61. Heathfield was an accountant. For Ricardo's opposition to redemption at par, see his speech of Dec. 16, 1819, S, V, 34. But cf. his brief note of March 5, 1822, to Foster: "I am of opinion that without a breach of national faith, the Government could not, if it had the means, pay off the 3 pcts. Stock at a less rate than one hundred pouds money for every one hundred pounds capital stock." S, IX, 173-74. What had occurred in the two years to induce this reversal of opinion?

[68] Acworth, p. 61.

conviction on his part that if the course of action was correct in principle, is was correct whatever the quantities.[69]

Precisely how the debt could legally be retired at its then market price was not explained by Ricardo; he could not have thought that merely because the market price was at 70, the entire debt could be bought up on the open market at that price, or at an average price close to it.

The whole operation should be carried through in the space of four or five years[70] (or two or three years).[71] According to the Hansard reporter, Ricardo proposed

For the discharge of the public debt ... checks [elsewhere, "a particular paper money," *i. e.*, "exchequer bills"][72] should be issued upon the government to each purchaser [each holder of the public debt],[73] which checks should be kept distinct from the ordinary circulating medium of the country, but should be received by the government in payment of taxes. Thus the debt might be gradually liquidated while the government continued gradually receiving the assessments upon capital to provide for that liquidation. He would not, however, dwell farther upon this chimerical project, as he understood it was considered by every one except himself....[74]

On this latter point, at least, Ricardo was not in error. His proposal "was regarded as a 'wild sort of notion' even by his own friends," remarks Sraffa.[75] Acworth expresses the opinion that when the House of Commons in 1822 "agreed with Baring that the Capital Levy scheme 'though

[69] Certain other advocates of such a levy spoke in terms of rates in (roughly) the 10 to 20 percent range. See Diehl, "Die einmalige Vermögensabgabe," pp. 53-54.

[70] Speech of Dec. 24, 1819, S, V, 39.

[71] In "Funding System," S, IV, 197.

[72] Letter of Sept. 15, 1820, Ricardo to McCulloch, S, VIII, 239.

[73] *Idem.*

[74] Speech of Dec. 24, 1819, S, V, 39.

[75] S, V, xx. See also Lord Brougham's opinion, reproduced *ibid.*, xxxiii; and the extracts from Mallet's diary, reproduced by Sraffa, at S, VIII, 147, note 1; S, VIII, 152, note 2; and S, X, 187, note 1. But Ricardo was not the only one to advocate a capital levy to retire the debt; see the publications cited by Gottlieb, "The Capital Levy and Deadweight Debt in England 1815-40," *J. Finance,* VIII (No. 1, March, 1953), p. 38. For still earlier proposals, see Acworth, Chapter V, Tayler, *History of the Taxation of England,* pp. 50-51, and Hargreaves, *The National Debt,* pp. 31-36. Frend favored only a gradual redemption of the debt; to this end, he proposed a continuing tax on capital and on income, with personal exemptions. The tax on capital would be at the rate of $^1/_5$ of 1 percent the first year, $^2/_9$ of 1 percent the second year, and so on, up to a maximum of 1 percent in the ninth year. *The National Debt in Its True Colours,* pp. 28-29; *Principles of Taxation,* pp. 12-13, 53, 57-61, 66-67.

ingenious in theory and obvious enough, was not very sound for practice,' it was for once in the right, and Ricardo in the wrong." [76]

The alternative method of gradual debt reduction by means of a sinking fund afforded, on the whole, few attractions to Ricardo; experience with sinking funds in Great Britain had disillusioned him, and his willingness, noted above, to countenance a sinking fund in time of war as a means of beneficial deception is a measure of his fear of debt financing. A sinking fund will be raided for expenditures that would not have been made in the absence of the temptation offered by the fund; and, if it is not raided, it is negated by the issuance of new debt, that is, the sinking fund is not accumulated from a true surplus of revenue over expenditure. The net effect is demoralizing: the sinking fund is "pernicious." [77] Ricardo could be "quite easy in recommending the measure of a sinking fund, if they had a different kind of parliament—one that moved in more direct sympathy with the people. He confessed his fear of the present parliament, and its disposition to ministerial compliance." [78]

In any event, "taxes raised in order to pay off debt, ought to be looked upon in a very different light, from those that were raised for the im-

[76] *Financial Reconstruction,* p. 65. Acworth is even a bit patronizing: "Ricardo's indifferent apprehension of the principles of public finance presents, of course, a striking contrast to his brilliant insight into currency problems." *Idem.*

[77] "Funding System," S, IV, 199. See also the following speeches by Ricardo in Parliament (numerals in parentheses are page numbers in S, V): June 9, 1819 (20-21); June 18, 1819 (24-26); June 9, 1820 (62); March 6, 1821 (79-80); April 5, 1821 (101); July 1, 1822 (220-23); Feb. 21, 1823 (250-51); Feb. 28, 1823 (259-66: an important speech, in which Ricardo's objection to a sinking fund is seen not to be based on temporary negation of it by increasing total debt); March 6, 1823 (267); and March 11, 1823 (270-71). See also the following letters: May 28, 1819, to Trower, S, VIII, 32-33; Sept. 25, 1819, to Trower, S, VIII, 78-79; Nov. 1, 1819, to Place, again not objecting to temporary negation, S, VIII, 118-23; Nov. 3, 1819, to Place, S, VIII, 124-25; Nov. 12, 1819, to Trower, S, VIII, 135; Jan. 14, 1821, to Trower, S, VIII, 332; March 5, 1822, to Trower, commenting on (1) Trower's proposal to allow individuals to compound for their "assessed taxes" and to use the capital sums thus obtained to pay off the debt, and (2) Parnell's plan to substitute life annuities for perpetuities by paying slightly more interest, S, IX, 174-75; March 25, 1822, to Trower, "To keep ... [the ministers] peaceable you must keep them poor," S, IX, 180. For a description of sinking fund concepts and practice in Ricardo's England, see Acworth, Chapter IV, and Hargreaves, *The National Debt,* Chapters VI-IX. Frend suggested that borrowing money in order to purchase annuities kept the rate of interest low (*The National Debt in Its True Colours,* pp. 20-21). In general, he did not share Ricardo's distaste for sinking funds.

[78] Speech of March 6, 1823, S, V, 269.

mediate services of the state. The one, we might be considered as paying to ourselves; the other was for ever lost to us." [79]

Ricardo sees no insuperable problems posed by his prescription of massive postwar taxation for prompt redemption of the public debt. In one place or another, he disposes of a number of objections that have been offered to his plan.

First, would not the special levy unfairly excuse from taxation those who possess little or no capital, but enjoy substantial incomes? This group would be relieved from the otherwise annually recurring taxation needed to service the debt.

Neither in the *Principles* nor in the essay, "Funding System," does Ricardo bring up this point when discussing his postwar levy; in a letter to McCulloch, he refers his friend to the statement in "Funding System" on heavy taxation while war is in progress. But we have seen that Ricardo there implies an extreme degree of mobility into and out of the professions; he seems himself uncertain of the strength of his argument on this score:

> Another objection which I have heard, and which I think is the most plausible, is that it would relieve from taxation all those who are in professions, and whose incomes are derived from wages or salaries. This I have endeavored to answer in my article ["Funding System"], but it requires your talents to give it weight.[80]

Second, would not property values be gravely impaired as business firms, holders of securities, and other taxpayers put their properties on the market in order to raise cash with which to pay the tax? But "the answer is plain: the national creditor, who is to receive [cash, in redemption of his government bond] ... will want an investment for his money, and will be disposed either to lend it to the landholder, or manufacturer, or to purchase from them a part of the property of which they have to dispose." [81]

Third, would not capital be destroyed? No, replies Ricardo, far from destroying capital, debt redemption by means of a tax on capital might well increase it. The erstwhile holder of government stock would almost

[79] Speech of Feb. 21, 1823, S, V, 250. [80] Letter of Sept. 15, 1820, S, VIII, 238.

[81] S, I, 248; G, 233. See also speech of Dec. 16, 1819, S, V, 34-35. For critical analyses of Ricardo's disposal of this problem, see Edgeworth, *A Levy on Capital for the Discharge of Debt*, pp. 15-16, and Gottlieb, "The Capital Levy," pp. 42-45. Ricardo did not refer to the argument advanced by Frend, *Principles of Taxation*, pp. 66-67, that the burden of a tax on capital would be lightened for the stockholder by a decline of commodity prices as taxes hitherto collected to service the debt were reduced, and for the landlords, as reductions in land taxes increased the value of land.

surely use the proceeds as capital, and the taxpayer might well pay some of the tax "out of revenue."[82] If instead he paid it "out of capital," there would be no net decrease of capital, only a transfer.[83] If total capital is increased, the country is better off; those who fear a glut of commodities from too much capital do not understand Say's law. Indeed, given free foreign trade, the country need not stop growing even when it has pushed cultivation to the point where the marginal dose barely returns the capital invested, for further increments of capital can be invested in manufactures and sent abroad for food: "it is difficult to say where the limit is at which you would cease to accumulate wealth and to derive profit from its employment."[84] The boundary line of the stationary state is fixed by the ability of the world, not the country in question, to produce foodstuffs.

The fourth and fifth objections are legal or administrative.

Fourth, would not the capital levy be evaded? "Some precautions," Ricardo admitted, "would be necessary to prevent people from concealing their property, or sending it abroad, to withdraw it from a share of the burden."[85] But he offers no concrete suggestions.

Fifth, what of Mr. Brougham's objection, that "The effect of such a measure would be to place the property for five years at the mercy of all the solicitors, conveyancers, and money-hunters, in the country"?[86] Change the law of title, says Ricardo.

> By act of Parliament the title of all land sold for the purpose of raising money necessary for the landholders contribution should be held to be a perfect title, whatever might be its insufficiency for any other sale. Suppose A paid it, and that hereafter it should appear to be the property of B—B would suffer no injury or injustice, for had he been before possessed of it, he must have equally with A, have [*sic*] contributed the portion to which the act has given a good title. No landed property in the country would have a better title, and it would therefore be preferred above all other by a purchaser—it could never require the interference or advice of low attornies.[87]

If, in place of a capital levy carried out in one year, we suppose a heavy tax to be imposed for a few years and then ended abruptly, there might

[82] For the meaning of this term, see Chapter III above.

[83] This reasoning is developed in discussing the rapid growth of a sinking fund, but it is of course applicable also to the capital levy proposal. "Funding System," S, IV, 177. See also *ibid.*, 183-84.

[84] S, IV, 179.

[85] Letter of Sept. 15, 1820, Ricardo to McCulloch, S, VIII, 239.

[86] Speech of Dec. 24, 1819, S, V, 41.

[87] Letter of Sept. 15, 1820, Ricardo to McCulloch, S, VIII, 239.

arise a problem of floor stocks. Ricardo did not discuss this issue in connection with a modified capital levy, but rather as a problem to be faced under the funding system. The abrupt reduction in tax is presumed to occur when the debt has finally been liquidated by sinking fund accumulations. Ricardo deals with the allegation that merchants with goods on their shelves on which excise or other taxes have been paid will suddenly be exposed to competition from tax-free goods that are produced as soon as tax repeal takes effect. Would such merchants be in danger of bankruptcy? The solution is simple, in principle; let a floor-stocks refund be given, just the reverse of the usual floor-stocks tax that is imposed when a manufacturers' excise is introduced.[88]

In summary: Ricardo's attitude toward a national debt, internally held, is composed of somewhat conflicting elements, but perhaps they can be largely reconciled by recalling that he feared two evils: repudiation, with all that would be implied for future dealings with the state; and heavy taxation.

> I cannot agree with you [Ricardo writes to McCulloch in 1819] in thinking so lightly of the extinction of our national debt. I should agree to no other means of getting rid of it, but by paying it, which would relieve us from many of the evils you enumerate, such as the encouragement to gambling &ca. We agree as to the evil, but not as to the remedy.[89]

5. ERRORS IN BUCHANAN AND SAY ON FARM TAXATION

The remainder of Chapter XVII of the *Principles*[90] is of quite a different order from the brilliant analysis of war taxation and borrowing; it offers nothing new to the reader who has followed Ricardo's doctrine of agricultural land rent, and who understands the implications of that doctrine for the taxation of agriculture. After some remarks on what he understands by "monopoly price," Ricardo deals with certain erroneous theorems propagated by Buchanan and Say.

Buchanan asserted that agricultural taxes affect rent and not prices of raw produce; he believed that all portions of raw produce yield a rent. Say appeared to assume, somehow or other, that the supply of agricultural produce from any given plot of land was quite inelastic with regard to price. Ricardo, working with his marginal concept, demolishes

[88] "Funding System," S, IV, 176, 182.

[89] Letter of Jan. 3, 1819, S, VIII, 4. But even McCulloch's remedy, Ricardo seemed to say to himself, as he jotted down notes on Malthus's *Principles of Political Economy*, would be better than nothing at all. See S, II, 451.

[90] S, I, 249-56; G, 234-41.

Say as readily as he does Buchanan. There is little point in attempting to summarize the work of demolition, or the lengthy passages that Ricardo reproduces from Buchanan, Say, and Smith. The parties to the contest are too far apart in their basic ideas of how the economic system works, and Ricardo's opponents are too inconsistent, too unskilled in system-building, to make the controversy fruitful. Thus Ricardo is able to agree completely with Smith and Buchanan when they lower their sights from grand generalizations about some widespread tax like one on raw produce to a common-sense analysis of a tax on a small item like malt. All three economists agree that a tax on malt will not lower the price of barley or barley land, but will instead be paid by the consumer of beer; no distinction is drawn between completely inelastic and partly inelastic demand.[91]

Ricardo's reference to "monopoly price" needs to be read in the light of his implicit definition of commodities not produced under unrestrained competition.[92] To him, a monopoly price is that price that clears the market of commodities or objects, the quantity of which cannot be increased by human effort. Significantly, he admits that "corn and raw produce" may themselves sell at a monopoly price, "for a time" [93]—presumably between one harvest and the next. He even visualizes a hypothetical condition in which they sell at a monopoly price "permanently": "when no more capital can be profitably employed on the lands, and when, therefore, their produce cannot be increased." [94] No practical importance can be attached to the latter statement, however; Ricardo at one point challenges Buchanan directly on this issue: "Is it possible that Mr. Buchanan can seriously assert, that the produce of the land cannot be increased, if the demand increases?" [95] But he notes that

[91] S, I, 252-54; G, 237-39. In 1816 the extra or war duty of 2*s*. per bushel of malt had been repealed, at a cost of about £2.7 million. Acworth, p. 33. Cf. C. W. Armstrong, of Newcastle, in *Thoughts on the Expediency of a Relaxation of the Corn Laws* (1822), p. 53, commenting on Ricardo's analysis: "But is it not perfectly evident, that a high tax upon malt must restrain, or lessen, the consumption of barley, and, therefore, be injurious to the landholder? No doubt the tax upon malt falls principally upon the consumer, but why?—Because the land adapted to barley might still be advantageously employed in the production of something else, and barley for malting would not be raised at all, were it not to afford the ordinary amount of rent."

[92] S, I, 12; G, 6-7. [93] S, I, 250; G, 235. [94] S, I, 250-51; G, 235.

[95] S, I, 252, note; G, 237, note. The argument Say employs to defend Buchanan, based chiefly on the possibility that all parcels of land in use are yielding rent (a possibility that Ricardo never denied), shows how little of the theory of rent Say had grasped, especially the concept of the intensive margin. Notes on Ricardo, II, 23-25. See Appendix B below.

in the unlikely if not impossible event that the produce of the land should encounter some kind of absolute block to its increase, the proceeds of the last dose of labor and capital would be large enough to allow payment of some rent, so that "At such a time too, any tax which may be imposed on the farmer, will fall on rent, and not on the consumer." [96]

[96] S, I, 251; G, 235.

CHAPTER XII

TAXES AND BOUNTIES ON FOREIGN TRADE

Foreign trade, oddly enough, is not treated in that group of eleven chapters on taxation that follow Ricardo's exposition of his economic system in Chapters I to VII of the *Principles* and that precede the somewhat disjointed chapters making up the last third of the book. Instead, the reader who has assimilated the discussion of poor rates in Chapter XVIII [1] must push on through analyses of sudden changes in the channels of trade, the distinction between value and riches, and the effects of accumulation on profits and interest, before regaining tax territory with "Bounties on Exportation and Prohibitions of Importation" (Chapter XXII). And he finds that this chapter is apparently not constructed with a view to complementing the core chapter, "On Foreign Trade" (VII) to the degree in which the chapter "Taxes on Wages" (XVI), for example, complements that "On Wages" (V).[2] But the gap is partly closed by analysis in other chapters of the *Principles,* and by a large amount of material in the other volumes of the *Works and Correspondence.*

[1] The material in that chapter is covered at the end of Chapter V above and in note 55 to the present chapter, below.

[2] Chapter XXII was apparently written not as a part of the "'inquiry into the subject of Taxation' (as [James] Mill described it)," but as one of what Sraffa terms "the group of controversial chapters which follows the chapters on taxation." S, I, xviii. Torrens, in claiming to be the originator of the doctrine of comparative costs, notes that "These principles Mr. Ricardo adopted into his very valuable work upon Political Economy and Taxation; and they form, in some measure, the ground-work of his chapters upon foreign trade, and of his doctrines on the influence of taxation upon the export and import of commodities." *An Essay on the External Corn Trade,* 4th ed., pp. vii-viii. See Seligman, "On

It is therefore convenient to analyze first Ricardo's treatment of export bounties and import duties in Chapter XXII, then to turn to corresponding fragments elsewhere in the *Principles* (VII, "On Foreign Trade"; XVIII, "Poor Rates"; XIX, "On Sudden Changes in the Channels of Trade"; and XXV, "On Colonial Trade"), and finally to interpret the material on taxes and bounties on foreign trade in the essay, *On Protection to Agriculture* (1822), all with the aid of numerous references to Ricardo's correspondence and speeches in Parliament. A few paragraphs at the end of the chapter cover Ricardo's brief treatment of domestic bounties financed by domestic taxes in his Chapter XXIII, "On Bounties to Production."

Ricardo did not treat explicitly of import bounties or export duties.

1. THE ANALYSIS IN CHAPTER XXII OF THE *Principles*

Right at the beginning there is internal proof that Chapter XXII was written as one of the "controversial" group rather than as a complement to the magnificent chapter "On Foreign Trade." Ricardo operates for several pages on an assumption that agriculture is in a state of constant returns, where the production of corn can be increased with no increase in the real cost per bushel. He is absorbed in refuting erroneous doctrine on export bounties and import duties. To this end, he finds it convenient to simplify the cost assumptions in order to focus attention on the mistake made by Adam Smith and Francis Horner in supposing that there would be no permanent movement of capital from manufactures into agriculture under an export bounty on corn.

Another peculiarity of Chapter XXII is the small amount of space devoted to import duties or import prohibitions. By far the larger part of the chapter has to do with export bounties, again because of Smithian error: "Perhaps in no part of Adam Smith's justly celebrated work, are his conclusions more liable to objection, than in the chapter on bounties."[3] The vehemence of this criticism may appear somewhat surprising, in view of the fact that Smith had reached a conclusion quite acceptable

Some Neglected British Economists," in *Essays in Economics*, p. 75; also in Econ. J., XIII (Nos. 51, 52), Sept. and Dec., 1903 (cf. Viner, *Studies in the Theory of International Trade*, pp. 441-44). The phrase "in some measure" must be emphasized; it is in fact surprising how little use Ricardo makes of the doctrine of comparative costs in analyzing the effects of import and export duties and bounties.

[3] S, I, 304; G, 288. See also the letter of Dec. 2, 1816, Ricardo to Mill, S, VII, 100, and of Dec. 16, 1816, Mill to Ricardo, S, VII, 107-108.

to Ricardo, namely, that no bounties should be granted on exports.[4] But Ricardo's reaction, after all, should not astonish us; his deepest interests were intellectual; faulty reasoning upset him as much as mistaken ends.

Smith had said that a bounty on the export of corn would not lead to an increase in the production of corn. To Ricardo this was nonsense.[5] There was agreement on the initial effect: The price of corn in the domestic market would rise, as corn was exported to meet the foreign demand enhanced by the fall in the foreign price consequent on the bounty. But then, said Smith, the money wages of labor would rise, including, of course, farm labor, because wages must rise when corn prices rise. Hence farming would be no more profitable than before. No, says Ricardo, the rise in the price of corn is a temporary rationing device, pending the flow of more capital from manufacturing into agriculture to meet the increased foreign demand for corn. Wages cannot rise to meet this temporary increase in the price of corn; if they did, they would push corn prices still higher by enabling laborers to bid more for corn. Anyway, Ricardo adds, corn is not the only necessary that the laborer consumes, hence, even supposing wages to rise enough to allow the worker the same market basket, they would rise by a smaller percentage than corn had risen. Thus, in either event, agricultural profits would increase for the time being.

As to manufacturers, they too would have to pay higher wages, said Smith, but would recoup this added cost by a rise in prices, hence their profits, too, would remain as before. According to Smithian doctrine, with profits in both agriculture and manufacturing back at their initial, pre-bounty levels, no motive would exist for a transfer of capital from the latter sector to the former.

This last step in Smith's reasoning is the greatest error of all, Ricardo implies. A rise in wages—granting that one occurs—affects not the prices of manufactured goods, but the level of manufacturing profits. "If no more labour than before be required to bring either cloth or gold to market, they will not vary in relative value . . .,"[6] that is, in natural value; and the export bounty on corn has no tendency to raise the market price of manufactures. Consequently, whether or not wages rise following the increase in corn price resulting from the export bounty, agricultural profits will for a time exceed those in manufacturing. If wages do rise,

[4] Ricardo spoke against export bounties in Parliament; see speech of June 8, 1820, S, V, 57-58.

[5] S, I, 304; G, 288-89. See also S, I, 413-14; G, 406-407.

[6] S, I, 309; G, 294.

they affect both sectors equally, but only in the agricultural sector will the price of the product increase for the time being, and it will do so whether or not wages rise.

Smith's fundamental error is thus his belief that "The money price of labour, and of every thing that is the produce either of land and labour, must necessarily rise or fall in proportion to the money price of corn."[7] This leads to the absurd conclusion that corn can never vary in value relative to all other commodities, even when margins of cultivation are in the area of diminishing returns. It is this error that vitiates the otherwise excellent analysis of "A writer in ... the Edinburgh Review" (Francis Horner)[8] on export bounties for corn.

Ricardo of course agrees that if the agricultural sector is experiencing diminishing returns at the margin, instead of being an industry of constant cost as he at first assumes, the higher corn price consequent on the enhanced foreign demand will be permanent, and wages will rise. But prices of manufactures will be unchanged, hence the initial differential in favor of agriculture remains, until the flow of capital into farming eliminates it by pushing farm production out to a more expensive margin. Rent will increase; landlords will benefit.

Smith thought that the "country gentlemen" were mistaken in hoping that they could increase their incomes under a bounty on the export of corn, or by restricting its importation; they were reasoning falsely by analogy with the manufacturing class, which did gain by such devices, applied to manufactures. But it was Smith who was mistaken, not the country gentlemen, in Ricardo's view. Owners of agricultural land always benefit from measures that push cultivation out to more expensive margins, thus increasing total corn rent. Manufacturers, on the other hand, operating under constant cost, have nothing permanent to gain by export bounties or import duties on manufactured goods.

By an extension of Ricardo's reasoning, the country gentlemen would be harmed by a bounty on the export of manufactures, or a restriction of their imports. Capital would flow into domestic manufacturing, from agriculture; the diminished production of corn would be accompanied by withdrawal to less expensive margins of cultivation, and a decrease

[7] S, I, 308; G, 293. Ricardo italicizes this passage. There are two slight inaccuracies in the passage as quoted by Ricardo. The correct reading, with corrections indicated by italics, is: "The money price of labour, and of every thing that is the produce either of land *or* labour, must necessarily *either* rise or fall in proportion to the money price of corn." *Wealth of Nations,* Bk. IV, Ch. V, C, II, 12; M, 477.

[8] S, I, 302 (see note 1 by Sraffa); G, 286.

in total corn rent. Ricardo did not, however, carry his analysis this far.[9]

Finally, Smith was wrong in concluding that his assumed rise in the general price level would permanently lower the volume of exports. Failure to maintain exports would lead to a specie flow abroad, which would pull the price level down to a point where international trade could continue in approximately the former volume.[10] And since a bounty on the export of corn would not force a rise in all prices anyway, Smith's point is not only erroneous, but irrelevant.

However, Ricardo implies that it is not entirely irrelevant. "It must ... be conceded, that the tendency of a bounty on the exportation of any commodity is to lower in a small degree the value of money. Whatever facilitates exportation, tends to accumulate money in a country. ..."[11]

Gonner seems somewhat partial to Smith in concluding that Ricardo "is hardly fortunate in his attempt to present the views of Smith, keen sighted though his criticism may be."[12] In any event, the reasoning summarized above is what Ricardo believed Smith's to be, and the vigor of Ricardo's reaction is a measure of the errors he thought he detected.

As always, Ricardo is concerned over the inefficient allocation of productive resources that results from interference with trade.

> The sole effect of high duties on the importation either of manufactures or of corn, or of a bounty on their exportation, is to divert a portion of capital to an employment, which it would not naturally seek. It causes a pernicious distribution of the general funds of the society—it bribes a manufacturer to commence or continue in a comparatively less profitable employment.[13]

Total product decreases.

Ricardo indicates how this loss of product may be computed.

> It is the worst species of taxation, for it does not give to the foreign country all that it takes away from the home country, the balance of loss being made up by the less advantageous distribution of the general capital. Thus, if the price of corn is in England 4 *l.* and in France 3 *l.* 15 *s.* [so that, initially, we may assume, no corn is exported to France from England], a bounty of 10 *s.* will ultimately reduce it to 3 *l.* 10 *s.* in France, and maintain it at the same price of 4 *l.* in England. For every quarter exported, England pays a tax of 10 *s.* For every quarter imported into France, France gains only 5 *s.*, so that the value of 5 *s.* per quarter is absolutely lost to the world, by such a distribution of its funds as

[9] S, I, 311-14; G, 296-99. [10] S, I, 310-11; G, 295-96.

[11] S, I, 316; G, 301. [12] G, 288, note.

[13] S, I, 314; G, 298-99. See also letter of May 20, 1822, Ricardo to Trower, S, IX, 197-98.

to cause diminished production, probably not of corn, but of some other object of necessity or enjoyment.[14]

During the Great War with France, imported wheat was subject to a scale of duties varying with the domestic price of wheat, in place of the nominal duty that had prevailed for some time before. Under the duties, and the exceptions made to them, the price of wheat fluctuated widely, on occasion reaching heights that induced the conversion of good pasture land into mediocre wheat land. With the coming of peace, a price collapse threatened, and Parliament, dominated by rural landowners, enacted in 1815 a new corn law that prohibited the import of wheat for domestic use unless the price exceeded 80 shillings a quarter (10 shillings a bushel). Above that price, wheat could be imported entirely free of duty,[15] and in the bad crop years of 1817 and 1818 a considerable amount was in fact imported.[16] "Under the law of 1815 no duty was paid at all, and it is impossible to calculate the indirect effects of a non-existent tax." [17]

McCulloch and Ricardo had a brief exchange on this issue, *i. e.,* to how large a tax is the system of corn-law restrictions equivalent? McCulloch calls Ricardo's attention to the computation he has published in an article in the *Edinburgh Review:*

I thought it was the best way in order to render the article *frappant,* and that you know either is or ought to be the great object of a Reviewer, to endeavour to shew the effect of the Corn laws as a tax. I do not think I have at all exaggerated the burden they impose on the country, and an arithmetical statement of the kind in question, if it is nearly correct, will make a more powerful impression than the best conducted argument.[18]

Ricardo was not wholly in agreement.

You say that the corn laws have the same effect as if a tax of 24 millions and a half were levied from the consumers of corn for the public expenditure. I should

[14] S, I, 314; G, 299.

[15] See Dowell, *History of Taxation and Taxes In England,* IV, 9-11.

[16] Acworth, *Financial Reconstruction in England, 1815-1822,* p. 80. For a critical appraisal of the wartime and postwar corn laws, see Alfred Marshall, *Industry and Trade,* pp. 77-83.

[17] C. R. Fay, "Corn Prices and the Corn Laws, 1815-1846," Econ. J., XXXI (No. 121, March, 1921), 19. Fay continues: "The calculation was no easier with the sliding scale introduced by the Act of 1828; for most of the corn was held up until the duty was nominal. In 1838, for example, out of 1.7 million quarters of imported wheat, 1.2 were entered at the duty of 1 *s*."

[18] Letter of March 19, 1820, McCulloch to Ricardo, S, VIII, 165. The article was in the *Edinburgh Review,* Jan. 1820, Art. IX. S, VIII, 165, note 2, and 172, note 2, by Sraffa.

add, provided the 24 millions and a half received by the landholders be all expended as revenue, and no part be added to capital.[19]

To this McCulloch replies,

I did not mean to say that the $24^1/_2$ millions went into the pockets of the landlords. This sum goes partly into their pockets, but by far the largest share, perhaps two thirds must be expended *en pure perte* on the increased cost of production.[20]

On the latter point, Ricardo is of course in general agreement with McCulloch; we have just noted his quantification of loss from a bounty; and in the *Principles* he says that the "mercantile system," the "whole aim" of which was "to raise the price of commodities, in the home market, by prohibiting foreign competition ...," was "no more injurious to the agricultural classes than to any other part of the community. By forcing capital into channels where it would not otherwise flow, it diminished the whole amount of commodities produced ...,"[21] and damaged manufacturers along with others.

Accordingly, both before and after enactment of the corn law of 1815, Ricardo denounced restriction as an impediment to economic progress. In Chapter XXII of the *Principles* his views on this score are clear enough, but their impact is softened by the attention Ricardo devotes to his doctrinal differences with Smith, Say, and Horner. His intense dislike for the corn laws can be perceived more readily in the two essays of 1815 and 1822, and in his Parliamentary speeches and letters.[22] The

[19] Letter of March 29, 1820, Ricardo to McCulloch, S, VIII, 172.

[20] Letter of April 2, 1820, McCulloch to Ricardo, S, VIII, 176.

[21] S, I, 316; G, 301.

[22] In addition to passages cited later in this chapter, and the two essays, *An Essay on the Influence of a Low Price of Corn on the Profits of Stock* (1815), S, IV, 1-41, and *On Protection to Agriculture* (1822), S, IV, 201-70, with notes by Sraffa, see speeches in Parliament: Dec. 16, 1819 (S, V, 33); Dec. 24, 1819 (S, V, 38); May 12, 1820 (S, V, 47); May 25, 1820 (S, V, 47-48); May 30, 1820 (an important speech; S, V, 48-56); Feb. 8, 1821 (S, V, 73-75); Feb. 26, 1821 (S, V, 78-79); March 7, 1821 (an important speech; S, V, 81-91); Feb. 18, 1822 (S, V, 133, 137-38); April 3, 1822 (an important speech; S, V, 151-54). See also the following letters: June 26, 1814, Ricardo to Malthus (S, VI, 108-109); July 6, 1814, Malthus to Ricardo (S, VI, 109-12); July 25, 1814, Ricardo to Malthus (S, VI, 113-15); Aug. 5, 1814, Malthus to Ricardo (S, VI, 115-18); Aug. 11, 1814, Ricardo to Malthus (S, VI, 119-21); Feb. 6, 1815, Ricardo to Malthus (S, VI, 173); Feb. 13, 1815, Ricardo to Malthus (S, VI, 177-78); Feb. 8, 1822, Ricardo to McCulloch (S, IX, 158); May 7, 1822, Ricardo to McCulloch (S, IX, 192); and letters cited in subsequent footnotes to this chapter.

latter sources also testify to his opposition to other types of protective duty.[23]

2. ANALYSIS ELSEWHERE IN THE *Principles*

Four other chapters in the *Principles* (VII, XVIII, XIX, XXV) contain isolated analyses of certain types of import-export measures.[24]

Only one passage in Chapter VII, "On Foreign Trade," specifically refers to import or export duties or bounties. Two others mention taxes in general. All three are concerned with the effect of such fiscal measures on the flow of monetary metals, that is, on the general level of money prices in the country taking the action, and in other countries.

> Beside the improvements in arts and machinery, there are various other causes which are constantly operating on the natural course of trade, and which interfere with the equilibrium, and the relative value of money. Bounties on exportation or importation, new taxes on commodities, sometimes by their direct, and at other times by their indirect operation, disturb the natural trade of barter, and produce a consequent necessity of importing or exporting money,[25] in order that prices may be accommodated to the natural course of commerce; and this effect is produced not only in the country where the disturbing cause takes place, but, in a greater or less degree, in every country of the commercial world.[26]

> ... we are now endeavouring to shew that besides the ordinary variations in the value of money, and those which are common to the whole commercial world, there are also partial variations to which money is subject in particular countries; and in fact, that the value of money is never the same in any two countries, depending as it does on relative taxation, on manufacturing skill, on the advantages of climate, natural productions, and many other causes.[27]

[23] See the following speeches in Parliament: April 5, 1821 (S, V, 103-104) and April 16, 1821 (S, V, 111), on timber duties; March 20, 1822 (S, V, 146-47), on duties on tallow and candles; May 17, 1822 (S, V, 189-90), on sugar duties, favoring West Indies against East Indies; June 20, 1822 (S, V, 218-19), on duty on butter; May 7, 1823 (S, V, 291), on duty on tallow again; May 12, 1823 (S, V, 294), on tallow once more; May 22, 1823 (S, V, 297-301), on sugar duty, favoring West Indies; June 6, 1823 (S, V, 305-306), on discriminatory duties on merchandise carried in foreign vessels. See also Ricardo's remarks before the General Court of the East India Company, June 12, 1822, and March 19, 1823 (S, V, 475-83), on sugar and cotton. On the timber duties, see J. Potter, "The British Timber Duties, 1815-60," *Economica* (New Series), XXII (No. 86, May, 1955), 122-36.

[24] As to Chapter XVIII of the *Principles,* see note 55 below, this chapter.

[25] Thus we have seen (note 11 above) that "the tendency of a bounty on the exportation of any commodity is to lower in a small degree the value of money."

[26] S, I, 141-42; G, 122-23. [27] S, I, 143; G, 123-24.

...although taxation occasions a disturbance of the equilibrium of money, it does so by depriving the country in which it is imposed of some of the advantages attending skill, industry, and climate.[28]

These passages reflect Ricardo's view that the monetary metals are distributed "in such proportions amongst the different countries of the world, as to accommodate themselves to the natural traffic which would take place if no such metals existed, and the trade between countries were purely a trade of barter."[29] The trade of barter would in turn be determined by the workings of the law of comparative costs.

For the purpose of making explicit Ricardo's views on the effect exercised on the country's gold stock by a general increase in taxation, that is, by an increase in the proportion of the country's labor force assigned to nonproductive ends, the working of the factors determining the amount of gold stock in the country may be illustrated as follows.

If both wine and cloth can be produced in Portugal with fewer hours of labor than in England, and abstracting from costs other than labor, but if Portugal's advantage in this respect is greater for wine than for cloth, then under a barter system trade will develop, Portugal becoming an exporter of wine and an importer of cloth. Under a money economy, if the hourly wage rate in terms of gold is the same in Portugal as in England, no Portuguese consumer has reason to import cloth; he can get it more cheaply from Portuguese workmen. England's imports must be paid for by shipping gold to Portugal, until the hourly gold wage is encugh higher in Portugal than in England, that the Portuguese consumer finds it less expensive to import cloth from England even though the cloth carries a larger labor-hour cost than if made in Portugal. At the same time, the higher hourly gold wage in Portugal will not bar the English consumer from importing wine rather than purchasing it domestically, in view of the very low labor-hour content of the Portuguese wine. In general, then, the low-cost country, in terms of labor input, has the higher hourly gold wage; if England and Portugal contain the same number of workers working the same number of hours, and if the velocity of circulation is the same in the two countries, Portugal must have a larger gold stock than England.

The significance of all this for tax policy is that an increase of taxation indicates an increase in the proportion of the economy's manpower that is used up in nonproductive ends; more man-years of labor must be supported than before, if the country is to turn out a given amount of final product, such as wine. The effect of an increase in taxation is therefore

[28] S, I, 145; G, 126. [29] S, I, 137; G, 117.

the same as if the productivity of those workers engaged directly in wine production fell for some reason, such as a worsening of the climate. In the case supposed here, the level of output of the final product would decline, as workers were shifted from vineyards to the army. Exports would diminish, gold would flow out. Thus the increase in the economy's cost of production represented by the increase in taxation would cause a decline in the country's share of the total stock of gold. The hourly wage in terms of gold would fall.[30]

Ricardo could therefore say, in testimony before a Parliamentary committee in 1819, "I think every tax has some influence upon the value of the precious metals, and either occasions their exportation or importation," and "... when I say the value, I do not mean the value as compared with paper, but the value as compared with commodities generally."[31]

And in "Funding System": "An injudicious tax may induce us to import what we should otherwise have produced at home, or to export what we should otherwise have received from abroad. . . ."[32] The context does not seem to presuppose import duties or export bounties.

And in the *Principles:* "A new tax too may destroy the comparative advantage which a country before possessed in the manufacture of a particular commodity..."[33]

In Chapter XIX, "On Sudden Changes in the Channels of Trade," Ricardo finds one occasion when an import duty on corn will be advisable, though only for a short period.

A country which normally imports food but which must become self-sufficient during a war, should, he argues, reopen the gates to foreign foodstuffs only gradually after the war. The farmers and landlords will then be willing to expand food production in the event of another war, without demanding a substantial addition to the price as a premium

[30] That added taxation will lower the gold stock is an inference drawn from Ricardo, not a paraphrase of an explicit statement, for he nowhere specifies the direction of movement, under a tax. For a critique of the Ricardian analysis, not with particular reference to taxation, see Viner, *Studies in the Theory of International Trade,* pp. 311-18; Angell, *Theory of International Prices,* pp. 68-70. For the contribution by Nassau Senior to the problem (but without specific reference to taxation), see Senior, *Three Lectures on the Cost of Obtaining Money,* Lecture I, "On the Cost of Obtaining Money."

[31] "Minutes of Evidence Taken Before the Secret Committee on the Expediency of the Bank Resuming Cash Payments," March 4, 1819, S, V, 374.

[32] "Funding System," S, IV, 189.

[33] Chapter XIX, "On Sudden Changes in the Channels of Trade," S, I, 263; G, 248.

against risk of ruin upon the return of peace. "Notwithstanding, then, that it would be more productive of wealth to the country, at whatever sacrifice of capital it might be done, to allow the importation of cheap corn, it would, perhaps, be advisable to charge it with a duty for a few years." [34]

Ricardo's recommendation seems to be on grounds not of equity, but of avoiding what would otherwise be a heavy insurance premium. He does not consider the problem of comparing the amount of potential wealth lost by continuing protection for a few years with the size of that premium.

In his chapter "On Colonial Trade" (XXV), Ricardo's analysis is almost entirely in terms of a "monopoly" of the trade of the colony by the mother country, which usually seems to imply, in this discussion, complete prohibition rather than partial obstruction by duties or bounties. However, the general conclusion, so far as it has relevance for such fiscal measures, is clear: Ricardo believes (regretfully, we may assume) that a mother country can extract some benefit for herself by distorting the trade relations of her colonies with the rest of the world. "Who can doubt, for example, that if England were the colony of France, the latter country would be benefited by a heavy bounty paid by England on the exportation of corn, cloth, or any other commodities?" [35] An explanatory reference is made to the numerical example given in Chapter XXII.[36]

The only other specific references to taxes or bounties in Chapter XXV are one in a quotation from Adam Smith, concerning the exemption of goods from duties under a commercial treaty,[37] and a reminder to the reader that taxes and bounties affect the international distribution of the monetary metals.[38]

3. ON PROTECTION TO AGRICULTURE

Ricardo devotes much of the essay, *On Protection to Agriculture*, published April 18, 1822,[39] to ascertaining the causes of the low price of corn prevailing in England. He attributes a fall of 10 percent to "the

[34] S, I, 268; G, 253. Ricardo wrote to Sir John Sinclair that he would continue the existing corn laws while his proposed capital levy to retire the war debt was being paid. Letter of May 11, 1820, S, VIII, 187.

[35] S, I, 339; G, 326. [36] See above, Section 1, this chapter. [37] S, I, 340; G, 327.

[38] S, I, 343; G, 330. With respect to Canada, see speech of March 13, 1822, S, V, 144-45.

[39] Note by Sraffa, S, IV, 203.

alteration in the value of the currency;" the rest of the decline has resulted from "a succession of good crops, ... an increasing importation from Ireland, and ... the increase of tillage which the high prices and the obstacles opposed to importation during the war occasioned?"[40] Taxation is not responsible for agricultural distress (see Chapter IV above).

Taxation and bounties should meet the test of economic neutrality: "It is for the interest of the public that [the home producer] should not be driven from a trade which, under a system of free competition, he would have chosen, and to which he would adhere if every other commodity were taxed equally with that which he produces."[41] "The greatest benefit results to a country when its Government forbears to give encouragement, or oppose obstacles, to any disposition of capital which the proprietor may think most advantageous to him."[42] "We cannot now help living under a system of heavy taxation, but to make our industry as productive to us as possible, we should offer no temptations to capitalists, to employ their funds and their skill in any other way than they would have employed them, if we had had the good fortune to be untaxed, and had been permitted to give the greatest development to our talents and industry."[43] The same prescription is put forcefully in a letter to McCulloch, two years before the essay was written: "My principle is that we may impose restrictions to restore things to their natural relation, but never to destroy it."[44]

Accordingly, cost-increasing forces that operate throughout the economy, like a "rise of wages, a tax on income, or a proportional tax on all commodities," furnish no occasion for import duties; they

> do not alter the relative value of goods, and therefore they do not subject us to any disadvantage in our commerce with foreign countries. We suffer indeed the inconvenience of paying the tax, but from that burthen we have no means of freeing ourselves.[45]

A tax that falls especially on the producers of a particular commodity is another matter. It justifies a countervailing import duty.

The distinction between the two cases had been developed clearly in

[40] *On Protection to Agriculture*, S, IV, 259-60. Cf. Sir Edward West's rebuttal of this argument. He attributed the fall in price wholly to "the diminished employment, and consequently diminished wages of the labouring classes ..." *Price of Corn and Wages of Labour* (1826), p. 16.

[41] *On Protection to Agriculture*, S, IV, 217.

[42] *Ibid.*, S, IV, 218. [43] *Ibid.*, S, IV, 244.

[44] Letter of March 29, 1820, S, VIII, 173.

[45] *On Protection to Agriculture*, S, IV, 217.

an exchange between Malthus and Ricardo in 1815. Malthus had asked: "If you would lay a tax on foreign corn on account of a tax on our own; does not the same principle apply to the indirect taxes that raise the price of labour?"[46] To this, Ricardo had replied:

> I think not because a tax on corn will raise the price of corn twice, once on account of the tax and a second time on account of the rise of wages, but as this second rise is common to all things in which labour enters and will be corrected by a new value of money, it will not be of long duration. The indirect taxes which only raise the wages of labour produce I think the same effects as the second rise in the price of corn of which I have just been speaking. Whenever a tax bore with unequal effect on the land, when it did not affect labour bestowed in other employments a countervailing duty on importation should I think be also imposed.[47]

The protectionists were objecting that "If the farmer ... could, before taxation [of the laboring classes], and the high wages which are the effect of it, compete with the foreign grower of corn, he can no longer do so now he is exposed to a burthen from which his competitor is free."[48] Their error, to Ricardo, was in deducing that prices would rise, following the rise in wages. Under Ricardian monetary theory, prices could not rise in these circumstances. Hence there would be no need for an import duty to ward off foreign competition. And even if farm prices did rise under pressure from the rise in wages, so would the prices of all other products domestically produced. In that event (the possibility of which Ricardo does not admit) there would still be no need for an import duty on corn alone. All commodities would need protecting duties; but this would help no one. "To impose protecting duties on all commodities would be absurd, because nothing would be gained by it; it would in no way alter the relative value of commodities; and it is only by altering the relative value of commodities that any particular trade is protected; not merely by an alteration of price."[49]

If the commodity subjected to discriminatory domestic taxation is an article of export, another type of countervailing action is called for: a

[46] Letter of March 24, 1815, to Ricardo, S, VI, 202.

[47] Letter of March 27, 1815, to Malthus, S, VI, 206. See also Ricardo's response to McCulloch's fears that Ricardo's proposals on countervailing duties and transitional duties were equivalent to giving up the principle of free trade: letters of March 13, 1821, McCulloch to Ricardo, S, VIII, 351-55, and of March 23, 1821, Ricardo to McCulloch, S, VIII, 355-57.

[48] *On Protection to Agriculture,* S, IV, 213.

[49] *Ibid.,* S, IV, 214.

drawback.[50] How does a drawback differ from a bounty on exportation, to which, as we know, Ricardo is opposed?

However large the aggregate amount might be of the drawback given to the exporter it would only be returning to him a tax which he had before paid, and which he must have to place him in a fair state of competition in the foreign markets, not only with the foreign producer, but with his own countrymen who are producing other commodities. It is essentially different from a bounty on exportation, in the sense that the word bounty is usually understood; for by a bounty is generally meant a tax levied on the people for the purpose of rendering corn unnaturally cheap to the foreign consumer, whereas, what I propose, is to sell our corn at the price at which we can really afford to produce it, and not to add to its price a tax which shall induce the foreigner rather to purchase it from some other country, and deprive us of a trade, which, under a system of free competition, we might have selected.[51]

Was the agriculture of England indeed subject to heavier taxation than any other trade in the economy, or than the average of all trades (Ricardo never made his measuring rod very explicit), and thus in need of a countervailing duty and drawback? At first, Ricardo thought not,[52] but later changed his mind. Writing to McCulloch in March, 1820, he says,

You must not have the least fear of my compromising my opinion on the Corn laws, I have already spoken out, on that subject, and shall again, if I can muster up courage to speak at all. You know however that I have always maintained that the growers of corn in this country should be protected from any peculiar burdens to which they may be subject, but then they should shew that they are so burthened—the fact I believe is that every other trade is taxed in a proportion greater than the growth of corn."[53]

A few weeks later, in a speech in Parliament, Ricardo gave ground a little. The essential details in this slight shift of position can be noted only by quoting in full the Parliamentary reporter: Ricardo

was surprised that the right hon. gentleman[54] who had expressed such liberal principles of political economy, and had so freely declared himself against the

[50] *Ibid.*, S, IV, 217. See also letter of March 23, 1821, Ricardo to McCulloch, S, VIII, 359.

[51] *On Protection to Agriculture,* S, IV, 243-44.

[52] To be sure, as early as the first edition of the *Principles* Ricardo speaks favorably of such a duty for a country that imposes the tithe: S, I, 179; G, 159-60. This passage is cast in general terms, however, and does not broach the question of whether non-agricultural branches of the economy are similarly subject to special domestic burdens of their own. Great Britain is not specifically mentioned.

[53] Letter of March 29, 1820, S, VIII, 172-73.

[54] Mr. Robinson, President of the Board of Trade (note by Sraffa, S, V, 44).

policy of our commercial restrictions, had yet made a reservation in favour of the corn laws. They were necessary, he said, to protect the agricultural interests; and he (Mr Ricardo) would admit the validity of the argument, provided it could be made to appear that the agriculturists suffered more burthens than other classes of the community. But what were their peculiar burthens? They did not suffer more from the malt-tax, or from the leather tax, or from any other tax with which he was acquainted, than any other class of men. These taxes were common to all, and all felt their pressure alike. But the poor-rates [the tax levied by the parish to support the poor], it was said, operated on them as a peculiar burthen. Well; if the poor-rates were really more oppressive to them than to other classes, and tended to raise the price of grain, he would recommend a countervailing duty on the importation of foreign corn, to the amount of the operation of that cause. He allowed that the poor-rates actually raised the price of corn, because they fell upon the land, and operated as a burthen solely upon agriculturists.[55] But if, while this burthen was felt by them, other classes of the community felt equal burthens, they were put to no disadvantage, and ought to receive no protection. He was fully prepared to admit, that the necessity for supporting the poor constituted the only or the best apology for the corn-laws. Tithes likewise were another burthen to the landed interest, and tended, he would allow, to a certain extent, to raise the price of grain, and for these he would have no objection to allow a countervailing duty. There was this difference between poor-rates and tithes—that while we must support the poor, whatever was the produce, the church could only claim a tenth of what was raised; for, whatever was the deficiency of produce, the clergy must conform to their proportion, and find it sufficient for their support.[56]

Two years later, when he wrote *On Protection to Agriculture,* Ricardo had completed his change of view. "The growers of corn are subject to some of these peculiar taxes, such as tithes, a portion of the poors' rate, and, perhaps, one or two other taxes, all of which tend to raise the price

[55] Cf. S, I, 258; G, 243: "The poor rates are professed to be levied on the farmer in proportion to his rent.... But I believe that it is not true; the poor rate is not levied according to the rent which a farmer actually pays to his landlord; it is proportioned to the annual value of his land, whether that annual value be given to it by the capital of the landlord or of the tenant." See also speeches in Parliament of May 8, 1821, S, V, 113-14; and of May 9, 1822, S, V, 178. The manufacturer, on the other hand, is rated "only according to the value of the buildings in which he works, without any regard to the value of the machinery, labour, or stock which he may employ." S, I, 260; G, 245. In some parishes, at least, the rates were substantial; Trower speaks of them as being "enormously high—more than 20/- in the pound on about $^2/_3$ of the real rent." Letter of Nov. 9, 1817, to Ricardo, S, VII, 209. For data on amounts expended by Poor Law authorities, see Acworth, pp. 129-30.

[56] Speech of May 8, 1820, S, V, 44-45.

of corn, and other raw produce. . . ." [57] He suggests that a countervailing import duty of 10 shillings a quarter would be more than ample, and that the drawback should be "to the same amount", [58] or perhaps somewhat less:

A duty of 10 *s.* per quarter, on importation, to which I wish to approach, is, I am sure, rather too high as a countervailing duty for the peculiar taxes which are imposed on the corn grower, over and above those which are imposed on the other classes of producers in the country; but I would rather err on the side of a liberal allowance than of a scanty one; and it is for this reason that I do not propose to allow a drawback quite equal to the duty.[59]

The countervailing duty should, of course, not be based on the difference in price of corn in England and abroad.[60]

In speeches in Parliament made shortly after the essay *On Protection to Agriculture* was published, Ricardo repeated the formula of 10 shillings duty and 7 shillings drawback,[61] but he made more specific his belief that he had been too generous to the farmer in suggesting a 10-shilling duty. As reported in Parliament, "in allowing a duty of 10 *s.*, he thought that he had made an ample allowance; and he had made that allowance, too, on the principle, that all the poor-rates as well as all the tithes fell exclusively upon the agricultural interest. He now stated, however, that the agricultural interest was not entitled to the full allowance of all the poor-rates, inasmuch as a part of them was paid by the manufacturers, although much the greater part, he would allow, was paid by the agricultural classes. He was persuaded that if he had kept to that principle, the allowance to the agricultural interest would not have been more than 7 *s.*" [62] And in the preceding year, in a letter to McCulloch, Ricardo had set the proper duty at 8 shillings.[63]

Mr. Brougham, in May, 1822, objected in Parliament that Ricardo had understated the degree of discriminatory taxation borne by agriculture, in view of the fact that "the agriculturists, more than any other

[57] S, IV, 217-18. [58] S, IV, 243.

[59] S, IV, 264. In a speech of May 30, 1823, Ricardo protested against a measure that would grant some exemption from the tithes in Ireland without a countervailing duty to English agriculture. S, V, 304.

[60] Speech of May 25, 1820. S, V, 47-48. Cf. note 50 to Chapter XVI below.

[61] Speeches of April 29, 1822, S, V, 156-59; May 7, 1822, S, V, 172-75; and May 9, 1822, S, V, 177-78.

[62] Speech of May 9, 1822, S, V, 178. See also letter of May 21, 1822, Ricardo to Cowell, S, IX, 200.

[63] Letter of July 8, 1821, S, IX, 8. For Ricardo's criticism of a proposal for a permanent duty of 20 shillings with a drawback of 18 shillings, see his letter to Trower, May 20, 1822, S, IX, 197.

class, were affected by the taxes imposed on those commodities which were consumed by the labouring classes, because more labour was used in producing the same amount of produce in value by the farmer, than by the manufacturer, or any other individual."[64] Ricardo replied that he agreed with the principle involved: "If the noble lord could substantiate such a proposition, he [Ricardo] would agree that he was entitled to the allowance he demanded." But Ricardo "doubted whether the proportion of labour was greater in agriculture than in manufactures,"[65] and gave his reasons for so thinking.

Will not imposition of a countervailing duty raise the price of the article in question, to the domestic consumer, from what is was under the discriminatory domestic tax and no countervailing duty? Does not that fact tell against the countervailing duty? In addressing himself to this question, Ricardo supposes that the domestic consumers purchase the commodity—cloth, in this illustration—entirely from domestic producers if there is neither tax nor duty, entirely from abroad if there is tax but no duty, and entirely from domestic producers if there are both tax and duty. The price of cloth is higher in the second case than the first, and higher still in the third.

The rise in price from the second case (tax, no duty) to the third (tax and duty) does not reflect a movement to a less advantageous position for the economy as a whole, for in the second case the state gets no revenue from the cloth trade, while in the third case it does. Best of all, we may infer, is the first case (no tax, no duty), but if there is to be a burden on cloth consumers, the state might as well benefit. "In the second case [the consumer of cloth] pays more than in the first, but all he pays in addition is not received by the State, it is an increased price caused by difficulty of production, which is incurred, because the easiest means of production are taken away from us, by being fettered with a tax."[66]

In the same vein, Ricardo seems to hint, in a somewhat cryptic passage in one of his letters to Malthus (1818), that repeal of a tax on domestic [?] corn along with abolition of restriction on importation would not be all pure gain; the loss of revenue to the state should be considered. Ricardo had just read Malthus's *Inquiry into the Nature and Progress of Rent,* and after four paragraphs of remarks not concerned with taxation he adds:

I will try if I have a little leisure to put my thoughts on this subject on paper,

[64] S, V, 176. [65] Speech of May 9, 1822, S, V, 177. [66] S, I, 179-80; G, 160.

and shall attempt to shew that the effects of a tax and of rent are very different as far as regards importation. It may be economical to grow corn if its price is raised merely by taxation, as by importing it a part of the tax would be wholly lost to the country [impor]ting. No such consideration should influence us w[ith regar]d to rent being lost.[67]

What of the transition period, from the existing system of prohibition (up to a price of 80 shillings a quarter) to Ricardo's 10-shilling countervailing duty and 7-shilling drawback? Ricardo believed that an abrupt change to the new system would be too damaging to the farmer, and suggested that when the price of corn reached 70 shillings a quarter—it was 50 shillings at the time[68]—the country be opened to imports of corn subject to a duty of 20 shillings, this duty then to be reduced 1 shilling a year until the 10-shilling level was reached.[69] He would also allow domestic sale of foreign corn then in bond, whenever the price of corn reached 65 shillings, subject to a duty of 15 shillings.[70]

On his proposals for a transition period, Ricardo met with resistance from one of his disciples. McCulloch wrote, "Would it not be better to abolish the restriction at once? I incline to think that this would be preferable to a gradually diminishing rate of duties." [71] To which Ricardo replied:

I do not quite agree with you about reverting at once to a free trade in corn. The price of corn is indeed low, but land has not gone out of cultivation. It would I think be desirable that the process by which it should be made to go out should be very slow—you would otherwise make the situation of the farmer irretrievable—he would be ruined past redemption.[72]

While believing that the prevailing low price of corn was attributable largely to abundant harvests and imports from Ireland, Ricardo could still hold the corn laws accountable to some degree. Any system that in ordinary years forces the domestic price of corn to a level notably above the world price leaves the farmer that much more vulnerable in the event of an abnormally large harvest. The farmer can get no relief from the glut by exporting a part of the crop, until the price has fallen by a very

[67] Letter of Feb. 6, 1815, S, VI, 173. Brackets indicate MS torn (note 3, Sraffa).
[68] S, V, 155, note 2 by Sraffa.
[69] Speech of April 29, 1822, S, V, 158-59. Ricardo expected that no corn would be imported under the 20-shilling duty. Speech of May 7, 1822, S, V, 173.
[70] Speeches of April 29, 1822, S, V, 158, and May 7, 1822, S, V, 173.
[71] Letter of April 17, 1822, S, IX, 188.
[72] Letter of May 7, 1822, S, IX, 194-95.

substantial percentage, to the level of foreign prices.[73] A protected agriculture is therefore subject to greater fluctuations in the prices of its products than one operating under free trade. Ricardo even tries to persuade the landlords that they would be better off with lower, but steadier, rents.[74]

At the other extreme, in the event of an unusually short domestic crop, the farmer is also vulnerable. Under the ordinary type of import restriction, a substantial fixed duty of a certain amount per bushel, the farmer is compensated in part for the short crop, since he obtains a higher price than he would get in the absence of a duty. Although foreign corn may be imported, if the price rises far enough, the imports will not drive the price down immediately. But under the peculiar system in force in Great Britain, the farmer is likely to be injured, for the corn law "prohibits importation till the price rises to 80 *s*.," and then, when the price reaches that level,

> the ports are now open for three months, for an unlimited importation of foreign wheat, duty free. With prices somewhat about 40 *s*. per quarter on the Continent, in average years, the temptation to import into this country, during the three months that the ports are open, must operate to the introduction of an enormous quantity.... By prohibitory duties [the home grower] is encouraged to employ his capital on the poorer lands of this country, which require a great expense for a small produce; and when he has an unusually short crop, and most stands in need of a high price, he is all at once exposed to the free competition of the grower of corn on the Continent ...[75]

[73] *On Protection to Agriculture,* S, IV, 241. See also speeches of Feb. 8, 1821, S, V, 73-74; April 3, 1822, S, V, 151; May 9, 1822, S, V, 182-83; and Feb. 26, 1823, S, V, 256.

[74] *On Protection to Agriculture,* S, IV, 238.

[75] *Ibid.,* S, IV, 242. See also speeches of April 3, 1822, S, V, 151; April 29, 1822, S, V, 157; and May 7, 1822, S, V, 172. For a summary of the economic background of the corn law of 1815, see Acworth, pp. 124-25. Fay has said that "the nobles of Poland and Russia grew [wheat] as a speculative surplus to be sold for what it would fetch on the best foreign market. This, hitherto [before 1815], had been England. In 1814, for example, England was computed to consume two-thirds of the total corn exports of Poland and to warehouse for a time a part of the remainder .... A rise of price, sufficient to open the English ports [under the corn law of 1815], was followed by an immediate flow from the Baltic ports of wheat which had been waiting patiently for its only good market. Sufficiently prolonged, low prices in England, instead of being met by a disposal of the produce elsewhere, might quite likely force the Polish nobility to revert to the production of staples such as rye and to retire from foreign production. The position for the moment seems to have been that rare one in which a tax imposed by the importing country would have been paid mainly by the for-

Consequently, Ricardo concluded that, if permanent protection were to be granted to corn (a step to which he remained, of course, unalterably opposed), a simple duty would be preferable to the existing system of alternate prohibition and free importation.[76] At first he seemed to lean toward a graduated duty, which would rise, in shillings per quarter, as the market price of corn fell below a price, say 80 shillings a quarter, at which the duty would be zero.[77] Later, Ricardo was reported in Parliament as opposed to that type of tariff.[78]

The fear of emigration from England of capital—and capitalists—that was aroused in Ricardo by the generally heavy taxes imposed to service the war debt[79] comes to the surface again as he contemplates the economic consequences of import duties on corn.

> There is no other way of keeping profits up but by keeping wages down.[80] In this view of the law of profits, it will at once be seen how important it is that so essential a necessary as corn, which so powerfully affects wages, should be at a low price; and how injurious it must be to the community generally, that, by prohibitions against importation, we should be driven to the cultivation of our poorer lands to feed our augmenting population.
>
> Besides the impolicy of devoting a greater portion of our labour to the production of food than would otherwise be necessary, thereby diminishing the sum of our enjoyments and the power of saving, by lowering profits, we offer an irresistable temptation to capitalists to quit this country, that they may take their capitals to places where wages are low and profits high.[81]

Protective duties on manufactures cannot justify protection for agri-

eigner. . . ." "Corn Prices and the Corn Laws, 1815-1846," *Econ. J.*, XXXI (No. 121, March, 1921), 22-23. Provided, we may infer, that the tax was not so large and not so long in force that it became equivalent to "sufficiently prolonged, low prices in England." Fay adds: "From 1815 right down to 1828 the thought of the Polish corn piled up in bond and ever piling up was a nightmare to the British farmer. Forth it would pour, at the first opportunity, heedless of the price it fetched. From the behaviour of the bonded corn under abnormal conditions it was erroneously inferred that there was a limitless supply growing in Poland which would be offered at the same low price were the trade in corn free." *Ibid.*, p. 23.

[76] Letters of March 2, 1821, Ricardo to Trower, S, VIII, 350, and of March 23, 1821, Ricardo to McCulloch, S, VIII, 359.

[77] Letter of Feb. 28, 1820, Ricardo to McCulloch, S, VIII, 158-59. See McCulloch's comment, letter of March 19, 1820, to Ricardo, S, VIII, 166.

[78] Speech of March 7, 1821, S, V, 82-83.

[79] See Chapter XI above, Sec. 3.

[80] "Keeping wages down" does not, in Ricardian terminology, in this context, imply a smaller market basket; quite the contrary. See Chapter II above.

[81] *On Protection to Agriculture,* S, IV, 237.

culture; Ricardo quotes Lord Grenville for support. Moreover, some of the duties on manufactures were in large part countervailing.[82]

So convinced, perhaps so obsessed, is Ricardo by his principles, that he persuades himself there is no case for protection for agriculture even if war is to be feared. The food-exporting countries upon which England would be depending would not dare to shut off exports to England, even, it is implied, if they were active enemies, because of the distress that such a measure would bring to their own farmers and landlords.[83] Had Ricardo forgotten what he had written in Chapter XIX of the *Principles?*[84]

4. SYMMETRY BETWEEN IMPORT AND EXPORT DUTIES

In the closing sentences of a letter to Malthus in 1815, Ricardo apparently anticipates the doctrine of symmetry between import and export duties.[85] The paragraph in which this passage occurs deserves quotation in full:

Sir F. Burdett and some others think that the high price of our corn is owing to enormous taxation, and that it ought not, nor cannot fall, without oppression to the landholders till our debt is diminished. If I could convince myself that any part of the price of corn was owing to taxation I should be in favour of a protecting duty to that amount. But if he were right, the high price would not be accompanied by high rents and by the cultivation of inferior lands. These I consider as unequivocal marks of the high price being caused by wealth and a scarcity of fertile land. Indeed my theory leads me to think that no taxes but those directly on the land, or on its produce, would raise the price of corn and even such taxes would have no effect if all exportable commodities were taxed in the same degree, for a tax on exportable commodities in a country which

[82] *On Protection to Agriculture,* S, IV, 250-52. See also speech of June 4, 1822, S, V, 197-98.

[83] *On Protection to Agriculture,* S, IV, 266. Such an event in fact occurred, but apparently from a different motivation. As Fay describes it, Napoleon tried to drain England of bullion, by encouraging exports of corn, especially from Poland, and prohibiting imports of British manufactures. But English export smugglers maintained the balance of trade. "Free Traders in later years recalled these feats of British industry when they wished to show the improbability of a total cessation of imported food, even in the event of war." Fay, "Corn Prices and the Corn Laws, 1815-1846," *Econ. J.,* LXII (No. 121, March 1921), p. 21.

[84] S, I, 266; G, 251-52.

[85] See, e. g., Lerner, "The Symmetry between Import and Export Taxes," in *Essays in Economic Analysis,* pp. 123-33; originally published in *Economica* (New Series), III (No. 11, Aug. 1936), 306-13.

imports corn does not act very differently from a duty on the importation of corn.[86]

5. DOMESTIC BOUNTIES FINANCED BY DOMESTIC TAXES

In his short chapter, "On Bounties on Production" (XXIII), Ricardo puts current policy questions aside to speculate on the consequences of a purely domestic tax-and-bounty combination, simply "to observe the application of the principles which I have been endeavouring to establish, with regard to [1] the profits of stock, [2] the division of the annual produce of the land and labour, and [3] the relative prices of manufactures and raw produce." [87]

First, as to profits. If a tax is levied on the production of all commodities other than corn to finance a bounty on corn (but gold production is implicitly exempt), prices change accordingly. The physical quantities of corn and non-corn commodities taken by consumers remain unchanged, for, "as there would be no alteration, either in the amount of capital or population, there would be precisely the same demand for bread and manufactures." [88] Price elasticity appears not to exist, or is negligible. Consumer disposable income remains unchanged, since the government dispenses in bounty what it collects in tax. There being no change in the physical amounts of corn and non-corn production, the price of corn will fall by enough and the prices of other commodities will rise by enough, to make profit rates in the two sectors equal, after tax and bounty.

Aggregate money profit might change, however. All depends on the composition of the worker's market basket. If the market basket consists mostly or entirely of the bountied commodities, the worker would of course benefit from the tax-bounty combination, if he could maintain his advantage. But this he cannot do. Wages will fall correspondingly, and profits rise, "to requite [the employer] ... for his payment ... of his labourer's [tax] ...," [89] that is, the tax (or further tax) the laborer would be paying if he spent as much on taxed goods as on untaxed goods.

At no point in this chapter are the qualifiers "natural" or "market" applied to profit rates or wage rates. It appears that Ricardo thought that the changes in wage rate and profit rate would occur at once; the implicit reasoning for the short period is analogous to that in the chapters on

[86] Letter of March 9, 1815, S, VI, 181.

[87] S, I, 321; G, 306. [88] S, I, 322; G, 307. [89] S, I, 323; G, 308.

raw-produce taxation and wage taxes.[90] We are to infer that the employer has less capital available because he must spend more of his accumulation on his own consumer goods. The employer, then, like the laborer, has a certain minimum standard of living that he will maintain—a certain "station in life"? An exception, worth only passing mention, is the "miser," who may avoid a commodity tax "by not consuming."[91]

The landlord, in this setting, affords Ricardo an opportunity for another elegant application of rent doctrine, analogous to that made in his raw-produce analysis. "On the same principles that a tax on raw produce would lower the corn rent of land, leaving the money rent unaltered, a bounty on production, which is directly the contrary of a tax, would raise corn rent, leaving the money rent unaltered."[92] The landlord would pay more for his manufactured goods, less for his corn; he would "probably"[93] be neither richer nor poorer in real terms. Indeed, even "probably" seems certainly out of place, in this economic system; if workers and employers are each neither richer nor poorer than before, the remaining claimant of the nation's produce, the landlord, must also be precisely as well off as before.

Similar reasoning on the three parties' shares is applied to the case where corn is taxed to finance a bounty on other commodities. "In this case too there would be a complicated measure producing no national result whatever."[94]

The conclusions are explicitly said to hold only for an isolated economy. If there were foreign commerce, production of the bountied commodities would expand, at the expense of the taxed commodities: "the natural distribution of employments" would be altered, "to the advantage indeed of the foreign countries, but ruinously to that in which so absurd a policy was adopted."[95]

[90] See Chapters IV and X above. [91] S, I, 324-25; G, 309.
[92] S, I, 322; G, 307. [93] *Idem.* [94] S, I, 325; G, 310. [95] S, I, 326; G, 311.

CHAPTER XIII

TAXABLE CAPACITY OF A NATION

In the first edition of the *Principles,* Ricardo defines the taxable capacity of a nation, chiefly in Chapter XXVI, "On Gross and Net Revenue." In the first edition also, but with much more assurance in the third edition,[1] he applies his definition of taxable capacity in analyzing the problem faced by a country which is considering measures that will lower the cost of food, and hence, on the average, the price level of commodities generally, but which hesitates to do so because it is committed to a heavy internal debt service that is fixed in money terms. The question at issue is whether the government bondholders would benefit, to the net disadvantage of the rest of the community. This problem is analyzed toward the end of Chapter XXXII, "Mr. Malthus's Opinions on Rent."

1. GROSS REVENUE AND NET REVENUE

The concepts of net and gross income, foreshadowed in the first of Ricardo's tax chapters (VIII, "On Taxes"), are introduced explicitly in the chapter on tithes (XI), but not defined; Ricardo merely remarks in passing that "it is from the net income of a country that all taxes are ultimately paid, either in a progressive or in a stationary country."[2] Now, in Chapter XXVI, Ricardo is reacting against certain passages in *The Wealth of Nations* that extol agriculture. In Smith's view, agriculture "puts into motion" the greatest quantity of productive labor and adds the greatest amount of value, per unit of capital invested.[3] To Smith this fact was important, since "The riches, and so far as power depends upon

[1] See his "Advertisement to the Third Edition," March 26, 1821, S, I, 8; G, 3-4.
[2] S, I, 178; G, 159.
[3] S, I, 347; G, 335-36. See *Wealth of Nations,* Bk. II, Ch. V; C, I, 343; M, 344.

riches, the power of every country, must always be in proportion to the value of its annual produce, the fund from which all taxes must ultimately be paid." [4] Ricardo considered this dangerously misleading. It promoted mistaken ideas about the relation of the price of corn to the taxpaying capacity of a nation.[5] "Adam Smith constantly magnifies the advantages which a country derives from a large gross, rather than a large net income." [6]

The gross income of a country, to Ricardo, is what today is termed net national income: the sum of wages, profits, and rent, in a Ricardian economy. His concept of the net income of a country, on the other hand, is the sum of profits and rent only; modern national income accounting has no corresponding term.[7] Wages, to Ricardo, constitute "the necessary expenses of production," at least if they are "moderate."

> Provided its net real income, its rent and profits be the same, it is of no importance whether the nation consists of ten or of twelve millions of inhabitants. Its power of supporting fleets and armies, and all species of unproductive labour, must be in proportion to its net, and not in proportion to its gross income.[8]

Two nations, one of ten million inhabitants, the other of twelve, have equal "power" in this sense, if the larger nation must employ seven of its twelve millions in producing food and clothing for the whole twelve millions, while the smaller nation need employ only five of its ten millions in producing food and clothing for the ten millions. In both cases, the number of laborers in excess of those needed to produce the food and clothing for the whole nation is just five millions. "The food and clothing of five millions would be still the net revenue," for the larger as well as the smaller nation.

To put it this way, that "the food and clothing" for the five millions is the net revenue, the surplus revenue available for war or other unproductive expenditure, may seem to blur the distinction, but here Ricardo must be viewed as looking at the product side of the national accounts. The food and clothing for the five million unproductive

[4] *Wealth of Nations,* Bk. II, Ch. V; C, I, 351; M, 352.

[5] Even apart from the considerations adduced in Section 2 of the present chapter, below.

[6] S, I, 347; G, 334.

[7] See Shoup, *Principles of National Income Analysis,* pp. 147-54.

[8] S, I, 348; G, 336. See also *Notes on Malthus,* S, II, 380-82, and Robbins, *The Theory of Economic Policy in English Classical Political Economy,* pp. 85-87. The computation quoted above from the *Principles* might better have been in terms of "families" than "inhabitants."

laborers is owned in the first instance not by the laborers but by capitalists; these goods are the embodiment of rents and profits gained in the immediately preceding period. The food and clothing are given to the five million in exchange for their labor.

The net revenue may be somewhat larger than the sum of profits and rent, for it may include a part of wages. In a footnote to his statement that wages, "if moderate, [constitute] ... always the necessary expenses of production," Ricardo says,

Perhaps this is expressed too strongly, as more is generally allotted to the labourer under the name of wages, than the absolutely necessary expenses of production. In that case a part of the net produce of the country is received by the labourer, and may be saved or expended by him; or it may enable him to contribute to the defence of the country.[9]

Other passages to the same effect can be found in the *Principles,* even though Ricardo does not emphasize the possibility of surplus wages when formulating his general laws of tax incidence. To the extent that the laborer's wage is in excess of this minimum wage, the laborer is like the landlord and the capitalist in being able to bear a part of the tax load, through a rise in the price of consumer goods, either necessaries or luxuries.

A memorandum bearing on this point was found inserted in a copy of the first edition of the *Principles,* at the close of Chapter VIII ("Taxes on Raw Produce"). Hollander thought the handwriting of the manuscript was Ricardo's,[10] but Sraffa believes that, although it is "similar in general appearance to that of Ricardo's, [it] differs in essential details and is unlikely to be his."[11] Moreover, the literary style seems not quite Ricardo's; and the statement on taxation departs from the analysis in the *Principles* (see Chapter IV above). Because of its relevance to the point under discussion, however, the memorandum is here reproduced in full:

The labourer is in the same situation which any other manufacturer is in. He gives his labours, and the food and necessaries which are actually necessary to support him is [*sic*] the price of that labour, while the additional luxuries and comforts which he can obtain are the profits upon his capital, the labour of his body. Then if we could by any means distinguish these two sums, *viz.* the price given him for labour and his profit upon it, the price given him for labour would be a standard measure of value. Suppose that in ——— the sum actually

[9] S, I, 348, note; G, 336, note.

[10] Hollander, ed., *Letters of Ricardo to McCulloch,* pp. 59-61, referring to letter of March 29, 1820.

[11] S, VIII, 173, note 2.

necessary to support a labourer was 3 quarters of wheat; that he receives £12 for necessaries and £12 for profits. Suppose that now he receives £14 for necessaries and £6 for profits. Though taxes on Raw Produce, etc. may finally fall upon the consumer and may not affect the interest of the manufacturer and the natural price of labour, yet they do most materially affect its market price, and the labourer will certainly be exposed to great inconvenience till the new state of things shall become established.

The analysis of taxable capacity in this Chapter XXVI may be integrated with that in Chapter VIII ("On Taxes"). There, it is said that taxes can be paid—that is, armies and navies can be supported—either out of revenue or out of capital. They are paid out of revenue by a diminution in unproductive private consumption or by an increase in total (net) production. Chapter XXVI is concerned only with the first option: a diminution of private unproductive consumption. Abstracting from growth, we are to imagine a country of 12 millions, in which 7 millions produce food and clothing for the 12 millions, while the other 5 millions, before the government comes on the scene, consume unproductively at private order, by producing goods and services for the well-to-do. Such a country could turn 5 million laborers into soldiers and sailors, or create by their labor arsenals and shipyards, and could maintain this degree of military effort indefinitely. The diversion of resources would be accomplished by absorbing profits and rent in taxation, directly or indirectly, thus forcing the well-to-do consumers to relinquish their demand for that part of the labor supply.

2. DOES MONEY NET REVENUE FALL WITH MONEY GROSS REVENUE?

Free importation of corn, like improvements in agriculture, would cause a fall in the price of corn, and therefore, on the assumption of an unchanged amount of corn consumed, a fall in the total value of corn consumed in the country. Total money rent would fall. What of the total net revenue of the country? If it decreased, might not the government bondholders benefit, and the remainder of the community be worse off than before? In this event, removal of the trade restrictions on corn could be opposed as far too unjust. But Ricardo concludes that in fact the money aggregate of the net revenue would not decrease at all. His line of reasoning may be paraphrased as follows.

As the market value, in gold, of the unchanged amount of corn falls, the total wage bill of the economy, in gold, declines by a like amount, under Ricardian wage doctrine. At the same time, the aggregate gold value of rent declines, as the margin of cultivation is drawn in (corn rent also falls, of course). As to profits, the aggregate in terms of gold rises; as wages decline, profits increase. In money terms, therefore, one element of net revenue (profits) rises, while the other (rent) falls. Ricardo's problem is to ascertain whether the increase at least matches the decrease; and, if it does not, whether the net decrease in money net revenue still reflects a real-income increase (owing to the fall in the price of corn) large enough to cover the increase in real tax burden caused by an unchanging tax bill in the face of a lower price of corn.

In the first and second editions of the *Principles* Ricardo goes no farther than to assert that "it is very highly probable"[12] that the money increase in profits will equal the money decline in rent. In the third edition he works out a numerical example that satisfies him that this outcome is certain.

Rent falls by the amount of labor cost saved; in his illustration rent falls from £5 million to £4 million; wages, from £10 million to £9 million. The total of wages-plus-profits remains unchanged at £15 million, since the number of workers is unchanged.[13] The fall in labor cost is reflected by an equal increase in profit, from £5 million to £6 million. Accordingly, the rise in profit equals the fall in rent. The net revenue of the economy in terms of money is therefore unchanged, at £10 million, although the gross income has declined from £20 million to £19 million. The tax bill, to service the debt, is also unchanged, at £2 million. But the unchanged net revenue of £10 million has a greater real value than it had before, since the price of corn has fallen. Consequently, the unaltered portion of this net revenue left after tax, the unchanged net disposable revenue in money terms (£8 million), also is of a greater real value than before. The tax bill is heavier, in real terms, than before, but the country is better able to bear it than before, and has more, in real terms, left over, after paying the tax.

All this Ricardo demonstrates even before allowing for a partial return of the general price level toward the initial position that will take place owing to the gold influx that must be expected as the result of cheaper corn.

There is, however, a flaw in Ricardo's reasoning. No one-to-one correspondence necessarily exists between the decline in the money wage

[12] S, I, 421, note 2.

[13] "... independently of rent, the same quantity of labour would always produce the same value." (Eds. 1 and 2 of *Principles;* S, I, 421-22, note 2.)

cost of the corn crop and the fall in the aggregate of money rent. The relation between the two decrements will vary with the pattern of diminishing returns. For example, if, initially, money rent happens to equal the aggregate wage cost of producing corn, a certain improvement might eliminate rent entirely, but some wage cost of producing corn would remain. Nevertheless, Ricardo may have wished simply to imply that he thought that in the usual case the fall in money rent would not exeed the fall in the wage cost of the corn crop.

Thus does Ricardo consider that he has achieved the aim announced in his "Advertisement to the Third Edition," that is,

> to place in a stronger point of view than before, the doctrine of the ability of a country to pay additional money taxes, although the aggregate money value of the mass of its commodities should fall, in consequence either of the diminished quantity of labour required to produce its corn at home, by improvements in its husbandry, or from its obtaining a part of its corn at a cheaper price from abroad, by means of the exportation of its manufactured commodities. This consideration is of great importance, as it regards the question of the policy of leaving unrestricted the importation of foreign corn, particularly in a country burthened with a heavy fixed money taxation, the consequence of an immense National Debt. I have endeavoured to shew, that the ability to pay taxes, depends, not on the gross money value of the mass of commodities, nor on the net money value of the revenues of capitalists and landlords, but on the money value of each man's revenue, compared to the money value of the commodities which he usually consumes.[14]

The moral is, then, do not be timid about repealing the corn laws, for fear that the fall in price of corn will enrich the government bond holder at the expense of the rest of the community.

> That the stockholder is benefited by a great fall in the value of corn, cannot be doubted; but if no one else [what of the landlords?] be injured, that is no reason why corn should be made dear .... If [the stockholders] are unjustly benefited, let the degree in which they are so, be accurately ascertained, and then it is for the legislature to devise a remedy....[15]

[14] S, I, 8; G, 3-4. In the absence of appeal to the argument in Chapter XXXII of the *Principles*, this last sentence is indeed difficult to interpret; cf. St. Clair, *A Key to Ricardo*, p. 122, note 3. In a letter to McCulloch, disapproving of McCulloch's proposal to reduce unilaterally the interest on the national debt, so that agricultural taxation might be lightened, Ricardo had said: "I firmly believe that if corn fell from 80 to 60/- the ability of the people to pay taxes would be increased instead of diminished." Letter of Dec. 4, 1816, S, VII, 104.

[15] S, I, 425; G, 417. The five paragraphs analyzing this problem, S, I, 421-25, G, 414-17, represent a substantial revision and expansion of similar material in the first two editions of the *Principles*. See note by Sraffa, S, I, 421-23.

3. FORCING OTHER COUNTRIES TO BEAR PART OF THE TAX BURDEN

Although he did not say so, Ricardo would presumably have agreed that a nation's taxpaying capacity includes the amount of taxes that it can shift to other countries, in view of its special position in the import-export complex. In his Chapter XVI, "Taxes on Wages," Ricardo recognizes the possibility of forcing the foreign consumer of domestic goods to bear a domestic tax. He describes it in terms that may not necessarily imply the existence of the law of comparative advantage that he had developed in the chapter on foreign trade (Chapter VII). The passage is ambiguous enough, and of enough significance, to call for quotation in full:

> Of all commodities, none are perhaps so proper for taxation, as those which, either by the aid of nature or art, are produced with peculiar facility. With respect to foreign countries, such commodities may be classed under the head of those which are not regulated in their price by the quantity of labour bestowed, but rather by the caprice, the tastes, and the power of the purchasers. If England had more productive tin mines than other countries, or if, from superior machinery or fuel, she had peculiar facilities in manufacturing cotton goods, the prices of tin, and of cotton goods, would still in England be regulated by the comparative quantity of labour and capital required to produce them, and the competition of our merchants would make them very little dearer to the foreign consumer. Our advantage in the production of these commodities might be so decided, that probably they could bear a very great additional price in the foreign market, without very materially diminishing their consumption. This price they never could attain, whilst competition was free at home, by any other means but by a tax on their exportation. This tax would fall wholly on foreign consumers, and part of the expenses of the Government of England would be defrayed, by a tax on the land and labour of other countries. The tax on tea, which at present is paid by the people of England and goes to aid the expenses of the Government of England, might, if laid in China, on the exportation of the tea, be diverted to the payment of the expenses of the Government of China.[16]

When Ricardo says: "Our advantage in the production of these commodities might be so decided," is he referring to comparative advantage, or absolute advantage? No doubt we are to interpret it as meaning comparative advantage, if we keep in mind the chapter on foreign trade. Ricardo did not, in that chapter, formulate a rule for the terms of trade; his illustration there leaves a zone of indeterminancy for international prices. Not having attempted to solve that problem, he probably relies on intuition in the passage just quoted.

[16] S, I, 240; G, 224.

CHAPTER XIV

MISCELLANEOUS TAX ISSUES

A number of miscellaneous tax issues raised by Ricardo may conveniently be grouped in this concluding chapter of analysis.

1. EXTRA BURDEN REPRESENTED BY INTEREST ON THE TAX

Say and Sismondi ("Simonde," in Ricardo) attributed a particular disadvantage to a tax levied at the manufacturing stage, rather than at retail or in the hands of the consumer. As Say put it, the manufacturer is under financial pressure, since he must pay the tax some time before he can recoup it from his vendee. Hence he must add to the price not only the tax, but something to cover interest on the tax money thus advanced, and those through whose hands the article passes before it reaches the consumer must do the same. This additional charge brings no benefit to the Treasury.

Ricardo agrees that the first objection is sound; the tax will often be "attended with considerable difficulty to a manufacturer of very limited capital and credit."[1] But Say's second point is invalid, for he fails to consider the alternatives facing the Treasury if the tax is not imposed at the manufacturing stage.

If the Treasury waits until the commodity reaches the final consumer before demanding payment of the tax, it must float a loan, and pay interest on it (which interest, Ricardo might have pointed out, necessitates correspondingly extra taxation at the end of the period). If the Treasury demands the tax at once from the consumer—in some other form than a commodity tax, impliedly—, the consumer loses interest for a year on

[1] S, I, 379; G, 370 (Chapter XXIX of the *Principles*, "Taxes Paid by the Producer").

the sum he could otherwise have retained, and indeed could have loaned to the manufacturer.[2]

If the interest rates for all parties are the same, say 5 percent, there is evidently no gain or loss to any one of them from having the Treasury wait a year for its tax. But Ricardo explores the case where the manufacturer can "add to his own real gains" by superimposing on the tax a percentage greater than the interest rate he pays. He and the Government can borrow at 5 percent; he charges the consumer 10 percent "interest" on the tax. Ricardo's only general comment on this result is that "the manufacturer and Government together gain, or save, precisely the sum which the consumer pays."[3]

Two remarks are called for, on this generalization.

First, the statement is true only in those cases where, as in Ricardo's numerical example, the Government and the manufacturer can borrow at the same rate. If the manufacturer borrows, say, at 8 percent and the Government could borrow at 5 percent, while the consumer is charged 10 percent on the tax, then Ricardo's general conclusion must be reworded to read: "the sum of the gains by the manufacturer, the Government, and the creditors equals the loss to the consumer," compared with what would have happened if the Government had borrowed. In the case just stipulated, some unspecified creditors gain 3 percent by lending to the manufacturer rather than the Government; the Government gains 5 percent by not having to borrow at all; and the manufacturer gets 2 percent more from the consumer than he pays in interest.

Second, Ricardo does not explain how a manufacturer is able to gain "5 per cent. on his advance over and above his usual profits. . ." If this extra charge reflects added real costs due to credit risks, record keeping, and so on, Ricardo would be expected to condemn the tax on grounds of inefficiency. If it must be made in order to keep in business manufacturers "of very limited capital and credit," a new element of rent is implicit in Ricardo's macro-economic system.[4]

[2] Von Falck raises the practical objection that the low-income individual, who is precisely the one asked to support the state through consumption taxes rather than an income tax (this is 1882) cannot possibly put out at loan the few pennies a day that for him are involved in this problem. *Kritische Rückblicke auf die Entwicklung der Lehre von der Steuerüberwälzung seit Adam Smith,* p. 68. Sismondi's error has been a common one; it is to be found, e.g., in Cournot, *Researches into the Mathematical Principles of the Theory of Wealth,* p. 70, and in Frend, *Principles of Taxation,* p. 43.

[3] S, I, 380; G, 371.

[4] *Idem.* Forte, in his extensive discussion of this issue, concludes that such a

The objection advanced by Sismondi to a tax at the manufacturing stage is said to follow "the same line of argument as M. Say,"[5] but it also contains an error of naïveté of which Say could scarcely have been guilty: Sismondi cumulated 10 percent on the tax, from one firm to another, as the commodity progressed from manufacturer to consumer, without noticing that he was using an annual rate, and should therefore have assumed that "five years elapsed between the first advance of the tax, and the sale of the taxed commodity to the consumer...."[6]

In speeches and evidence given in Parliament, and in pamphlets and papers, Ricardo commented briefly on other issues in taxation. These fragments are assembled here chronologically.

2. LOTTERIES

Ricardo spoke in favor of a motion made May 4, 1819, to abolish State Lotteries, pointing out "the evils which arose from the drawings of the lottery so often in the year."[7]

3. TAXATION OF MACHINERY

In June, 1820, a member of the House moved

> for a select committee to inquire into the means of relieving the distress of the cotton weavers. Amongst the plans to be considered he mentioned: the taxing of 'a machine called "a power-loom"' which competed with the simple loom of the individual weaver ('the capital of the poor man, which consisted in the labour of his two hands, must bear the burden of taxation, since those articles, without which he could not exist, were taxed; while the large capital of the wealthy manufacturer, which he invested in a machine, was suffered to escape any contribution to the revenue')....[8]

Ricardo is reported, briefly, to have spoken against the proposal, making

differential interest charge is incompatible with Ricardo's theory of profits; sooner or later, capital will be attracted to the industry to a degree sufficient to eliminate this excess profit. Francesco Forte, "Su di alcune proposizioni del Ricardo riguardanti gli effetti di imposte pagate dal produttore," *Riv. di Diritto Finanziario,* XVI (No. 2, Pt. 1, June 1957), p. 152.

[5] S, I, 380; G, 371.

[6] S, I, 381; G, 372. Brougham apparently fell into the same error, in Parliamentary debate, and was corrected by Ricardo, in his speech of Feb. 18, 1822, S, V, 137.

[7] Speech of May 4, 1819, S, V, 3. See also a report by *The New Times,* in note by Sraffa, *ibid.,* pp. 3-4.

[8] Note by Sraffa, S, V, 68.

no reference to the considerations that he was to advance in the third edition of his *Principles,* on the possibility of injury to the working class through rapid adoption of machinery on a large scale.[9]

4. SALT TAX

The tax on salt was extremely heavy, reportedly some 16 times the amount of the price before tax.[10] Ricardo, addressing Parliament in March, 1822, acknowledged that the salt tax was "undoubtedly very burthensome," but thought it was not the one that "most demanded reduction." The taxes on law proceedings were entitled to that distinction.[11] Two months later, Ricardo was more favorably disposed toward reduction of the salt tax, the measure in question being one offered by the Government that would reduce "the duties on salt (from 15*s.* to 2*s.* per bushel) and on leather," and would repeal "the Irish window tax and the tonnage duty on ships." [12] His reason was on the despairing side: "He regretted much that any portion of the salt tax was continued, he did not wish that any nucleus should remain, because they well knew with what vigour, under the management of the exchequer, it would spread. [Hear, hear.]." [13]

5. TAX ON ABSENTEES

A petition from "600 respectable inhabitants of Somerset" was presented in May, 1822 "praying for a tax on absentees who had taken up their residence in foreign parts." The member of the House presenting the petition "said that it was calculated that in Paris alone there resided 10,000 families of English, Irish and Scots; they were spending large sums and by transferring the money to France they gained an advantage of 25 per cent." [14]

Ricardo chided the petitioners for taking wrong measures toward a desirable end. Let the cost of living in Britain be reduced by repeal of the corn laws, and by redemption of the war debt through a contribution from all sorts of property, and "we should find that capital would come hither from all corners of the civilized world." Meanwhile, any tax "on the property or income of absentees, would hold out a direct encouragement to them to take away their capital, as well as their persons. Now,

[9] Speech of June 29, 1820, S, V, 68-69. [10] Speech of March 7, 1821, S, V, 84.
[11] Speech of March 20, 1822, S, V, 147. [12] As summarized by Sraffa, S, V, 191.
[13] Speech of May 24, 1822, S, V, 192. [14] As summarized by Sraffa, S, V, 186.

we had at any rate their capital, which was useful, though not so useful as if they also stayed at home." [15]

6. TAX ON BEER VERSUS TAX ON MALT

Mr. Denison, in presenting a petition from the table beer and ale brewers of London, suggested that the tax should be removed from beer and placed on malt. 'This would place the poor man and the rich on an equality. At present, the poor man, who could not brew his beer, paid a tax from which the rich man was exempt.' [16]

Ricardo agreed with this proposal, since individuals

would be at liberty to brew what quality of beer they pleased. The hardship was very great on the poor man, who was obliged to purchase his beer at a high rate from the public brewer; whereas all those who possessed facilities for brewing were exempted from the burden.[17]

He repeated this sentiment [18] when the matter came up again some days later, on Mr. Maberly's motion to appoint a committee " 'to inquire into the present mode of taxing malt and beer separately, and whether it would not be expedient to collect the same amount on malt alone.' " [19] And on June 13, 1823, he opposed a bill that "added to the two kinds of beer, then taxed respectively 10*s*. and 2*s*. per barrel according to strength, an 'intermediate beer', to be taxed 5*s*., and prohibited the brewing of different kinds of beer on the same premises." [20] Ricardo objected to the restrictive feature of the bill.[21]

7. OTHER ISSUES

For the sake of completeness, the following references to minor taxes, duties, etc., are given:

a. Coastwise duty on coal: a complaint by Collieries at Forest Dean is supported by Ricardo.[22]

b. Free port: Ricardo supports a bill "to permit foreign manufactures and produce to be deposited in British warehouses and taken out for exportation without payment of duty".[23]

[15] Speech of May 16, 1822, S, V, 187. [16] As summarized by Sraffa, S, V, 294.
[17] Speech of May, 12, 1823, S, V, 294-95. [18] Speech of May 28, 1823, S, V, 301.
[19] As summarized by Sraffa, *idem.*
[20] As summarized by Sraffa, S, V, 322. The bill became law.
[21] Speech of June 13, 1823, *idem.* [22] Speech of March 21, 1823, S, V, 275.
[23] As summarized by Sraffa, *idem;* speech of March 21, 1823. See also speech of June 21, 1822, S, V, 220.

c. Scotch linen laws: Ricardo presents and supports a petition "from the Merchants and Manufacturers of the Burgh of Arbroath against the present regulation, which imposes a stamp, and inflicts a tax upon the manufacture of that article . . . ," a stamping which "afforded no security whatever as to the quality of the cloth. . . ."[24]

[24] Speech of May 7, 1823, S, V, 290.

CHAPTER XV

RICARDO AND THE BRITISH TAX SYSTEM OF HIS DAY

Ricardo's first published contribution to economics dealt with specific matters of policy.[1] The notable pamphlets of his later years were powerful pleas for economic reform. Several parts of the *Principles,* including those having to do with money and foreign trade, for example, are related to current issues. But does he approach taxation from a similar point of view? Are Ricardo's chapters on taxation in the *Principles,* and his references to taxation in his other writings, aimed at the tax policy of the England of his day? Or did Ricardo write in a policy vacuum, analyzing taxes that might mean nothing to the current Chancellor of the Exchequer?

Certainly, Ricardo was not wholly detached from the debates on tax policy. The minor references given in Chapters XI and XII above are testimony on this score. His concern over the aggregate weight of British taxation is evident in his analyses of taxable capacity (see Chapter XIII above) and of the interest charge on the national debt that had been incurred in the struggle with France (see Chapter XI above). With respect to taxation, at least, we must dissent from an assertion that "Ricardo was writing as though there were no war...."[2] But the question remains, was he writing without reference to the tax structure of Great Britain, and its particular problems? Accordingly, we seek to ascertain which of the taxes discussed by Ricardo were not to be found in the British fiscal system, and which of that system's taxes, in turn, Ricardo ignored.

[1] The anonymous contribution to the *Morning Chronicle,* "The Price of Gold," Aug. 29, 1809. Note by Sraffa, S, III, 3.

[2] Hope-Jones, *Income Tax in the Napoleonic Wars,* p. 111.

1. TRANSFER TAXES

In the first of the chapters on taxation in the *Principles*, Chapter VIII, "On Taxes," we have seen that Ricardo refers disparagingly to certain British transfer taxes: taxes on "the probates of wills, ... the legacy duty, ... taxes affecting the transference of property from the dead to the living." Smith, quoted by Ricardo, refers to taxes "on the sale of land," and "stamp duties, and duties upon the registration of bonds and contracts for borrowed money," as well as "duties of the same kind upon law proceedings." [3] These, too, were in force in England when Ricardo wrote, but at low rates; they supplied a very small part of the tax revenue.[4]

(a) *Taxes on Passage of Property at Death.* On passage of property at death three taxes applied, but only two, the stamp tax on probates of wills, and the succession duty, were significant; the legacy stamp duty on receipts given by legatees or successors, introduced in 1780 by Lord North, had been avoided on a large scale by dispensing with the receipts. The stamp tax on probates was a rudimentary form of ad valorem tax, a step-scale levy of fixed amounts of tax according to the range of values within which the estate fell. Prior to the War of American Independence it had been merely a flat tax of 10*s*. The succession duty, introduced by Pitt in 1796, was in Ricardo's time a tax ranging from 1 percent to 10 percent, depending on the degree of relationship; transfers to spouse were not taxed. In 1815, out of a total tax yield of £74½ million for the United Kingdom, all these duties on transfer at death produced less than £2 million, partly because they applied only to transfer of personal property; landed property was exempt from all death duties until 1853.[5] Ricardo objected in Parliament to this exemption; he was reported as

[3] S, I, 153-54; G, 134-35.

[4] For the luxury-tax aspect of these levies, see Kennedy, *English Taxation, 1640-1799*, p. 157.

[5] See Dowell, *A History of Taxation and Taxes in England from the Earliest Times to the Year 1885*, II, 173-74, 213-15, 257-59, and III, 125-30, 133-35. The present chapter depends chiefly on this great work of Dowell's for its historical material. Buxton's book, *Finance and Politics, an Historical Study, 1783-1885*, published in the same year as Dowell's second edition (1888), is too impressionistic and biased for the period 1783-1827 (his Chapter I), and adds virtually nothing to the other sources cited here. Tayler, in *The History of the Taxation of England, with an Account of the Rise and Progress of the National Debt* (1853), offers little for the reader who now has at his disposal not only Dowell, but also Acworth and Kennedy. A wealth of detail for the several excises is available in Fine, Production and Excise in England, 1643-1825.

declaring that "The landed interest had already too many regulations in their favour. For instance, the commercial interest had to pay five per cent. upon all property transferred upon the death of the owner; and this was not required of the landed interest." [6]

(b) *Taxes on the Sale of Land.* "Taxes on the sale of land," disapproved of by Smith and Ricardo,[7] were levied on a minor scale. Pitt had failed to gain assent to his proposal in 1797 for an ad valorem tax on deeds of conveyance;[8] Addington and subsequently Pitt failed again in 1804.[9] But Perceval in 1808 put through a step-scale tax on conveyances of property on a private (non-auction) sale, ranging from 15*s.* for purchases under £50 in value, up to £500 tax on those of £50,000 value or more. Vansittart extended the upper limit, in 1815.[10] Not until 1850 was the tax put on a simple ad valorem basis (1/2 of 1 percent).[11] This tax was a part of the stamp duties.

An older stamp tax on the transfer of land, also modest, was included in "the deed duty," which was a fixed absolute amount "for every piece of paper upon which was engrossed or written any—'Indenture, lease, bond, or deed not otherwise specially charged.'" Since "the number of words or 'folios' to be written on a single skin [sheet] of parchment was ... limited by law," the tax was in fact one "on deeds by reference to their length." After a series of increases over the decades, the deed duty was raised in 1815 to £1 15*s.* for the first skin, and £1 5*s.* for each additional skin, where it remained during Ricardo's lifetime.[12]

There was also a minor tax on sale of property, including land and houses, at auction.[13]

All of the stamp duties together yielded only £2.7 million in 1815,[14] and it appears that sales of land contributed much less than half the total.

(c) *Taxes on Mortgages, Bonds, Notes.*[15] "Duties upon the registration of bonds and contracts for borrowed money" had existed within the

[6] Speech of May 7, 1823, S, V, 291. William Frend had objected strongly to this discrimination, in 1817: "... the legacy tax; an odious tax most assuredly, for an unjust distinction is made between personal and real property, the former only being subjected to, and the latter screened from it; whereas, if any distinction is to be made, it ought to be in favour of the former, not of the latter." *The National Debt,* pp. 11-12.

[7] S, I, 154-55, 204; G, 134-36, 184. [8] Dowell, II, 218. [9] *Ibid.,* II, 232.

[10] *Ibid.,* III, 295-96. [11] *Ibid.,* III, 299. [12] *Ibid.,* III, 290-96.

[13] *Ibid.,* III, 141-43.

[14] *Ibid.,* II, 258 (bills and notes, £841,000; receipts, £210,000; other instruments, £1,692,000).

[15] *Ibid.,* III, 291-96.

stamp tax structure ever since the stamp tax was introduced into England in 1694. In 1714 they were evidently classified under the "deed duty" subhead, the amount of tax depending on the length of the document, as explained above. Pitt had the tax on "bonds for money" put on an ad valorem step-scale basis, ranging from 10*s*. for bonds not exceeding £100 to £5 for bonds of £5,000 or more. In 1804 an ad valorem scale of charge (step-scale, apparently) was introduced for mortgages, the upper limit of which was extended in 1815.

Duties on inland bills of exchange and promissory notes had been added by North to the stamp list in 1782. These were raised several times subsequently, the last increase in Ricardo's lifetime being in 1815.

(d) *Taxes on Law Proceedings.* Finally, "Duties ... upon law proceedings," which, as we have seen, were Ricardo's candidate for the worst tax, had been levied in the period 1670-80, and reintroduced as part of the Stamp Act of 1694.[16] Had Ricardo lived one year more he would have had the satisfaction of seeing these duties repealed; the government gave up about £275,000 of revenue in this manner in 1824.[17]

Ricardo wrote at a time when the stamp duties in Great Britain were on a level to which they had moved by gradual steps over many decades. His quoting of Adam Smith therefore had a base in current policy. Still, the issue was a minor one, quantitatively, if not qualitatively; taxes on the transfer of property seem to have been scarcely high enough to cause significant misallocation of resources, or serious encroachment on capital. But the tax of this group that Ricardo perhaps feared the most, that on the transfer of property at death, developed a century later to a level that would have dismayed him.

2. TAXES ON RAW PRODUCE

(a) *Specific Tax per Bushel.* If Ricardo's powerfully reasoned chapter on taxation of raw produce (Chapter IX) had any connection with current policy, the link was only indirect, through the tithes, or the import duty on corn, for a specific tax per bushel on home-grown produce was unknown to England. The other English taxes that were special burdens on agriculture differed substantially from the specific tax per bushel in that they exerted little or no pressure at the margin of cultivation: the land tax and the agricultural horse tax. The land tax had by this time lost all of its marginal impact.[18] The agricultural-horse tax, not analyzed by Ricardo, although mentioned in

[16] *Ibid.*, III, 287. [17] *Ibid.*, III, 297; II, 277-78 (£200,000 revenue loss).

[18] See Section 3 below, this chapter.

passing in his essay, *On Protection to Agriculture*,[19] was a flat tax per horse used for agriculture or for purposes of trade, introduced in 1796 at 2 shillings the horse, but subsequently increased several times until it reached 17*s.* 6*d.* for husbandry horses and £1 1*s.* for trade horses; ponies and the horses of small farmers were taxed at lower rates. Nearly a million horses came under this tax in 1815. The tax on agricultural horses was repealed in 1821. Dowell reports that the horse tax was equivalent to a tax of 1½ percent of the rent on light soils, and 3 percent on "strong heavy soils."[20]

No doubt Ricardo thought of the specific tax per bushel as a useful device for illustrating some of the more important features of his macroeconomic system. Moreover, we know that he was disturbed by Smith's erroneous reasoning regarding a special tax on farm profits, reasoning that was applicable also to a tax on gross farm product.

(b) *Tithes.*[21] On the nature of tithes in England, we get no assistance from Dowell's four-volume classic; he considers them to be outside the tax system, presumably because they were paid to the established church, not to the Government. Dowell merely remarks that among the reforms instituted by the Whigs in the ten years they were in power, to 1841, there was the Tithe Commutation Act, which had "reformed the laws relating to the payment of the clergy."[22] From other sources, however, it is apparent that the tithe was an important issue in Ricardo's day.[23] McCulloch, using data from the income tax returns, estimates that in 1813 about two thirds of the farm land, by rental value, in England and Wales was subject to the tithe; but if Scotland, where the tithe had, in effect, ceased to operate, is taken into account, it appears that only about half the cultivated land of Great Britain was affected by this levy.[24]

Clergymen evidently differed considerably as to the rigor with which they enforced their rights to tithes; in many cases, therefore, the levy must have been much less than one tenth of the produce. Relative to a tax on rent, the tithe was however quite heavy in some circumstances;

[19] S, IV, 255.

[20] For further details, and a denunciation of the tax, see Dowell, III, 226-28.

[21] See Chapter VI above.

[22] Dowell, II, 320. Tithes taxable under Schedule A of the income tax in 1842 were estimated at £3.5 million, but turned out to be only £2.0 million. *Ibid.*, III, Appendix, 311.

[23] We may recall that James Mill, who seemed not much excited by the prospect of reading a Ricardian manuscript on taxation, nevertheless did say, "I long to hear you on tithes." See footnote 15, Chapter I above.

[24] *Taxation and the Funding System*, p. 176.

McCulloch quotes an observer who asserts that the tithe of an acre of hops "is worth 3 *l.* or 4 *l.* after the charge for drying and the duty are deducted; while, perhaps, the rent of the land is not more than 40*s.* or 50*s.*; and he adds that he had known the tithe of an acre of carrot-seed worth from six to eight guineas grown on land not worth 20*s.*!" [25]

The existence of tithe-free land, and the uneven degree to which tithes were exacted from the remaining land, must have made the economic impact of the levy even more difficult to trace than Ricardo's analysis would indicate; of these complicating circumstances Ricardo took no notice.

Some time after Ricardo wrote, the tithe lost most of its character of a levy at the margin by being commuted into fixed quantities of produce.[26]

3. AGRICULTURAL LAND TAX

"A tax on rent would affect rent only . . . ," but "A tax on rent, as rent is constituted, would discourage cultivation. . . ." [27] The "land-tax," in Ricardo's time, was neither of these. It was the frozen remains of what had started more than a century before as an annual tax on income from all property. The land tax was a good example of "that comfortable English compromise which had made every tax in the past a fixed, and generally a diminishing, charge." [28] It applied to both farm and non-farm real estate.

The tax was introduced near the end of the seventeenth century to replace a still earlier tax that had atrophied in much the same way as this one was destined to do.[29] The new tax was imposed at a rate of 20 percent on the full rental value of real estate and on an imputed income of 6 percent of the capital value of all personal property, including money, but excluding stock on land, and household property. Stipends from offices,[30] except naval or military, were taxable. The yield proved so disappointing, owing to inadequate administration, that in 1697 Parliament reverted

[25] *Ibid.*, p. 180.

[26] See the article, "Tithes," by Eleanor G. Powell, in *Palgrave's Dictionary of Political Economy*, III, 543-45, and the note on "Terms of Commutation," in the act of 1836, by Rev. A. Caldecott, *ibid.*, III, 545-46.

[27] S, I, 173; G, 154.

[28] Hope-Jones, p. 68. See also Kennedy, pp. 16-17, on the "stereotyping" of early English taxes.

[29] Dowell, II, 47, and III, 81; and Kennedy, pp. 38-50.

[30] "Offices and employments," Dowell says later (III, 83), and, for 1698, "public office or employment of profit," *ibid.*, p. 84.

to an earlier technique by fixing a total sum to be raised by the tax, and apportioning this sum among the several counties and towns. The total revenue to be obtained was computed on the basis of what it was thought a 15 percent tax rate should yield. Within a county or a town the sum apportioned to it was to be raised by a 15 percent tax on imputed income from personal property plus a tax on real estate of whatever rate was necessary to yield the balance of the apportioned sum. Thus Parliament was assured of a sum certain from each town or county, but within a town or county, evasion of the tax with respect to personal property automatically put up the rate applicable to real property.[31] The apportionment among towns and counties was, from the start, notoriously unfair, whatever the base of the tax might be taken to be.[32]

In 1698 Parliament apportioned the tax further down, stipulating, in effect, the absolute total to be obtained from each district or division within a county or town.

For the next hundred years the rate of the tax, "rate" being interpreted as described above, fluctuated from 10 percent to 20 percent (5 percent under Walpole in 1731 and 1732).

Before long, personal property had slipped out of assessment through evasion and laxity in administration, as it had done in earlier centuries under the "fifteenths and tenths" and the "Subsidy" system. The tax thus became one virtually on real estate alone. In 1798, under Pitt, the tax that was then being levied (nominal rate, 20 percent) on each parcel of real estate was fixed at that absolute amount forever, and was made subject to redemption by the owner of the land, or even by a stranger (1803), upon payment to the Government of a capital sum, in cash, or in the form of public bonds at the current price.[33] Almost one quarter of the land tax was redeemed in 1798-99.[34] On the remaining taxed parcels of real estate it was a fixed amount. If we exclude from consideration land that may have been driven out of use by overassessment so drastic that the effective rate was more than 100 percent, the land tax of Ricardo's day emerges as a species of tax on pure land rent. It was not, to be sure, a tax that varied with variations in pure land rent, but it had no impact on the margin of cultivation.[35] If, instead, we look back in

[31] See also Cannan, *History of Local Rates in England,* p. 118.

[32] See, e. g., Kennedy, pp. 44-46.

[33] This summary of land-tax history is based on Dowell, III, 67-91.

[34] *Ibid.,* II, 223.

[35] Kennedy observes that "the real justification for maintaining the Land Tax in its stereotyped condition was that by long continuance it had come to be a rent charge rather than a tax," and, since much land had changed hands at prices

time, and take account of those parcels that may have been forced out of use, the tax resembles rather the fixed tax per acre that Ricardo analyzes in his Chapter XII, "Land-Tax," except that it was not of a uniform amount per acre. Finally, if we consider the intention of the Legislature in 1692, the tax was "a tax on rent, as rent is constituted," thus including the profit on the landlord's improvements, rather than a tax on pure rent.

In summary, Ricardo was not dealing with any existing British tax when he analyzed taxes on pure rent, or on rent as commonly defined, or on acrage; but the land tax of his day was a bit of all three, depending on the place in time from which it is viewed.[36]

Ricardo's only specific reference to the British land tax is in Chapter XII, where he comments critically on the views expressed by Smith and Say. " 'A land-tax,' says Adam Smith, 'which, like that of Great Britain, is assessed upon each district according to a certain invariable canon, though it should be equal at the time of its first establishment, necessarily becomes unequal in process of time, according to the unequal degrees of improvement or neglect in the cultivation of the different parts of the country.' " On this, Ricardo comments:

> If the tax be shifted by the tenant not on the landlord [as Smith believed] but on the consumer [as Ricardo believed], then if it be not unequal at first, it can never become so; for the price of produce has been at once raised in proportion to the tax, and will afterwards vary no more on that account.[37]

This conclusion seems in error, or at least places a strained interpretation on the term "equal," for it implicitly disregards possible changes in productivity of the various acres. Once the tax becomes fixed on each acre in amount, a certain acre, losing some fertility or advantage of position, may prove unprofitable to cultivate, in view of the tax attaching to it, even after the subsequent rise in price that is needed to induce an extension of the margin of cultivation if the inelastic demand is to be satisfied. The landlord whose acre has thus been forced out of cultivation will not agree to Ricardo's concept of "equal."

A similarly unsympathetic interpretation of Say is to be found in Ricardo's comment: "M. Say appears to me to have mistaken the nature

set to allow for the tax, "The abolition of the tax ... would have amounted to a gift to the landlord class...." *English Taxation,* p. 128.

[36] For the possibility that Ricardo may have had in mind Schedule A of the income tax that had just been repealed, see Section 8 below, this chapter.

[37] S, I, 185-86; G, 166. *Wealth of Nations,* Bk. V, Ch. II, Pt. II, Art. I, C, II, 312-14; M, 780.

and effects of the English land-tax, when he says, 'Many persons attribute to this fixed valuation, the great prosperity of English agriculture.' "[38] Ricardo proceeds as if Say were maintaining that agriculture derived a positive benefit from the tax; but this was not Say's point. Ricardo also attributes to Say a belief that the English Government had promised agriculture it would never have to pay any further tax of any kind, aside from the frozen land tax; but even if Say can be so interpreted, his point remains, though somewhat weakened. The agriculturist would surely be impressed by the fixity of the land tax, and in deciding whether to make improvements would not be so pessimistic as to assume that this stability would be completely offset by new taxes on agriculture. Of course the issue tends to disappear anyway, under Ricardo's assumption of a quite inelastic demand for farm produce, and his belief that one tax of general scope is about as bad as another, their only important effect being to diminish the amount of productive capital available in future years.

4. TAXES ON GOLD

Ricardo's Chapter XIII, "Taxes on Gold," was perhaps a device for extending his analysis of money, and foreign trade, or for illustrating the importance, to tax shifting, of "the facility with which . . . [a commodity] can be reduced in quantity."[39] Great Britain produced no gold or silver, and no tax on these monetary metals had been imposed or was contemplated. The taxes levied on silver plate (1720-1758) and later on both gold and silver plate[40] might be thought of as partial, indirect taxes affecting the supply of money, since plate could be melted into coinable bullion; but this is not what Ricardo seems to have had in mind.

5. TAXES ON HOUSES

Chapter XIV of the *Principles,* "Taxes on Houses," is on so general a plane that it seems to have little bearing on current policy. Moreover,

[38] S, I, 186; G, 167. [39] S, I, 191; G, 171.

[40] See Dowell, IV, 360-75. In France a tax was imposed on plate (1672, 1674) "to check the progress of a manufacture which threatened to deprive the Mint of silver for coinage." In England, in 1697, prohibition of the use of plate for certain purposes had the same end in view. *Ibid.,* IV, 363. A tax on gold and silver wire was in force from 1712 to 1826. Fine, Production and Excise in England, pp. 226-27.

[41] Dowell, III, 172-73. The English window tax was reduced by one half in 1823, and was repealed in 1851.

the window tax, which Ricardo does not mention, was yielding more than twice as much as the tax on annual rental value of houses, in 1815.

The precursor of these taxes was the hearth-and-chimney tax of the Restoration period, which was repealed in 1688. In 1696 there was introduced a tax of two shillings on each house, with higher amounts on houses having more than a stated number of windows. This was preferred to the hearth tax because it was assessable with less invasion of the privacy of the householder. It was later refined to vary directly with the number of windows; thus in 1815 it ranged from 6*s.* 6*d.* on houses with not more than six windows, if under the value of £5 a year, to £93 2*s.* 6*d.* for a house with 180 windows, with a further charge of 3*s.* for each window over 180. The yield in 1815 was £2 million a year.[41]

Both the hearth tax and the window tax exempted the poorer class of dwelling, *viz.*, those not subject to church and poor rates.[42]

The tax on the annual rental value of inhabited dwellings[43] was introduced during the War of American Independence by Lord North, who is said by Dowell to have obtained the idea from Adam Smith. Initially (1778) it exempted houses with an annual value of less than £5; the rate was 5 percent (2½ percent for houses in the range £5 to £50). In general, the tax did not apply to business properties or farmhouses. The top rate rose to slightly over 14 percent during the war with Napoleon. The yield in 1815 was less than £900,000.

The window tax and the house tax were included in the group of taxes that in 1785 constituted the "assessed taxes," the forerunners of the income tax. Dowell concludes that both taxes were levied primarily to compensate for the failure of the property tax to reach movables effectively.[44]

6. SPECIAL TAX ON GROUND RENTS

"Adam Smith considers ground rents as peculiarly fit subjects for taxation."[45] The passage that Ricardo quotes from Smith refers both to "ground rents, and the ordinary rent of land," apparently meaning pure rent of building land and pure rent of agricultural land, respectively. No

[42] In 1743 Sir Matthew Decker proposed a single tax on houses, exemption to be granted to houses of some half a million of the poorest people. Kennedy, p. 114.

[43] Dowell, III, 178-92. The house tax was repealed in 1834, but was reintroduced, in modified form, in 1851.

[44] *Ibid.*, III, 153. [45] S, I, 203; G, 183.

tax like this existed in Great Britain, unless the land tax could by that time be put in that category.

7. TAXES ON LUXURIES

Only a few passages in the *Principles* refer to the taxation of luxuries in general; they occur in Chapters XV ("Taxes on Profits"), XVI ("Taxes on Wages"), and XVII ("Taxes on Other Commodities than Raw Produce"). Scattered references occur in Ricardo's other writings and his Parliamentary speeches.[46]

Ricardo finds no need for an extensive analysis of luxury taxes; they fall entirely on the consumers. He gives as examples taxes on wine, pleasure horses, coaches, and servants.[47] We may also assume that Ricardo has "luxuries" in mind when referring to taxes on malt, barley, beer, or ale.[48] The same inference may be drawn from his remarks concerning the tax on tea,[49] his brief references to gold used in manufactures,[50] and the quotation from Smith that touches on "country villas." [51]

Ricardo does not refer at all to the tax on sugar, an important source of revenue, or to the even more important tobacco tax.

In Parliamentary debate, however, Ricardo had one occasion to apply his conclusions to a policy issue, when in 1819 the Chancellor of the Exchequer proposed to increase the taxes on malt, tobacco, tea, and certain other commodities. Ricardo seemed to view these taxes as falling partly on luxury expenditures of the laborer, partly on necessaries; his analysis has been reproduced in Chapter IV above. Perhaps the relative lack of attention that Ricardo gave to luxury taxes reflected simply an acceptance by him of the general opinion that they were unobjectionable; at least in the eighteenth century, according to Kennedy, "the disposition of opinion raised [taxes on luxuries] . . . to the position of the one satisfactory kind of tax." [52]

(a) *Alcoholic Drinks.* From the incidental manner in which Ricardo refers to them, the British taxes on alcoholic drinks might appear to have been of little importance, yet in yield they dwarfed the land tax and

[46] S, I, 205 (G, 186), 233 (217), 235 (219), 241-42 (225-26), 243-44 (228); S, V, 45, 137 (malt); S, V, 294-95, 301, 322 (beer and malt); and S, VIII, 177 ("wines, silks and velvets").

[47] For wine, S, I, 153 (G, 134), 205 (186), 235 (219), 241 (225), 242 (226), 253 (237-38); for horses, S, I, 153 (G, 134), 205 (186), 241 (225), 242 (226); for servants, S, I, 153 (G, 134), 242 (226).

[48] S, I, 219 (G, 202), 252-54 (237-39). [49] S, I, 240 (G, 224).

[50] S, I, 193-94 (G, 174), 200 (180). [51] S, I, 202 (G, 182).

house tax combined. In 1815 the three beer taxes produced £9.6 million;[53] the tax on wine, £1.9 million;[54] and the tax on spirits, £3.5 million[55]—a total of £15 million. The malt tax was the most important of the beer taxes (£6 million). But for it, and the tax on hops (£0.2 million), the extensive private brewing on the consumer's premises would have escaped taxation.

When Adam Smith was writing, the three beer taxes were yielding only £2.5 million (1774). But the malt tax in England was subsequently raised from 9*d.* the bushel to 1*s.* 4½*d.* in 1780, to 2*s.* 5*d.* in 1802, and, when war broke out again following the Peace of Amiens, to 4*s.* 5*d.*, where it stayed until reduced to 2*s.* 5*d.* in 1816; but it was raised to 3*s.* 7½*d.* in 1819, and lowered only to 2*s.* 7*d.* in 1822. The tax on beer, which ranged in 1782 from 1*s.* 4*d.* the barrel to 8*s.*, depending on strength, was raised in 1802 to 10*s.*, with a reduced rate of 2*s.* for table beer. These rates remained essentially unchanged, apparently, until the beer tax was repealed in 1830.[56]

Was beer a necessary or a luxury? It "was in fact both a necessary and a luxury to the poor," says Kennedy, who adds that it was usually regarded as a necessary (eighteenth century).[57] Here, however, we follow Adam Smith,[58] and class it as a luxury.

All wine was imported. The rate on Spanish and Portuguese wines was raised, in several stages, from 2*s.* 11*d.* a gallon, in the 1780s, to 7*s.* 7*d.* by 1815 (French wines, from 3*s.* 9*d.* to 11*s.* 5*d.*).[59]

The tax on spirits (distilled alcoholic drinks) assumed importance in the early eighteenth century, when the discovery of a cheap way to make gin had led to serious trouble. A heavy tax of five shillings a gallon was imposed on this spirit in 1729 ("Act against geneva"). But the tax stimulated invention of another distilled liquor that was found to be outside the taxing act; it was "termed, in derision of the legislature, 'Parliament Brandy.'"[60] Parliament responded in 1733 by repealing the

[52] *English Taxation*, p. 129; see also *ibid.*, pp. 152-57, and Shehab, *Progressive Taxation*, Chapter II.

[53] Dowell, IV, 78. [54] *Ibid.*, IV, 130. [55] *Ibid.*, IV, 181.

[56] *Ibid.*, IV, 75-80. A slightly lower set of rates is reported in Fine, Production and Excise in England, p. 238. An intermediate grade of beer, bearing a 5*s.* tax, was authorized in 1823. Dowell, IV, 79; see Chapter XIV, Section 6, above.

[57] Kennedy, p. 145.

[58] *Wealth of Nations*, Bk. V, Ch. II, Pt. II, Art. IV, C, II, 355; M, 822.

[59] The gallon was the old wine gallon, 231 cubic inches, not the "imperial gallon" of 277.274 cubic inches, adopted in 1825. Dowell, IV, 129-31.

[60] *Ibid.*, IV, 169. See also Kennedy, pp. 137-41.

tax on gin; there ensued the orgies pictured by Hogarth: "Drunk for a penny, and dead drunk for twopence. Clean straw for nothing."[61] In desperation, Parliament passed Jekyll's "Act against spirituous liquors," in 1736, imposing the extremely heavy tax of £1 per gallon on all retailed spirits, and a license tax of £50 a year on each retailer.[62] Evasion, however, forced a reduction in the taxes a few years later (1743); subsequently, in the seesaw battle against drunkenness, the rates were increased again.

Revenue considerations gained in importance; during the Great War with France the rate was trebled. By 1811 it had reached a level equivalent to 10*s.* 2¾*d.* the imperial gallon, and in 1819 it was raised to the equivalent of 11*s.* 8¼*d.* the imperial gallon. From this peak it was reduced, in 1825, two years after Ricardo's death, to 7*s.* per imperial gallon of proof spirits.[63] Other rates applied to foreign spirits.

(b) *Nonalcoholic Drinks.* In 1815, the tax on tea yielded £3.6 million in Great Britain, and the tax on coffee £0.3 million.[64]

The English trade in tea was virtually monopolized by the East India Company, from 1677 to 1834. Not until the third quarter of the eighteenth century had tea-drinking become usual among the farming class and artisan class.[65] In 1770, Arthur Young observed: "All united in the assertion that the practice [of using tea and sugar] *twice a day* was constant [among the poor], and it is inconceivable how much it impoverished them."[66] To lower the cost, dealers in tea adulterated it with sloe leaves, licorice leaves, used tea leaves, leaves of other trees (especially ash and elder), shrubs, or plants mixed or colored with terra japonica, sugar, molasses, clay, copperas, and logwood.

Tea was taxed upon importation throughout the eighteenth century, with fluctuating degrees of success against smugglers. By 1784 the tax amounted to 119 percent; Pitt slashed it to 12½ percent, and to everyone's surprise, tax-paid consumption increased so much that the revenue dropped only a little more than one half. By 1801, however, the tax rate was back up to 50 percent, and by 1806 to 96 percent (6 percent cus-

[61] Dowell, IV, 169. [62] Kennedy, p. 139.

[63] Other rates applied in Scotland and Ireland. Proof spirit is that which, at 51 degrees Fahrenheit, weighs $^{12}/_{13}$ parts of an equal measure of water. Dowell, IV, 182, note.

[64] *Ibid.*, IV, 225, 235. For the rates on coffee, see *ibid.*, IV, 234-36.

[65] *Ibid.*, IV, 214-17. See also Kennedy, p. 161, note 2.

[66] Quoted by Dowell, IV, 218.

toms, 90 percent excise). There it remained, virtually unchanged, until 1834.[67]

(c) *Tobacco.*[68] By the 1720s, use of tobacco was widespread among all social and income classes, and was already a significant contributor to tax revenue. In Pitt's tariff of 1787, the tobacco tax—levied as a customs duty—was 1*s.* 3*d.* a pound on colonial tobacco, equivalent to an ad valorem tax of nearly 400 percent on the leaf. By 1815 the rate was 3*s.* 2*d.*, and the yield slightly over £2 million. A further increase in tax rate, to 4*s.*, was enacted in 1819.

(d) *Sugar.*[69] Among the articles taxed by Britain as luxuries, but which Ricardo does not note, is sugar. At least it was considered a luxury by Arthur Young and Adam Smith, and in 1829 Huskisson, President of the Board of Trade, asserted that, under the high price caused by the duty, "two thirds of the poorer consumers of coffee drink that beverage without sugar." [70]

The duty on sugar was raised seven times during the Great War with France, and by 1815 was yielding £3.0 million, at 30*s.* the cwt. At the close of the war Vansittart reduced the tax by 3*s.* The duty of 27*s.* was about equal to an ad valorem tax of 100 percent. Protecting duties against noncolonial sugar were practically prohibitive. After further reductions, the sugar tax was repealed in 1874.

(e) *Pepper, etc.*[71] Other food luxuries subject to tax but unimportant in their yield were: pepper, on which the rate of tax rose from 4*d.* the pound in 1722 to 2*s.* 6*d.* the pound by the end of the war with Napoleon (Gladstone repealed the tax in 1865); raisins, currants, oranges and lemons, and olive oil and vinegar.

(f) *Horses, Carriages, Servants, etc.* "After visiting with a tax the whole round of luxuries; after laying horses, carriages, wine, servants, and all the other enjoyments of the rich, under contribution," [72] Ricardo says; but he might have also specified: sporting licenses, hair-powder, dogs, and armorial ensigns, the taxes on which, together with the three items he mentioned (leaving wine to one side in a category of its own) were initiated between 1747 and 1798, and extended, some of them, up

[67] Dowell, IV, 224-25. [68] *Ibid.*, IV, 257-58.

[69] *Ibid.*, IV, 22-25, 29. Shehab, *Progressive Taxation*, p. 70, appears to be in error in saying that the sugar tax was raised after the war; the authority cited (Dowell, II, 239-59, 1884 ed.) does not make that statement.

[70] Quoted by Dowell, IV, 32.

[71] Dowell, IV, 35-44. The olive oil duty was repealed in 1845, the vinegar excise in 1844.

[72] S, I, 242; G, 226.

to the time Dowell wrote his *History of Taxation and Taxes in England from the Earliest Times to the Year 1885*. Several of these taxes—those on carriages, menservants, horses, hair-powder, dogs, and clocks, together with the window tax and the inhabited-house tax—were known as "the assessed taxes," and it was the failure of these taxes to respond well to heavy rate increases under the so-called "Triple Assessment" of 1798 that decided Pitt to venture on the untried income tax.[73] Dowell groups these taxes under the label, "in respect of domestic establishments, with others that resemble them in principle," as a subdivision under "Taxes Analogous to a Property Tax." The group includes three that were repealed before Ricardo wrote (on the household plate chest, female servants, and clocks and watches).[74]

The tax on carriages,[75] which was introduced in 1747 simply as an annual tax of £4 on all four-wheeled carriages and £2 on two-wheeled carriages, had by 1812 developed a complex schedule at considerably higher rates: progressive on owners of four-wheeled carriages (£12 if one carriage; £13 per carriage if two carriages; and so on), and at various lower rates for more modest types. The carriage tax in fact yielded nearly half a million pounds sterling in 1815. This tax, like the others described in this subsection, were imposed on the basis of taxing luxury expenditure as a measure of ability to pay; it had nothing to do with the construction or maintenance of roads.

Pitt introduced a complementary tax in 1784: an annual tax on the owner, "for every horse kept and used for the saddle or for driving in a taxable carriage."[76] This new tax, along with the tax on carriages, was put under "the commissioners of taxes" (the carriage tax had been administered by "the excise commissioners"), to be assessed and collected as one of the "assessed taxes." The rate was only 10*s*. a horse in 1784, but by the end of the war with France it had been made progressive, at a much higher level: £2. 17*s*. *6d*. a year for one horse, £4. 14*s*. *6d*. for each of two horses, and so on, up to a maximum of £6. 12*s*. a horse for the owner of twenty or more saddle or carriage horses. Thus the marginal rate on the second horse was £6 11*s*. *6d*. Ricardo ventured the observa-

[73] Dowell, III, 153-62, and II, 188-91, 220-22. For a reference by Ricardo to the assessed taxes, see S, III, 241. The "Triple Assessment" was more complex than a mere tripling of all amounts due the previous year under the assessed taxes; for a detailed description, see Seligman, *The Income Tax*, pp. 65-72.

[74] Dowell, III, ix. [75] *Ibid*., III, 195-209.

[76] *Ibid*., III, 226. A tax on racehorses, imposed in 1784, produced a negligible amount of revenue. *Ibid*., III, 231-34.

tion that "many would pay a tax of 5 *l.* for the enjoyment which a horse affords, who would not pay 10 *l.* or 20 *l.*"[77]

In 1815, about a quarter of a million saddle and carriage horses were being charged under this tax. The tax was repealed in 1874.[78]

"The multiplicity of men servants has ever been a remarkable feature in our domestic establishment," said Dowell, writing toward the end of the nineteenth century.[79] About a hundred years earlier, in 1777, Lord North had introduced an annual tax of a guinea for every servant kept, excluding all those employed in any trade or business activity. By 1812 the tax had developed a progressive rate scale of two branches, one for nonbachelors keeping servants, the other for bachelors. The highest rate was £9 13*s.* per servant in the establishment of a bachelor keeping more than ten servants. The yield of the tax was £600,000 in 1819. It involved many more difficulties of definition and administration than might at first be thought.[80]

A tax on female servants proved a failure. Pitt introduced it in 1785; it was repealed in 1792.[81]

The sporting license tax produced only £132,000 in 1815;[82] the annual tax on users of hair-powder (1795-1869) declined rapidly from £210,000 in 1796;[83] the annual tax on dogs, introduced in 1796 (Pitt was searching desperately for revenue in the early days of the Great War, before he brought himself to recommend an income tax), produced £160,000 in 1815;[84] the tax on every person "using or wearing" any "armorial bearing or ensign," introduced in 1798, was yielding only £42,000 a year by the close of the war[85]—altogether, Ricardo may be credited with a sense of proportion in failing to specify these four taxes as among those on "the luxuries of the rich."

(g) *Playing Cards, Dice, etc.* In 1801 the tax on cards was raised to 2*s.* 6*d.* the pack, and that on dice, in 1804, to £1 the pair. These rates were continued to 1828.[86]

8. TAX ON PROFITS; INCOME TAX

Oddly enough, Ricardo devotes no chapter, no paragraph even, to the income tax,[87] although he had just lived through a period when it had

[77] S, I, 241; G, 225. [78] Dowell, III, 227-30. [79] *Ibid.*, III, 215.
[80] *Ibid.*, III, 216-23. [81] *Ibid.*, III, 223-25. [82] *Ibid.*, 244. [83] *Ibid.*, III, 258-59.
[84] *Ibid.*, III, 264. [85] *Ibid.*, III, 279. [86] *Ibid.*, IV, 315.

[87] For passing references, generally unfavorable, to an income tax, see *Principles*, S, I, 152, 153, 161, 242 (G, 133, 134, 142, 226); *Reply to Bosanquet*

played the leading role in the British wartime tax drama. Enacted in 1799, and repealed in 1802, it had been reenacted in 1803, "with a fresh label as the 'Property Tax,'" although "The new name did not deceive anyone and the 'Income Tax' remained its ordinary and popular title."[88] The tax was repealed finally in 1816, in an atmosphere of intense political excitement,[89] just a few months before Ricardo wrote his chapters on taxation. The Government had proposed to continue the tax for two years at a 5 percent rate, in place of the wartime rate of 10 percent, but Parliament rebelled. In 1842 the income tax was reimposed and has continued in force, without lapse, to the present day.

Moreover, income as a standard for distribution of the tax burden had been the goal of fiscal legislation in the seventeenth and eighteenth centuries, though the attempts had degenerated into simple land taxation.[90] The assessed taxes, too, were to some extent considered indirect attempts to tax according to income, or income in excess of the subsistence level, not merely according to expenditures.[91]

Ricardo's seeming unconcern with the income tax, almost indeed an apparent unawareness of the very existence of the tax, is by itself enough to give to his chapters on taxation an air of detachment from policy problems. Ricardo, like the taxing authorities, may have fallen into the habit

(1811), S, III, 240-42; "Funding System," S, IV, 187-88; Speeches of June 9, 1819 (S, V, 20-21), and May 16, 1822 (S, V, 187), and letter of Jan. 28, 1820, Ricardo to Trower, S, VIII, 154. The passage in the *Reply to Bosanquet* gives the only reasoned account of the incidence of a general income tax to be found in Ricardo's writings: "The income tax, were it fairly imposed, would leave every member of the community in the same relative situation in which it found him. Each man's expences must be diminished to the amount of his tax; and if the seller would wish to relieve himself from the burthen of the tax by raising the price of his commodity, the buyer for the same reason would wish to buy cheaper. These contending interests would so exactly counteract each other, that prices would undergo no alteration." (The tax status of the gold mines is not stipulated.) S, III, 241.

[88] Hope-Jones, p. 20. See also Farnsworth, *Addington, Author of the Modern Income Tax*, Chapters 3-5.

[89] See Acworth, *Financial Reconstruction in England, 1815-1822*, Chapter III; Hope-Jones, pp. 1-2 and Chapter VII; Kennedy, p. 146, note 5; Shehab, pp. 60-69. A detailed description of the 1799-1802 income tax is given in Seligman, *The Income Tax*, pp. 72-82; of the 1803 tax and subsequent modifications to 1816, *ibid.*, pp. 89-106; and of the circumstances attending repeal of the tax, *ibid.*, pp. 106-114. Ricardo's name does not appear in the index to Seligman's exhaustive work.

[90] Kennedy, pp. 38-50. [91] See Shehab, pp. 30-37, 42-45.

of thinking in terms of schedules: parts of total income. Under the first income tax (1799-1802), the taxpayer had had to submit a return in a form that revealed, or rather might reveal, his total income for the year.[92] When the tax was reimposed in 1803,

> No general return of income from all sources was required. The obligation to make such a return, involving, as it did, a disclosure of the taxpayer's circumstances in life, had been regarded as the chief objection to the tax. Addington now substituted, in lieu of a general return, *particular returns of income from particular sources.*[93]

Another reason for the use of schedules was the introduction of collection at source.[94]

Consequently we might infer that Ricardo, when writing Chapter XV, "Taxes on Profits," had in mind Schedule B (farm profits) and Schedule D (income not specified elsewhere, and particularly profits from trade and manufacture). In this view, Ricardo's Chapters XII and XIV, "Land Tax" and "Taxes on Houses," deal in effect with Schedule A of the income tax; but the existence of the old land tax and special taxes on houses makes this extension of the interpretation dubious.

Chapter XVI, "Taxes on Wages," to be noted below, might at first be thought of as a commentary on Schedule D, so far as that reached

[92] Dowell, III, 97. According to Farnsworth, the taxpayer had to file, not a statement of his income, in the first instance, but merely a declaration that "... I am willing to pay the Sum of ———, ... and I do declare that the said Sum of ——— is not less than One Tenth Part of my Income...." The Commissioners could demand details of income only if they had reason to think the statement incorrect, and, in fact, they called for such data only infrequently. Farnsworth, pp. 17-18 (quotation from p. 17). Cheats and honest men gained no secrecy by this provision; and philanthropists could scarcely be identified. But William Frend, for one, was reassured that "honour still remains, and may it ever remain in the breast of an Englishman," when, upon expiration of the income tax in 1802, the returns "were carefully collected and cut into pieces with large stationer's sheers, then thrown into large bags, and conveyed with equal care to a paper manufactory, where, under the inspection of a commissioner, they were committed to the mash tub: and he did not leave them till they were reduced to a pulp." *The Principles of Taxation*, p. 3. But bureaucracy had vanquished honor; some hundred years later J. H. Clapham and A. Hope-Jones discovered in the Public Records Office duplicates of all the returns, which had been duly sent to that exquisitely named official, the King's Remembrancer. Hope-Jones, pp. ix-x, 1-3.

[93] Dowell, III, 99.

[94] Farnsworth, Chapters 2 and 3; Seligman, *The Income Tax*, p. 90.

salaries and wages, and Schedule E (income from public office or employment of profit); but the early British income tax was not a mass tax as are those of Great Britain and the United States today. The tax of 1799-1802 exempted incomes under £60 a year, hence struck only "the middle class and the rich." [95] Certain reliefs were allowed in respect of children.[96] The exemption limit remained at £60 under the 1803 tax, at first, but was lowered to £50 in 1806 (and now limited to incomes derived from labor, for daily or weekly wages).[97] An abatement of tax for families with more than two children, made part of the 1803 act, was repealed in 1806.[98] That these exemption limits were sufficient to exclude from the income tax virtually all the laboring class and most of the small business men is indicated by the yields of the several schedules; from 1806 to 1815 the yield of Schedule D fluctuated not far from the level of £3.5 million a year, while the total revenue from the income tax was climbing irregularly from about £13 million to nearly £16 million a year.[99]

In any event, if the income tax Schedule D is not what Ricardo had in mind in his Chapters XV and XVI, we must consider him to be analyzing in the abstract, for there is nothing else in the British tax system, in earlier years or in his time, to which his analysis seems germane. In particular, his speculations on what would happen "If the profits of all trades were taxed, excepting the profits of the farmer," [100] or if "the profits of the farmer only should be taxed, and not the profits of any other capitalist," [101] must be taken simply as an intellectual exercise within the framework of his macro-economic system.

The incidental references to "A tax on hats," "a tax on shoes," and "a tax on the profits of the clothier," with which Ricardo opens Chapter XV are only hypothetical illustrations—unless he was recalling the short-lived tax on hats, of 1784-1811,[102] a distinct possibility, in view of his remark in Chapter XVI ("Taxes on Wages"): "Nothing is more common, than to see hats or malt rise when taxed. . . ." [103]

Perhaps, on the other hand, Ricardo's failure to deal with the income tax reflects, not a schedular point of view, but an intense dislike of the

[95] Kennedy, p. 171. [96] Dowell, III, 94.

[97] On the reason for lowering the exemption from £60 to £50, see Hope-Jones, p. 27.

[98] Dowell, III, 101-103. [99] Hope-Jones, pp. 77, 78, 118; Dowell, III, 104-105.

[100] S, I, 210; G, 192. [101] S, I, 212, footnote; G, 195, footnote.

[102] Dowell, IV, 388-90. See also speech of March 7, 1821, S, V, 84.

[103] S, I, 219; G, 202.

whole levy, so pronounced as to place the tax outside the limits of discussion—much as the excess profits tax has disappeared from modern public finance literature once the wars that have given rise to it have ended. A passage in his Chapter IX, "Taxes on Raw Produce," may reflect firsthand experience: "... the obnoxious measure of prying into every man's concerns, and arming commissioners with powers repugnant to the habits and feelings of a free country."[104] Kennedy makes the following remark: "The commercial tradition which Adam Smith represented opposed both taxes on income and [because they raised wages, hence costs] taxes on necessaries, but of the two it disliked taxes on income most."[105]

Precisely the opposite thesis has been advanced by Giraudeau:[106] that Ricardo thought of his tax chapters, and hoped they would be regarded, as "a more or less discreet plea for the return of the income tax."[107] The four points on which this provocative interpretation is based seem subject, however, to substantial qualification. (a) "Ricardo always remained firmly opposed to any tax on capital...,"[108]—but Ricardo's objection was not to the form of tax, whether technically on capital or income, but to its effect. (b) Ricardo's theorem that taxes could be paid only from the nation's net revenue, not its gross, "seems to imply that he advocates taxation of the nation's income,"[109] but again, this consideration does not require that the individual be taxed, technically speaking, on his income. (c) Ricardo was disturbed by Vansittart's failure to reduce the national debt, and so probably wished for a return of the income tax; but rather, we should say, hoped for a capital levy, or for reduced governmental expenditures. (d) "Ricardo's stand in favor of direct taxation is in the Anglo-Saxon tradition, according to which consumption taxes can only be considered supplementary to the

[104] S, I, 161; G, 142. The tone is reminiscent of William Frend, to whom the income tax was "oppression," if not "terror." *The Principles of Taxation*, pp. 5-6.

[105] Kennedy, p. 148.

[106] Roger Giraudeau, "La théorie de l'impôt chez Ricardo," *Revue de Science et de Législation financières*, XLIII (No. 2, April-June, 1951), 319-39.

[107] "Il peut être ... possible que l'ouvrage de Ricardo ... ait put être ... considéré par son auteur comme un plaidoyer plus ou moins discret en faveur du retour de l'income tax." *Ibid.*, p. 320.

[108] "Ricardo est toujours demeuré solidement hostile à tout impôt sur le capital...." *Ibid.*, p. 335.

[109] "...paraît le poser en partisan de l'imposition du revenu national...." *Ibid.*, p. 336.

other taxes";[110] but we have seen that the English tradition of Ricardo's day was strongly in favor of indirect taxation, and we lack evidence that Ricardo himself broke with this tradition, except for his proposal to redeem the war debt by a capital levy. In any event, it may be agreed that Ricardo's attitude toward income taxation remains a subject for further study.

The rate of income tax was 10 percent from 1799 to 1802, on incomes above £200. On incomes between that amount and the exemption level of £60, a series of lower rates applied. When the tax was reimposed in 1803, the rate was set at 5 percent. Between £150 and £60, lower rates again applied.[111]

> In 1805 Pitt added one-fourth to all the rates; and in 1806, after the battle of Austerlitz and the death of Pitt, the tax was raised by the Grenville Coalition ministry to 10 per cent. . . . The rate of allowance in abatement of tax for incomes under 150 *l*. . . . was fixed at 1*s*. for every 20*s*. by which the income was less than 150 *l*.[112]

The 10 percent rate remained in force until repeal of the tax in 1816.

9. TAXES ON WAGES

In the history of British taxation up to Ricardo's time, there is no record of successful wage taxation on a large scale, if exception is made for occasional poll taxes from 1640 to 1700,[113] which are not of course taxes directly on wages. We have seen that the wartime income tax did not reach the bulk of wage payments. And Adam Smith had spoken disparagingly of wage taxation abroad.[114] Accordingly, in writing Chapter XVI of the *Principles*, "Taxes on Wages," Ricardo must have been stimulated by something other than Britain's inland revenue policy.

10. TAXES ON NECESSARIES

The stimulus to the wage-tax analysis was doubtless the taxation of necessaries, for Ricardo frequently equates taxes on wages with taxes on

[110] ". . . la position de Ricardo, partisan de l'impôt direct, de préférence, est bien dans la ligne anglo-saxonne pour qui l'impôt de consommation ne saurait que faire l'appoint de l'autre impôt." *Ibid.*, p. 337.

[111] Dowell, III, 94, 101. [112] *Ibid.*, III, 102.

[113] See Kennedy, pp. 18-22, for attempts to tax large numbers of laborers in the thirteenth to sixteenth centuries, and p. 50 for the poll taxes.

[114] *Wealth of Nations*, Bk. V, Ch. II, Pt. II, Art. III; C, II, 350; M, 817. See also *ibid.*, C, II, 359; M, 826; S, I, 227; G, 210; and Gonner's note 2, *idem*.

necessaries.[115] The corn laws, particularly, raised the cost of the most important necessary in the worker's budget. Ricardo also refers, briefly, to taxes on leather, salt, soap, and candles, as did Adam Smith,[116] and to a hypothetical "tax on bread," [117] but he devotes no separate chapter to the taxation of necessaries in general. The specific-rate tax on raw produce that is the subject of Chapter IX of the *Principles* was not to be found in British history; only the tithes came close to being a generalized tax on the worker's necessaries.

Moreover, Great Britain had never imposed a general sales tax of the old Spanish *alcavala* type.

The taxing of superfluities while sparing necessaries had thus become a generally accepted canon in Britain by the middle of the seventeenth century.[118] The reasons why this attitude prevailed are somewhat mixed. It was not, at that time, believed that taxes on necessaries inevitably led to an increase in wages and a decrease in profits. Opposition to taxes on necessaries, from those in power, was grounded simply on compassion, or a desire to avert social unrest.[119] And toward the end of the seventeenth century, the scope of the compassionate motive seems to have narrowed. Thus Kennedy concludes that by that time the idea that the poor, but not the paupers, should pay some tax had become well established, in contrast to "the Elizabethan and Stuart tradition of exempting the poor man from taxation." [120] Moreover, taxation of necessaries implied a network of agents and inspectors that was distasteful to the business community.[121]

The idea that taxes on necessaries would be passed on by the worker through higher wages seems to have developed systematically, from about 1730, in the minds of the manufacturing and trading classes, who used it to oppose Walpole's proposal to raise the salt tax as a means of permitting a decrease in the rate of the land tax.[122] This argument, although somewhat inconsistent with that based on compassion for the very poor, was employed along with it, and the two together "led to the condemnation of taxes on necessaries." This condemnation

[115] S, I, 215 (G, 198), 227 (210), 232 (216), 233 (217), 235 (219).

[116] S, I, 234 (G, 218); see also S, I, 237 (G, 220), salt; speeches of May 8, 1820 (S, V, 45), leather; March 7, 1821 (S, V, 84-85), salt; Feb. 18, 1822 (S ,V, 137), salt and soap; March 20, 1822 (S, V, 147), candles and salt; May 24, 1822 (S, V, 192), salt; letter of April 8, 1820, Ricardo to McCulloch, S, VIII, 177, "corn and clothing."

[117] S, I, 254; G, 239. [118] Kennedy, pp. 26-33. [119] *Ibid.*, p. 80, note 1.

[120] *Ibid.*, p. 49. [121] Fine, Production and Excise in England, pp. 139-42.

[122] Kennedy, pp. 107-111, and Chapter VII, *passim.*

came gradually to be almost universally accepted and constituted the most important element of the eighteenth-century view of the ideal tax, the tax on luxuries. This result was achieved, however, in spite of and not by overthrowing the doctrine that every man should pay taxation and that a just tax must be general. The new theory was therefore not directly the result of a view of distributive equity in taxation but rather of two ideas of non-tax policy, compassion for the poor and the advantage of low wages in the interest of trade.[123]

Kennedy concludes that when Adam Smith enunciated this doctrine, that a tax on the laboring poor would inevitably be shifted to others, he merely gave "the sanction of a name which had great weight with certain kind of people to a view which was already influential." Thus, "two negative and inconsistent principles—the one of commercial, the other of social policy—joined together to place the negative maxim that taxes should not be on necessaries in the position of a first principle of tax policy."[124]

The principle was fairly well observed in the Great War with France; aside from the import duties on wheat, taxation of necessaries was restricted largely to the four commodities mentioned by Adam Smith,[125] salt, candles, leather, and soap, and to coal or its transport.[126] Of these, only salt was called on to contribute significantly increased revenue in the war period.

(a) *Salt.* Of the salt tax, Dowell says that it

proved a burden to the poor, and injurious in its operation on many of our manufactures, and was extremely unpopular, no doubt in a considerable degree from its resemblance to the hated *gabelle* of France, a country always regarded by Englishmen as the hotbed of oppressive taxes. Repealed by Walpole for these reasons in 1730, it was, only two years after the repeal, revived with a view to enable him to keep the land tax at a low rate.[127]

At that time (1732) a Parliamentary opponent of the salt tax estimated that it would take 4*s.* 6*d.* a year from a poor man earning a shilling a day, with a wife and three children to support.[128]

The tax rate was driven to extreme heights in the Great War with

[123] *Ibid.*, pp. 111-12. [124] *Ibid.*, pp. 122-123.

[125] S, I, 234; G, 218. *Wealth of Nations*, Bk. V, Ch. II, Pt. II, Art. IV, C, II, 357; M, 825.

[126] Dowell, IV, 397-403.

[127] *Ibid.*, IV, 3-4. Kennedy attaches importance to this revival of the salt tax. *English Taxation*, p. 99. For the earlier history of salt taxation in Britain, see *ibid.*, pp. 14, 58-60.

[128] Kennedy, p. 105.

[129] Dowell, IV, 4. About sixteen times, Ricardo implies, in 1821. S, V, 84.

France. From 5*s.* the bushel on domestic salt, during the War of American Independence, it was raised to 10*s.* and then to 15*s.* in 1805, a tax thirty times the price of salt.[129] In 1815 the yield was £1.6 million. In 1822, the year before Ricardo's death, the 15*s.* rate was reduced to 2*s.*, and in 1825 the tax was repealed.[130]

Ricardo was aware of the extraordinary rate of the tax on salt, using it to demonstrate that under a discriminating tax, no matter how heavy, "a sufficient profit"[131] is left for the producer—at least, we might add, for those producers who remain in the trade.

(b) *Candles, Leather, Soap.*[132] In the War of American Independence, candles, leather, and soap, which had been taxed since the early eighteenth century, were spared the rate increases that were applied to most of the excises. These exceptions were made "in accordance with the rule established by Adam Smith, North's master in matters of taxation, that these taxes, if continued, should be kept at the lowest possible rate."[133] Moreover, these three specific-rate taxes remained virtually unchanged through the Napoleonic Wars. Accordingly, they were minor sources of revenue in Ricardo's day. In 1815 they yielded £354,000 (candles), £698,000 (leather), and £748,000 (soap).

The tax on candles had been 8*d.* the pound for wax candles and 1*d.* the pound for tallow candles, from 1711 to 1779. After a few rate readjustments, the tax became stabilized at 3½*d.* for wax candles and 1*d.* for tallow candles; these rates remained unchanged throughout the Napoleonic Wars and until the tax was repealed in 1832.[134]

The tax on leather, too, remained unchanged at 1½*d.* the pound from 1711 to 1812, when Vansittart doubled it; this wartime increase was rescinded in 1822, and the tax itself was repealed in 1830.

The soap tax was raised in 1782, to 1¾*d.*-2¼*d.* the pound, from a uniform rate of 1½*d.* the pound imposed in 1712, but was kept unchanged throughout the Napoleonic Wars. When the income tax was repealed in 1816, Vansittart raised the rate on hard soap from 2¼*d.* to 3*d.* This made the tax about 100 percent of the price. The soap tax was repealed in 1853.

(c) *Other Manufactures.* Other manufactured articles that yielded

[130] Dowell, IV, 4. [131] S, V, 84-85. See Chapter XIV, Section 4, above.

[132] Dowell, IV, 287, 309-19. According to Fine, Production and Excise in England, p. 215, the candles excise was introduced in 1710 and the rates were doubled in 1711.

[133] Dowell, IV, 283-84.

[134] Fine, Production and Excise in England, pp. 215-16.

appreciable excise revenue in 1815 were: paper, printed goods, newspapers, starch, glass, and bricks and tiles.[135]

There were also taxes on certain raw materials.[136]

(d) *Meat, Butter, and Cheese.* The import duties on meat, especially on bacon, and on butter and cheese may be included in the taxes on necessaries, though their quantitative role was apparently minor.[137]

(e) *Corn.*[138] From being an exporter of corn in the first half of the eighteenth century, England changed to an importer, taking one year with another. In 1791 the restrictions on imports of corn were transformed into a sliding-scale duty, varying with the domestic price. At less than 50*s.* the quarter, the duty was 24*s.* 3*d.*; from 50*s.* to 54*s.*, the duty was 2*s.* 6*d.*; and if the domestic price rose above 54*s.* the duty was only 6*d.* In certain years these charges were in fact reduced or suspended; but the dividing lines were moved up in 1804 (to 63*s.* and 66*s.*).

In 1815 this almost prohibitory import duty was yielding £28,000. It was repealed in that year and replaced by the famous Corn Law of 1815:

> Corn was now allowed to be imported, warehoused and exported, free of duty, so that the country might be an entrepôt for corn; but until the price of wheat reached 80*s.* the quarter, an absolute prohibition was imposed on the delivery of wheat out of warehouse, and the importation of it, for home consumption.[139]

11. TAXES ON EXPORTS

Ricardo's recommendation that taxes be imposed on the export of commodities that, "either by the aid of nature or art, are produced with peculiar facility," [140] was not reflected in English tax policy. In the seventeenth century, export duties were levied indifferently along with import duties, both being imposed, in principle, as benefit taxes on the consumers, at home and abroad, of goods in international trade (in those days largely luxuries), to help defray the cost of the Navy, which made such traffic possible.[141] But "under the influence of Mercantile ideas, duties on exports were gradually reduced and repealed," [142] and in 1721 Walpole repealed "practically all the remaining duties on exports except those on raw materials." [143]

[135] *Idem.* For details, see Dowell, IV, 290-303, 323-60, 376-84. Newspapers were regarded as a luxury by Pitt: Kennedy, p. 156.

[136] For details, see Dowell, IV, 394-444. [137] *Ibid.*, IV, 13-16.

[138] *Ibid.*, IV, 6-12.

[139] *Ibid.*, IV, 11. [140] S, I, 240; G, 224. [141] Kennedy, pp. 10-16, 24-28.

[142] *Ibid.*, p. 27. [143] *Ibid.*, p. 28, note 1. See also *ibid.*, p. 35.

Yet a tax on selected exports, said Ricardo, was a way to force the foreigner to bear part of England's tax burden, just as the Chinese, if alive to their opportunity, could call on the English tea drinker to finance the Chinese Government.

12. IMPORT DUTIES

Import duties have been largely covered in the sections of the present chapter above, except as they were prohibitive, or virtually so, in which case they do not fall under the topic here being discussed (with the important exception of the corn laws). Import duties developed markedly in the eighteenth century, as export duties were repealed; the benefit-tax concept of the early seventeenth century disappeared. "Customs duties in the eighteenth century thus became taxes almost entirely on imported commodities, levied at high rates, regarded for the most part as falling on superfluities, and imposed for two purposes, both of which were important, revenue and trade policy."[144]

13. BOUNTIES

No attempt is made here to describe the system of bounties in force in Great Britain in or shortly before Ricardo's time, and to compare them with the types of bounty that Ricardo analyzes. Such a description and comparison must await a scholarly work on English subsidies comparable to Dowell's treatise on taxes.

In passing, however, we note that bounties were not restricted to exports.

> In the worst years [of the war with France] the British Government went out of its way to bring in foreign food. . . . Between September, 1795, and September, 1796, a bounty, varying from 10 *s.* to 20 *s.* per quarter, was offered on imported foreign wheat. . . . In 1800 . . . importers were guaranteed the difference between the average price of English wheat in the second week after importation and a price of 90 *s.* (extended in 1801 to 100 *s.*). But inasmuch as the price continuously exceeded 100 *s.* in both of these years, the measures, while lending confidence to importers, cost the Government nothing.[145]

[144] *Ibid.*, p. 37. See also *ibid.*, pp. 135-37.

[145] Fay, "Corn Prices and the Corn Laws, 1815-1846," *Econ. J.*, XXXI (No. 121, March, 1921), pp. 20-21.

14. POOR RATES

The poor rate, to which Ricardo devoted a separate chapter, was a local tax, established by a statute of 1601 which declared that the money required for poor relief should be raised in each parish "by taxation of every inhabitant, parson, vicar, or other, and of every occupier of lands, houses, tithes impropriate, propriations of tithes, coal-mines, or saleable underwoods." [146] Over the years the tax became narrower in scope than this prescription would imply, finally being limited to occupiers of real estate; and the basis of the tax, not specified in the 1601 statute, became annual income, actual or presumed. The impost became a "rate" in the sense that the rate of the tax was not fixed at a round or even figure that usually remained unaltered from year to year—as in the national tax on inhabited houses—but was determined anew each year by dividing the aggregate taxable income of the parish into the revenue needs for poor relief. The rate of course varied from one parish to another. Thus, under a "rate," or "rates," the aggregate tax base must be known to the law-makers at the time they decide how much to spend.

Thus "a system of taxation according to ability estimated by persons acquainted with the circumstances of the taxpayers" gradually changed into "a system of taxation according to the annual value of lands and tenements occupied." [147] Ability was from the beginning associated with income from property; any one who had income only from wages or salaries was not likely to be able to contribute substantially to the support of the poor.[148] Concentration of the poor rate upon real estate was another matter. "The history of the omission of profits derived from movables or personal property ... extends from 1601 to 1840." [149] From 1795 on, following a King's Bench decision, "there could be no doubt that the law required stock-in-trade to be rated, but it does not appear to have been rated any more than before." [150] Not until 1840, when Parliament enacted a prohibition against including profits from stock-in-trade in the poor-law base, was the question settled.[151]

From all this it is clear that Ricardo, when he commented on the poor rates, not only knew the law, but was familiar with the way in which the tax was in fact being assessed.[152]

[146] Quoted from Cannan, *The History of Local Rates in England*, p. 3. For the history of local rates prior to 1601, see *ibid.*, Chapters I-III.

[147] *Ibid.*, p. 80. [148] *Ibid.*, pp. 22, 81. [149] *Ibid.*, p. 85. [150] *Ibid.*, p. 97.

[151] *Ibid.*, p. 100.

[152] S, I, 257-60; G, 242-45. See also note 55 to Chapter XII above.

15. OTHER LOCAL RATES

Ricardo nowhere refers to local rates other than the poor rates, unless we may so interpret a reference in his letter of January 28, 1820, to Trower, where he approves of "Taxes for the benefit of trade itself such as for Docks, canals, Roads. . . ." [153] Perhaps he has the local highway-rate in mind, and the sewer tax.

The omission is the less significant in that by Ricardo's time many of the local rates, including the highway-rate, had come "to be little but additions to the poor-rate," [154] or at least were levied on virtually the same base. The church-rate was on its way to becoming a voluntary contribution.[155] The "sewers-rate," which at the beginning of the nineteenth century "was widely applied to the purposes of house and street drainage," was a benefit charge, administered by "commissions of sewers"—seven of them in London.[156] What remained of the land tax was a national levy, although Cannan, writing in 1898, insists that "it has the essential features of a rate and a local rate," because "it is a sum determined beforehand, and levied at different rates in different localities." [157]

16. CAPITAL LEVY

Ricardo's proposal for a capital levy to retire the war debt was based on no experience with such a tax in Britain, nor upon any proposal seriously considered by Parliament. No capital levy was imposed in Great Britain even after the First or Second World War.

17. OTHER TAXES

The present chapter has touched on all the taxes that were in existence when Ricardo wrote, or that had been levied not long before, with certain minor exceptions: Pitt's tax on shops, repealed in 1789; annual license taxes on attorneys, note bankers, auctioneers, those engaged in the coaching trade (including a mileage tax) or keeping post horses for hire, and certain other professions and businesses; a tax on property sold by auction (1777-1845), which produced nearly £300,000 in 1815; the tax on fire insurance (1782-1869), which yielded over £500,000 in 1815, at a rate of 3*s.* per £100 insured; the tax on insurance from sea

[153] S, VIII, 155.
[154] Cannan, *History of Local Rates in England,* pp. 102, 119-30.
[155] *Ibid.,* p. 108. [156] *Ibid.,* p. 112. [157] *Ibid.,* p. 114.

risk (1795-1885), giving about £400,000 a year in the later years of the Great War; and a few minor taxes on manufactures.[158]

In addition, the heterogeneous mass of taxes known as "stamp duties" has not been fully described in this chapter,[159] nor have all the taxes on raw materials been mentioned by name;[160] and certain minor aspects of liquor and soft drink taxation have been omitted.[161]

18. MISCELLANEOUS[162]

No tax on machinery, such as that proposed in 1820, which Ricardo condemned, was ever adopted in Britain. Apparently, too, no tax on absentees (nonresident citizens) was enacted. Ricardo spoke briefly against lotteries in 1819, but the present chapter does not describe that branch of British revenue, owing to lack of data.

19. RELATIVE IMPORTANCE OF THE SEVERAL NATIONAL-GOVERNMENT TAXES

In the detail given above, it is easy to lose sight of the relative importance of the several taxes in the national revenue system of Ricardo's day.

First, the grouped data as given by Acworth for each of the years 1816-1823 afford a general sense of proportion; they are reproduced in Table 5.

Table 5. *YIELD OF MAJOR TAX GROUPS, 1816-1823*[a]

(in millions of pounds sterling)

	1816	*1817*	*1818*	*1819*	*1820*	*1821*	*1822*	*1823*
Customs and excise	43.8	38.8	36.6	40.2	39.5	41.5	42.6	42.0
Income tax[b]	14.6	11.8	2.3	.6	.2	—	—	—
Other revenue[c]	20.7	18.7	18.7	18.7	18.4	18.4	19.0	17.9
Total receipts	79.1	69.3	57.6	59.5	58.1	59.9	61.6	59.9
Total expenditures	99.5	71.4	58.7	57.6	57.5	58.4	58.4	56.5
Surplus	—20.4	—2.1	—1.1	1.9	.6	1.5	3.2	3.4

[a] Acworth, *Financial Reconstruction in England, 1815-1822,* p. 137. All years end on January 5.

[b] Called "the property tax" after 1803. Repealed in 1816.

[c] Includes "the receipts of the Post Office, which brought in over £2 millions a year—the cost of the department was rather more than £1/2 million." Acworth, p. 137, note 2.

[158] Dowell, III, 8-63, 142-48; IV, 281-384.

[159] *Ibid.,* III, 285-309. [160] *Ibid.,* IV, 394-444.

[161] *Ibid.,* IV, Book II and Appendix. [162] See Chapter XIV above.

Second, the tax yields given by Dowell for 1815, the last year of the war, are presented first in summary form in Table 6 and then in detail in Table 7.

Table 6. *SUMMARY OF TAX SOURCES IN GREAT BRITAIN, 1815*[a]

(in millions of pounds sterling)

I. *Direct Taxes*		
Land	1	
Houses and establishments	6	
Income	15	
Property passing at death	1	
Property insured	1	
Property used in public transportation of persons	[b]	
Other	[b]	
Total, direct taxes		25
II. *Taxes on Specific Commodities*		
Salt, sugar, currants, etc.	5	
Beer, malt, hops, licenses	10	
Wine	2	
Spirits	7	
Tea	4	
Coffee	[b]	
Tobacco	2	
Coal, other raw or semi-finished goods	6	
Manufactured goods	4	
Total, taxes on specific goods		40
III. Stamp Duties		3
Total tax revenue		68

[a] Dowell, *History of Taxation*, II, 249-59.
[b] Not over £0.5 million.

Table 6 reveals that the British national government of 1815 subsisted largely on mankind's addiction to stimulants and depressants: taxes on alcoholic drinks, caffein beverages, and tobacco produced 37 percent of the total. Taxes on a miscellany of articles, only a few of which could be called luxuries, yielded another 22 percent. The income tax and the house and establishment taxes, which were at least aimed at, if not imposed upon, the general economic capacity of the individual or the family, contributed 31 percent. Stamp duties, on the other hand, were a minor source of revenue. Finally, it is somewhat surprising how small were the revenues from the land tax and the tax on property passing at death: not over 2 percent of the total, in each case.

Table 7. *TAX SOURCES IN GREAT BRITAIN, 1815, IN DETAIL*

(in millions of pounds sterling)

I. *Direct Taxes*			
Land tax		1.2	
Window tax, inhabited-house tax, and "taxes on establishments" (carriages, menservants, saddle and carriage horses, race-horses and dogs, hair-powder, armorial bearings): a group of "taxes on persons by reference to their expenditure"[a]		6.5	
Income tax at 10 percent		14.6	
Taxes on property passing at death (probate and legacy duties)[b]		1.3	
Taxes on property against risk from fire		0.5	
Taxes on property insured against sea risk		0.4	
Tax on property sold at public auction		0.3	
Taxes on persons providing means of locomotion for the public		0.5	
Tonnage tax on shipping		0.2	
Total			25.5
II. *Taxes on Specific Commodities*			
Salt, at 15 *s.* the bushel		1.6	
Sugar, at 1 *l.* 10 *s.* the cwt.		3.0[c]	
Plum puddings, raisins for dessert, currant dumplings, pepper, vinegar		0.5	
Beer and ingredients:			
Beer	3.3		
Malt	6.0		
Hops	0.2		
Licences, brewers and maltsters	0.2		
Total, beer taxes		9.8[d]	
Wine		1.9	
Distilled spirits:			
Domestic spirits (gin, whisky, British brandy)	3.5		
Foreign and colonial (brandy, rum)	2.9		
Licenses	0.3		
Total, distilled spirits taxes		6.7	
Tea, at 96 percent of price		3.6	
Coffee		0.3	
Tobacco and snuff		2.0	
Coal and culm, slates and stones, carried coastways		0.9	
Timber of various sorts, and in various stages of manufacture		1.8	
Cotton wool[e]		0.8	
Raw and thrown silk		0.4	
Hemp		0.3	

Barilla, indigo, pearl and potashes, bar iron, skins and furs	0.3	
Leather	0.7	
Soap	0.7	
Bricks and tiles	0.3	
Glass	0.4	
Candles	0.4	
Printed goods (textiles)	0.4	
Paper	0.5	
Newspapers	0.4	
Advertisements	0.1	
Gold and silver plate	0.1	
Starch, stone bottles, wire, medicine, cards and dice	0.1	
Tariff on imports not included above	1.2	
Duties on exports	0.4	
Total		39.6
III. *Stamp Duties*		
Bills of exchange and promissory notes	0.9	
Receipts	0.2	
Other	1.7	
Total		2.8
Total, all taxes		67.9

[a] Dowell, *History of Taxation*, II, 250.
[b] Landed property was exempt from these taxes.
[c] After subtracting drawbacks and bounties of £1.6 million.
[d] Constituent items rounded to nearest £100,000.
[e] Not "Cotton, wool".

20. NATIONAL TAX MEASURES, 1816-1829

Parliament granted tax relief on a lavish scale in the first postwar year, 1816, subtracting nearly £18 million annually from the Exchequer's resources. The largest item was the repeal of the income tax, £14 million.

From then until Ricardo's death, seven years later, there were no tax reform measures of substance, nothing important enough to justify essays from Ricardo's pen. Scattered increases in rates in 1819 helped the Government out of financial difficulties attributable partly to the impetuosity of the 1816 Parliament; scattered tax reductions in 1822 and again in 1823 more than counterbalanced the 1819 measures. It was not an exciting period in taxation, once the income tax had been disposed of.

No doubt Ricardo was depressed by the necessity for tax increases only three years after the end of the war, but he almost surely preferred the higher rates then voted on malt, spirits, and tobacco to a return of the income tax. Nor can we picture him as especially pleased, or displeased either, with the choice of malt, salt, and windows for tax relief in 1822 and 1823.

Table 8 lists chronologically all the tax measures noted in Dowell for the years 1816-1829 inclusive.

Table 8. NATIONAL TAX MEASURES IN GREAT BRITAIN, 1816-1829

(in thousands of pounds sterling)

		Estimated gain (+) or estimated loss (—) based on current yield[a]
1816	Repeal of 10 percent income tax	—14,320
	Repeal of war malt duty	— 2,790
	Repeal of war customs and spirit duties	— 1,000
	Increases in port duties and excises:	
	Increase in soap tax, from $2^1/_4d.$ to $3d.$ a pound	+ 230
	Other	n.s.
	Total, net, for 1816	—17,880
1817	No change	
1818	No change	
1819	Increases in rates of tax on	
	Malt	+ 1,400
	Domestic spirits	500
	Tobacco	500
	Coffee and cocoa	130
	Tea (from 96 percent to 100 percent)	130
	Pepper	30
	Consolidation of customs duties, including £200,000 increase in duty on foreign wool	500
	Total, for 1819	+ 3,190
1820	No change	
1821	Repeal of agricultural horse tax	— 450
1822	Repeal of all but 2 *d.* of the additional duty on malt voted in 1819	— 1,400
	Reduction of tax on leather, by one half	— 300
	Reduction of salt tax from 15 *s.* the bushel to 2 *s.* (complete repeal scheduled for 1825)	— 1,400
	Repeal of tonnage tax on shipping	— 150
	Repeal of Irish hearth money and window taxes[b]	— 240
	Total, net, for 1822	— 3,490

1823	Reduction of windows tax by one half Repeal of assessed taxes on establishments with carriages, menservants, and horses	—	2,500
	Repeal of all "establishments" taxes, and dog tax, in Ireland	—	100
	Reduction in spirit duties in Scotland and Ireland		[c]
	Partial repeal of Union duties between Great Britain and Ireland (see below)		
	Total for 1823	—	2,600
1824	Reduction of duties on imported raw and thrown silk	—	460
	Complete repeal of Union duties	—	300
	Repeal of bounties on exportation of silk manufactured articles		n.s.
	Reduction of duties on imported wool	—	350
	Reduction of duty on coal imported into London	—	200
	Reduction in duty on rum	—	150
	Repeal of stamp duties on law proceedings	—	200
	Imposition of export duty of 1 *d.* the pound on wool		n.s.
	Total, net, for 1824	—	1,660
1825	Inadvertent repeal of one fourth of duty on tobacco, owing to error in drafting law		[d]
	Repeal of remnant of salt tax, as scheduled in 1822		n.s.
	Exemption of houses with rent under 10 *l.* a year from inhabited-house duty Exemption of houses with not more than seven windows from windows tax	—	220
	Other minor exemptions	—	50
	Reduction of import duty on hemp by one half	—	100
	Reduction in taxes on coffee, cocoa, and cider	—	150
	Reduction of wine duty from 11 *s.* 5 *d.* the gallon (French) and 7 *s.* 7 *d.* (other) to 6 *s.* and 4 *s.* respectively	—	230
	Reduction of tax on domestic distilled spirits, from 11 *s.* 8¼ *d.* the gallon to 7 *s.*[e]	—	750
	Miscellaneous reductions in tariffs on imports	—	250
	Total, 1825	—	1,750
1826	No change		
1827	No change		
1828	No change		
1829	Reduction in duty on silk		n.s.

[a] "n.s." means "not stated by Dowell."

[b] As of January 17, 1817, the revenues of Great Britain and Ireland were consolidated. "The separate revenue from Ireland was only 4,500,000 *l.*, as against a charge for the funded and unfunded debt of 6,400,000 *l.*, including therein the sum of 2,400,000 *l.* as the sinking fund applicable to the reduction of the

debt." Dowell, *A History of Taxation,* II, 266, note 1. "The revenue from taxes in Ireland in ... 1815 ... was in British currency as follows:—

	£
Customs	2,356,544
Excise[1]	3,298,309
Specially appropriated duties	43,209
Stamps	560,661
	6,258,723

[1] This includes quit-rents and other revenue under the management of the commissioners of excise." *Ibid.,* p. 259.

[c] Gain in revenue, owing to reduction in smuggling.

[d] Smuggling thereupon decreased so much that the reduction was regularized in 1826.

[e] There was a simultaneous reduction of the duty on rum; and the revenue loss was recouped in two years, owing to increased consumption of tax-paid spirits.

21. LOCAL TAXATION IN THE POSTWAR PERIOD

The national budget contained nothing, or virtually nothing, for education, public relief, the maintenance of roads and bridges, the administration of justice, and the police. So far as these functions were performed at all by government, they were at the charge of the local units, financed on a parochial level. By 1818 local rates amounted to £9 million a year. Changes in the local rates during the period here under consideration, 1815-1829, were not significant for purposes of the present analysis.[163]

[163] See Cannan, *History of Local Rates in England,* Chapters IV and V.

CHAPTER XVI

AN APPRAISAL OF RICARDIAN TAX ANALYSIS

Although the body of Ricardian tax doctrine is found in the *Principles*, we have seen that the correspondence, the speeches, and some of the essays and articles contain passages that add to our understanding of the theorems propounded in the book, and touch on a number of other, if usually minor, issues. The order in which these elaborations and additions have been presented in the preceding chapters has necessarily obscured the chronological development of Ricardo's thoughts on taxation. A survey of this development will reveal the extent to which Ricardo had worked out on paper the analysis that took form in the taxation chapters composed from mid-October to mid-November of 1816, and the degree to which the material in those chapters was modified or contradicted by his later thinking.

1. THE RECORD PRIOR TO OCTOBER, 1816

Prior to the composition of the *Principles*, Ricardo wrote little on taxation; moreover, what he did write did not maintain a high level of quality. In both quantity and quality it stands in contrast to his monetary analysis. There is nothing in Ricardo's pre-1816 tax material comparable to his letters published in the *Morning Chronicle* in 1809 and 1810 on "The Price of Gold," and on "Report of the Bullion Committee," or to his essay, *The High Price of Bullion* (1811). The only items of significance are a single chapter in the *Reply to Bosanquet*, and four contributions in his correspondence.

Ricardo's *Reply to Mr. Bosanquet's Practical Observations on the Report of the Bullion Committee* was written in November and December of 1810, and published early in January, 1811.[1] In this booklet of nearly a hundred pages (Sraffa edition) Ricardo devotes Chapter VIII (of only nine pages) to the topic: "Mr. Bosanquet's Opinion—that Years of Scarcity and Taxes have been the sole Cause of the Rise of Prices, excessive Circulation no Cause—considered." There is nothing else on taxation in the *Reply*.

This Chapter VIII, when set against the analysis six years later in the *Principles*, is evidence that Ricardo did some rethinking over that period. Of the three contributions to tax theory in the *Reply*, only one remains unaltered in the 1817 edition of the *Principles:* the distinction between taxes paid out of income and those paid out of capital.[2] A general tax on commodities will fall entirely on consumers, according to the *Reply*,[3] rather than chiefly on profits, as is stated in the *Principles*. And if the prices of commodities are increased by taxation, "it does not appear necessarily to follow that more money will be requisite to circulate them";[4] but we have seen that this view was abandoned in the first and second editions of the *Principles*, to be taken up again in the third. Finally, the *Reply's* conclusion that an income tax would have no effect on prices[5] never gets into the *Principles*.

The four contributions of substance in the correspondence prior to October, 1816, are found in: (1) an exchange of letters in which Ricardo does not quite convince Malthus that taxes on raw produce do not fall on the landlord;[6] (2) a series of exchanges, again with Malthus, in which Ricardo insists that the prevailing high price of corn is not due to taxation, and affords no grounds for a protecting duty, while Malthus stumbles in attempting to extend the compensating-duty concept to taxes of general scope;[7] (3) a page by Ricardo to Malthus on the effects of a subsidy in stimulating exports;[8] and (4) a brief assertion in a letter to McCulloch that no matter how heavy their taxes, farmers will still get the general rate of profits, since all taxes fall ultimately on the consumer (McCulloch is not sure that he knows what that statement means).[9] Some light is cast on Ricardo's view of current tax policy; he hopes

[1] S, III, 11. [2] S, III, 243-44. [3] S, III, 241, 243. [4] S, III, 243. [5] S, III, 241.
[6] S, VI, 173, 175-76. See Appendix B below. [7] S, VI, 181, 202, 206, 224, 256.
[8] S, VI, 73.
[9] S, VII, 38, 94. Other passages on taxation in Ricardo's letters, S, VI, and S, VII, prior to October, 1816, are remarks on acceptance of bank notes in payment of taxes (S, VI, 53), taxation an alleged cause of high prices (S, VI, 54), the effect on profits of restrictions on imports of corn (S, VI, 108-9, 119), a comment on the disadvantage of a heavy government debt (S ,VI, 345), a criticism

Trower will petition against the income tax, though that levy would be acceptable if the Government's protestations that it would be retained for only a short period could be believed[10] (Trower thought that the income tax never should have been repealed).[11]

Thus we lack evidence from the written record that Ricardo had developed much of his tax analysis before he set about writing the middle group of chapters of the *Principles.* The rapidity with which those chapters were composed suggests the contrary conclusion. It seems unlikely that this question will ever be settled, but the weight of evidence favors the thesis that Ricardo worked out his tax analysis almost *de novo,* with facility, immediately after he had constructed the framework of his economic system in the first seven chapters of the *Principles.*

2. THE RECORD FROM OCTOBER, 1816, TO SEPTEMBER, 1823

In assessing the further development of Ricardo's thinking on taxation after 1816, we are again struck by the lack of pamphlet or essay material. There are only two items of interest. The article, "Funding System," written in 1819 for the Encyclopaedia Britannica, and published in 1820, has a good deal to say on taxation, but only in relation to the public debt. *On Protection to Agriculture,* 1822, contains several pages devoted to taxation, but they are scattered through the pamphlet, and the tax system is not the focal point.

(a) *Correspondence.* The correspondence for the period from October, 1816, to the end of 1818 in Volume VII of the *Letters* does not add much to Ricardian tax analysis. In fact, the only analytical contribution of substance is that in Ricardo's letter of November 20, 1816, to Mill, in which he corrects an error in the manuscript then in the hands of Mill; he had argued—erroneously, he now concludes—that a general tax on profits would affect landlords adversely. He had fallen into the error of regarding such a tax as if it acted in the same manner as a proportionate tax on gross produce. It was now clear to Ricardo that a tax on profits always leaves corn rent unaltered, while a tax on raw produce,

of McCulloch's plan for forcible reduction of interest on the public debt (S, VII, 37), and a plea for economy and a balanced budget (S, VII, 38). The only other references to taxation by his correspondents concern the taxation of necessaries versus luxuries (Malthus, S, VI, 118); the amount of stamp duty on Bank of England notes (Grenfell, S, VI, 261, 265, 275, 282, 286); and doubt on what to say on bounties (Malthus, S, VI, 289, and VII, 68).

[10] S, VII, 27; see also 25. [11] S, VII, 142, 149.

tithes, etc. affects corn rent, but not money rent.[12] The other passages of more than incidental interest are those in which Ricardo again disagrees with McCulloch on the latter's plan for reducing interest forcibly on the public debt,[13] informs Mill that he has altered some views on taxation (without saying which ones),[14] informs Malthus that he has reverted to his former views on taxes on raw produce (again, not specifying what the changes are),[15] declares to McCulloch that if the price of corn fell the ability of the nation to pay taxes would increase and the farmers themselves would automatically have a lighter money tax bill,[16] and voices to Mill and Trower his misgivings about a flow of capital from Great Britain stimulated by the heavy taxation needed to service the huge public debt.[17]

More or less in passing, Ricardo declares that rigid economy in government expenditure is needed[18] and that relief works to employ the poor on roads are harmful, since they divert capital from better uses (this, dated January 3, 1817, in a year of commercial crisis),[19] but that the poor law itself must be changed only gradually.[20] The year 1818 was also the one in which Ricardo did his best to satisfy McCulloch on the issue of government extravagance.[21]

While it is clear from the letters of this period—October, 1816, to December, 1818—that Ricardo's thoughts on taxation had undergone some change, and that he was developing a significant theorem to be elaborated later (capacity to pay taxes, under a lower national money income), little detail is given; we get hints rather than explanations.

The third volume of Ricardian correspondence, covering the period 1819 through June, 1821, contains more solid analysis than the others: Ricardo's letter to Trower on the effect of taxation on the price level,[22] his letter to McCulloch on taxation and the accumulation of capital with its implications for the laboring class,[23] the exchange of correspondence between McCulloch and Ricardo on the consequences of a tax imposed to pay a subsidy abroad,[24] and discussion of the corn laws.[25] But both the problems and the conclusions reached by Ricardo are all to be found in the *Principles.*

A greater interest attaches to the reactions of the letter writers to the

[12] S, VII, 90-92. [13] S, VII, 103, 104-106. [14] S, VII, 88. [15] S, VII, 115.
[16] S, VII, 104. [17] S, VII, 171, 260. [18] S, VII, 90.
[19] S, VII, 116; see also 135, and Trower, 209. [20] S, VII, 248.
[21] S, VII, 281, 286, 337, 349. For other references to taxation in S, VII, from October, 1816, see pp. 75, 84, 86, 99, 100, 107-108, 151, 154, 228, and 253.
[22] S, VIII, 153-56. [23] S, VIII, 168-73. [24] See Section 3, Chapter IV above.
[25] See Sections 1 and 3, Chapter XII above.

economic and social crisis of 1819. To McCulloch, the situation of the country was now "critical in the extreme—With ignorant and despotic ministers, a million of paupers, a taxation three times as oppressive as in any other country in the world, and corn laws forcing the cultivation of the poorest soils...."[26] Ricardo, Trower, Malthus, and Brown were originators or recipients of persuasive arguments on the need for sound tax policy, and, to this end, for a study of the British tax system in the light of basic principles.[27]

Ricardo entered Parliament in 1819, and there expounded his proposal for paying off the national debt by a capital levy, but less controversy over this plan is found in the correspondence than might have been expected. Some details are filled in, and taxation for a sinking fund is frequently discussed.[28]

The correspondence is enlivened by remarks of James Mill on the relation of parliamentary reform to taxation,[29] and it is significant that both Ricardo and McCulloch express the opinion that the income tax need not be revived.[30] McCulloch is meanwhile struggling with his article on tithes.[31] Finally, we note that Ricardo was writing his article on "Funding System" in 1819,[32] was disturbed by Malthus's ideas on government spending,[33] and still was of the view that the prevailing distress of the farmers could not be laid at the door of taxation resting especially on agriculture.[34] There is nothing of the unexpected for us in these bits and pieces.

References to taxation decrease in the last volume of the correspondence, covering the period from July, 1821 through 1823. Of the three topics given more than cursory treatment, two are quite familiar by now: the importance of applying the principles of political economy to the practice of taxation, and of providing some treatise that will show the way;[35] and the lack of connection (according to Ricardo) between taxation and the prevailing distress in agriculture.[36] The only new issue raised is how to value tithes for redemption.[37] The topics noted in passing

[26] Letter of Dec. 5, 1819, to Ricardo, S, VIII, 139.

[27] S, VIII, 71, 79, 101, 130-31, 132.

[28] For references to Vol. VIII of the Sraffa edition on this point, see Chapter XI above.

[29] S, VIII, 9, 53. [30] S, VIII, 190, 196. [31] S, VIII, 203, 214, 222, 229, 237.

[32] S, VIII, 75-77, 127. [33] S, VIII, 185.

[34] S, VIII, 357. For other references by Ricardo to taxation in VIII, see pages 2, 135, 147, 277, 302, 369, and 371.

[35] S, IX, 68-69, 87. [36] S, IX, 152, 160, 165-67, 188, 199-200.

[37] S, IX, 31, 39-40, 70, 88.

are also familiar: how the stockholder fares under changes in the price level;[38] poor rates and the poor law;[39] governmental extravagance;[40] and ot course the corn laws.[41] All of these references carry a date prior to June of 1822. From July to December of that year Ricardo and his family toured the Continent. His letters en route make almost no reference to taxation.

The correspondence of 1823 contains few passages on taxation, and none of consequence.[42] There is no evidence here that Ricardo's mind was occupied with the subject in the months preceding his death in September, 1823. Did he remember the promise made to Trower in November, 1819, "on some future day ... [to] bend my whole mind to the consideration of this subject [the construction of an ideal tax system]?"[43] If so, his will may have been weakened by ill health, but this is merely conjecture. The moving passage in a letter to Mill in which Ricardo expresses a conviction that "general happiness would be best promoted if death visited us on an average at an earlier period than he now does,"[44] occurs three years before his own death; and there is little reference to the state of his health in the correspondence from that time on.[45] A more likely explanation for the lack of tax analysis in the 1823 correspondence is that Ricardo was occupied with another problem: "The difficult subject of value has engaged my thoughts but without my being able satisfactorily to find my way out of the labyrinth."[46] His next to last letter, written to Malthus on the day his fatal illness began, and containing the implicit farewell, "And now my dear Malthus I have done,"[47] was devoted entirely to the subject of value.

(b) *Speeches.* The record of Ricardo's speeches in the House of Commons, March, 1819, to July, 1823, is somewhat more rewarding than the correspondence. This fact may appear the more surprising, in that we do not have here Ricardo's own words, by his own hand, and the questions and reactions of his friends, but instead only a transcription

[38] S, IX, 39, 73. [39] S, IX, 40, 52-53, 181, 201. [40] S, IX, 120, 122, 124, 180.

[41] See references in Chapter XII above. See also S, IX, 17.

[42] See S, IX, 267, 269, 276, 342, 345, 362, 369, and 372.

[43] S, VIII, 132. [44] Letter of Sept. 25, 1820, S, VIII, 253.

[45] See the passing reference in letter of May 20, 1822, Ricardo to Trower, S, IX, 196. Cf.: "Mr. Ricardo never appeared more cheerful, or in better health, than he did during his last retirement in the country, just previous to his death" (A Memoir of David Ricardo, by one of his brothers, presumably Moses Ricardo), S, X, 12.

[46] Letter of Aug. 8, 1823, Ricardo to McCulloch, S, IX, 330.

[47] Letter of Aug. 31, 1823, S, IX, 382. "The malady commenced with a pain in

or paraphrase of Ricardo's verbal exposition, by newspaper reporters. The problems Ricardo discussed were frequently difficult for them to understand, and he complains that "they often represent me as uttering perfect nonsense."[48] Some of the reports in Hansard were based on material supplied directly by Ricardo, but most of them were compilations by T. C. Hansard from newspaper accounts. "Thus, from the picture that we have of parliamentary reporting at that time, it seems clear that we cannot read Ricardo's speeches with the same confidence in their authenticity as we can his writings, or even his evidence."[49]

No doubt caution is justified in using this source; but for matters of taxation, at least, or the associated problems of public debt and expenditure, the Parliamentary reports seem reasonably accurate and complete, and there are no instances of "utter nonsense."[50] This conclusion is based on the test of consistency with Ricardo's writings in these fields, and the further test of ability to remove ambiguities in, or add illuminating details for, passages in the *Principles* and in the letters. Furthermore, the style of the paraphrases is commonly vigorous, trenchant, and lucid.

Taxation and collateral problems of public finance account for the major part of Ricardo's speeches in Parliament; and within this category the range of subjects is wide. Thus in the 1819 session, his first, Ricardo dealt with the following proposals, in the order given: Poor rates misapplication bill, resumption of cash payments, state lotteries, sinking fund, poor rates misapplication bill again, resumption of cash payments again, exchequer bills, the budget, bank advances to the government, and excise duties.[51] In the next session, 1819-1820, Ricardo broadened his interests, or his willingness to expose himself, speaking on seditious meetings, and Mr. Owen's plan, but in the third of his sessions, that of

the ear, which resembled a common ear-ache, and which they treated as the effect of some little cold. He suffered somewhat on the sunday night..." ["31 August," notes Sraffa]. Letter of Sept. 19, 1823, Mill to McCulloch, S, IX, 390, and note 2. Ricardo died Sept. 11, 1823.

[48] S, V, xxix, and references there cited.

[49] Sraffa, in S, V, xxx-xxxi.

[50] Except the report that Ricardo advocated "a countervailing duty to the home grower, to recompence all the additional charges which he had to pay in taxes above the charges borne by the foreign grower...." Speech of March 7, 1821, S, V, 82. Fay implies that the error was Ricardo's, not the reporter's; see his review of S, V, in *Econ. J.*, LXII (No. 247, Sept. 1952), p. 665. Cf. note 60 to Chapter XII above.

[51] S, V, 1-27. For the debate on the excise tax bill of 1819, see Hansard, XL, 1207-21, June 18, 1819.

1820, it is again purely the financier who takes the floor. The same is true of the 1821 session, with minor exceptions; the subject of bank cash payments was then the preponderant one for Ricardo.[52]

In contrast to the correspondence, the speeches show no decline of interest in taxation, public debt, and government expenditures in the last two years of Ricardo's life.

In 1822, his speeches were centered largely on one topic, this being the supreme one of agricultural distress, how to relieve it, and to what extent taxation was responsible for it. Nothing in the speeches in the other years, with the possible exception of his observations on "Mr. Western's Motion Respecting the Resumption of Cash Payments," in 1823,[53] matches for length and depth of analysis the report of Ricardo's speech on the "Motion for a Committee on the Agricultural Distress,"[54] or of his participation in the debate on the "Agricultural Distress Report";[55] and even the cash-payments speech of 1823 is at least equaled by two long speeches on the same topic in June and July, 1822.[56]

The speeches in the session 1823 cover a broader range of public finance topics: Financial situation of the country; Agricultural distress—Surrey petition; Mr. Whitmore's motion respecting the corn laws; Mr. Maberly's motion for the reduction of taxation; National debt reduction bill; Coal duties; Warehousing [for re-export] bill; Military and naval pensions bill; Scotch linen [quality stamp tax] laws; Tallow [import duty]; Beer duties bill; East and West Indies sugars [import duties]; Malt and beer tax; Irish tithes composition bill; Reciprocity of duties.[57]

The wealth of material on taxation, and on debt and expenditure, to be found in the speeches makes impractical the kind of summary statements given above for the letters; but references to the speeches have been given at the appropriate places in the preceding chapters. The public finance material is more abundant here than in the letters probably because the floor of Parliament was scarcely the place to discuss abstruse questions of value, and of distribution of the national product among profits, interest, and rent. Nor could an explanation of the law of comparative advantage have been reproduced in intelligible form by the newspaper reporters. To be sure, international trade theory and the doctrine of the stationary state are presented incidentally as Ricardo speaks against the corn laws, but there are fewer speeches on this subject than might have been expected. Those that he did give are notable for

[52] S, V, 28-122. [53] June 11, 1823; S, V, 309-22.
[54] Feb. 18, 1822; S, V, 129-38. [55] May 7, 9, 13, 1822; S, V, 162-86.
[56] S, V, 198-218; 231-45. [57] S, V, 246-331.

depth of analysis and scope.

The passages on taxation in the speeches are remarkable in their consistency with the doctrines already advanced in the *Principles.* They do not add to the theory appreciably. The net impression left by a reading of both the correspondence and the speeches is therefore that Ricardo's tax analysis can be appraised almost entirely in terms of what we find in the *Principles.* Ricardian tax doctrine was set down, in all its essentials, in October and November of 1816.

(c) *Other Sources.* In his evidence given before Parliamentary committees on the usury laws and on the resumption of cash payments by the Bank, Ricardo makes only three references, and those brief ones, to taxation, debt, or government expenditures.[58] They have been cited at the relevant points in the chapters above. Similarly, the few speeches "on various occasions" contain only two brief references to these matters.[59] In the "Two Papers on Parliamentary Reform" no such references occur; and in the Appendices in Volume V of Sraffa, only a brief one.[60]

In the engrossing collection that constitutes Volume X of the Sraffa-Dobb *Works and Correspondence,* the public finance student, unfortunately, will find almost nothing of professional interest. The entire "Journal of a Tour of the Continent" contains only two references to taxation.[61] The available information on Ricardo's library gives no hint of interest in taxation and, of his "commonplace book" excerpts, only two lie in that field.[62]

However, Ricardo's experiences on the Stock Exchange—and "stock," in those days, meant government bonds, aside from the stock of a few great chartered companies—will interest the student of debt-management techniques; and the information on his personal investment policy should have meaning for the analyst of private finance.[63]

Ricardo's early acquaintance with William Frend has been referred to in Chapter I above.[64]

[58] S, V, 374, 385, 386.

[59] S, V, 472 (national debt oppressive), 485 (restrict elective franchise to those who pay direct taxes, or are fairly called householders).

[60] If the price of wheat falls, the money wage of farm labor will fall, and "If the real value of the farmer's taxation as a grower be increased he can [pass on] that increase to the consumer." S, V, 525.

[61] On smuggling, S, X, 189 (see note 62, Chapter XI above); and on rejection by the States General of Holland of a proposal to lay a general tax on the grinding of corn, S, X, 202.

[62] S, X, 396. [63] S, X, 67-106. [64] S, X, 34. See note 10, Chapter I above.

3. PROBLEMS AND SOLUTIONS

An evaluation of Ricardo's tax analysis may be based on his choice of problems and on the degree of success with which he attacked them.

Ricardo did not attempt to prescribe a tax policy, or a budgetary policy, for the difficult years of 1815-1823, a period, on the whole, of falling prices and unemployment. He was surprised by the length and intensity of the depression, but this fact alone does not account for his air of aloofness from the current scene of distress. Nor was he entirely preoccupied with long-run problems; his demand for repeal of the corn laws and his advocacy of a capital levy to retire the war debt were based largely on the immediate benefits that would ensue or the immediate dangers that would be averted. An ingrained belief that government was incapable of mitigating economic fluctuations, or at any rate that the government in power was incompetent to do so, is the most likely explanation. But ultimately we must give weight to the fact that the economic model that Ricardo had constructed by the end of 1816 was not addressed to the problem of short-period fluctuations, and since Ricardo remained preoccupied with refining and defending this model to the end of his life, he had no set of tools with which to attack the current depression.

The details of tax technique, upon the mastery of which any workable program of tax reform must rest, were even less congenial to Ricardo's mind. The "amiable but incompetent Vansittart" [65] was in charge of the nation's finances, and "the financial structure that Pitt had built up was in ruins. . . . The work of financial reform, at which Pitt had made a beginning, had been suspended—taxes had been piled on incoherently with a sole view to revenue." [66] Yet Ricardo seems almost entirely unaware of the need for tax reform, and he scarcely ever analyzes technical problems, even those that bear directly on his general theorems. For example, we never learn from Ricardo that the fall in farm prices in 1816 gave farmers ground for claiming that in many cases they could not continue to pay an income tax on farm profits under Schedule B, which defined profits as a fraction of the rent, for the rent paid or imputed might not have decreased, while the actual profits had fallen considerably. Vansittart had conceded that if the income tax were retained, the Schedule B farm profits should be set at only one third of the rent instead of three fourths.[67] We may doubt that Ricardo was ever

[65] Acworth, *Financial Reconstruction in England, 1815-1822,* p. vi; see also *ibid.,* pp. 11, 12, 47, 52, 130, 131.
[66] *Ibid.,* p. 10. [67] *Ibid.,* p. 30.

truly committed in his own mind to writing a treatise on taxation, or on tax reform, of the type that has been alluded to above. What we do get from him is an opposition to all taxation that at times seems almost irresponsible.

Equity issues in taxation appear now and again in Ricardo's writings and speeches, as in his remarks on taxes on law proceedings, and on special taxation of land rent. But he makes no coordinated assault on the problems of justice in distribution of the tax burden. Thus he shows no interest in the issues of progressivity versus proportionality in taxation, allowances for size and composition of family, or earned versus unearned income.[68]

Finally, outside the field of taxation proper, we get from Ricardo no help on management of the public debt—for example, perpetuities versus short term debt—, and no theory of public expenditures.

Turning now from the negative to the positive aspects of Ricardo's choice of taxation problems, we find that his chief interest lies in the broad economic consequences of taxes in general, particularly with respect to: a) distribution of the national income among landlords, capitalists, and laborers; b) accumulation of capital and the allied problem of a nation's taxable capacity; and c) the price level. He also shows some concern over the influence of any one tax on the allocation of resources. Finally, Ricardo feels obliged to expose the errors that he finds in the tax analysis of those whose opinions carry weight, notably Smith and Malthus and, to a lesser degree, J. B. Say.

Ricardo's eleven tax chapters, following as they do the initial seven of the *Principles,* are closely keyed to his macro-economic system. The system itself, with all its gaps and inconsistencies, is an astonishing intellectual achievement, and the degree of consistency that the tax analysis maintains with it is no less remarkable. Moreover, we have seen that Ricardo's passages on taxation in his other writings after October, 1816, and in his speeches leave the impression each time that he has just come from rereading some part of the *Principles.* Given the economic world that he had created in his mind, Ricardo succeeds brilliantly in demonstrating the effects of taxation on the distribution of income among the three major claimants.[69]

[68] If Ricardo was stimulated to tax analysis by William Frend, he seems not to have shared the latter's concern for taxing income from "personal industry" at a lower rate than income from land or government obligations. See Frend, *The Principles of Taxation,* pp. 34-36.

[69] Wesley C. Mitchell, as reported in the unauthorized *Lecture Notes on Types of Economic Theory* (p. 149), thought that in comparison with modern treatises,

The extent of this achievement is somewhat obscured for the reader by an unexciting conclusion, inherent in the workings of a Ricardian economy. Aside from a tax on pure land rent, it makes very little difference, except in the short period, what major tax is imposed. Wealthy consumers of luxury products may pay a small amount of the total tax bill; the rest will come out of profits. Our attention is caught here and there by a certain looseness in Ricardo's reasoning. He seems occasionally to confuse the short run with the long run. Also, the implications of a market rate of wages in excess of the natural rate are not uniform throughout the analysis, for they sometimes include and sometimes seem to exclude the possibility that the worker has a certain amount of taxable capacity, that is to say, inability to shift the tax. These problems aside, the policy implication of Ricardo's distributive findings appears to be that any amateur can construct an optimum tax system. The total amount of taxation is what matters, not the structure. From this viewpoint, Ricardo's lack of interest in tax techniques is quite understandable.

The restraint that taxation may exert on the accumulation of capital is important to Ricardo if only because it might bring the stationary state uncomfortably close. A recurring theme is the tendency of almost all taxes to impede capital accumulation, since they absorb, for unproductive use by the state, funds that would have been employed productively by capitalists. There are exceptions, indeed, as shown by the distinction between taxes paid out of capital and those paid out of revenue.

An allied problem is a flight of capital or even capitalists that may be induced by the prospect of a long period of high taxation to service a heavy war debt.

On capital accumulation and taxable capacity, Ricardo must be credited with another intellectual success, this time not only in terms of his own macro-economic system but also with respect to more subtle implications of the daily conduct of various taxpayers. Thus the reaction of the man of means to a luxury excise is distinguished from that to be expected to a death duty. And Ricardo's warnings on the possible flight of capitalists abroad reflect his assessment of the strength of motives

"Ricardo's *Principles* seems like an assembly of mechanically disconnected parts." The judgment may be too severe, but for present purposes it is significant because it is immediately qualified with respect to the taxation chapters: "In just one respect Ricardo's treatise is highly integrated. His views concerning the incidence of taxation are closely reasoned corollaries from his theories of distribution. From the technical point of view, Ricardo's discussion of the incidence of certain taxes is perhaps the most remarkable part of all his speculations." *Ibid.*, p. 150.

difficult to appraise, but perhaps fairly well known to him from the circles in which his professional life had been spent.

Still, it must be confessed that for the most part the conclusions on taxation and capital are again inherent in Ricardo's economic system, and are correspondingly simplified.

A distinctive feature of the taxation chapters is the analysis of the effect of taxation on the general level of prices, and on relative prices. The conclusions are foreshadowed in earlier sections of the *Principles*, but not as clearly as in Ricardo's treatment of the problem of capital accumulation. They are more definite and more plausible with respect to changes in relative prices than when they deal with the general price level. An example of the former is Ricardo's proof that the effect on prices of a uniform tax on profits is not uniform. While this conclusion was implicit in the analysis of Chapter I, "On Value," it is developed remarkably in Chapter XV, "Taxes on Profits."

The effect of a broad-based tax on the level of prices is an issue on which, as we have seen, Ricardo never quite made up his mind. His very inconclusiveness, however, stimulates our interest as we trace his thoughts in the text of the *Principles*, in the footnotes, and in his correspondence with Trower. It is even somewhat refreshing to find Ricardo at a loss, for once. He may not have found the answer, but his mastery of international trade analysis and monetary theory enabled him to touch on most of the considerations with an astuteness that has not since been excelled.

Certain types of tax exert a pronounced effect on the allocation of resources. Here, Ricardo is sometimes helpful (taxes on transfer of property), sometimes not (allocation of resources to the professions under a capital levy), but always suggestive.

Ricardo did not engage in criticism for its own sake, but an intellectual error on the part of anyone he took seriously caused him so much discomfort that he could not let it pass unnoted. Despite his esteem for Smith, particularly in the field of taxation, Ricardo is unable to resist the challenge of the complex errors that he discovers in *The Wealth of Nations*. Here, surely, Ricardo succeeds as well as in any of the tasks he set himself. He was a fair critic, with occasional exceptions, but a sharp one.[70] It is easy to underrate the importance of this kind of activity for the advancement of economics. Ricardo never convinced Malthus of his errors, but he made them pretty clear to the rest of the world. Ricardo's

[70] Gonner seems unduly harsh: "Ricardo is a singularly unsympathetic critic." G, xxv.

usually generous and sympathetic interpretation, coupled with a rigid self-discipline in good manners, merely heightened the impact of his criticism.

In summary, then, Ricardo must be said to have reached most of his intellectual goals in tax analysis. He may not have chosen for study what to us would be the most important problems; his unwillingness to discuss tax policy in terms of the postwar economic depression is a case in point. The macro-economic system that he had to construct before he could reach conclusions on taxation or any other policy problem now seems vastly oversimplified, yet it represents a remarkable achievement; and how much more simplified is it than subsequent macro-economic constructs derived from economies more complex than the England of 1817?

Nevertheless, the student of Ricardian tax doctrine comes away with mingled feelings of gratification and disappointment.

4. THE RICARDIAN INTELLECT

Ricardo's passion for intellectual exercise shows in his tax analysis as clearly as anywhere. Difficult problems attract him; the exploration of hitherto unobserved connections between propositions in different sectors of economics delights him. Having explained the doctrine of rent, Ricardo sees at once its implications for shifting and incidence theory. More difficult linkages, such as that between the quantity theory of money and the effect of taxation on the price level, cause him more trouble but, we may infer, give him correspondingly more satisfaction. The implications of the lack of mobility of labor and capital that characterizes international trade are skillfully pursued with respect to taxation. Construction of new connections between branches of the science lends an air of excitement to Ricardo's otherwise dry and unemotional style. Ricardo has a system-building mind; he is an intellectual architect of the first order. Malthus may have had more insight than Ricardo on particular economic problems, a more fruitful intuition, and a broader grasp of the social environment in which economic forces operate, but Malthus never took the trouble, or never was able, to link his observations into a closely articulated whole.

The discomfort Ricardo experienced at the failure of others to maintain consistency is but another aspect of his propensity to explore. Thus he writes to Malthus,

I diff[er to]o, as you know, as to the effects of taxati[on] on the growth of produce. You appear to me not quite consistent in admitting as you unequivocally do that the last portion of land cultivated, yields nothing more than the profits of stock,—no rent, and yet to maintain that taxes on necessaries or on raw produce fall on the landlord and not on the consumer.[71]

An analyst of Ricardo's macro-economic system has something to gain technically from a study of the Ricardian tax material: for example, the discussion of productive and unproductive consumption in Chapter VIII of the *Principles*. At least one of the tax chapters seems to have almost no function other than an elaboration of his general economic and monetary theory: Chapter XIII, "Taxes on Gold."

The very tightness and occasional obscurity of Ricardo's writing offer a challenge, usually rewarding, to the reader who is willing to believe that Ricardo is consistent, intellectually powerful, and almost always working on an issue of some importance. Puzzling out some of the Ricardian passages becomes almost the game of solving cryptograms. The reader can bear down on Ricardo's more difficult sentences or paragraphs with the reasonable expectation that if he persists he will discover the point that Ricardo wants to make. This kind of mental exercise ordinarily does not pay with obscure passages in Malthus or even in Adam Smith. When Smith or Malthus have a valid point they are usually clear and explicit; Ricardo may or may not be.

Beneath Ricardo's sweet reasonableness in controversy, his almost unfailing courtesy, and his apparent desire to consider all sides of a question with an open mind, there lies a certain rigidity. Ricardo was probably impressed, more than he would admit to himself, by the closeness of his own reasoning, the power of his own intellect, and his own architectural skill. He must have felt that he had constructed a system that was not to be demolished by any passing critic. As long as the principles of this system stood, all the corollaries were valid. The reader gets the impression that no one, however skillful and systematic, could have persuaded Ricardo to alter the foundations of his macro-economic structure, once the edifice had been reared. Ricardo was willing to change a detail here and there, and in one instance he inserted a major revision: the chapter "On Machinery" in the third edition of the *Principles*. But this reconstruction was made largely on his own initiative; it was not primarily a concession to criticism.

Ricardo's frequent concern with the short period and his almost total lack of interest in problems of friction are difficult to reconcile. Perhaps

[71] Letter of Feb. 6, 1815, S, VI, 173. MS. torn at bracketed portions (note by Sraffa, *idem*).

they derive from his experiences as a speculator in stocks. The rapidity with which external events are reflected in short-period fluctuations in the prices of securities has no counterpart in the labor market or in the market for capital instruments. Ricardo was of course aware of this fact and even acknowledged it now and then, but could not bring himself to dwell on the consequences. He would have been gratified if someone else had done so, preferably in the treatise on taxation that he and Trower hoped for.

A disturbing emotional overtone marks some of Ricardo's analytical passages, notably those concerned with the total weight of taxation and with his proposal for a capital levy to retire the public debt. Ricardo's usual courtsey in controversy, to judge from these passages, must have been the product of great self control. He felt deeply that those who differed with him on these important points were essentially and fundamentally in error, sometimes dangerously so. This belief blinded him occasionally to the very nature of the problem that his opponents were struggling with. Thus he seems unable to understand what Malthus is groping for in viewing taxation and government expenditures against the background of unemployment and falling prices. Another emotional charge enters at this point: Ricardo was so irritated by Malthus's patchy logic that he made little effort to understand.[72] Again, Ricardo did not do Say justice with respect to the latter's comments on the English land tax.[73] The occasional complimentary references to Malthus and Say do not mean that Ricardo respected their intellectual powers. Smith, indeed, Ricardo truly admired, but even so, he was not always careful to be fair —witness his comments on the alleged spiral effect of the wages tax, under Smithian doctrine.[74] To McCulloch, on the other hand, Ricardo yielded too readily, not because he thought McCulloch a superior intellect, but because McCulloch was himself most concerned with the problems that also moved Ricardo deeply, and because McCulloch shared some of Ricardo's firmest convictions, or prejudices, notably with respect to the extravagance of government. James Mill, to whose advice Ricardo was always attentive, had almost nothing to offer him on taxation, or public finance generally.

Ricardo's distrust of government was almost absolute. He had good short-run reasons; he was a strong supporter of parliamentary reform, and was in a position to observe the uninspired leadership of the Tory party of that time. The fact that he had purchased his own seat in

[72] See *Notes on Malthus's Principles of Political Economy*, S, II, 433-45.

[73] See Section 3 in Chapter XV above. [74] See Section 2 in Chapter X above.

Parliament did not obscure for him the shortcomings of a system that allowed this. Ricardo became a country squire, but he was able to see the bias in the actions of a Parliament controlled by that group. Even a body only quasi-governmental in character, like the Bank of England, seemed committed to bungling.

Still, Ricardo's refusal to recognize any possible extension of governmental functions that would benefit the commonwealth is a subtle but effective irritant. We are made to feel that this is a pathological sector of economic analysis, and after a time become correspondingly depressed. There are occasional glimpses of a better world, but they are few.[75] More characteristic is the remark reported in Parliament in 1822: "He had voted for every reduction of taxes that had been proposed in the course of the session, because he was anxious for the repeal of taxes, feeling that every tax must prove a burthen upon the public."[76]

5. RICARDO'S INFLUENCE ON JOHN STUART MILL

The influence exerted by Ricardo's tax analysis in the period following his death may be tested by examining from this point of view the chapters on taxation in John Stuart Mill's *Principles of Political Economy*. McCulloch we leave out of account as being both a disciple and a contemporary of Ricardo's in his writings on public finance. The first edition of Mill's *Principles* (1848) appeared thirty-one years after the *Principles* of Ricardo, and revisions were made in the taxation chapters through the seventh and last edition of 1871. Even for the first edition, enough time had elapsed for Mill to have easily ignored or disavowed Ricardo if his tax theorems had come to appear unimportant or erroneous.

This Mill did not do; the staples of Ricardian tax doctrine are intact in the 1848 *Principles*, and also in the edition of 1871. A tax on wages of the lowest kind will come out of profits, and so too will a tax on

[75] See his remark on taxes earmarked for financing transportation facilities, S, VIII, 155.

[76] Speech of April 3, 1822, S, V, 154. See also speech of May 7, 1822, S, V, 168. Ricardo's expression of willingness to follow James Mill in believing that "legislation" may "improve society" seems rather an inadvertent by-product of a desire to offer congratulations to his friend (Mill had sent Ricardo a copy of his *History of British India*) than an indication of his convictions. See the letter of Dec. 18, 1817, Ricardo to Mill, S, VII, 227-29, referred to by Hutchison, "James Mill and the Political Education of Ricardo," *Cambridge Journal*, VII (No. 2, Nov. 1953), p. 88.

necessaries.[77] Such taxes cannot raise the general level of prices.[78] A tax on rent falls on rent.[79] A specific or ad valorem tax on corn lowers corn rent but leaves money rent unchanged.[80] Mill even followed Ricardo in forgetting to specify whether an income tax is shifted, though the implication is clear that no shifting occurs, if the tax carries an exemption for a minimum of subsistence. Like Ricardo, Mill considers the income tax inherently unworkable, though both men had lived or were living under an income tax that did work.[81]

Mill, to be sure, is more cautious than Ricardo. He equivocates, as though fearing the enlightened or sophisticated reader's reaction to dicta of the Ricardian type, stripped of qualifications. A possible consequence of a tax on wages is a permanent lowering of "the standard of comfortable subsistence in the minds of the poorest class." [82] Similarly, a tax on corn may "lower the condition of the labouring classes. . . ." [83] The context, however, indicates that Mill considered these to be the less likely consequences. The same kind of population growth under the progressive state that we may infer from Ricardo [84] is implied by Mill.[85]

Moreover, when Mill attempts to extend Ricardo's doctrines of shifting and incidence, the results are not always happy. Mill assumes a separation of the tax on house rent into two parts—the part on land rent and the part on rent paid for the building:[86] an assumption that no true marginalist deriving from Ricardo should have made.[87] From the valid, or at least plausible, conclusion that a general tax on the sale of all commodities could not raise the general level of prices, Mill moved to the dubious proposition that the distribution of the burden of such a tax depended on its initial impact: "if levied from the sellers, it would be a tax on profits, if from the buyers, a tax on consumption; and neither class could throw the burthen upon the other." [88] We can scarcely imagine Ricardo reasoning that the economic burden of the tax would depend simply on its legal point of impact, and he surely would not have

[77] J. S. Mill, *Principles of Political Economy*, Ashley ed., pp. 827-28, 839-40.
[78] *Ibid.*, pp. 466-67, 837. [79] *Ibid.*, pp. 823-24. [80] *Ibid.*, pp. 840-42.
[81] *Ibid.*, pp. 829-30, 867-68. [82] *Ibid.*, p. 828.
[83] *Ibid.*, p. 840. See also *ibid.*, p. 868.
[84] See Chapter II above.
[85] J. S. Mill, *Principles*, p. 828. [86] *Ibid.*, p. 832.
[87] See Edgeworth, "The Pure Theory of Taxation," in *Papers Relating to Political Economy*, II, 83-85, and Bickerdike, "Taxation of Site Values," *Econ. J.*, XII (No. 48, Dec., 1902), 472-84; see also note 29 to Chapter VIII above.
[88] J. S. Mill, *Principles*, p. 858. Edgeworth, in "The Pure Theory of Taxation," p. 68, is generous indeed to Mill.

made the mistake of thinking that an unchanging price level made such a conclusion a logical necessity.

When Ricardo fell into error, it was owing more to a failure to extend his reasoning than to illogical breaks in the chain already developed; and these Ricardian errors are not caught by Mill. Ricardo's conclusion respecting a flat tax per acre, for instance, is repeated without question by Mill.[89]

But Mill was too vigorous and too original a thinker to leave Ricardo's tax-distribution analysis quite unaltered, though his changes were additions to the structure rather than replacements. Mill's masterly analysis of the effects of taxes on imports and exports [90] goes far beyond anything that Ricardo offers, and indeed fills a notable gap that, as we have seen, exists in the tax section of Ricardo's *Principles,* which contains no chapter devoted to such duties. Here, of course, Mill is applying to taxation the great advances he had made on Ricardo's doctrine of international trade, which had stopped with the law of comparative advantage, leaving unexplored the determinants of the particular terms of trade that would emerge.

On one major issue we may possibly discern a true difference of opinion between Mill and Ricardo: the imminence of the stationary state. Ricardo had expressed a belief that England might not reach the stationary state within any calculable future, if she allowed free entry of corn. Mill, in his taxation chapters, repeatedly suggests that England is already at that state, or close to it.[91] This belief leads him to explore far more intensively than Ricardo the effects, of taxation of wages or necessaries, on the shares going to wages, profit, and rent. Following Senior, Mill notes that since disposable profits and wages must settle at certain minimum levels in any event, taxes on these shares can scarcely result in a lower net wage or a lower net rate of profit, once the stationary state is reached.[92] The true sufferers, then, are the landlords, for taxation brings the economy to the stationary state at a lower level of population.

Mill's belief that in England the rate of profit was already so low that further accumulation of capital for safe domestic use could not be expected is reflected in a lack of concern on his part for the effects of taxes imposed on legacies and inheritances. He agrees that these taxes come out of capital, but believes that they simply prevent the coming into

[89] J. S. Mill, *Principles,* p. 842. [90] *Ibid.,* pp. 847-56.

[91] *Ibid.,* pp. 821-22, 826, 845.

[92] *Ibid.,* pp. 825-26, 842-44, 849-50. See Senior, *Political Economy,* 6th ed., rev., 1872, pp. 120-28 (first edition, 1836).

existence of capital that would have gone abroad[93] or, we may infer, would have been "wasted in unprofitable speculations."[94]

So, though we say that Ricardo greatly influenced John Stuart Mill, that Mill accepted Ricardo on tax doctrine, yet, Mill's Book V has little of the flavor of Ricardo. In all of Mill's taxation chapters, Ricardo is mentioned only once,[95] and argued with not at all. Contrast, in this respect, Ricardo's attitude toward Smith. Here there emerges a curious difference between Mill and Ricardo. Ricardo, the hitherto practical man of finance, with no pretensions as a scholar, filled his pages with quotations from Smith, Buchanan, Say, and Malthus, and disputed them endlessly; but on practical taxation issues of his day he was largely silent. Mill, reared as a scholar, cited few and quarrelled with none of his great predecessors[96] in his chapters on taxation; but he was strongly attracted to the type of technical question around which tax policy is constructed. Should taxation be concentrated on interest, dividends, and land rent, as "realized property?"[97] Should life annuities be subject to income tax without deduction for the continual fall in their present value as the termination date approaches?[98] Should a Belvoir residence be valued for local rates at what it had cost, or at what it would now fetch in the market?[99] Mill's preoccupation with such problems arose from a consuming interest in equity, an interest not to be found in Ricardo, who was only drawn inadvertently, now and then, below the surface of a macro-economics that made all taxes come to about the same in any case. Here is where Mill's great contributions to tax theory are to be found, as in his analysis of the double taxation of saved income under an income tax, and his consequent advocacy of a spendings tax.[100] Mill's thoughts on equal and minimum sacrifice have suffered obsolescence, and indeed are in some respects technically in error,[101] but he was an impressive pioneer in this difficult country.[102] And Mill would not give up so readily, or settle so comfortably to a dogmatic conclusion, on equity issues, as would Ricardo in those few moments when he noticed them: compare the two analyses of a special tax on land rent.[103] Mill's scorn of

[93] J. S. Mill, *Principles*, p. 822. [94] *Ibid.*, p. 825.

[95] In reference to a tax on capital, *ibid.*, p. 822.

[96] But he did initiate the tradition that no treatise on public finance dare fail to reproduce Adam Smith's four maxims, appropriately mutilated, of course. J. S. Mill, *Principles*, pp. 802-803.

[97] *Ibid.*, p. 809. [98] *Ibid.*, p. 811. [99] *Ibid.*, p. 836.

[100] *Ibid.*, pp. 812-13, 829-31.

[101] See Pigou, *A Study in Public Finance*, p. 57.

[102] J. S. Mill, *Principles*, pp. 804-809. [103] *Ibid.*, pp. 817-21.

competitive consumption may have been matched by Ricardo's, but Mill let it crystallize in tax proposals that Ricardo never could have endorsed; an example is publicity for tax returns.[104]

In truth, Mill was closer to Adam Smith than to Ricardo. An entire chapter devoted to "Comparison between Direct and Indirect Taxation" contains a mixture of administrative, ethical, psychological, and sociological considerations that are never found in Ricardo. But in Mill we feel that the discussion is controlled by implicit adherence to a framework of economic theory, thus avoiding that fascinating but somewhat disorderly flowering of ideas and illustrations from everywhere that is so characteristic of the *Wealth of Nations.* Such order as is imposed by Smith on his treatment of the several taxes is due to repeated reference to his four maxims. Mill's disciplined exposition has a sterner origin: David Ricardo.

[104] *Ibid.*, pp. 829-30; see also *ibid.*, p. 869.

APPENDIX A

1. WHEWELL ON PERCENTAGE TAXES ON GROSS PRODUCE (CHAPTER VI)

Further details are presented here of Whewell's analysis of a percentage tax on gross produce, given in pp. 205-19 of his first paper, "Mathematical Exposition of some Doctrines of Political Economy" (see p. 85 above).

Whewell agrees with Ricardo on the effects of a flat-rate percentage tax, uniform on all the produce, under completely inelastic demand (*ibid.*, p. 208). He then examines variant cases: graduated tax rates, demand of various degrees of elasticity (though of course he does not use the word), patterns of increasing cost. Much of his analysis seems vitiated, however, by omission of reference to a no-rent intensive margin of cultivation. "In general, we shall have to consider only the *average* produce and rate of all the soils, except the last quality; the last quality being that which is brought into cultivation, or thrown out, by the changes which we have to consider" (*ibid.*, p. 206). Perhaps we are to use the term "soil" or "acre" in the imaginative sense that Whewell employs earlier, when, clearly recognizing the phenomenon of intensive cultivation, he says, "We may consider the acre as consisting of two acres, one *superimposed,* on the other; one cultivated with a capital of 100 and produce of 150, the other with a capital of 100 and produce of 115" (*ibid.*, p. 198). See also *ibid.*, pp. 217-18.

The conclusions for the variant cases are:

a. ". . . if the poorer soils be taxed at a lower proportional rate than the average, the tax will so far fall on rent, and be taken from price. . . . If the poorest soil pay no tax, the whole of the tax levied on other soils falls on rent. . . ." (*ibid.*, p. 209). This still assumes a completely inelastic demand. These conclusions appear invalid, once an intensive no-rent margin is postulated. Price must rise, if the intensive marginal doses are to earn a normal profit. If this rise in price permitted more intensive cultivation of the hitherto no-rent land, there would be somewhat less intensive cultivation of the taxed acres. Here the term soil can hardly be used in the imaginative sense noted above, for it would be quite impracticable to isolate the product of the intensive marginal dose for a special low or zero tax rate.

b. If "there is no soil in cultivation of the limiting quality," the tax will cause no change in price. "The cost of production does not affect prices in this case, because there is nothing produced which barely pays the cost of production with profits. . . . In this case, the tax falls wholly on rent" (*ibid.,* p. 209). Whewell does not note that this conclusion is invalid for a tax rate beyond a certain height.

c. If the demand is not completely inelastic, and if cultivation has been pushed to a no-rent margin, two cases may be distinguished:

(i) The elasticity of demand is, as we should say, − 1. Here, "the consumer pays no more [viz., spends no more] than he did before the tax. The tax is taken entirely from rent and profits. The consumer however receives less for his money" (*ibid.,* p. 212). In modern terminology, the tax is shifted in part to the consumer. Price rises, but by less than the tax.

(ii) The percentage increase in price is "a multiple of" the decrease in quantity demanded; Whewell takes the multiple to be 3. Assumptions are then made regarding the relative productivity of the best, average, and poorest soils. Conclusions are reached regarding the percentage increase of price and decrease in amount consequent on a stipulated percentage tax, and regarding the portions of the tax revenue coming from "rent, profits, and prices" (*ibid.*, pp. 209-17).

2. RISE IN PRICE UNDER PROFITS TAX IF GOLD MINE IS UNTAXED (CHAPTER IX)

The extent to which the spiral effect of prices on wages, and wages on prices, touched off by a tax on profits, would proceed in the absence of a tax on the profits of the gold mining industry is indicated by the following formula:

p_1 = price level for commodities in terms of gold in Period 1, before the tax is introduced

p_2 = price level under the tax

r = ratio of profit to sales in Period 1
t = percentage tax rate on profits

Postulates:

a. Aggregate wages in gold mining rise by the same percentage as commodity prices.

b. Ratio of disposable profits to sales, in the commodities industries, equals the ratio of profits (untaxed) to sales in the gold mining industry, in Period 2.

c. Ratios of profits to sales are equal, in the two sectors, in Period 1.

d. Total wage bill as a percentage of sales, in the commodities industries, is the same in Periods 1 and 2.

Then, if there is to be no change, from Period 1 to Period 2, in the physical volume of commodities, or in the physical volume of gold produced, it can be shown that:

$$p_2 = \frac{p_1[1 - r(1 - t)]}{1 - r}$$

$$\frac{p_2}{p_1} = \frac{1 - r(1 - t)}{1 - r}$$

Using the figures employed in the text above assuming a 10 percent tax on profits, setting p_1 equal to 1, and assuming that the share of profits is 30 percent,

$$p_2 = \frac{1[1 - .3(1 - .1)]}{1 - .3} = 1.04286$$

Thus, the sales volume of commodities likewise would be 4.286 percent higher under the tax, or 10,429 *l.*, not 11,000 *l.* Wages in the commodities industries would rise from 7,000 *l.* to 7,300 *l.* Profits before tax in those industries would be 3,129 *l.*, and the tax would take 313 *l.* Disposable profit after tax in the commodities industries would be 2,816 *l.*, a decline even in absolute terms, from the first-period level.

3. SPIRAL EFFECT OF WAGES TAX IN ADAM SMITH'S SYSTEM [1] (CHAPTER X)

In general: if t is a fixed absolute amount taken in wages tax, the increase in the wage bill is found by summing the series, $t + \frac{1}{2} \cdot \frac{2}{5} t + \frac{1}{25} t \ldots$ to infinitely many terms. The sum of this geometric progression is $\frac{t}{1-r}$, where $r = \frac{1}{5}$. Hence the wage bill increases from 400 to 450. Manufacturers' sales increase by the sum of the series $\frac{t}{2} + \frac{t}{2} \cdot \frac{1}{5} + \frac{t}{2} \cdot \frac{1}{25} \ldots.$, or by 25. Rent declines by the same sum.

[1] See p. 134 above.

Ricardo's failure to understand that he was dealing with a geometric progression that did not extend "without any assignable limits" was noted by Whewell, who formulated such a progression in terms of a percentage tax rather than a tax fixed in absolute amount:

Let wages rise to the whole amount of the tax; say $^1/_{10}$; and let this rise in wages produce a rise of $^1/_{20}$ in the price of manufactured goods; (not so much as $^1/_{10}$, because only a part, say $^1/_2$, of the *value* of goods is wages;) and let this rise of $^1/_{20}$ in the price of goods produce a rise of $^1/_{40}$ in wages (not so much as $^1/_{20}$, because only a part, say $^1/_2$, of the labourer's *consumption* is manufactures;) and so on. Then it is manifest that the whole rise in wages is $^1/_{10}$ + $^1/_{40}$ + $^1/_{160}$, &c. and that the whole rise in goods is $^1/_{20}$ + $^1/_{80}$ + $^1/_{320}$, &c. And the simplest principles of systematic arithmetic inform us, that these are not quantities having "no assignable limit," but that according to these suppositions, the whole rise of wages will be $^4/_{30}$, and the whole rise of manufactured goods $^2/_{30}$.

Whewell notes that the rise in wages would have to be $^1/_9$, if the tax rate of $^1/_{10}$ is assumed applicable to wages as increased by reaction to the tax. He also reaches the result "directly," "by expressing the conditions algebraically," in a note. The "effect on the price of goods,"

$mx = \frac{mk}{1-k-mn}$ where m is "the portion of the value of goods which depends on wages," so that "[manufactured] goods before the tax consist in value of *m* wages, and 1-*m* raw produce" (Whewell thus abstracts from profits), k is the rate of tax on wages, and n is "the labourer's consumption of manufactured goods [expressed as] ... a fraction ... of his whole consumption." (By a printer's error, or a slip of the pen, m and n are transposed in Whewell's definitions.) In terms of his illustration, a tax of $^1/_{10}$ puts wages up by $^2/_{13}$ and prices of manufactured goods, $^1/_{13}$.[2]

Two years later Whewell returns to this case with a more sophisticated analysis,[3] which allows for a possible difference in capital-turnover ratios between agriculture and manufactures, and in which he concludes that the ratio in which the wages tax will fall on (rich) consumers and on capitalists is indeterminate, in Ricardo's system:

In fact we suppose both the consumer and the capitalist to be entirely passive, so as to have no power of throwing their loss on any other person, and on this

[2] Whewell, "Mathematical Exposition of some Doctrines of Political Economy," pp. 192-93, 229-30.

[3] Whewell, "Mathematical Exposition of some of the Leading Doctrines in Mr. Ricardo's 'Principles' ", pp. 181-85.

supposition it is manifest, that there is nothing to disturb the equilibrium, whatever be the amount of this loss in either case.

It will be seen however, that the result which Mr. Ricardo appears to have inferred, viz. that the whole tax *in each case* would be taken from profits, cannot possibly be true. For in such a case it would differently affect profits in different employments, according to the proportion of fixed capital: and hence some succeeding adjustment must necessarily take place, in order to bring back profits to an equality.[4]

Whewell notes that Ricardo's error had been pointed out by "Col. Thompson."[5]

[4] *Ibid.* pp. 182-83. [5] *Ibid.*, p. 181.

APPENDIX B

REFERENCES TO TAXATION BY RICARDO'S CORRESPONDENTS

Passages dealing with taxation that are to be found in the letters written to Ricardo, published in Vols. VI to IX in the Sraffa edition of Ricardo's works, but which have not been quoted in the text of this volume, or which have been noted only in passing, are referred to or quoted below. The passages are given in chronological order.

MALTHUS, Aug. 5, 1814, S, VI, 118:

"My objection to taxes upon necessaries compared with taxes on luxuries and income taxes on the higher classes of society, is, that they must diminish capital and produce, though I dont think they would diminish profits and interest."

MALTHUS, Oct. 9, 1814, S, VI, 140:

An incidental reference only.

MALTHUS, Feb. 12, 1815, S, VI, 175-76:

To understand this passage it is necessary to reproduce a paragraph from a letter from Ricardo to Malthus, Feb. 6, 1815, written just after he had read Malthus's *An Inquiry into the Nature and Progress of Rent:*

I diff[er to]o, as you know, as to the effects of taxati[on] on the growth of produce. You appear to me not quite consistent in admitting as you unequivocally do that the last portion of land cultivated, yields nothing more than the profits of stock,—no rent, and yet to maintain that taxes on necessaries or on raw produce fall on the landlord and not on the consumer.[1]

In his reply to the letter from which this passage is taken, Malthus says, *inter alia:*

[1] S, VI, 173. MS. torn at bracketed portions.

With regard to the tax *being thrown off on* the Landlord I did not certainly express myself as I meant. I intended to alter it before I left Town but forgot it. It is now corrected. I think however there are often cases where taxes are thrown off on the landlord, and I meant to say that those which had not already been thrown off on the consumer would then be thrown off on the landlord (S, VI, 176). (Italics Malthus's).

In the same letter there is another passage, intelligible alone:

I shall like much to see your written opinions on the influence of taxation upon cultivation. You say very justly that it sometimes tends to clear up these matters, to put money out of the question. Upon this plan I would ask whether a man who was going to take some poor land into cultivation, might not be at once deterred from it, if for every six quarters of corn which he raised from it he was obliged to pay one for the support of the state. If the land were very poor the remainder might not be sufficient to support the labourers upon it, or pay the expences of cultivation (S, VI, 175).

MALTHUS, May 5, 1815, S, VI, 224:
An incidental reference to "the necessary and permanent rise of price occasioned by taxation."

MALTHUS, Aug. 26, 1815, S, VI, 256:
"Without some such peculiar advantages ["facility of production in manufactures, or in some peculiar natural products"], difficulty of production, or taxes on labour, would not permanently raise prices, relatively to other countries."

GRENFELL, Sept. 8, 1815, S, VI, 265-67; and Sept. 28, 1815, S, VI, 286:
Information for Ricardo on the stamp duty on bank notes, relevant to the gain made by the Bank of England in paying relatively little by way of composition for this tax over the past years. See Ricardo's letter of Sept. 10, 1815 to Malthus, S, VI, 267-69.

GRENFELL, Sept. 20, 1815, S, VI, 275; and Sept. 24, 1815, S, VI, 282:
A passing reference to the rate of income tax, evidently relative to the profits made by the Bank of England.

TROWER, March 18, 1817, S, VII, 142:
Trower proposes to "quicken the demand for labor," in order to induce a rise in wages, by "reducing, or repealing those taxes which affect most heavily our aggricultural (*sic*) and commercial interests. I am aware, that the Revenue forbids this to any extent unless the [other?] taxes are imposed, and I should not hesitate to recommend a new Income tax; a tax which ought never to have been repealed." See also letter from Trower of April 28, 1817, S, VII, 149.

MALTHUS, Feb. 24, 1818, S, VII, 253:

For myself, I own, I am quite satisfied with your own concessions; and if as you yourself acknowledge, taxation, foreign materials, and the different quantities of fixed and circulating capitals employed, all prevent the exchangeable value of commodities from being determined by the labour which they have cost in production, I should say, it followed that your theory was only true *caeteris paribus,* which might be equally said of the cost of the materials.

Given the wages of labour, the profits of stock, and the taxes, the exchangeable value of commodities will vary with the cost of the materials.

MILL, Jan. 14, 1819, S, VIII, 9:

Retrenchment (and tax reduction) without parliamentary reform is an absurd hope, says Mill.

TROWER, May 21, 1819, S, VIII, 30:

So we are to have another loan! If Ministers had proper firmness and resolution they would raise the money by *taxes,* and if they had the confidence of the Country they would be supported.—If the People wont bear an *income tax,* let *necessaries* be taxed, and thus the money might be easily raised. It is a folly to attempt raising any considerable sum by taxing Luxuries, and yet, the cry of the day *in Parliament* is that *necessaries must not be taxed,* because they fall on the poor; and so they would deprive us of the few productive taxes we have left.

MILL, Aug. 14, 1819, S, VIII, 53:

A passing remark on the inclination of even a representative government to overtax dependencies in order to relieve the "home population."

MCCULLOCH, Nov. 2, 1819, S, VIII, 127:

McCulloch urges Ricardo to make his article for the *Encyclopaedia Britannica* one on "the Funding System" rather than "only on the Sinking Fund":

You would have an opportunity not only of tracing the comparative advantages and defects attending the providing for extraordinary expences by means of loans, as contrasted with the advantages and defects attending the providing for them by means of a sudden increase of taxation; but would also be enabled to point out the ruinous effects attending the accumulation of a large debt.

SAY, 1819-1820:

Say, in his *Notes on Ricardo,* I, 249-50, commenting on the first paragraph of Ricardo's chapter on "Taxes on Gross Produce," had said:

Toute terre cultivée paye toujours un fermage, quelque faible qu'il soit. Un propriétaire, ne fût-ce que par mauvaise humeur, ne laisserait pas cultiver sa terre, si elle ne lui rapportait absolument rien. ... Il faudrait qu'un nouvel impôt sur les produits des terres fût considérable au point de faire abandonner des terres actuellement en culture, pour qu'il fît augmenter le prix de blés.... Tout impôt de ce genre, à moins qu'il ne soit exagéré, ne peut donc que diminuer les profits du propriétaire et ceux du cultivateur, sans faire renchérir le produit des terres.

Writing to Say on January 11, 1820 (S, VIII, 149-50), Ricardo said:

You appear to me to have mistaken also an opinion of mine on which you comment in a note of the translation of my book. My argument respecting rent, profit and taxes, is founded on a supposition that there is land in every country which pays no rent, or that there is capital employed on land before in cultivation for which no rent is paid. You answer the first position, but you take no notice of the second. The admission of either will answer my purpose.

Say replies, in a letter of March 2, 1820 (S, VIII, 161):

Vous blâmez une des notes que j'ai mises à la traduction française que Constancio a donnée de votre ouvrage (je crois que c'est celle de la page 249, tome I du français). J'avoue que je ne vois pas trop comment la seconde partie de la proposition fait passer la première. N'importe: si la critique est juste pour cette première partie, je conviendrai volontiers que vous avez raison pour la seconde. En effet, quand un fermage ne sert absolument qu'à payer l'intérêt du capital qu'un propriétaire a répandu sur sa terre, et qu'un impôt survient, le propriétaire n'abandonnera pas sa terre, et par conséquent le profit que rend son capital, pour ne pas payer l'impôt. Dès-lors l'impôt ne porte pas sur le propriétaire en tant que propriétaire, et il augmente les frais de production, et par conséquent le prix des produits bruts. C'est un cas qui montre, en dépit des physiocrates, que tout impôt ne retombe pas sur les terres.

Say appears to be confused; his last two sentences reverse, without reason, the conclusion implied by those preceding.

McCULLOCH, May 15, 1820, S, VIII, 190:

But although I am of opinion that it is better to impose taxes on luxuries than on necessaries, I should object to any scheme for repealing the taxes on commodities and substituting a property or income tax in their stead. Such a measure would most certainly add to the public distresses. It might no doubt give a momentary relief; but it would widen the basis of taxation, and enable ministers to divert a much greater portion of the wealth of the country into the coffers of the Treasury.

MILL, Dec. 28, 1820, S, VIII, 327:

"... I have been making good progress with my School Book of Political Economy [*Elements of Political Economy*] ... Of the whole subject, I have not much [remaining?] to consider, except the topic of *consumption,* including the doctrine of taxes."

TROWER, Feb. 16, 1821, S, VIII, 348:

Landlords are loud in their calls for a robbery on the public creditor; but they take care never to admit to the *only true* remedy; a fall in Rents, a fall in Tithes, and a fall in the *expences* of Husbandry. These, however, will come, in spite of the left handed honesty of these clamorous landlords; who silently fattened upon the distresses of the annuitants and the consumers, for many years; and who now call out, lustily, when forced to disgorge a portion of their unnatural acquirements!

TROWER, April 1, 1821, S, VIII, 363:

"Test, and Corporation Acts, Tithes, Church Establishment, these are the real foundation of the alarms attributed to 'the Old Whore of Babylon'!"

TROWER, July 22, 1821, S, IX, 30:

"How have you found matters in your part of the Country? Are rents, tithes, poor rates, wages and tradesmen's Bills coming down? These are the points to attend to—but the grumbling stupid farmer is looking only for increased prices."

SAY, July 19, 1821, S, IX, 33:

"Les circonstances qui occasionnent des frais sans production d'utilité, comme les impôts, ne produisent pas de la richesse; et lorsqu'on les fait payer au consommateur, on lui fait payer un prix pour lequel on ne lui donne rien en échange."

TROWER, Jan. 10, 1822, S, IX, 146:

The question of Tithes is, no doubt, one that cannot be overlooked; but it is beset with difficulties, and dependent, as it seems to me, in some measure, upon the question of Catholick Emancipation....

It seems probable, that, in some shape or other, you will have the Agricultural question before Parliament again. The Landlords and Farmers will cry aloud for a delivery from the Malt Tax; the benefit of which reduction would be felt principally by the *consumers*. Surely it would be much wiser to take off taxes, which would give a stimulus to our general trade, and diminish that horrible warfare that is carrying on against the smugglers. As to any immediate relief to the farmers the case does not admit of it; beyond that natural and obvious relief, which ought to be afforded, and which is now in operation all over the Country, in the diminutions of Rents and Tithes. And as to the Landlords, as a body, I do not much sympathise in *their* condition; they are now called upon to make sacrifices, which they are very capable of making, and which it is but justice, that they should make.

MCCULLOCH, Feb. 12, 1822, S, IX, 159-60:

This [agricultural] distress unquestionably arises from the low price of the principal articles of farming produce, and it is an utter absurdity to suppose that low price can ever be caused by excessive taxation.... Neither do I think that our prosperity can ever rest on a firm basis while our taxation is so oppressive.... I have promised to write an article for the forthcoming Review on the comparative effects of high and low taxes on the Revenue. In this article I should like to notice as particularly as I could the effects which the different taxes have had on the revenue in Ireland. Sir John Newport made some curious statements on this subject in the course of last session.... (See note by Sraffa and Dobb, *ibid.*, note 2.)

McCulloch, April 17, 1822, S, IX, 185-88:

I have made considerable use of these accounts [from Sir John Newport] in the forthcoming No of the Review (185). (See note 1 by Sraffa and Dobb, *idem.*)

Perhaps if he [Sir John] approves of what I have already done he may be induced to send me some more statements of the same kind. I should especially like to be possessed of all the attainable information respecting Irish tithes (185-86).

I have written an article on the Corn Laws for the forthcoming Review ... (186). (See note 3, *idem*, by Sraffa and Dobb.)

In the Article in the Review I have taken exactly the same view that you have taken of the effects of taxation, and have stated distinctly that it is impossible it can be the cause of the *peculiar* distress experienced by the agriculturists. Would it not be better to abolish the restriction at once? I incline to think that this would be preferable to a gradually diminishing rate of duties (188).

McCulloch, Aug. 11, 1823, S, IX, 342, 345:

After I came home Jeffrey pressed me to write an article on the Navigation laws, and I have since been so incessantly occupied with Taxation, that I have never been able to resume the consideration of the grand subject of value.... I will use the liberty to send you the proofs of the more difficult parts of my article on Taxation....

Trower, Aug. 26, 1823, S, IX, 372:

Trower suggests that a special tax might be imposed on the proprietor of any Irish lands that are leased by subdivision into small holdings, in order to encourage a more efficient use of the land. Ricardo, in answering Trower's letter (Aug. 31, 1823, S, IX, 376-79) does not touch on this point.

BIBLIOGRAPHY

Acworth, A. W. Financial Reconstruction in England, 1815-1822. London: P. S. King & Son, 1925.

Angell, James W. The Theory of International Prices: History, Criticism, and Restatement. Cambridge: Harvard Univ. Press, 1926.

Bastable, C. F. Public Finance. 3rd ed., rev. & enl. London: Macmillan, 1903.

Baumol, William. Economic Dynamics. New York: Macmillan, 1951.

Baumstark, Ed., trans., *see* Ricardo, David.

Beck, Morris. "Ability to Shift the Corporate Income Tax: Seven Industrial Groups," *National Tax Journal,* III (No. 3, Sept., 1950), 248-56.

——— "Ability to Shift the Corporate Income Tax: Correction," *National Tax Journal,* III (No. 4, Dec., 1950), 353.

Bentham, Jeremy. A Protest Against Law Taxes, shewing the peculiar mischievousness of all such impositions as add to the expense of appeal to justice. London: John M'Creery, Printer, n.d.

Bickerdike, C. F. "Taxation of Site Values," *Economic Journal,* XII (No. 48, Dec., 1902), 472-84.

Blaug, Mark. "The Empirical Content of Ricardian Economics," *Journal of Political Economy,* LXIX (No. 1, Feb., 1956), 41-58.

———. Ricardian Economics. A Historical Study. New Haven: Yale Univ. Press, 1958.

Bonar, James, and J. H. Hollander, eds. Letters of David Ricardo to Hutches Trower and Others, 1811-1823. Oxford, Clarendon Press, 1899.

Buxton, Sidney. Finance and Politics, an Historical Study, 1783-1885. 2 vols. London: Murray, 1888.

Cabiati, A. "La finanza di A. De Viti De Marco," *Giornale degli Economisti e Rivista di Statistica,* LXVIII (No. 11, Nov., 1928), 881-98.

Caldecott, Rev. A. "Terms of Commutation [of Tithes]," in: Palgrave's Dictionary of Political Economy (Henry Higgs, ed.), III, 545-46.

Cannan, Edwin. A History of the Theories of Production & Distribution in

English Political Economy from 1776 to 1848. 3rd ed. London: Staples Press, 1917.

———. The History of Local Rates in England. 2nd ed. London: P. S. King & Son, 1927.

Cassels, John M. "A Re-interpretation of Ricardo on Value," *Quarterly Journal of Economics*, XLIX (No. 3, May, 1935), 518-32.

Clewing, Ruth. Die finanzwissenschaftlichen Ansichten von David Ricardo. Unpublished dissertation, Rechts- und Staatswissenschaftliche Fakultät der Rhein, Friedrich-Wilhelms-Universität, Bonn a. Rhein, 1951.

Cournot, Augustin. Researches into the Mathematical Principles of the Theory of Wealth, trans. by Nathaniel T. Bacon. New York, Macmillan, 1929.

Deane, Phyllis. "Contemporary Estimates of National Income in the First Half of the Nineteenth Century," *Economic History Review* (second series), VIII (No. 3, April, 1956), 339-54.

Diehl, Karl. "Die einmalige Vermögensabgabe," in *Die Neuordnung der deutschen Finanzwirtschaft,* ed. Heinrich Herkner, *Schriften des Vereins für Sozialpolitik,* CLVI (No. 1, 1918), 1-83.

———. "David Ricardo und der finanzielle Wiederaufbau Englands nach den napoleonischen Kriegen," *Bankarchiv,* XIX (No. 9, 1920), 106-109, and XIX (No. 10, 1920), 122-27.

———. "Ricardo," in Handwörterbuch der Staatswissenschaften, 4th ed. 1926.

———. Socialwissenschaftliche Erläuterung, *see* Ricardo, David.

Dowell, Stephen. A History of Taxation and Taxes in England from the Earliest Times to the Year 1885. 4 vols. 2nd ed. London: Longmans, Green, 1888.

Du Puynode, Gustave. Etudes sur les principaux économistes: Turgot—Adam Smith—Ricardo—Malthus—J. B. Say—Rossi. Paris: Guillaumin et cie., 1868.

Edgeworth, F. Y. A Levy on Capital for the Discharge of Debt. Oxford: Clarendon, 1919.

———. Papers Relating to Political Economy. 3 vols. London: Macmillan, 1925.

Einaudi, L. "Dalla leggenda al monumento," *Giornale degli Economisti e Annali di Economia* (new series), X (Nos. 7-8, July-Aug., 1951), 329-34.

Encyclopaedia of the Social Sciences. Edwin R. A. Seligman and Alvin Johnson, eds. 15 vols. New York: Macmillan, 1930-35.

E. R., *see* R., E.

Falck, Georg von. Kritische Rückblicke auf die Entwicklung der Lehre von der Steuerüberwalzung seit Adam Smith. Dorpat: Schnakenburg, 1882.

Farnsworth, A. Addington, Author of the Modern Income Tax. London: Stevens & Sons, 1951.

Fay, C. R. "Corn Prices and the Corn Laws, 1815-1846," *Economic Journal,* XXXI (No. 121, March, 1921), 17-27.

———. "Speeches and Evidence, Vol. V in The Works and Correspondence of David Ricardo," *Economic Journal,* LXII (No. 247, Sept., 1952), 664-65.

Fine, Selma E. Production and Excise in England, 1643-1825. Unpublished doctoral dissertation, Cambridge, Radcliffe College. 1937.

Földes, Béla. "Ricardo. Mit besonderer Berücksichtigung der kriegswirtschaftlichen Probleme," *Jahrbücher für Nationalökonomie und Statistik,* CXIV (3rd series, LIX, No. 6, June, 1920), 481-535.

Forte, Francesco. "Su di alcune proposizioni del Ricardo riguardanti gli effetti di imposte pagate dal produttore," *Rivista di Diritto Finanziario e Scienza delle Finanze,* XVI (No. 2, Pt. I, June, 1957), 140-68.

Frend, William. The Principles of Taxation: or Contribution according to Means; in which it is shewn, that if every man pays in proportion to the stake he has in the country, the present ruinous and oppressive system of taxation, the custom house, and the excise office, may be abolished, and the national debt gradually and easily paid off. 2nd ed. London: Printed for J. Mawman, 1804.

———. The National Debt in Its True Colours, with Plans for Its Extinction by Honest Means. London: Printed for J. Mawman, 1817.

Fubini, R. "Contributo alla determinazione del concetto di imposta generale sul reddito," *Giornale degli Economisti e Rivista di Statistica,* LXXII (No. 5, May, 1932), 297-327.

———. "I dui tipi fondamentali di indagine nell'ambita dell'economia finanziaria," *Giornale degli Economisti e Rivista di Statistica,* LXXIII (No. 12, Dec. 1933), 883-89.

———. "Francesco Ferrara e David Ricardo," *Giornale degli Economisti e Rivista di Statistica,* LXXV (No. 2, Feb., 1935), 85-101.

Gale, Samuel. An Essay on the Nature and Principles of Public Credit. London: 1784.

Gayer, Arthur D., W. W. Rostow, and Anna Jacobson Schwartz. The Growth and Fluctuation of the British Economy, 1790-1850. 2 vols. Oxford: Clarendon, 1953.

Gide, Charles, and Charles Rist. A History of Economic Doctrines. New York: Heath, n.d.

Giraudeau, Roger. "La théorie de l'impôt chez Ricardo," *Revue de Science et de Législation Financières,* XLIII (No. 2, April-June, 1951), 319-39.

Gonner, E. C. K. "David Ricardo," in: Palgrave's Dictionary of Political Economy (Henry Higgs, ed.), III, 308.

———, ed., *see* Ricardo, David.

Gottlieb, Manuel. "The Capital Levy and Deadweight Debt in England—1815-40," *The Journal of Finance,* VIII (No. 1, March, 1953), 34-46.

Greuling, Wilhelm. Die Steuerlehre Ricardos. Inaugural-Dissertation, Friedrich-Wilhelms-Universität, Berlin. Idstein i. Taunus: Buchdruckerei Georg Grandpierre, 1927. (Copy in the University of Pennsylvania Library.) (See note 76 to Chapter I above.)

Griziotti, Benvenuto. "La diversa pressione tributaria del prestito e dell'imposta," *Giornale degli Economisti e Rivista di Statistica,* LIV (Nos. 3 and 5, March and May, 1917), 129-64 and 313-14.

———. Studi di Scienza delle Finanze e Diritto Finanziario. 2 vols. Milan:

Giuffrè, 1956.

Guillebaud, C. W. "The Evolution of Marshall's *Principles of Economics*," *Economic Journal*, LII (No. 208, Dec., 1942), 330-49.

Hargreaves, E. L. The National Debt. London: Edward Arnold & Co., 1930.

Held, Adolf. "Zur Lehre von der Überwälzung der Steuern," *Zeitschrift für die gesammte Staatswissenschaft*, XXIV (Nos. 3-4, 1868), 421-95.

Higgs, Henry, ed., *see* Palgrave's Dictionary of Political Economy.

Hollander, Jacob Harry. David Ricardo, A Centenary Estimate. Baltimore: Johns Hopkins Press, 1910.

———, ed. Letters of David Ricardo to John Ramsay McCulloch, 1816-1823. Publications of American Economic Association, Vol. X, Nos. 5-6, Sept. & Nov., 1895.

———, ed. Letters of John Ramsay McCulloch to David Ricardo, 1818-1823. Baltimore: Johns Hopkins Press. 1931.

Hope-Jones, Arthur. Income Tax in the Napoleonic Wars. Cambridge: Cambridge Univ. Press, 1939.

Hutchison, T. W. "Some Questions about Ricardo," *Economica* (new series), XIX (No. 76, Nov., 1952), 415-32.

———. "Ricardo's Correspondence," *Economica* (new series), XX (No. 79, August, 1953), 263-73.

———. "James Mill and the Political Education of Ricardo," *The Cambridge Journal*, VII (No. 2, Nov., 1953), 81-100.

Jarach, C. "Gli effetti di una imposta generale ed uniforme sui profitti," *Atti della R. Accademia delle scienze di Torino*, XLVI (1910-1911), 286-301.

Johnson, Alvin, ed., *see* Encyclopaedia of the Social Sciences.

Kaizl, Josef. *Die Lehre von der Überwälzung der Steuern*. 1882.

Kaldor, Nicholas. "Alternative Theories of Distribution," *Review of Economic Studies*, XXIII (No. 61, 1955-56), 85.

Kennedy, William. English Taxation, 1640-1799. London: G. Bell & Sons, 1913.

Knight, F. H. "The Ricardian Theory of Production and Distribution," *Canadian Journal of Economics and Political Science*, I (Feb. and May, 1935), 3-25 and 171-96.

Lawrence, T. J. "William Whewell," in: Palgrave's Dictionary of Political Economy (Henry Higgs, ed.), III, 665.

Lerner, Abba P. "The Symmetry between Import and Export Taxes," *Economica* (new series), III (No. 11, Aug., 1936), 306-13.

———. Essays in Economic Analysis. London: Macmillan, 1953.

Longfield, Mountifort. Lectures on Political Economy, delivered in Trinity and Michaelmas Terms, 1833. Dublin: Richard Milliken and Son, 1834. (No. 8 in Series of Reprints of Scarce Tracts in Economics and Political Science. London: The London School of Economics and Political Science [University of London], 1931.)

McCulloch, John Ramsay. "Taxation and The Corn Laws," Art. IX, in *Edinburgh Review*, Jan., 1820, pp. 155-87. Review of the following three items: 1.

Remarks on the Report of the Select Committee on the House of Commons on the Poor Laws, by J. H. Mogridge, Esq. 2. Observations on the Circumstances which Influence the Condition of the Labouring Classes of Society, by John Barton, Esq. 3. Observations on the Rise and Fall of the Manufacturing System of Great Britain.

———. A Treatise on the Principles and Practical Influence of Taxation and the Funding System. London: Longman, Brown, Green, and Longmans, 1845.

———. "Taxation," in: Encyclopaedia Britannica, 8th ed., 1860. Reprinted separately.

McKinley, Erskine. "The Problem of 'Underdevelopment' in the English Classical School," *Quarterly Journal of Economics,* LXIX (No. 2, May, 1955), 235-52.

Mann, Fritz Karl. "Überwälzung der Steuer," in: *Handwörterbuch der Staatswissenschaften,* Vol. 8. 4th ed. 1928.

———. "Die Wandlungen des Finanzliberalismus," *Schmollers Jahrbuch,* LIX (No. 3, 1935), 271-97.

———. "Geschichte der angelsächsischen Finanzwissenschaft," in Handbuch der Finanzwissenschaft. Vol. 1. 2nd ed. 1950.

Marcet, Mrs. Jane. Conversations on Political Economy; in which the Elements of that Science are Familiarly Explained. 4th ed. London: Longman, Hurst, Rees, Orme, and Brown, 1821.

Marshall, Alfred. Principles of Economics. 8th ed. London: Macmillan, 1920.

———. Industry and Trade. London: Macmillan, 1920.

Martineau, Harriet. Illustrations of Political Economy. 25 vols. London: 1832-34.

———. Poor Laws and Paupers Illustrated. 10 vols. London: 1833-34.

———. Illustrations of Taxation. 5 vols. London: 1834.

Mill, James. Elements of Political Economy. 3rd ed. London: Printed for Baldwin, Cradock, and Joy, 1826.

Mill, John Stuart. Principles of Political Economy, with some of their applications to social philosophy, ed. by Sir W. J. Ashley. London: Longmans, Green and Co., Ltd., 1926. (First printing, Ashley ed., 1909.)

Mitchell, Wesley C. Lecture Notes on Types of Economic Theory. Taken down stenographically by John Myers in the fall of 1934 and the spring of 1935 (responsibility disclaimed by Mitchell), ed. by J. M. Gould and A. M. Kelley. 2 vols. New York: Augustus M. Kelley, 1949.

Musgrave, Richard A. The Theory of Public Finance: A Study in Public Economy. New York, Toronto, and London: McGraw Hill, 1959.

Nachimson, M. "David Ricardos Steuertheorie," *Die Neue Zeit* (29th Year), I (No. 8, Nov. 25, 1910), 244-54.

Palgrave's Dictionary of Political Economy, ed. by Henry Higgs. 3 vols. New ed. New York: Macmillan, 1923-26.

Pantaleoni, Maffeo. Teoria della Traslazione dei Tributi: Definizione, Dinamica e Ubiquità della Traslazione. Rome: Paolini, 1882.

Paquet, André. Le conflit historique entre la loi des débouchés et le principe de la demande effective: La méthode de l'équilibre et l'intégration progressive de la monnaie et du temps dans l'explication jusqu'à J. M. Keynes. Thèse pour le doctorat, présenteé et soutenue le 28 juin 1952, Université de Paris, Faculté de Droit. Paris: Imprimerie Nationale, 1953.

Pigou, A. C. A Study in Public Finance. 3rd (rev.) ed. London: Macmillan, 1949.

———. The Political Economy of War. New an rev. ed. New York: Macmillan, 1941.

———, ed. Memorials of Alfred Marshall. London: Macmillan, 1925.

Political Economy Club. Centenary Volume. Minutes of Proceedings, 1899-1920; Roll of Members and Questions Discussed, 1821-1920, with documents bearing on the history of the club. Vol. VI. London: Macmillan and Co., 1921.

Potter, J. "The British Timber Duties, 1815-60," *Economica* (new series), XXII (No. 86, May, 1955), 122-36.

Powell, Eleanor G. "Tithes," in: Palgrave's Dictionary of Political Economy (Henry Higgs, ed.), III, 543-45.

Pressnell, L. S. Country Banking in the Industrial Revolution. Oxford: Clarendon, 1956.

R., E. An Essay on Some General Principles of Political Economy, on Taxes upon Raw Produce, and on Commutation of Tithes. London: 1822.

Read, Samuel. Political Economy: An Inquiry into the Natural Grounds of Right to Vendible Property or Wealth. Edinburgh: 1829.

Ricardo, David. Des principes de l'économie politique, et de l'impôt, trans. F. S. Constancio, with annotations by Jean-Baptiste Say. 2 vols. Paris, 1819.

———. Oeuvres complètes de David Ricardo, trans. by F. S. Constancio and Alcide Fonteyraud, with notes by Jean-Baptiste Say, and new notes and commentaries by Malthus, Sismondi, Rossi, Blanqui, etc. ... Paris, Guillaumin et Cie., 1847. (Copy in University of Chicago Library.)

———. David Ricardo's Grundgesetze der Volkswirtschaft und Besteuerung, trans. by Ed. Baumstark. Leipzig: Engelmann, 1877; Sozialwissenschaftliche Erläuterung, by Karl Diehl. 2 vols. Leipzig: Engelmann, 1905.

———. The Works of David Ricardo with a Notice of the Life and Writings of the Author, ed. by J. R. McCulloch. New ed. London: Murray, 1888.

———. Principles of Political Economy and Taxation, ed. by E. C. K. Gonner. London: G. Bell and Sons, 1925.

———. The Works and Correspondence of David Ricardo, ed. by Piero Sraffa, with the collaboration of M. H. Dobb. 10 vols. Cambridge: Cambridge Univ. Press, for the Royal Economic Society, 1951-1955.

Robbins, Lionel. The Theory of Economic Policy in English Classical Political Economy. London: Macmillan, 1952.

Robertson, Ross M. "Mathematical Economics before Cournot," *Journal of Political Economy*, LVII (No. 6, Dec., 1949), 523-36.

St. Clair, Oswald. A Key to Ricardo. New York: Kelley & Millman, 1957.

Say, Jean-Baptiste. Notes on Ricardo, *see* Ricardo, *Des principes de l'économie politique....*

Schneider, Gustav. Die Steuerlehre Ricardos. Unpublished doctoral dissertation, Albert-Ludwigs-Universität, Freiburg i. Br., 1923. (See note 76 to Chapter I above.)

Seligman, Edwin R. A. "On Some Neglected British Economists," *Economic Journal,* XIII (Nos. 51, 52, Sept. and Dec., 1903), 335-63, and 511-35.

———. The Income Tax. A Study of the History, Theory and Practice of Income Taxation at Home and Abroad. New York: Macmillan, 1911.

———. Essays in Economics. New York: Macmillan, 1925.

———. The Shifting and Incidence of Taxation. 5th ed. New York: Columbia Univ. Press, 1926.

———, ed., see Encyclopaedia of the Social Sciences.

Senior, Nassau W. Three Lectures on the Cost of Obtaining Money and on Some Effects of Private and Government Paper Money. London: John Murray, 1830. (No. 5 in Series of Reprints of Scarce Tracts in Economic and Political Science, London: The London School of Economics and Political Science [University of London], n.d.)

———. Political Economy. 6th ed. London: Charles Griffin and Company, 1872.

Sensini, G. "La teoria di Ricardo sui diversi effetti del prestito e dell'imposta," *Giornale degli Economisti e Rivista di Statistica,* LX (No. 2, Feb., 1920), 57-74.

Shehab, F. Progressive Taxation. Oxford: Clarendon, 1953.

Shoup, Carl S. Principles of National Income Analysis. Boston: Houghton Mifflin, 1947.

———. "Incidence of the Corporation Income Tax: Capital Structure and Turnover Rates," *National Tax Journal,* I (No. 1, March, 1948), 12-17.

———. "Ricardo on the Taxation of Profits," *Public Finance (Finances Publiques),* V (No. 2, 1950), 101-118.

———. "Some Considerations on the Incidence of the Corporation Income Tax," *The Journal of Finance,* VI (No. 2, June, 1951), 187-96.

———. "Ricardo and Taxation," *Finanzarchiv,* XVIII (No. 1, 1957), 13-24.

Shove, G. F. "The Place of Marshall's *Principles* in the Development of Economic Theory," *Economic Journal,* LII (No. 208, Dec., 1942), 294-329.

Sidgwick, Henry, "Political Economy: Method," in: Palgrave's Dictionary of Political Economy (Henry Higgs, ed.), III, 136.

Smith, Adam. The Wealth of Nations. Cannan edition. 2 vols. London: Methuen, 1904. Modern Library edition. New York: The Modern Library, 1937.

Smith, G. Barnett. "John Ramsay McCulloch," in: Palgrave's Dictionary of Political Economy (Henry Higgs, ed.), II, 657-58.

Steve, S. "Sul concetto di imposta generale," *Giornale degli Economisti e Annali di Economia* (new series), VI (Nos. 11-12, Nov.-Dec., 1947), 573-626.

Stigler, George J. "The Ricardian Theory of Value and Distribution," *Journal of Political Economy,* LX (No. 3, June, 1952), 187-207.

———. "Sraffa's Ricardo," *American Economic Review,* XLIII (No. 4, Pt. I, Sept., 1953), 586-99.

———. "Ricardo and the 93% Labor Theory of Value," *American Economic Review*, XLVIII (No. 3, June, 1958), 357-67.

Taussig, F. W. Wages and Capital: An Examination of the Wages Fund Doctrine. New York: Appleton, 1899.

Tayler, William. The History of the Taxation of England, with an account of the Rise and Progress of the National Debt. London: Hope & Co., 1853.

Thompson, T. Perronet. "On the Instrument of Exchange," *Westminster Review*, I (No. 2, April, 1824), 171-205.

Toma, A. de. "Ricardiana," *Giornale degli Economisti e Annali di Economia* (new series), XI (Nos. 3-4, March-April, 1952), 211-28.

Torrens, Robert. An Essay on the External Corn Trade. 1st ed., London: John Hatchard & Son, 1815; 4th ed., 1827.

Viner, Jacob. Studies in the Theory of International Trade. New York: Harper, 1937.

West, Sir Edward. Price of Corn and Wages of Labour, with Observations upon Dr. Smith's, Mr. Ricardo's, and Mr. Malthus's Doctrines upon those Subjects. London: John Hatchard and Son, 1826.

Whewell, William. "Mathematical Exposition of Some Doctrines of Political Economy," No. IX in Transactions of the Cambridge Philosophical Society, III, 191-230. Cambridge: Univ. Press, 1830. (Paper dated Trinity College, March 30, 1829.)

———. "Mathematical Exposition of some of the Leading Doctrines in Mr. Ricardo's 'Principles of Political Economy and Taxation.'" No. V in Transactions of the Cambridge Philosophical Society, IV, 155-98. Cambridge: J. Smith, printer to the Univ., 1833. (Paper dated Trinity College, May 7, 1831.)

Wicksell, Knut. Finanztheoretische Untersuchungen. Jena: Fischer, 1896.

———. Zur Lehre von der Steuerincidenz. Upsala, 1895.

INDEX

Bei Fragen zur Produktsicherheit wenden Sie sich bitte an:
If you have any questions regarding product safety,
please contact:

Walter de Gruyter GmbH
Genthiner Straße 13
10785 Berlin
productsafety@degruyterbrill.com